VI. SOCIAL, ETHICAL, LEGAL, AND HUMAN ISSUES

Teachers understand the social, ethical, legal, and human issues sur...
in PK–12 schools and apply those principles in practice. Teachers:

A. model and teach legal and ethical practice related to technology
B. apply technology resources to enable and empower learners with ...tics, and abilities
C. identify and use technology resources that affirm diversity
D. promote safe and healthy use of technology resources
E. facilitate equitable access to technology resources for all students

Reprinted with permission from National Educational Technology Standards for Teachers—Connecting Curriculum and Technology, copyright © 2000, ISTE (International Society for Technology in Education), 800.336.5191 (U.S. & Canada) or 541.302.3777 (International), iste@iste.org, www.iste.org. All rights reserved. Permission does not constitute an endorsement by ISTE.

ISTE National Educational Technology Standards for Teachers (NETS•T) Performance Standards covered in *The Computer as an Educational Tool*, 5/e by Richard Forcier and Don Descy.

Chapter:	Ch 1	Ch 2	Ch 3	Ch 4	Ch 5	Ch 6	Ch 7	Ch 8	Ch 9	Ch10	Ch11	Ch12
Foundation Standard NETS•T												
I. Tech Op/Concept	✓	✓	✓	✓	✓	✓	✓	✓	✓	✓	✓	✓
A. Tech Op/Concepts	x	x	x	x	x	x	x	x	x	x	x	x
B. Continued Growth	x	x	x	x	x	x	x	x	x	x	x	x
II. Plan and Design	✓	✓	✓	✓	✓	✓	✓	✓	✓	✓	✓	✓
A. Appropriate Opps	x			x		x	x	x	x	x	x	x
B. Current Research			x	x								
C. Identify/Locate Resources	x	x		x			x					x
D. Management of Resources	x	x	x	x	x							x
E. Manage Learning	x	x	x	x	x							x
III. Teach, Learn, Curriculum	✓	✓	✓	✓	✓	✓	✓	✓	✓	✓	✓	✓
A. Address Content Standards	x	x	x			x	x	x	x	x	x	x
B. Diverse Needs of Students	x	x	x	x		x	x	x	x	x	x	x
C. Higher Order Skills						x	x	x	x	x	x	
D. Technology Enhanced	x	x		x	x	x		x				x
IV. Assessment/Eval	✓	✓				✓	✓	✓	✓	✓	✓	✓
A. Assess Learning	x	x						x				
B. Collect, Analyze, Interpret						x	x	x	x	x	x	x
C. Multiple Evals	x	x										
V. Product/Prof Practice	✓		✓	✓	✓	✓	✓	✓	✓	✓	✓	✓
A. Ongoing Development	x		x		x	x	x	x	x	x	x	x
B. Evaluate and Reflect	x		x	x				x	x			
C. Increase Productivity	x				x	x	x	x	x	x	x	
D. Communicate, Collaborate	x				x	x	x	x	x	x	x	x
VI. Social/Ethic/Legal/Human	✓		✓	✓	✓	✓	✓		✓		✓	✓
A. Legal and Ethical				x			x		x		x	x
B. Empower Learner	x		x	x		x	x		x		x	x
C. Affirm Diversity				x								x
D. Promote Safe Healthy Use				x	x						x	x
E. Equitable Access				x								

✓ = Overall standard is covered in this chapter.
x = Specific standard is covered in this chapter.

TEACHER PREP

MERRILL
PRENTICE HALL

Teacher Preparation Classroom

Your Class. Their Careers. Our Future. Will Your Students be Prepared?

We invite you to explore our new, innovative and engaging website and all that it has to offer you, your course, and tomorrow's educators! Preview this site today at *www.prenhall.com/teacherprep/demo*. Just click on "go" on the login page to begin your exploration.

Organized around the major courses pre-service teachers take, the Teacher Preparation site provides media, student/teacher artifacts, strategies, research articles, and other resources to equip your students with the quality tools needed to excel in their courses and prepare them for their first classroom.

This ultimate on-line education resource will provide you and your students access to:

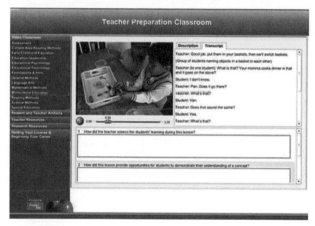

Online Video Library. More than 250 video clips—each tied to a course topic and framed by learning goals and Praxis-type questions—capture real teachers and students working in real classrooms.

Student and Teacher Artifacts. More than 200 student and teacher classroom artifacts—each tied to a course topic and framed by learning goals and application questions—provide a wealth of materials and experiences to help your students observe children's developmental learning.

Lesson Plan Builder. Step-by-step guidelines and lesson plan examples support students as they learn to build high-quality lesson plans.

Articles and Readings. Over 500 articles from ASCD's renowed journal *Educational Leadership* are available. The site also includes Research Naviagtor, a searchable database of additional education journals.

Strategies and Lessons. Over 500 research-supported instructional strategies appropriate for a wide range of grade levels and content areas.

Licensure and Career Tools. Resources devoted to helping your students pass their licensure exam; learn standards, law, and public policies; plan a teaching portfolio; and succeed in your first year of teaching.

The Computer as an Educational Tool

Productivity and Problem Solving

Fifth Edition

Richard C. Forcier
Western Oregon University

Don E. Descy
Minnesota State University, Mankato

PEARSON
Merrill
Prentice Hall

Upper Saddle River, New Jersey
Columbus, Ohio

14221
LIBRARY
Argosy University
San Francisco Bay Area
1005 Atlantic Ave.
Alameda, CA 94501

Library of Congress Cataloging-in-Publication Data

Forcier, Richard C.

  The computer as an educational tool : productivity and problem solving / Richard C. Forcier, Don E. Descy.—5th ed.

    p. cm

   ISBN 0-13-243396-6

1. Education—Data processing—Study and teaching (Higher) 2. Computers—Study and teaching (Higher) 3. Computer managed instruction. 4. Computer-assisted instruction. I. Descy, Don E. II. Title.

  LB1028.43.F67 2008

  378.1'734—dc22   2007004115

Vice President and Executive Publisher: Jeffery W. Johnston
Executive Editor: Darcy Betts Prybella
Development Editor: Amy Nelson/Elisa Rogers
Production Editor: Kris Roach
Photo Coordinator: Maria B. Vonada
Production Coordinator: Carlisle Publishing Services
Design Coordinator: Diane C. Lorenzo
Cover Designer: Terry Rohrbach
Cover Image: Jupiter Images
Production Manager: Susan Hannahs
Director of Marketing: David Gesell
Marketing Coordinator: Brian Mounts

This book was set in Garamond by Carlisle Editorial Services. It was printed and bound by Edwards Brothers. The cover was printed by Phoenix Color Corp.

Chapter Opener Photos: Patrick White/Merrill, Chapters 1 and 3; Liz Moore/Merrill, Chapters 2, 7, and 8; Krista Greco, Chapters 4 and 12; Maria B. Vonada, Chapter 5; Pearson Learning Photo Studio, Chapter 6; Lori Whitley, Chapter 9; David Young-Wolff/Photo Edit Inc., Chapter 10; Prentice Hall School Division, Chapter 11.

Pearson Education Ltd.
Pearson Education Singapore Pte. Ltd.
Pearson Education Canada, Ltd.
Pearson Education—Japan

Pearson Education Australia Pty. Limited
Pearson Education North Asia Ltd.
Pearson Educatión de Mexico, S.A. de C.V.
Pearson Education Malaysia Pte. Ltd.

10 9 8 7 6 5 4 3
ISBN 13: 978-0-13-243396-9
ISBN 10: 0-13-243396-6

Preface

The Computer as an Educational Tool: Productivity and Problem Solving, Fifth Edition, is based on the authors' long-held view that technology should be used to support learning and be as transparent as possible—that is, the use of technology should not call attention to itself but should be a means to an end. The computer should empower the user to solve problems effectively and efficiently.

Our goal is to lead teachers and those aspiring to be teachers to become proficient at applying the computer to solve problems, to infuse the computer into the curriculum in order to help students do the same, and to encourage both teachers and learners to integrate technology into their professional, academic, and personal lives in useful and meaningful ways. Those who are successful will indeed come to see the computer as an extension of their human capability. The computer will allow them to do more, to do it faster, and to do it more creatively and more accurately.

A PROBLEM-SOLVING FOCUS

The Computer as an Educational Tool: Productivity and Problem Solving, Fifth Edition, provides a current, comprehensive look at the computer's role in education, as well as the application of the computer as a tool of the mind. Topics are organized into specific areas of interest to illustrate how the computer contributes to solving everyday problems and handling tasks encountered in everyday work and personal environments. Problem-solving models are included to encourage an increase in computer productivity and to clarify the application of the computer in a thoughtful and deliberate manner, reinforcing the concept of the computer as an extension of the mind.

A LINK TO NATIONAL STANDARDS

The authors have always promoted the importance of technology standards for both students and teachers in the classroom environment. Our long-time adopters remember that *The Computer as an Educational Tool: Productivity and Problem Solving* linked its material directly to the International Society for Technology in Education standards as soon as they were published. Whereas the evolution of several national technology standards are discussed in the text, two sets of standards developed by ISTE and cosponsored by the U.S. Department of Education, NASA, and computer industry representatives are stressed. These are the National Educational Technology Standards for Students (NETS•S) and the National Educational Technology Standards for Teachers (NETS•T). Knowledge of and the ability to perform well on tests of both of these sets of standards are paramount for classroom teachers, media specialists, guidance counselors, and administrators in school settings. Students who read this text will be able to incorporate the standards in their teaching and evaluate their students on the NETS•S standards. They should also perform well on any examinations that include the NETS•T standards. Applicable NETS•T standards are listed at the beginning of each chapter, and NETS•S portfolio development exercises are included at the end of each chapter. The complete set of each set of standards is found on the inside covers, along with grids showing which NETS•S and NETS•T standards are emphasized in each chapter.

NEW IN THIS EDITION

- The new *Let's Try It* feature consists of tutorials to develop the reader's skills with Inspiration®, Kidspiration®, Photoshop Elements®, The Print Shop® Deluxe, Kid Pix®, Microsoft Excel®, Microsoft Word® (to create a web page), and Microsoft PowerPoint®. They allow the reader to construct basic applications in software with which they might not be comfortable. We chose these programs because they are readily available and because most readers are less familiar with this software than they are with standard word processing programs.

- A new *Take-Along CD* packaged in the front of the book contains copies of all the tutorials listed above, plus one for Netscape Composer® and FileMaker® Pro as well as an expanded tutorial for Photoshop Elements®. It also contains files of the *actual examples* used in the word processing, spreadsheet, and database chapters, allowing the reader a hands-on experience with the examples and an ability to modify and extend them. The guidelines folder includes sample forms, guidelines, and checklists. Fourteen *All Aboard the Internet* columns from *TechTrends*, the magazine of the Association for Educational Communications and Technology (AECT), were chosen to supplement the information regarding the Internet and the World Wide Web found in Chapters 11 and 12. A *test item database* with 20 sample questions is included on the CD to allow readers to construct their own true–false and multiple choice tests.

- This *Take-Along CD* is a wonderful tool designed not only for the instructor but also for the students to use in their own classroom. A *Take-Along CD* icon is found in the margin of the text to indicate that there are resources on the CD that relate to the material being discussed in the chapter.

- This edition has an even *greater emphasis on curriculum applications,* with the addition of numerous examples, model lessons, and suggestions for integrating the computer into educational curricula.

- We expanded the discussion of computer literacy to include other literacies: media, information, technological, and visual literacy.

- Recognizing the growing popularity of digital cameras, we wanted to emphasize their use as a communication tool. In this edition there is a brief discussion of some basic photographic elements of lighting and composition leading up to an examination of the use of *Photoshop Elements®* and photo editor.

OTHER HIGHLIGHTS OF THIS REVISION

An improved *Companion Website* serves as a resource to the instructor and as a reference to the student. It includes:

- *New! Demo Central* activities build around the guidelines, checklists, rubrics, and evaluation forms that are in the text
- *New! Activity Central* links to vendor demos/trial versions of software mentioned in the book
- *Chapter Objective* outlines key topics and concepts in each chapter
- *Self assessment* multiple choice and true/false questions with automatic grading provides immediate feedback for students
- *Let's Practice* allows students to electronically answer the questions from the text's end-of-chapter feature *Let's Practice*
- *Web resources* offer students website links to explore, including supplemental information resources for assessment, portfolio development, and standards
- *Professional Development web links* provide website links to professional organizations, magazines, and journals
- *Digital Portfolio* allows students to electronically answer the questions from the text's end-of-chapter activities and submit them electronically to their professor
- *Web extensions* provide a topic or situation related to chapter content and includes a designated web link or links along with meaningful activities/questions
- *Lesson Ideas* include electronic versions of the lesson plan ideas that appear in the text
- *Selection Rubrics* include downloadable versions of rubrics listed throughout the text
- *PowerPoint Slides* provide PowerPoint presentations for each chapter for students to use as a study guide

A *Companion Website* icon in the margin of the text indicates that there are resources on the website that relate to the material being discussed in the chapter.

Teachers and students will find that the strengths of the book have been retained in its fifth edition:

- A balance of up-to-date and cutting edge factual information, research, theory, and application
- Highly readable, student-friendly prose
- Technical matters explained clearly for the nonexpert audience
- Direct and meaningful standards-based integration of software and hardware applications into the classroom for both students and teachers
- A chapter on Internet resources, including strategies for using search tools, especially filtered search engines. We present the basics of web page construction and the use of commonly found editors.

With the help of feedback from professors and student users in an extensive review process, this book has been revised significantly. We have made meaningful changes to more effectively demonstrate the computer's capacity as an educational tool for problem solving and to show to a greater extent the range of classroom applications of computer technology available to teachers and learners.

TEXT ORGANIZATION

Woven throughout this text is the value of the computer as a personal productivity and problem-solving tool for the teacher in an instructional role, as well as for the student in a learning role. The text is divided into two parts. The first deals with foundational issues and underlying theory. The second part addresses practical classroom applications of the computer. The text, therefore, is organized with the following thematic frameworks:

- *Issues in information technology.* A number of issues are examined, including copyright, intellectual property, equitable computer access, and gender equity.
- *Learning theory and instruction.* Theoretical structures are established as a way of looking at the computer's role in teacher-centered instruction and to examine student-centered learning. Both *behaviorist* and *constructivist* perspectives are examined. Underlying principles and theories of education are reviewed and applied to discussions of computer applications in instruction and learning.
- *Strategies for computer use.* The computer as a productivity tool is applied to tutorial, drill and practice, simulation, and multimedia formats. The Internet, word processing, graphics, databases, and spreadsheets are seen as problem-solving tools in the curriculum. Furthermore, the text is organized to provide thorough coverage of computer knowledge and educational applications, including the following:
  - *Word processing.* Curriculum applications are suggested, along with sample lessons to illustrate them. Mail merging is explained.
  - *Graphics.* Instruction on using the computer to generate graphics for charts and graphs, signs, posters, bulletin boards, and projected presentations is given. Tutorials on Photoshop Elements® and Print Shop® Deluxe lead the reader through basic applications.
  - *Spreadsheets.* Detailed instructions for creating spreadsheets are presented. Curriculum applications are suggested, along with sample lessons to illustrate them. Proper selection of chart types and the interpretation of data represented by graphs are explained. A tutorial on Microsoft Excel® shows the reader how to create a grade book.
  - *Databases.* The organization and retrieval of information are examined. Detailed instructions for creating databases are presented. Curriculum applications are suggested, along with sample lessons to illustrate them. A tutorial on FileMaker® Pro shows the reader how to create an address book.
  - *Multimedia.* Multimedia applications can help to organize thoughts and ideas and to communicate them to others. The chapter on multimedia tools covers how to produce instructional materials to fit students' varied learning styles. A tutorial on PowerPoint® shows the reader how to create a multimedia presentation.
  - *Internet.* Several Internet tools (including the World Wide Web) and their practical application are described in this chapter. Searching the Web and evaluating Web information are examined. The proper way of citing Internet information is explained. A tutorial on Microsoft Word® shows the reader to create a Web page.

■■■ CHAPTER FEATURES

This edition maintains the style of the fourth edition, which drew acclaim from students for presenting important and useful information in a highly readable format. The following features are included in each chapter:

- Each chapter begins with an *advance organizer* and, in this edition, *applicable* **NETS-T Standards,** followed by an overview called **Let's Look at This Chapter.**
- *Charts and line drawings* are used to illustrate concepts in a concrete manner.
- Direct, practical applications of concepts discussed are highlighted in the feature called **Let's Go into the Classroom,** which were contributed by teachers throughout the United States as well as Canada, Australia, Japan, and a military school in Germany.
- *Screen displays* illustrate application software in, as much as possible, a nonspecific hardware platform.
- *Basic tutorials* called **Let's Try It** introduce students to popular software in the graphics, spreadsheet, database, and multimedia chapters.
- Each chapter ends with a summary in a feature called **Let's Review.**
- *Exercises* called **Let's Practice** allow the student the opportunity to process the information presented in the chapter and apply it in a practical manner, using higher-order thinking skills.
- Important terms are printed in boldface when they are introduced to the reader. They are then defined in the **Chapter Glossary** and in the **glossary** at the end of the book, as well as included in the **index** to facilitate reference.

■■■ ACKNOWLEDGMENTS

We would like to acknowledge the significant contributions that the following people made to the creation and development of this text.

- Glenna Descy, for her wonderful support and thoughtful suggestions.
- Peggy Forcier, for her unflagging support and careful consideration of the ideas presented in the manuscript. A special thanks for working through the tutorials.
- Susannah Groves, for her meticulous examination of the last edition and helpful suggestions to improve it.
- Kathy Schrock, for sharing her practical wisdom in the inspiring Prologue to the text.
- Doug Johnson, for contributing his useful strategy *"The Upgrade: Easing into Technology Integration"* in Chapter 3.
- David Warlick, for his thoughtful contribution of *"Literacy: In a Time of Rapid Change"* (Chapter 3) and for his challenging look at the school of tomorrow in the Epilogue.
- Users of our previous editions, both instructors and students, who accepted our suggestion and emailed us their thoughtful comments.

We would also like to express our gratitude to the reviewers who so thoughtfully read and offered constructive criticism to the work in progress. Their expertise contributed greatly to the strength of this book and to its potential usefulness in a course dealing with computers in education. They include Jeremy Dickerson, East Carolina University; Loretta Enlow, Indiana Wesleyan University; Patricia Hess, Illinois Central College; Donna Jurich, Knox College; Robert Lipton, Pennsylvania State University; Jeff Newell, University of Illinois, Springfield; Shannon Scanlon, Henry Ford Community College; Toni Stokes-Jones, Eastern Michigan University; and George Weimer, University of Indianapolis.

Brief Contents

Contents

Part 2 Classroom Applications as Learning Tools 169

About the Authors

RICHARD C. FORCIER

My formal education consists of a B.S. degree in science education from Westfield Massachusetts State College, an M.S. in instructional technology from the University of Massachusetts, and a Ph.D. in educational administration from Michigan State University, where I worked as a curriculum developer.

After succeeding as a classroom teacher at the elementary and secondary level and as a school principal, I embarked on a college teaching career that spanned 27 years at the University of Wisconsin and at Western Oregon University. I taught undergraduate and graduate courses in a variety of technology applications on campus as well as to remote locations by two-way video conferencing. As Assistant Dean in the College of Education where I have been an administrator, I continue to teach courses and consider myself first and foremost a teacher.

DON E. DESCY

My education consists of a B.S. and M.S. in biology education from Central Connecticut State University and a 6th year certificate and Ph.D. in educational technology from the University of Connecticut.

After receiving my first two degrees I taught biology, earth science, and general science for 17 years. It was during this time I achieved my 6th year degree. Realizing that I needed a new challenge, I decided to pursue my doctorate. I knew immediately that I wanted to study instructional technology. I was motivated by the fact that this field makes learning more enjoyable for both the student and teacher. In fact, one of the most rewarding ongoing experiences that I have is reading all of the positive feedback we get from users of this text. I came to the University of Minnesota in Mankato in 1989 and have since written profusely and presented all over the world including Canada, France, Japan, Okinawa (as a guest of their state department), and China (as a guest of the People's Republic of China Liberation Army).

Together, we promote the concept borrowed from Marshall McLuhan that a tool is an extension of a human's potential. In the current edition of our textbook, we describe the computer as a tool of the mind that allows the user to create, store, access, retrieve, analyze, and disseminate information. Although we respect the behaviorist viewpoint, we believe in a constructivist philosophy and teach accordingly, relying heavily on cooperative learning techniques and the construction of projects as a way of meeting learning goals. The textbook was written with this in mind.

A Message to the Reader

"We are living in the Information Age" is a saying that has been overused to the point that we don't appreciate what it really means. The authors believe, however, that each one of us will have our own "aha!" moment, where we will reach a personal understanding of the true impact of its meaning. We venture to guess that this personal understanding will relate in some manner to shifting paradigms associated with teaching and learning and to the effective use of technology

Do not take the term *Information Age* at face value, but dig deeply to derive your own personal understanding. Let this insight guide your teaching behaviors. It is our fervent hope that each one of you, as readers of this text, will sharpen your skills dealing with the creation, storage, access, retrieval, analysis, synthesis, and dissemination of information—and pass that skill along to your students.

The title of this book has been carefully chosen to reflect our view of the computer as a tool—a tool to increase our productivity and problem-solving abilities. We hope that the title alone will challenge you to seek a deeper definition of productivity than the one based on the old factory-model meaning of the efficient creation of products. Think of productivity as encompassing effectiveness as well. Include quality, quantity, time, and space in your definition. Think of productivity when you read the following quote from the noted Canadian philosopher and scholar Marshall McLuhan, "All media are extensions of some human faculty." The computer is one of the most powerful of such media.

In our profession, change is not only inevitable but it is also rapid and significant, and it is upon us all, both as a new generation of teachers and as seasoned professionals. Two quotes come to mind as we close this message: "It takes all the running you can do, to keep in the same place," from *Through the Looking Glass and What Alice Found There;* and "Who dares to teach, must never cease to learn," carved above the entrance to the instructional technology building at Western Oregon University.

Based on the belief that teachers are also perpetual learners, we have significantly expanded the Take-Along CD accompanying this book. We have included material that we believe will benefit you as you approach your first teaching position or continue in your present one. We present the outline of its contents on the following page for your consideration. We encourage you to use these resources.

The computer places us in a looking glass of change: a place that is rapidly changing even as you read this. Change is not something to fear but rather to embrace. We must always seek the unknown so that we will grow and be able to provide the information and the guidance necessary to allow our students to create new knowledge and understanding. The computer can become the productivity tool that extends our human capability as we teach and continue to learn.

Richard C. Forcier
Don E. Descy

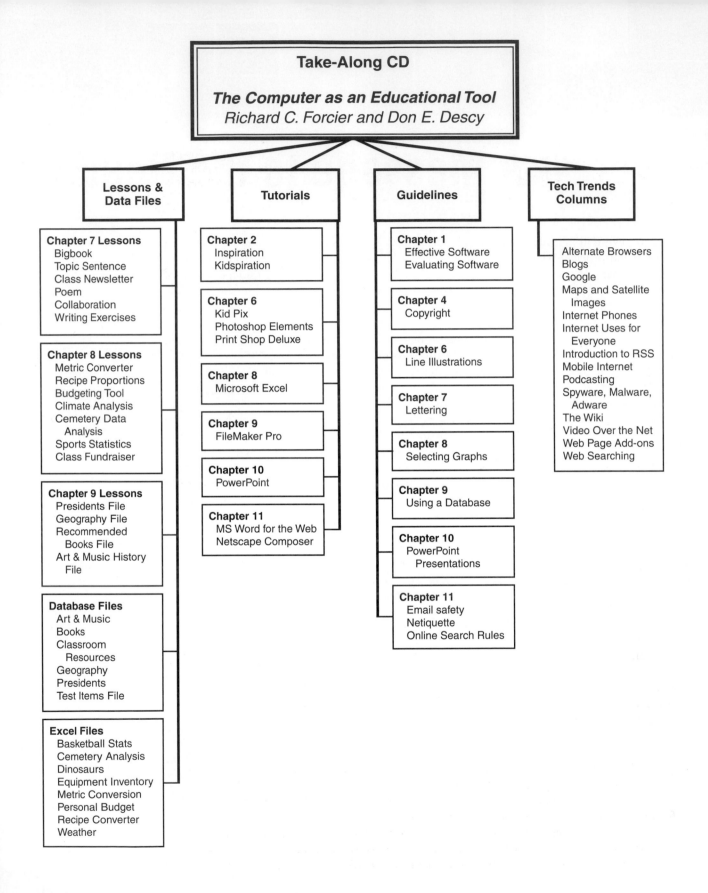

Take-Along CD

The Computer as an Educational Tool
Richard C. Forcier and Don E. Descy

Lessons & Data Files

Chapter 7 Lessons
Bigbook
Topic Sentence
Class Newsletter
Poem
Collaboration
Writing Exercises

Chapter 8 Lessons
Metric Converter
Recipe Proportions
Budgeting Tool
Climate Analysis
Cemetery Data
  Analysis
Sports Statistics
Class Fundraiser

Chapter 9 Lessons
Presidents File
Geography File
Recommended
  Books File
Art & Music History
  File

Database Files
Art & Music
Books
Classroom
  Resources
Geography
Presidents
Test Items File

Excel Files
Basketball Stats
Cemetery Analysis
Dinosaurs
Equipment Inventory
Metric Conversion
Personal Budget
Recipe Converter
Weather

Tutorials

Chapter 2
Inspiration
Kidspiration

Chapter 6
Kid Pix
Photoshop Elements
Print Shop Deluxe

Chapter 8
Microsoft Excel

Chapter 9
FileMaker Pro

Chapter 10
PowerPoint

Chapter 11
MS Word for the Web
Netscape Composer

Guidelines

Chapter 1
Effective Software
Evaluating Software

Chapter 4
Copyright

Chapter 6
Line Illustrations

Chapter 7
Lettering

Chapter 8
Selecting Graphs

Chapter 9
Using a Database

Chapter 10
PowerPoint
  Presentations

Chapter 11
Email safety
Netiquette
Online Search Rules

Tech Trends Columns

Alternate Browsers
Blogs
Google
Maps and Satellite
  Images
Internet Phones
Internet Uses for
  Everyone
Introduction to RSS
Mobile Internet
Podcasting
Spyware, Malware,
  Adware
The Wiki
Video Over the Net
Web Page Add-ons
Web Searching

Prologue

Things you need to know about educational technology

by Kathy Schrock

As a pre-service teacher, planning for your own classroom sometimes seems overwhelming. What type of discipline model is best for what situation? How do I both adhere to required content standards and include creativity in my lessons? What lesson or unit plan methodology and assessment information do I need to be familiar with in order to succeed? These concerns have not changed in the quarter century since I completed my student teaching and received my education degree from Rutgers College. However, there is another aspect of classroom teaching and learning that I did not have to worry about in 1979—that of technology use. Since the first IBM PC did not come out until 1981 and personal computers were intended primary for business use, there were no examples of using this technology to affect student learning. The first Apple II came on the market a bit earlier, in 1977, but, due to the high cost of any desktop computer, they were not often seen in classrooms.

I feel privileged to have been in education while this technology revolution has taken place. I lived through the era of educational technology when formatting a floppy disk was the important skill to attain. There were no books, classes, or information about using the personal computer, except for creating word processed notes home to parents, making banners for Open House Night, and allowing students access to educational software programs such as *Oregon Trail*. I dialed up to the Internet via a 2400 baud modem in 1992, and used a text-based browser to find material for my students located on Gopher servers housed at universities around the country. I was confused when the World Wide Web showed up as a menu option in this text-based browser in 1993. However, when I first viewed the Web through the graphical Web browser Mosaic and saw the images and text that were viewable, I immediately knew this was going to be an important resource for educators and students! I learned to write HTML from a book, and mounted my site on the growing World Wide Web on July 1, 1995.

Over the past ten years, the growth in the amount of material on the Web, the advances in technology that allow access to many formats of material via the Internet, the affordable price of personal computers, and the expansion of broadband Internet access to schools and homes has created a huge information source for educators and students. From the use of online subscription databases to locate information, to the creation of blogs as an avenue for peer evaluation of writings, there are a few important skills you need to feel comfortable with as you begin your journey into the classroom. I am not worried about your technology skills—most of you have probably grown up using a computer. However, from one who creates materials for teachers and students, has made hundreds of mistakes over the last ten years, and is trained as an information specialist, I feel qualified to give you some helpful suggestions for using technology in support of teaching and learning.

You need to become familiar and conversant with the International Society for Technology in Education's (ISTE) National Technology Standards for Teachers (NETS*T), as described in the first chapter of this textbook. This important document contains the set of technology standards that all new teachers should acquire. These standards are not about creating columns or using a spreadsheet. They are a set of pedagogically based and practical ideas for how educators can best use technology to reach all learners. In preparation for your upcoming job interviews, I suggest that you create an e-portfolio, arranged by the NETS*T standards, demonstrating your competencies in each of the areas. Many school districts are now asking in-service teachers to choose a NETS*T standard as one of their personal and professional yearly goals, so you will shine at an interview with your e-portfolio!

The other things you need to be very comfortable with are the basic information literacy skills of creating the good questions, choosing the best information source for your information need, searching for your information source on the Web, critically evaluating the information you find and comparing it to your question, and communicating this information in a meaningful way. Pay attention to the search rules and the section on evaluating Web information in Chapter 11 of this text. There are also plenty of sites on the Web to help you understand these concepts, including Jamie McKenzie's Questioning Toolbox (*questioning.org*), my own Guide for Educators site (*discoveryschool.com/schrockguide/*), and Debbie Abilock's site (*www.noodletools.com/debbie/literacies/information/5locate/adviceengine.html*). As a classroom teacher, it is up to you to mentor the choice of good resources, to demonstrate proper searching techniques, to require your students to validate and cite information, and to demand ethical use of others' intellectual property.

You are fortunate to have hundreds of online tools at your disposal to help you in the classroom. Take advantage of them. Communication to parents via email is the accepted method used in classrooms today. Posting the classroom homework on a site dedicated to that purpose, or on a Web page or blog you create, is easy to do and only takes a little time to maintain. Allowing students the chance to create podcasts of their stories, music creations, or interviews is another way you can share student work with your community. You can "invite" the community to hear and see the exciting things you and your students are doing.

Another area you should think about is your responsibility to keep your students safe on the Internet. Whether you are teaching second graders what to do when an inappropriate site slips through the content filter or posting artwork created by middle school students on a website, safety is an important aspect to consider. I do not recommend posting student pictures, even in groups and unidentified, or full student names on the Web. Use initials or have students design their own avatar to "identify" themselves. You need to remember that the Web reaches a much larger audience than your local newspaper!

The last thing I want you to remember is to be creative! Apply for grants to fund the innovative technology unit you are planning. Attend as many conferences as you can to bring back successful ideas and practices for use in your classroom. Consider the sample lessons presented in the application chapters in this textbook as idea starters for your own unique lessons. Offer to showcase some of your technology lessons for your colleagues and ask for suggestions on how you can make them better.

You have access to an entire world of information that was not available when I was a beginning teacher and I am jealous. Remember to use it often (and wisely) for both personal and professional practice!

Kathy Schrock is the Administrator for Technology for the Nauset Public Schools in Orleans, Massachusetts, and the creator of *Kathy Schrock's Guide for Educators*. She may be reached via email at *Kathy@kathyschrock.net*

Foundations and Theory

LET'S LOOK AT FOUNDATIONS AND THEORY

A computer does not exist in a vacuum, neither should its use. As teachers we have the responsibility to make good use of the computer as a teaching tool or as an effective tool in the proper learning environment.

To set the stage for effective computer use, we examine in some detail Behaviorist and Constructivist perspectives on learning. We also discuss how students learn and relate that to the selection, evaluation and use of computer software.

To appreciate the role of the computer, we scrutinize a wide variety of applications in education and refer to specific software appropriate to these applications.

As computer use has spread in the classroom, standards for its effective use have emerged and gained national prominence. As its use has evolved, we can learn from its past, appreciate present use, and look for an exciting future. We are fortunate in having nationally known experts assist us in this task by contributing their thought in this section of the textbook.

If we, as teachers, are to use the computer effectively, we must consider legal and ethical issues surrounding its use. We must give thoughtful consideration to social contexts for computers in the classroom and the obligations and expectations in a computer literate society.

Finally, in this first section of the textbook we take a careful look at the computer itself. We are not suggesting that readers become technicians, but rather, that you become technologists capable of understanding the equipment well enough to know what to choose and when and how to use it most effectively. Our hope is that its use will become transparent to the task to which it is applied in a problem solving fashion.

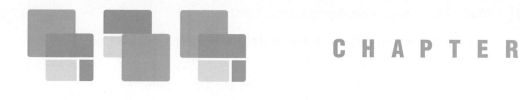

CHAPTER 1

Learning and Instruction

1. What are the basic tenets of behaviorism?

2. What are the basic tenets of constructivism?

3. How can the computer support each perspective?

4. How is information acquired?

5. What is the relationship between concrete and abstract experiences?

6. How can the presentation of the message be enhanced using computer software?

7. How can we use cooperative learning in the classroom? How does this differ from a learning community?

8. What are the benefits of using authentic assessment in the classroom?

9. What role can rubrics play in classroom assessment?

10. How do portfolios aid in the authentic assessment of our students?

11. What are some steps in developing a useful digital portfolio?

12. What are the types of intelligences described by Gardner and how might these help you when teaching your students?

13. What should be considered in the evaluation and selection of software?

NETS•T Foundation Standards and Performance Indicators Addressed in this Chapter

I. Technology operations and concepts
   A. demonstrate introductory knowledge, skills, and understanding of concepts related to technology (as described in the ISTE National Education Technology Standards for Students)
   B. demonstrate continual growth in technology knowledge and skills to stay abreast of current and emerging technologies

II. Planning and designing learning environments and experiences
   A. design developmentally appropriate learning opportunities that apply technology-enhanced instructional strategies to support the diverse needs of learners
   D. plan for the management of technology resources within the context of learning activities
   E. plan strategies to manage student learning in a technology-enhanced environment

III. Teaching, learning, and the curriculum
   A. facilitate technology-enhanced experiences that address content standards and student technology standards
   B. use technology to support learner-centered strategies that address the diverse needs of students
   D. manage student learning activities in a technology-enhanced environment

IV. Assessment and evaluation
   A. apply technology in assessing student learning of subject matter using a variety of assessment techniques
   B. use technology resources to collect and analyze data, interpret results, and communicate findings to improve instructional practice and maximize student learning
   C. apply multiple methods of evaluation to determine students' appropriate use of technology resources for learning, communication, and productivity

V. Productivity and professional practice
   A. use technology resources to engage in ongoing professional development and lifelong learning
   B. continually evaluate and reflect on professional practice to make informed decisions regarding the use of technology in support of student learning

C. apply technology to increase productivity
D. use technology to communicate and collaborate with peers, parents, and the larger community in order to nurture student learning
VI. Social, ethical, legal, and human issues
B. apply technology resources to enable and empower learners with diverse backgrounds, characteristics, and abilities

▮▮▮▮▮ LET'S LOOK AT THIS CHAPTER ▮▮▮▮▮

This chapter establishes the groundwork for looking at the computer's role in instruction and examines its role in student learning. Recognizing that there are several theories of learning, that classroom practice is often based on one or more of these theories in combination, and that this text does not purport to be an instructional theory textbook, we review behaviorist and constructivist theories of learning and instruction that are covered in greater depth in courses dealing with pedagogy. The intent here is to demonstrate that the computer can be a practical tool used in concert with multiple teaching strategies that have a solid theoretical basis.

Much learning in the classroom is teacher directed and is based on behaviorist theories that purport that learning takes place in small incremental steps. We present an introduction to this theory and describe ways that computers are used in this approach. Acknowledging that there is a growing interest in constructivist theories of learning, this chapter also presents an overview of a moderate constructivist perspective so that the use of the computer as a productivity tool can be better understood in that environment. The thoughtful application of the computer can make students more productive in the construction of their knowledge through problem solving.

Many of the problems that educators face could be solved with the assistance of a computer. If the computer is to be an effective tool in increasing productivity, then the teacher must begin with answers to the following fundamental questions: When do I use a computer? Will using a computer save time? Will it allow me to perform tasks that might otherwise be beyond my skills? Can I get better, more complete, and more accurate information by using a computer or will it only complicate my life?

Using computers in education depends on the effective use of software that can increase productivity. As computer users, we need to be thoroughly familiar with the process of problem solving. Most of us will never choose to become computer programmers, but as educators we need to be good users of computer programs, and we need to acquire skills to develop problem-solving specifications.

Looking beyond our own needs as educators, problem-solving proficiency is an essential skill that we must help our students develop. According to **constructivism,** students interact with the real-life experiences that surround them, and they construct mental structures that provide an understanding of their environment. If students are to build these mental structures, they must refine the skills needed to solve the problems they will encounter, whether they are working individually or in cooperative learning groups.

Not all people's thinking patterns and learning styles are alike, although many different cognitive processes and intelligences are valid and should be valued. This chapter gives an overview of perception and communication to emphasize the importance of analyzing our student population and matching instructional materials to student needs.

PERSPECTIVES ON TEACHING AND LEARNING

Every learning environment has an implied method of information presentation. Learning activities are based on a belief of how students best learn. Of the many philosophical doctrines, two stand out rather clearly as examples related to software development, selection, and use: the behaviorist perspective and the constructivist perspective.

Behaviorism uses a teacher-directed approach that is based on theories developed by B. F. Skinner, Robert Gagné, Richard Atkinson, Lee Cronbach, and David Ausubel. Behaviorists view the teacher as the manipulator of the environment that is experienced by the learner. B. F. Skinner, well known for his work in behavior modification through operant conditioning, was a proponent of programmed instruction. Skinnerian-style lessons use carefully planned steps of stimulus–response pairing and reinforcement to reach a goal. The lessons and their accompanying drills are administered in small, incremental steps to minimize the likelihood of incorrect responses. The techniques used reflect a belief that, by tightly structuring the environment, the behavior of the organism (the student) can be shaped to achieve desired changes (learning). **Linear** programmed instruction is an example of this concept of education, where the accumulation of knowledge is preparing the student for predicted future needs. Traditional classroom instruction has included strong components of this behaviorist theory, which is referred to at times as objectivist. The teacher, with the prescribed textbook, is the source of information. Behavioral objectives are identified, lessons are planned, instruction is delivered, guided practice is provided, retention and transfer of learning activities are encouraged, and testing the information taught is the standard means of assessment.

In direct contrast to the behaviorist viewpoint is the perspective espoused by constructivists, who view education as inseparable from ordinary life. Constructivists base their model on work by Jerome Bruner, Seymour Papert, Jean Piaget, and Lev Vygotosky. Through developmental exploration and play, students assume control of educational activities by making choices related to individual interests. The students discover rules and concepts during the course of interactions in an environment that encourages the use of problem-solving strategies, which in turn are developed while learning how to think. The teacher learns along with the students and becomes a guide, a facilitator, and a supportive partner in this educational process. Education is considered a guided tour of preparatory experiences in which students practice making decisions by simulating real-world situations. The teacher becomes the facilitator of education by selecting the experiences that offer the appropriate practice to the students. In this way students construct their own knowledge and gain skills that will be needed in a future environment, which may be quite different from the present one. If reduced to a single overriding distinction, it could be said that constructivism encourages the learner to pose a problem and then solve it, whereas according to behaviorism, the role of the teacher or other external source is to pose the problem to be solved. It should, therefore, be noted that the teaching of problem-solving strategies is important in both perspectives.

Software may reflect one or both of these approaches and may make assumptions about the teaching and learning style that will be used in the classroom. Different techniques are selected to achieve educational goals in relation to different philosophical perspectives. Teachers must learn to identify the instructional approaches embodied in particular software if they are to effectively harness the power of the computer in their classrooms.

The Behaviorist Perspective on Learning

Robert Gagné (Gagné, Briggs, & Wager, 1992, pp. 54–66) lists types of intellectual skills in a linear scheme, ranging from simple discriminations to complex problem-solving processes.

Maria B. Vonada/Merrill

This approach is predicated on the belief that the acquisition of knowledge at any stage depends on what has been learned at an earlier one. Thus, a learner must master the lower-level abilities before tackling the higher orders.

Elements of a Good Lesson. A great deal of research has gone into identifying the components of a good learning situation. Gagné views learning theory as technology—a set of rules that can be followed in the design of instructional events. His point of view draws on many theories of outstanding psychologists and resulted in the formulation of the following instructional events as elements of a good lesson (Gagné et al., 1992, p. 190).

1. Gaining attention: Stimulation to gain attention to ensure the reception of stimuli
2. Informing learner of the objective: Informing learners of the learning objective to establish appropriate expectancies
3. Stimulating recall of prerequisite learning: Reminding learners of previously learned content for retrieval from long-term memory
4. Presenting the stimulus material: Clear and distinctive presentation of material to ensure selective perception
5. Providing learning guidance: Guidance of learning by suitable semantic encoding
6. Eliciting the performance: Eliciting performance involving response generation
7. Providing feedback about performance correctness: Informing students about correctness of responses
8. Assessing the performance: Following the opportunity for additional responses, informing the learner of mastery, and giving further directions
9. Enhancing retention and transfer: Arranging variety of practice to aid future retrieval and transfer of learning

Wedman (1986) found it quite revealing to examine the elements of a good lesson as they relate to the instructional functions provided by computer-assisted instruction (CAI) software. By describing common ways in which software provides each of the instructional events, he offers a method of analyzing a program's strengths and weaknesses relative to the elements in a good lesson as described by Gagné and colleagues. Wedman then examines the teacher's role in complementing the instruction provided by the software to provide a complete instructional unit. The chart presented in Figure 1–1 displays the CAI software and teacher techniques related to each instructional event.

Figure 1–1 CAI and teacher techniques

Teacher techniques and computer applications related to events of instruction *(Wedman, 1986. Courtesy of The Computing Teacher. Reprinted with permission.)*

Events of Instruction	CAI Techniques	Teacher Techniques
1. Gaining attention	• Graphics • Sound • Games	• Demonstrate relevance of content • Present high-involvement problems • Use related, highly attractive media • Assign groups to use software
2. Informing learner of objectives	• Pretest • Textual statement of objectives • Graphic illustration of objectives • Brief interactive demonstration	• Pretest • Tell the learner what is expected • Demonstrate use of the content
3. Stimulating recall of prerequisites	• Pretest for prerequisites • Textual review of prerequisites • Graphic display of prerequisites	• Test prerequisite content • Review prerequisite content and vocabulary
4. Presenting stimuli	• Textual display of new content • Graphic display of new content • Learner control over presentation sequence and display rate • Reference to non-CAI material	• Use other media to present new content
5. Providing guidance	• Attention focusing devices (e.g., animation, sound, pointers) • Help screens • Examples and illustrations	• Organize peer tutoring • Cross-reference difficult content to examples and remediation in other materials
6. Eliciting performance	• Questions on new content • Applications of new content to solve problems or control situation (e.g., flight simulator)	• Ask questions • Create performance tasks where the learner applies the new content (e.g., lab experiment)
7. Providing feedback	• Display score or correct answer • Help screens for incorrect answers • Additional information or examples	• Provide answer keys • Provide reference materials coordinated with correct answers • Provide outcome guides coordinated with performance tasks (e.g., lab experiment check sheet)
8. Assessing performance	• Test questions • Limited response time (for memory-level questions) • Recordkeeping	• Give paper-and-pencil tests • Conduct performance tests • Use computers for context-rich testing
9. Enhancing retention and transfer	• Repeating content not mastered • Applying new content to a different, but related situation	• Provide alternative instructional materials for content not mastered • Create situations (not involving a computer) where students must apply new content

A diagram of these events as they might occur in a computerized lesson using the program *Odell Down Under*® (The Learning Company, Inc.) is provided in Figure 1–2. This example, set in Australia's Great Barrier Reef, is a worthy successor to the award-winning *Odell Lake* and uses all the instructional events described by Gagné and colleagues.

Figure 1–3 is an example of the high-quality graphics used to gain attention. Animation is also present on the computer screen. Some software, of course, uses only certain instructional events. In such cases, the teacher must provide the missing events for the lesson.

Human Factors. A great deal of attention has been given to individual responses during interactions with computers. These effects are critical to the effectiveness of a program, because they influence the learning events of a good lesson. Early writings by Gagné and Briggs (1974, p. 11) recognized eight human factors affecting the learning event. These factors, identified as external and internal stimulus factors and internal cognitive factors, are listed in Figure 1–4.

The three external stimulus factors are contiguity (time relationship between stimulus and response), repetition (frequency and rate of exposure to a stimulus), and reinforcement (follow-up to the reception of a stimulus). The three internal cognitive factors are factual information (from memory or external sources), intellectual skills (ability to manipulate

Figure 1–2 Elements of a good science lesson

The application of the events of instruction to a science lesson using *Odell Down Under*, a simulation of a predator/prey model *(Courtesy of TLC Properties, Inc., a subsidiary of the Learning Company, Inc. Reprinted with permission.)*

Gaining attention

A reef is shown with fish swimming around and music playing.

Stating the objective

The student is informed that the object is to discover the relationship between fish, which to eat, which to avoid, and which ones will clean off parasites.

Stimulating recall of prerequisite learnings

The student is reminded to use all of the information presented in the picture and to make choices. The student can interrupt the program at any time to review information about the various reef dwellers.

Presenting the stimulus material

When the student has chosen a fish and read the given information, the computer generates a picture of the reef with the chosen fish shown in some situation.

Eliciting the performance

The student is asked to control the fish's behavior by moving the mouse, clicking when appropriate, or pressing the spacebar.

Assessing the performance

The computer indicates whether the chosen behavior was correct, incorrect, or indifferent.

Providing feedback about the performance

The action in the given reef situation is carried out demonstrating the behavior chosen by the student.

Enhancing retention and transfer

Another situation is presented to the student based on past performance.

Figure 1–3   Odell Down Under

A screen shot showing quality graphics *(Courtesy of TLC Properties Inc., a subsidiary of The Learning Company, Inc. Reprinted with permission.)*

Figure 1–4   Human factors

Eight external and internal factors affecting the learning event

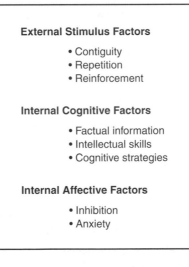

External Stimulus Factors

- Contiguity
- Repetition
- Reinforcement

Internal Cognitive Factors

- Factual information
- Intellectual skills
- Cognitive strategies

Internal Affective Factors

- Inhibition
- Anxiety

information), and cognitive strategies (ability to process or interpret into meaningful information). Added to these are the internal affective factors of inhibition (reluctance to react to a stimulus) and anxiety (a tension often stemming from a lack of confidence).

These factors relate to a theory of how information is stored in and retrieved from short-term and long-term memory. Gagné and Briggs believe that information that is sensed is held in the auditory, visual, or tactile register for only a second before it is disregarded or sent to short-term memory. There it is encoded for about one-half minute before storage in long-term memory. Because of the short periods involved, a stimulus must be limited to one idea, and there must be enough time to process and store the information without interference or overload. Meaningful repetition is believed to contribute to control of the processes and, in turn, to learning. The effectiveness of a lesson depends on the internal responses to a stimulus, the senses used, and the ease of use of the computer so as to minimize distractions during computer-assisted learning.

Behaviorists favor software designed for drill and practice or tutorial instruction. Popular titles of this type of software on the market today include *Math Blaster® 6–8; Math Munchers Deluxe®; Word Munchers Deluxe®; Read, Write & Type;* and *Mavis Beacon Teaches Typing®*.

The Constructivist Perspective on Learning

Cognitive psychologists as early as Whitehead (1929) have insisted that learning is an active and highly individualized process. They clearly point out that learners must actively construct new knowledge based on their own individual experiences and understandings. This constructivist model of learning is based on the concept that knowledge is produced by the individual learner rather than processed from information received from an external source. The student becomes the producer rather than the consumer of information. The teacher becomes the guide and facilitator of learning rather than the director of instruction. Goals are still set, but the learner is given significant freedom in how to attain them. Assessment is still performed, but benchmarks are established and the teacher employs authentic measures such as evaluating a product or examining a portfolio.

A foundation for some of the current constructivists' beliefs can be found in the work of Jean Piaget. He is best known for proposing four stages of development in a child's cognitive abilities: (1) from birth to about age two, the sensorimotor stage (when children begin to explore their environment and to differentiate themselves from the world around them); (2) from age two to about seven, the preoperational stage (when language and intuitive thought develop); (3) from age seven to about 12, the **concrete** operational stage (when classifying and ordering of items and inductive reasoning develop); and (4) from about age 12 on, the stage of formal operations (when more **abstract** and formal thought, control of variables, and proportionality can be managed). Piaget attributed these stages to a naturally occurring process of maturation and the appropriate exposure to experiences that encourage development.

The idea that children learn without being taught is central to this learning theory. Long before children enter school, they have mastered the complexities of language and speech enough to understand and communicate with those around them. They have gained a sense of intuitive body geometry that enables them to move around in space, and they have learned enough logic and rhetoric to convey their desires to parents and peers. Children learn all these things effectively without formal teachers and a curriculum, and without explicit external rewards or punishments. They learn by simply interacting with their environment, relating what is new to what they know from past experience.

For example, a very young child can build a cognitive structure or a concept of "dogness": dogs look, feel, sound, and smell a certain way. Whenever a dog is encountered, the child attempts to make sense of the experience by calling on a previously formed cognitive structure of "dog." Piaget calls this assimilation. But a new dog may be different from the one met before. As new elements are encountered (a curly tail instead of a straight one; long, shaggy hair instead of short hair; and so on), the cognitive structure for "dog" must be modified and enlarged to encompass the new information, a process Piaget called accommodation.

If we think of learners in Piagetian terms, as the active builders of their own cognitive structures, we should consider the kinds of experiences and material our culture provides for use in this building process and examine the potential contribution of the computer.

Figure 1–5   Comparison of behaviorism and constructivism

Predominant differences between their perspectives

Behaviorist	Constructivist
Teacher-centered	Learner-centered
Teacher as expert	Teacher as member of learning community
Teacher as dispenser of information	Teacher as coach, mentor, and facilitator
Learning as a solitary activity	Learning as a social, collaborative endeavor
Assessment primarily through testing	Assessment interwoven with teaching
Emphasis on "covering" the material	Emphasis on discovering and constructing knowledge
Emphasis on short-term memorization	Emphasis on application and understanding
Strict adherence to fixed curriculum	Pursuit of student questions highly valued

Figure 1–5 summarizes the predominant differences between the behaviorist and constructivist perspectives. They should be viewed as points on a continuum, not as absolutes. Though the trend in the United States is toward constructivism, most classrooms exhibit some characteristics of both.

Saunders (1992) illustrated the constructivist perspective with the model shown in Figure 1–6. He states, "Constructivism can be defined as that philosophical position which holds that any so-called reality is, in the most immediate and concrete sense, the mental construction of those who believe they have discovered and investigated it." The conflict between expectations (what we think will happen) and observations (measures of what actually happens) causes disequilibration. The problem is resolved through accommodation, or learning—the process of reconciling new information with previously held ideas and beliefs. Explained this way, it becomes clear that constructivism is a philosophy in which problem solving is a central element.

From a constructivist perspective, learners must be provided with a rich environment of sensory experiences, to which they will respond in a problem-solving fashion to build understandings. The computer, through its use of text, sound, graphics, animation, and multimedia, is ideally suited to present such a rich environment. In a constructivist classroom, technology is encountered that will enable the student the opportunity to experiment with it, construct individually and in groups, and reconstruct models and simulations that aid them as they build their own ideas and beliefs. Many of the computer applications that we discuss in this textbook will be useful tools for students to help them construct their own knowledge. We stated in the beginning that computers are simply a tool to help people perform tasks easily and more efficiently. Students who have ownership in a product take care as they construct their own knowledge. This sometimes poses a dilemma for teachers who have been successful in their schooling using the older behaviorist approach. Many may feel that they are losing control of learning rather than understanding that they are co-controlling learning now with their students.

Constructivists favor software designed to pose problems and construct scenarios designed to make students active participants in their learning. Popular titles of this type of software on the market today include *Hot Dog Stand*®, *SimCity2000*®, *Where in the World Is Carmen Sandiego?*®, *Inspiration*®, and the ever-popular *Oregon Trail*®.

The shifting paradigms of computer applications denote a transition from a centralized environment to a personalized one, with the user in command of the computer, and then to an interpersonal one, where users interact with one another. A distinct move has occurred

Figure 1–6   A constructivist learning model

The constructivist perspective illustrated by Saunders's model *(Reprinted with permission from School Science and Mathematics Association.)*

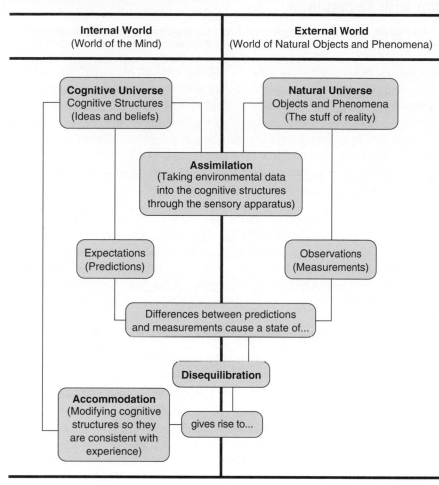

from the computer operator to the end user interacting directly with the computer and then to a networked community of users interconnected electronically. Finally, we have moved away from a fascination with huge amounts of stored data to a concern for the value of the information and the development of knowledge. Every one of these paradigm shifts parallels the shift in philosophical foundations of education toward a more constructivist approach emphasizing problem solving.

Compared with behaviorist approaches to instruction, in which "covering the material" is emphasized, constructivist approaches to instruction focus on students "discovering the material." When students are actively engaged with other students and teachers in the process of learning through the completion of authentic tasks, they need both problem-solving tools and problem-solving skills to assist them.

COOPERATIVE LEARNING

All learning takes place in one of three ways: individually or students working alone, competitively or students working against each other, and cooperatively or students working

LET'S GO INTO THE CLASSROOM
Constructivist Teaching with Technology

New technologies are particularly well suited to support constructivist teaching and learning; in fact, they are some of the most exciting tools available to educators today. We only have to think about what computers do well to imagine their possibilities in the constructivist classroom. New technologies meet their real promise when they are used as tools by the students to help them in the process of difficult, complex, but meaningful learning. New technologies can then be used as exciting, cutting-edge tools to assist teachers in providing curriculum for students that is authentic, connected to the real world, and challenging.

The ideas expressed below will hopefully help teachers to generate new ideas and uses limited only by their own creativity and the development of new technologies for the constructivist classroom:

- **Connecting the Classroom to the World.** Authentic inquiry—learning that is connected to the world—allows students to pursue their curiosity about science, history, literature, mathematics, or virtually any subject they desire. When used judiciously, the Internet—along with the many educational programs that have been developed to take advantage of it—can provide students with authentic connections to projects that pique their curiosity. Students and teachers can take advantage of searchable scientific, demographic, or informational databases, and millions of images that may be used for research on nature, history, or art.

- **Cognitive Assistants.** Writing and editing is far smoother and simpler with word processing software than with pencil and paper. The student can brainstorm more easily, draft writing and discard it, cut and paste, exchange drafts or ideas with students and teachers by email, write collaboratively, receive feedback electronically, and file and organize the writing. Spreadsheet or database programs that organize, manipulate, and represent data allow students to see patterns or generate and test hypotheses in a fraction of the time it takes to do the same work manually. Graphing software lets students explore how various equations are represented visually as they experiment with data. When technology is used in this way, it is a cognitive assistant that takes what we already know how to do and makes it easier, allowing us to focus more fully on developing powerful ideas.

- **Platforms for Representing and Linking Knowledge.** When students create hyperlinked media such as web pages or wikis, they are learning to represent knowledge symbolically, combining language and images. Through hyperlinking, they learn that language can and should be defined, and that knowledge on one topic can easily be linked to knowledge on other topics. When students create a website to report on and assess their learning on a complex topic area, they are in fact creating a 3-dimensional representation of knowledge. Wikis are an excellent example of how that knowledge can be made public and collaborative, while its accuracy is subject to the scrutiny of others. Wikis can represent a publicly agreed upon body of knowledge, and as such, they allow students to learn about the sociology of knowledge creation at the same time as they express what they know about a particular topic.

- **Simulations.** Simulations provide a way to bring fascinating, real-world problems into the classroom. Simulations allow students to experiment with altering the variables of a particular situation in ways that the real world does not. In a simulation of Newtonian physics, students can wonder how acceleration would change if they make the ball go faster or slower, and see the immediate effects of their actions. They can experiment with what happens in a city if there is a major fire or hurricane, or if a new business moves into town. With this bounded experimentation, they can learn a lot about phenomena that are extremely complex in the real world, because the teacher can help them to introduce that complexity one step at a time. Finally, together to accomplish shared learning goals. While all three should be part of a child's education, Roger Johnson and David Johnson, codirectors of the Cooperative Learning Center at the University of Minnesota, recommend that the cooperative mode play the dominant role. Cooperative learning—or collaborative learning, as it is sometimes called— activities tend to promote the development of communications skills, higher-order thinking skills, positive self-esteem, social awareness, improved motivation, and a greater tolerance of individual differences (Johnson & Johnson, 1994).

A productive environment must be created by carefully grouping students and monitoring the behavior of groups to prevent students from "slacking off" and riding the coattails

Anthony Magnacca/Merrill

of more able partners and to prevent higher-ability students from lowering their own effort and achievement because of a feeling of being used by others. True collaboration must provide for structured sharing in creation and decision making, resulting in a negotiated product. Teachers must prepare students for collaborative computer activities by issuing specific directions relating to each group member's role and expected interaction with others and the computer. Individual and group assessment must be considered. Individual student journals or portfolios may be used, along with an evaluation of the product produced by the group. Individual assessment tends to keep the individual student on task, while product assessment fosters peer tutoring and a feeling of responsibility to the group.

Cooperative learning prepares the student for the world of work, where some measure of collaboration is found in nearly every job situation. Research indicates that cooperative learning supports task-oriented behavior and improved peer relations. It provides social skill benefits, with achievement benefits for low achievers and no penalty on high achievers (Schlechter, 1990). Thus, cooperative learning, correctly implemented, is one way teachers can effectively stretch scarce computer resources.

Technology can serve an important role in cooperative learning environments. The teamwork needed to plan and produce a technology-enhanced lesson or project allows students with diverse skills, backgrounds, and abilities to work together as a team and be successful in their individual roles. Most schools do not have enough computers or equipment to allow for individual work on projects so cooperative learning, with all of its benefits, is an excellent way to change a computer-poor situation into a learning-rich one.

LEARNING COMMUNITIES

More and more, school systems are embracing the idea of learning communities on both a small and large scale. Learning circles or communities of learners are groups of individuals—be they teachers, students, preservice teachers, or professors of education—who aid one another in the learning process. According to Collay, Dunlap, Enloe, and Gagnon (1998), the six essential characteristics of purposeful, sound learning communities include: "1. Building community, 2. Constructing knowledge, 3. Supporting learners, 4. Documenting reflection, 5. Assessing expectations, and 6. Changing cultures."

Productive learning circles build community first by establishing *how they are unique* from other groups associated with instruction and learning. Distinctions often include the approach that learning circles take to opening their sessions, inviting participation, or setting core values around which the group revolves. Where, for example, an average study session of teachers might simply begin their work perfunctorily, the learning circle group generally begin their interactions with a ritual of sorts (bringing and sharing of food, a check-in of participants' feelings, and so forth). *Group construction of knowledge* is an integral part of genuine learning communities. Similarly, where many classrooms or learning settings still function through rote learning, true learning circles stress active engagement and participation. Learning circles *support learners* through encouragement, support groups and positive conversations, and interactions. Although these might seem to be characteristics true of any classroom or group of learners, they are often overlooked entirely. The fourth essential characteristic of effective learning communities entails *documenting reflections* on all parts of the learning process and results.

As with all productive learning environments, learning circles also depend on *assessment of expectations.* The group of learners involved must determine the degree to which they have or have not met their specified goals. In essence, this is assessment of expectations criteria of learning communities. Last, the underlying purpose of learning circles is to *understand the culture* of the communities in which they serve and work, and how their work fits in and/or changes this community.

ASSESSMENT

It is important to assess student learning accurately if we are to truly measure progress. Many teachers do not feel that traditional paper-and-pencil testing and measurement accurately reflect the amount of student learning actually taking place. One increasingly popular way to improve the accuracy of the measurement of student learning is **authentic assessment** or **performance-based assessment.** Authentic assessment refers to assessment tasks that resemble real-world situations. Authentic assessment does not encourage passive testing or rote learning but rather focuses on the student being able to integrate learning to overcome a real-world problem. Authentic assessment encourages students to use higher-order thinking skills to solve problems by utilizing *performance samples* such as open response questions, short investigation of problems, performance assessment, portfolios, and self-assessment. Authentic assessment allows students to not only understand information but also develop this understanding in real-world skills that are much easier to transfer to the outside world. Assessments usually reflect learning over time and enable instructors to better evaluate performance and achievement in a way not available with standard paper-and-pencil examinations. Project development also can be documented to show learning over time.

Project-based learning is an authentic assessment model for teaching in which projects are used to assess student learning. Students involved in this model actively construct their own knowledge, complete meaningful tasks, create realistic projects, and/or solve real-world projects. Checklists, rating scales, rubrics, and portfolios are all authentic assessment methods of evaluating student learning.

Checklists are simple ways of observing and categorizing behaviors in a bimodal (observed/not observed) manner. **Rating scales,** on the other hand, are more complex. Each observation is placed on a scale, usually of numerical values that measure the degree to which a student completes a task.

Another way to score authentic assessment projects is with a **rubric,** a scoring matrix that differentiates the quality of learning using a graduated scale of exemplar behaviors. These benchmarks assist teachers by providing objective guidelines to evaluate student performance on a task. The behaviors may be correlated with qualitative or quantitative scores. Rubrics are used to place student achievement at a point on a scale that enables the student to see what is needed to achieve mastery. Many times rubrics are distributed beforehand to help students plan and measure their learning.

Well-constructed rubrics:

- Present learners with explicit guidelines concerning the expectations of their teacher,
- Supply a model for the learners to impart emphasis, focus, and detail to refine their capabilities,
- Present learners with a sequential progression of behaviors that guide them to a higher level of knowledge,
- Allow learners to pattern their own education to meet the expectations of their teacher,
- Enable the teacher to accurately assess learning on a predetermined scale.

The following is a partial rubric that might be used to evaluate a web page.

Digital Portfolios

The school reform movement that has been gaining momentum over the past years is changing some of the basic ways schools and students interact. As stated, in many school systems, evaluation of student learning using paper-and-pencil tests and quizzes is being

GUIDELINES TO EVALUATING A WEB PAGE

Authority

- **Level 1:** No author or email contact is listed.
- **Level 2:** No author is listed but an email address is given.
- **Level 3:** An author is listed but there is no way to find out about credentials.
- **Level 4:** An author is listed along with credentials that are appropriate for the material on the page.

Dating

- **Level 1:** There is no way to tell when the web page was produced or updated.
- **Level 2:** Information on the page was updated within the past two years but still seems to be relevant.
- **Level 3:** Information on the page was updated within the past year and seems to be up to date.
- **Level 4:** Information on the page was updated within the last three months and reflects up-to-date knowledge on the subject.

Bias

- **Level 1:** The information on the page discusses only one point of view with generalizations and seemingly unprovable assumptions.
- **Level 2:** The information on the page discusses only one point of view with little reference to known authorities in the field.
- **Level 3:** The information on the page discusses only one point of view with references to known authorities in the field.
- **Level 4:** The information on the page seems fair and balanced.

Purpose

- **Level 1:** It is difficult to understand the purpose of the web page.
- **Level 2:** The web page seems to have a purpose but contains information that does not seem relevant to it.
- **Level 3:** The purpose is somewhat clear though it contains some distracting elements.
- **Level 4:** It is easy to define the purpose of the web page.

supplemented with more authentic means of assessment. The use of portfolios is a popular means of authentic assessment. Many educators believe that a portfolio is a truer representation and documentation of learning. Portfolios fit into the constructivist view of learning because they contain representations of knowledge that the students themselves have synthesized and constructed. A portfolio is not simply an assortment of a student's work used as examples to show how they met specific requirements. Rather, it is a selected collection of student work designed to demonstrate the degree to which a student achieved specific standards (Figure 1–7). An important component of this collection is the inclusion of reflective commentary and self-assessment articulated by both the teacher and student as they fit each piece of the portfolio into the larger framework of standards and achievement. This creates a much richer tool, adding insight into the abilities of the student. True portfolios are never completed but rather continue to grow and change as the student continues to grow and learn. Barrett (2000) sums it up, "An electronic portfolio is

LET'S GO INTO THE CLASSROOM
A Grading Rubric for the 28 State Assignment*

Grading Rubric			Student: Trip Through the 28 States East of the Mississippi			
Table	**A Quality 18–20 Points**	**B Quality 16–17 Points**	**C Quality 14–15 Points**	**D Quality 12–13 Points**	**Your Points**	
	• City-to-city route is complete • Full state names listed • Miles are completely accurate • Columns are left aligned except for mileage (centered)	• City-to-city route is complete • Some abbreviations used in state names • Miles are completely accurate • Columns are aligned properly	• Some cities are missing in route • Some errors traveling to contiguous states • Miles are complete & accurate • Some misalignment in columns	• Many errors in either route, mileage, state names • Table is incomplete, misaligned, etc.		
Map	**A Quality 9–10 Points**	**B Quality 8 Points**	**C Quality 7 Points**	**D Quality 6 Points**	**Your Points**	
	• All states are labeled with the correct abbreviation • Title • Used a ruler • Route is clearly marked • Mississippi River follows the correct route & is labeled • No spelling errors • No more than 5 distinctly different colors were used	• Title • Used a ruler • Two or less errors in labeling states and/or spelling • Route is clearly marked • Mississippi River follows the correct route & is labeled • Used more than 5 colors or colors weren't distinctly different • A few contiguous	• Title messy or incomplete • Some ruler • More than three errors in labeling states or spelling • Route is marked but may have some confusions • Mississippi River isn't clearly marked • Used more than 5 colors or colors were not distinct or different	• Final product messy or incomplete • Smudges on product are distracting • Erasures are messy • Words are illegible or incorrect • Cartographic rules have been ignored • Route isn't complete or is difficult to follow		

(Continued)

	• Outlining/ shading • Map is free of erasures & smudges • Writing is clear & legible	states same color • Very few erasures or smudges • No outlining or shades, if present it is messy • Very little of the writing is illegible	• Contiguous states same color • Coloring is missing or incomplete • Smudges or erasures	• Mississippi River path is confusing or missing	
Chart	**A Quality** **14–15 Points**	**B Quality** **12–13 Points**	**C Quality** **11 Points**	**D Quality** **9–10 Points**	**Your** **Points**
Cover Sheet	**A Quality** **5 Points**	**B Quality** **4 Points**	**C Quality** **3 Points**	**D Quality** **2 Points**	**Your** **Points**
	• All required information is included • Border is neatly printed • Paper is free of erasures & smudges • No spelling errors • Writing is clear & legible	• All required information included • Border may be somewhat messy • Very few smudges, erasures • No spelling errors • Writing is crooked, somewhat unclear, or illegible	• Some information missing • No border • Some smudges or erasures that detract • 1–2 spelling errors • Writing is crooked, unclear, or illegible	• Numerous smudges or erasures • Incomplete • Numerous errors • Writing is crooked, unclear, or illegible	
Total Points					**50**

Paula Conley
Skyway Elementary School
Coeur d'Alene, Idaho

*This rubric was used to grade students for the **Let's GO INTO THE CLASSROOM:
Technology Enhanced Lessons Make Learning Fun** found in Chapter 3.*

Figure 1–7 Digital portfolio

Elementary schools are using digital portfolios to demonstrate student growth and achievement. This one, on a CD, also acts as a yearbook for the student to treasure

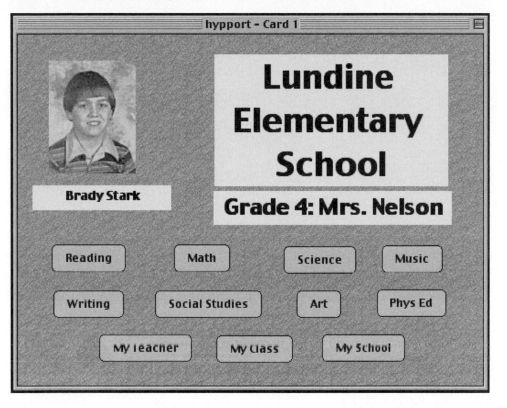

not a haphazard collection of artifacts (i.e., a **digital** scrapbook or multimedia presentation) but rather a reflective tool that demonstrates growth over time" (p. 41).

Computers have proven themselves to be useful tools in the collection, development, and presentation of portfolios. Their power enables individuals to compactly store and quickly locate information at the click of a mouse. We use the term **digital portfolio** to designate one stored on a computer disk, CD-ROM, or DVD. You may encounter the term **electronic portfolio** elsewhere. Electronic portfolios may contain components such as a videotape that are in an electronic analog format but perhaps not stored digitally on a computer storage medium. Digital portfolios may contain written words along with movies, still images, sounds, and interactive examples of a student's work all digitized for use by the computer, allowing pages of information and boxes of artifacts to be neatly stored on a small USB flash drive, CD-ROM, or DVD. Many university students (Figure 1–8) produce interactive digital résumés that highlight their achievements and store them in a convenient format for prospective employers. More and more teachers and students are placing portfolios on secure websites or on DVDs, both of which can be accessed using either Macintosh or Windows computers instead of CD-ROMs that are platform specific and may limit access to the platform on which they were made. Two different spheres of knowledge are tapped when developing a digital portfolio. These are portfolio development and multimedia production. Understanding both of these spheres will enable teachers and students alike to design, develop, and produce powerful tools that easily communicate the level of knowledge and achievement attained by the students.

Portfolio development contains several steps. The first step is the assembly of a collection of documents and artifacts (i.e., videos, images, text and text files, models, and sound)

Figure 1–8 Electronic resume

University students use digital portfolios as electronic resumes. Some universities save copies of these as examples of student mastery of standards for accreditation

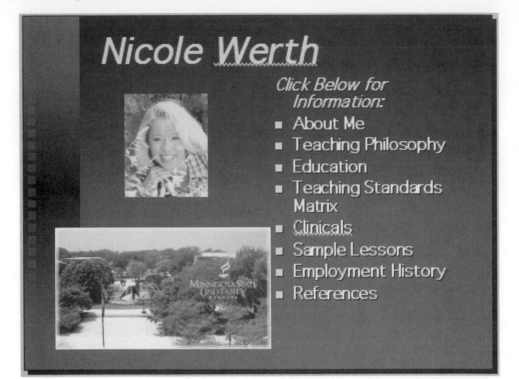

that demonstrate the achievement of a specific standard. This step contains several smaller steps: the identification and understanding of the standards, the collection of documents and artifacts, and the selection of documents and artifacts that best exemplify the achievement of the standards. The second step involves thoughtful reflection on the documents and artifacts by both the student and the teacher. At this stage collaborative discussions may take place to discuss past, present, and future progress.

Several steps are involved in the multimedia development phase. First, the parameters of the portfolio must be established. The two considerations at this point are how to store and present the information, and what software and hardware are available to do this. Of course, these are closely related. Software selection need not be an issue. Hardware decisions hinge on equipment available for digitizing (e.g., scanners, digital cameras, video digitizers) and final method of storage (e.g., USB flash drive, CD-ROM, DVD).

The second step in the multimedia development phase consists of setting up the standards within the software package, digitizing documents and artifacts, and assembling the final product. As stated, an important part of this phase is the evaluation and reflective commentary of the artifacts by the student. The portfolio exercises at the end of each chapter are linked to one or more of the NETSS•standards.

Portfolio Programs. Software is not an issue. Specific portfolio management tools such as *The Portfolio Builder*™, The *Grady Profile*™, and *The Portfolio Assessment Kit*™ may be used. Wonderful portfolios have also been developed using *PowerPoint*® (explored in Chapter 10), *FileMaker Pro* (explored in Chapter 9), and even *Microsoft Word*® (discussed in Chapter 7). Portfolio management programs are specifically designed to easily store and display student work, link the work to standards, and shed a new light on the terms *evaluation* and *assessment.* Some of the programs are linked to or are add-ons to other programs. For example, *The Portfolio Builder* is designed to work with *PowerPoint,* and *The Portfolio Assessment Toolkit* is designed to interface with *HyperStudio.* Linked or not, they all serve as a repository for student work. Many of the portfolio programs have several layers of information each accessed by one or more passwords for students, teachers, or administrators and can serve as a complete record of the student's time and progress in school.

LET'S GO INTO THE CLASSROOM
Starting Right with Portfolios

I have been implementing standards-based electronic portfolios for three years with my fourth graders. It has been one of the most rewarding projects I have done with my students each year, and their reflections on the project, along with the benefits I have seen demonstrated in my research, make it all worthwhile. I became interested in electronic portfolios while going through graduate school, and pursued implementing them as a topic for my thesis. The procedure I used for implementation was Dr. Helen Barrett's (2000) electronic portfolio process. This process guided my research, and it still guides my process today.

The electronic portfolios my students create are based on my school district's reading and writing standards. Many elementary electronic portfolio examples today are simply digital scrapbooks due to missing the standards component. In the beginning of the process, students use a template I created for them in PowerPoint. The template contains all of the basic elements of the portfolio, and students add their own work and personal touches as they go along. Each portfolio contains slides for: a cover, table of contents, purpose statement, goals, "All About Me," and three slides for each trimester of reading and writing (one for reading and two for writing). Students record a reading clip for each trimester, in addition to linking reading captions and two writing pieces with captions for each trimester. An additional component I have added over the past two years has been artwork. Students take digital camera pictures of the artwork they truly feel shows their art progress. Then, they have one slide at the end of the year that is their art reflection. Once everything is linked, and students have added their own personal touches, portfolios are burned to CDs for students to take home. PowerPoint viewer is also burned onto the CD for those students who do not have PowerPoint at home.

The benefits to using electronic portfolios are numerous. First, and foremost, students have captured their reading, writing, and artwork in a way that will allow them to keep it indefinitely. Having this work stored on a CD is a treasure for the students and their parents. Second, students gain increased technology skills. In this process, students become familiar with many different software applications, the digital camera, and the scanner. They are gaining skills that have lifelong implications, in addition to gaining confidence in their skills. Students become more reflective in their reading and writing. By having this purposeful collection of their work, students are able to look back on it, and make accurate assessments of their abilities and areas they need to grow in. In addition to becoming more reflective about their reading and writing abilities, they become more confident in their reading and writing abilities. Using the technology is exciting for the students, which in turn creates additional enthusiasm for reading and writing.

To effectively manage electronic portfolios in your classroom, there are several important recommendations to consider. First, choose several students to be PowerPoint (or whatever software you have chosen as the medium) trainers. By doing this you have empowered the students to teach each other, and it takes a lot of the pressure off you. Give each trainer a class list of highlighted names with tasks written at the top for them to check off. Second, develop instruction sheets for how to do different aspects of the portfolio on the computer. This makes students more responsible for themselves by requiring them to use the instruction sheets after they've already learned how to do something

(Continued)

23

before asking you or the trainers. Next, utilize the parent volunteers in your classroom who are willing to help with the project. Offer to train parents, and then have them work with individuals or small groups of students. By having one parent devote an entire morning or afternoon to helping with the portfolios, the entire class could complete a specific component in one day. Finally, develop a schedule for when the different aspects of the portfolio need to be done. Having a set schedule will keep you more disciplined with the process and will allow you to see what needs to be done in the future.

By sticking to your schedule, in addition to implementing the above recommendations, electronic portfolios will not be so overwhelming and time won't be such an issue. It is a challenging process, and roadblocks encountered along the way cause frustration at times. However, by looking at the big picture, the outcome of electronic portfolios is amazing, and the positive effect it has on the students is incredible. I feel I am proof that electronic portfolios can work in an elementary classroom. Is it worth it? Absolutely.

Lori Kiene
4th Grade Teacher
West Des Moines Community School District (IA)

It is easy to see how technology can aid the teacher and the student in an authentic assessment environment. The student can match goals, outcomes, and standards with work accomplished using databases and electronic portfolios. Teachers can use technology in many of the same ways matching students, progress, and projects in databases, spreadsheets, and electronic storage systems.

INSTRUCTION AND LEARNING

Just as problem-solving strategies vary among individuals, so do types of intelligence, perception, and motivation. Good teachers always try to individualize their instruction, even when dealing with 30 students in a classroom. They attempt to know each student as an individual; to recognize strengths and weaknesses; and to identify, accommodate, and respect different types of intelligence and different learning styles. The computer is becoming an invaluable tool, aiding the teacher in each of these ways. Good teachers also understand the role of perception and motivation in learning, and how computer software can increase both faculties. Understanding students as individuals allows teachers to make intelligent and informed decisions when choosing software for their classrooms.

Learning Styles—Types of Intelligence

Howard Gardner proposes that there are at least eight intelligences: linguistic, logical-mathematical, spatial, musical, bodily-kinesthetic, interpersonal, intrapersonal, and naturalist. Gardner has also proposed that other intelligences might exist including spiritual and existential (Gardner, 1999). Your students may exhibit one type of intelligence in particular or may have several strengths. Gardner defines intelligence as "a set of skills of problem solving—enabling the individual to resolve genuine problems or difficulties that he or she encounters and when appropriate, to create an effective product; it also entails the potential for finding or creating problems, thereby laying the groundwork for the acquisition of new knowledge" (Gardner, 1983, pp. 60–61). Gardner believes that intelligence defines not only how people acquire information but also how they process this acquired information—how they learn best. Although many people tend to think of intelligence more narrowly, it is important to recognize and support individual aptitudes by ensuring that all students have resources to help cultivate their full range of talents and intelligences. Unfortunately, today's schools usually address only two of Gardner's intelligences: linguistic and logical-mathematical (Ross & Olsen, 1995). Reflecting on these intelligences and seeking to create a computer environment supportive of all students, Eichleay and Kilroy (1993–1994) suggest types of software appropriate to each intelligence.

Not all students will react alike to the same piece of software. A study of Figure 1–9 will suggest ways in which a variety of software can be applied to meet the needs of different

Figure 1–9 Multiple intelligences and software types

(Adapted with permission from "Hot Tips for Inclusion with Technology" by K. Eichleay and C. Kilroy, December/January, 1993–94, The Computing Teacher, 21(4), pp. 38–40. Modified by Forcier in 1998 and Descy in 2006.)

Forms	Description	Software
Linguistic	Able to express abstract ideas and concepts in words and language	Word processors, word games, software with speech output, crossword puzzle generators, label makers, prompted software programs, books on CD-ROM
Logical-mathematical	Able to solve problems with analytical, logical reasoning. Using numbers to test hypothesis, infer, categorize and make generalizations	Spreadsheets, database, problem-solving software, concept mapping software, simulations, computer programming, logo, probeware, strategy game formats
Spatial-visual	Able to form mental pictures and models of the spatial world and use these pictures and models to help solve problems	Graphic production, drawing and painting software, three-dimensional modeling, desktop publishing, concept mapping Software hypermedia, mazes and puzzles, logo, maps, charts and diagrams, multimedia
Musical	Able to use music to express ideas, and recognize patterns and sounds	Song creation, hypermedia, music concepts/skills, story and song combinations, multimedia, recording music, singing or rhymes with microphone
Bodily-kinesthetic	Able to express concepts and solve problems using parts or the whole body. Able to move the body with control and skill	Alternative input devices, keyboarding/word processing, science and math with manipulatives and probes, programs where the user can move objects on the screen
Interpersonal	Able to understand, communicate, interpret and interact with other people	Telecommunications, interactions with characters in simulations and adventures, programs about social issues, group participation/decision-making programs, two or more player games
Intrapersonal	Able to internalize and use this to relate to the world. Is aware of oneself and uses this for personal understanding	Tutorial, self-paced games played against the computer, self-awareness/self-improvement building programs, programs where students work independently
Naturalist	Able to recognize, relate, and categorize the natural world and interpret cause-and-effect relationship in this world	Spreadsheets, databases, image capture software, problem-solving software, concept mapping software, probeware, simulations, strategy games

learners. More information on expanding Gardner's theory into effective classroom practice can be found in Campbell, Campbell, and Dickinson (1999).

Cognitive Styles—How We Think. Cognitive style is another factor that influences student learning. Unlike the learning styles proposed by Gardner that describe the conditions under which we learn most comfortably and efficiently, cognitive style deals with how we think. Each person seems to have a set of measurable preferences. One of the most widely used instruments to measure cognitive style was based on the work of Katherine Briggs and extended and developed by her daughter Isabel Briggs Myers and husband Peter B. Myers. The Myers-Briggs Type Indicator (MBTI) is based on a constructivist view of learning. Students answer a series of questions based on their learning preferences. After that, their responses are categorized and clustered onto a continuum of one of four sets of opposing cognitive styles: extrovert (E) or introvert (I), sensing (S) or intuitive (N), thinking (T) or feeling (F), and judging (J) or perceiving (P). The characteristics of each style are described in the following table. The results contain one factor from each set. One person might be ENFJ (extrovert, intuitive, feeling, judging) and another may be INTP (introvert, intuitive, thinking, perceiving). Teachers and students alike have preferences in each of these four polar opposites. Understanding and awareness of a students' cognitive style will better enable you to design instruction to meet students' needs. Several sites on the Web contain the MBTI, review the meaning of each cluster of styles, and discuss famous people with these styles. You will find it fun and interesting to check yours!

MBTI Type	Characteristics
Extrovert (E)	interested in people and relationships, act first/think later, needs interaction with outside world, extrinsic motivation
Introvert (I)	interested in self, needs "private time," thinks first/acts later, intrinsic motivation, inner world, prefers one-to-one relationships
Sensing (S)	likes clear concrete information, solid facts, reality, lives in the present, uses common sense and practical solutions, uses concrete past experiences, real objects, and solid facts
Intuitive (N)	comfortable with ambiguous information and data, theoretical constructs, possibility, lives in the future, uses connections, patterns and contexts, personal meanings
Thinking (T)	analyzes facts, logical decision making, accepts conflict and normal part of living, critical analysis, detached
Feeling (F)	uses subjective views and values, sensitive to people's needs, conflict is unsettling, decisions based on impact on people and personal feelings, attached
Judging (J)	task-related actions, planned, organized, controlled, works best and less stress if ahead of deadlines
Perceiving (P)	likes multitasking, variety, works best close to deadlines, avoids commitments that interfere with freedom, flexibility, actions without plans, plans on the fly

Perception

What we know about the world we have experienced through our senses. Free of any physical impairments, we usually gain information through all five senses. Infants are intrigued by the wondrous variety of sounds, sights, and smells to which they are exposed, and they seek to explore every sensory stimulus. As we mature, our visual and aural senses assume an overwhelming importance in the acquisition of knowledge. Indeed, a great deal of the information we possess as adults has been acquired through the sense of sight.

Perception is relative, not absolute. Sensory stimuli are accepted by the learner and given meaning based primarily on past experiences. Thus, sensory experiences result in perceptions. Because perceptions, in turn, are organized into understandings, the quality of the visual and aural stimuli embodied in software assumes great importance.

As an infant, the concept of "fiveness" might be acquired by handling five items (units), gradually seeing them represented by five fingers (digits), and then processing the meaning as the numeral 5 (symbol). Once a child has been exposed to a variety of concrete experiences, pictorial and then verbal experiences are an effective and much more efficient way of building understandings. These more abstract expressions of ideas must have a concrete basis. Examining well-designed software, we find that computer graphics, visuals, and certainly multimedia serve as more concrete referents to meaning than do written words. Because visuals resemble the items they represent, they offer the viewer concrete clues to meaning. To enhance the perception of visual information in software, research by Guba, Wolf DeGroot, Kneneyer, VanAtta, and Light (1964) and others has shown that, in good graphic design, distracting elements must be kept to a minimum. This point is particularly important, because the learner is constantly bombarded by a multitude of sensory inputs. Software must be designed to limit distraction and guide the learner's attention to the essential information. Visual and aural cues should give order to the message, and difficult concepts should be broken down into easily digested steps providing concrete reference points familiar to the learner.

Motivation

Research strongly suggests a positive correlation between achievement and the amount of time students spend on an instructional task. Motivation is an essential element in instruction. One challenge we face as teachers is to understand learners and to elicit maximum responses from them. Motivation can be intrinsic as well as extrinsic. Some students are motivated to learn by forces internal to themselves. They have a strong belief in the acquisition of knowledge. Others seem to respond more positively to external stimuli in their learning environment.

The ARCS Model. John Keller (1987) designed a useful model to define the components of motivation. This is known as the **ARCS model** after the first letter of the word that describes the four essential parts:

Attention	Is the instruction interesting and worth paying attention to?
Relevance	Will this instruction meet a personal goal or need?
Confidence	Can I succeed in learning this?
Satisfaction	Is there an extrinsic or intrinsic reward for me after the instruction?

Communication

Because a learner cannot experience everything on a direct, purposeful, firsthand basis, a great deal of knowledge is gained through vicarious experiences. To select teaching materials that will provide appropriate vicarious experiences, we must understand the process of communication.

Communication is often defined as the transmission or sharing of ideas based on common understandings in one of three major modes: oral, visual, or written. Direct, face-to-face communication usually is oral. The visual mode often spans greater distances and has a sense of permanency. This is also true of the written mode, the most abstract of the three. It is often suggested that communication implies an interaction, give and take, or feedback. This is immediate and easily accommodated in verbal. It is a bit more difficult and delayed in visual and written communication.

A meaning resides in the individual, not in the message—the structure of contextual clues and stimuli designed to evoke a desired response (meaning). Communication in the classroom can be seen as the transmission of this structured information organized to produce learning. The source of such a transmission might be a student or teacher speaking or demonstrating a skill or procedure. It might also be materials, such as textbooks, films, videos, or computer courseware.

Communication Models. An early model first proposed by Claude Shannon and Warren Weaver (1949), two mathematicians employed by Bell Telephone Laboratories, was quite technical and appropriate for understanding telephone or radio communication. A popular song, for example, might be selected by a disc jockey (information source), encoded by equipment (transmitter) into radio waves, received by a radio (receiver), and heard as music reaching your ear (destination). **Noise** might be static in the atmosphere or, as the authors defined it, anything that deteriorates the quality of the signal. It might even be visual distractions.

Wilbur Schramm (1954), concerned with the instructional communication potential of education television, adapted the Shannon-Weaver model as seen in Figure 1–10 to reflect the interpretation of meaningful symbols. For communication to take place, the fields of experience of the sender and of the receiver must overlap. The signal that is shared is subject to each party's perceptions. The sender encodes the message according to skills possessed, biases, cultural influences, attitudes, and so on. The receiver calls on like factors to decode (understand) the message.

Because meanings cannot be transmitted, the model illustrates that the message designed under the influence of meanings, which reside in the sender, must elicit accurate and appropriate meanings in the receiver. In turn, the message being communicated is embodied in the instructional materials. The decoding (understanding) of the message depends on meanings that reside in the field of experience of the student. The medium carries the message, serving as a channel or bridge between fields of experience. The more accurately the instructional media express meanings in each field, the better the communication. The message will be degraded or distorted if the content is perceived by the user as incorrect, biased, or incomplete. It will suffer if the sequencing is wrong, if it is too fragmented, or if too much information is presented to be absorbed by the user. The message will be lost if the presentation is boring. Distractions will enter as

Figure 1–10   Revised Shannon-Weaver model
Schramm adapted the model to reflect meaningful symbols

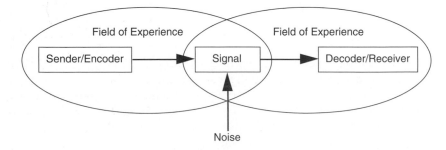

"noise" in the communication process if the predetermined pacing is wrong (too slow or too fast) for the user, or if the presentation employs verbal or visual techniques that are foreign to the user.

Taking communication theory into account, it is possible to postulate that effective teaching materials must have the following qualities.

- Materials must stimulate a high degree of interest in the learner.
- They must have a basis in concrete experience.
- They must make optimum use of the visual and, where appropriate, the aural sensory channels to strengthen the reality of the experience.

Bloom's Taxonomy

Over the years, several educators and educational technologists have tried to classify the different thinking skills used as we go about learning and processing information. One of the most important classification schemes was developed in 1956 by researchers led by Benjamin Bloom. Bloom's Taxonomy (Bloom, 1956) contains six levels of cognition ranging from knowledge acquisition (recalling, memorizing, and recognizing information) in its simplest level to knowledge evaluation (critiquing and assessing information) at the most complex level as illustrated in the following table. It is useful to keep Bloom's Taxonomy in mind as you write student objectives. Each level of progression requires a higher level of cognitive ability and critical thinking. Even though some of the objectives

Level	Action Verbs	Description	Questions
Knowledge	define, identify, label, list, match, memorize, name, order, recognize, recall, repeat, reproduce, state, write	simple recognition or recall of information, principles and ideas	What is the information I found?
Comprehension	arrange, classify, compare, describe, discover, discuss, explain, match, recognize, relate, restate, select, translate	translate or understand information based on prior learning	I have a problem. What exactly is it? How do I solve it?
Application	apply, choose, classify, demonstrate, discover, interpret, modify, sketch, solve, use	choose and use appropriate prior learning to complete a task	How do the pieces fit together? How can I organize and present this information in an appropriate and meaningful way?
Analysis	analyze, associate, compare, contrast, discriminate, dissect, distinguish, examine, infer, test	examine and pull apart information into its component parts	What is it exactly that I am trying to discover? What are the most efficient and effective search methods and tools to use?
Synthesis	arrange, assemble, combine, compose, construct, collect, create, design, develop, originate, organize, plan, theorize, write	combine and integrate knowledge into a construct new to the individual	How can I integrate and summarize this information into a usable form?
Evaluation	appraise, assess, collect, compare, contrast, critique, defend, estimate, evaluate, judge, predict, support, value, weigh	appraise and critique information based on specific criteria or standards	Is this credible information? Are there any underlying biases or motives present?

will be at the lower cognitive levels, strive to write objectives using cognitive skills that are higher up on the list. This will enable students to develop a broader range of thinking skills and increase their understanding of the information.

The ASSURE Model

It is important to place all knowledge of learning theory in a strong framework as we construct learning experiences for students. One popular framework is the **ASSURE model,** which consists of five component parts: (A) **A**nalyze learners, (S) **S**tate objectives, (S) **S**elect methods, media, and materials, (U) **U**tilize media and materials, (R) **R**equire learner participation, and (E) **E**valuate and revise. You may want to search the Web to get more information on this model.

████ ▌ FROM THEORY TO APPLICATION

Good practice should be based on an understanding of sound theory. As we study theories of learning, reflect on experiences, and examine self motivations—as well as those of students—we should seek to develop a knowledge base and a skill level that will enhance application of computers to the classroom. This knowledge and skill will guide us through many decisions related to curriculum, teaching and learning strategies with the computer, equipment purchases, and computer software selection.

Appropriateness of Software

Because the learning theory on which software design is based dictates the role of the computer, the role of the teacher, and the role of the student, recognizing these elements is an important first step toward making good use of the computer in the classroom. Instructional objectives will be met only if the software and the intent of the lesson are closely related.

To understand why the computer lesson must be consistent with the kinds of learning students have come to expect, consider the following example. Imagine that we have prepared a lesson plan calling for practice on the subtraction of whole numbers less than 100. Surveying a curriculum resource guide for software to use, we find a program that presents a subtraction algorithm. This software on subtraction is designed for discovery learning. That is, when a student misses the answer, the software branches back to work that should have been mastered earlier and presents a different problem. However, if our classroom method prior to this lesson has been directive, replete with examples, some students would be frustrated by the computer lesson, because it fails to give them the information they expect. Clearly, in this case, our students would be better served by software built around a more linear approach.

Effectiveness of Software

In assessing the effectiveness of software, keep in mind that the internal responses to a stimulus correspond closely with the events of a good lesson. The student is alerted or motivated, perhaps by curiosity, to interact with the program. The objective of the program sets an expectancy for performance that interests the student. The student must be able to retrieve prerequisite information that provides meaning to the activity.

Liz Moore/Merrill

The stimulus of new information must be perceived selectively over time, or through repetition, from processing to memory. Feedback in the form of favorable reinforcement should bolster self-worth. The information should have relevance to the student's environment for generalization and transfer of learning to occur. If the progression of these responses is not smooth, the chain of events is interrupted, and the lesson is less effective.

Teachers must appeal to multiple senses to gain students' attention and keep them interested. As with other classroom activities, a variety of events is more effective than one or two continuously repeated actions. Variety can be achieved by offering, for example, interaction through the tactile response of typing on the keyboard; using different sounds, bright colors, and interesting graphics; and introducing new topics to challenge reasoning. In addition, students should interact at the appropriate level to avoid frustration or boredom.

When evaluating software, remember that the process of interacting with the computer must be simple, so students can concentrate on the content of the program. Elements that contribute to ease of use center on a simple means of input and a simple presentation of output. To simplify input, a mouse click, single-key command, and single-key selection of activities from a menu of options limit typing errors and speed program execution. Error-free programs (no bugs) and error-trapped designs (in which mistakes are correctable or not accepted at all) prevent frustration with stalled or prematurely terminated lessons.

Clarity in eliciting responses from the student also avoids confusion when interpreting what or how to respond. Output can be simplified, for example, by limiting the field of perception using uncluttered displays on one page at a time, double-spacing text for readability, grouping ideas for easy understanding, formatting the screen to focus on one point, and highlighting major points by effectively using color, animation, and sound. Most of these features are encountered frequently in films, slides, textbooks, and other instructional materials.

Based on an understanding of learning theories and an awareness of factors dealing with intelligence, perception, and motivation, when considering effective software, it is possible to postulate the following guidelines.

 A copy of these
guidelines may
be found in the
Guidelines folder in the
Take-Along CD

GUIDELINES FOR
EFFECTIVE SOFTWARE

- Software must stimulate a high degree of interest in the learner.
- Software must contribute to developmental learning and, thereby, increase the permanence of that learning.
- Software must be based in concrete experience to enhance understanding.
- Software must make optimum use of the visual and, where appropriate, the aural sensory channels to strengthen the reality of the experience.

Software Evaluation

Keep in mind that the fundamental reason for using computer software is to enhance teaching and learning. The fundamental reason for software evaluation is to determine whether it fits the educational goals. D'Ignazio (1992) states:

> Technology has the potential to dramatically improve the performance of teachers and students, and enrich the learning environment. However, in order to produce these outcomes, technology must be used to support the "best practices" for teaching and learning.
>
> Technology must be used by teachers to create a classroom that encourages:
>
> - Heightened student attention, engagement, and enthusiasm for learning
> - Inspired teaching
> - Students taking responsibility for their learning and for coaching fellow students
> - Student authoring, publishing, and presentations
> - Cooperative learning
> - Problem solving, critical thinking, questioning, and analysis
> - Collaborative inquiry, research, and investigation. (pp. 54–55)

When evaluating software, keep some kind of permanent record that describes the product and lists its features and potential applications. Enter the information from the evaluation into the school's electronic resource guide to media available in the school or into the public access catalog of the school library's automated system if the software is purchased.

Some of the criteria for evaluation are general to all software, whereas some of the evaluative criteria are specific to types of software: drill and practice, tutorial, simulation, or tool. The following sections consider the evaluation process, first according to general criteria, and then according to criteria related to software type.

General Criteria. Familiarize yourself with the total software package. Read the instructions to the teacher and to the user. Look over the manuals, if available. Pay attention to the organization and layout of the written material.

Run the program following the written or on-screen directions to determine whether the program leads you through the material in a well-organized fashion. Notice whether the program lets you correct mistakes or whether it traps data entry errors. Can you exit the program at any point without difficulty? Are there any dead ends or blind alleys? Is the information accurate, free from stereotyping, and unbiased? Are the displays well organized and easy to understand?

After you are familiar with the intent of the program, use the following guidelines to determine the soundness of the software. The actual worth of the program is determined

We, as educators, are faced with a vast array of educational software. Some of it is excellent and some of it is worthless. It is not enough that we purchase software based on brightly colored advertisements in our professional publications or the words of vendors at a conference or even based on how many awards the software has received. We must spend time with the software: using it, dissecting it, and evaluating it. We must find out for ourselves if it matches our needs, our students' needs, our goals and objectives, and the time and technology that we have available.

It is important that we evaluate software in a systematic way. There are many evaluation forms available. They can be found in textbooks, professional periodicals, and on the Internet. I have used several. Following is an example of a typical evaluation form that I have found useful.

Title of Software: Kid Works 2
Publisher: Davidson and Associates, Inc.
Subject Area: Language arts and fine arts
Specific Topics: Writing, spelling, speaking, and drawing
Grade Levels: Kindergarten, first grade
Objectives: Students can exercise their creativity and improve their language skills with this program.
Prerequisite Skills: Students need to know how to use the keyboard and the mouse.
Teacher Options: I could not find any.
Nature of Program: Tutorial, art, and "story writer"

Opinions

Feedback Strengths: After students type in their stories, they can click an icon and have the computer read them out loud. They can hear what they wrote.

Feedback Weaknesses: The program reads misspelled words, and students may not know that they misspelled a word.

Self-Paced: Yes

Graphics/sound Quality: This program has great graphics and sound. There are pictures that represent many different nouns, verbs, and adjectives, and the pictures are all identified in writing underneath, so the program is very conducive to learning. There are sounds for all of the different icons that you push, which adds to student involvement and enjoyment. The program can also read out loud what students type.

Nonsexist: Yes. There doesn't seem to be anything in this program that would be considered sexist.

Reflects Racial/ethnic Diversity: Marginal. This program lacks cultural diversity. Although there are some African American people in the pictures, most of the people are Caucasian. There are no other ethnic groups represented.

Appropriate for ESL Students: This is a great program for ESL students. The different pictures are labeled so when they look at a picture of a dog, for example, they can read the word "dog" displayed underneath it. Also, the program can read the words out loud to the student so the student can hear the word as he or she learns to read and speak basic English nouns, verbs, and adjectives.

Appropriate for Students with Special Learning Needs: Yes. Students use this program at their own pace. There are also no right or wrong answers in this program, so it will not discourage slow students.

Recommendation: This seems to be a wonderful program. I highly recommend it. It will fit the present needs of my class.

(Continued)

by the school's curriculum needs. A program can be very good technically but may not develop the needed goals, or it may be of fair technical quality but very good in terms of its approach to subject and content.

Many programs can be used in a variety of settings. Individual interaction focused on gathering information for a group promotes cooperation and teamwork, enhancing the development of problem-solving techniques. Group interaction, whether as an entire class or as a small group of students in a lab setting, can encourage communication and sharing, which leads to a broader range of ideas. Team interaction can occur in either a cooperative or competitive situation. When reviewing software, consider the possible settings in which the program may be used.

Many factors are viewed differently depending on the classification of the software as drill and practice, tutorial, simulation, or as a construction tool for word processing and creating databases. The following general guidelines will help to measure the soundness of a program and to gather information about a piece of software in the drill and practice, tutorial, and simulation formats. After examining these guidelines and considering the information presented in a later section of this chapter, develop an evaluation instrument specifically designed for your school or classroom.

A copy of these guidelines may be found in the Guidelines folder in the Take-Along CD

Evaluating the Use of Graphics and Sound. As we contemplate general characteristics in the evaluation of educational software, we must look beyond text as the carrier of the message. The computer as a tool for instruction and learning must first gain a student's attention and then hold that interest to satisfy a curiosity. Students today are from the MTV™, video game, cell phone, iPOD and beyond generation. Addressing the student's interest by using the computer's capabilities of graphics and sound yields the optimum presentation of the software's message in a drill and practice, tutorial, or simulation format. The use of graphics and sound has become so ubiquitous in educational software that it deserves special consideration in the evaluation process.

Sound can enhance the learning experience by adding a degree of realism and by holding the user's attention. It can be used as a reward or reinforcement. Sound can help to highlight key concepts. Music and speech synthesis are important factors in some software. Conversely, sound can be distracting in a classroom or in a room full of computers.

GENERAL EVALUATION GUIDELINES FOR EDUCATIONAL SOFTWARE

A copy of these guidelines may be found in the Guidelines folder in the Take-Along CD

1. Documentation
   a. Is a manual included?
   b. Are the instructions clear and easy to read?
   c. Are goals and objectives clearly stated?
   d. Are suggested lesson plans or activities included?
   e. Are other resource materials included?
2. Ease of use
   a. Is minimum knowledge needed to run the program?
   b. Are potential errors trapped?
   c. Is text easily readable on the monitor screen?
   d. Can the user skip on-screen directions?
   e. Can the student use the program without teacher intervention?
3. Content
   a. Is the content appropriate to the curriculum?
   b. Is the content accurate?
   c. Is the content free of age, gender, and ethnic bias or discrimination?
   d. Is the presentation of the information interesting and does it encourage a high degree of student involvement?
   e. Is the content free of grammar and punctuation errors?
   f. In a simulation, is the content realistic?
4. Performance
   a. Does the program reach its stated goal?
   b. Is the goal worthwhile?
   c. Does the program follow sound educational techniques?
   d. Does the program make proper and effective use of graphics and sound?
   e. Does the program present appropriate reinforcement for correct replies?
   f. Does the program handle incorrect responses appropriately?
5. Versatility
   a. Can the program be used in a variety of ways?
   b. Can the user control the rate of presentation?
   c. Can the user control the sequence of the lesson?
   d. Can the user control the level of difficulty?
   e. Can the user review previous information?
   f. Can the user enter and exit at various points?
   g. In a tutorial, is the user tested and placed at the proper entry level?
   h. In a tutorial, is there effective remedial branching in the instruction?
   i. In a simulation, can the instructor change random and control factors?
6. Data collection
   a. Is the program's data collection and management system easy to use?
   b. Can student data be summarized in tables and charts?
   c. Is the student's privacy and data security ensured?

The ability to turn sound on or off is desirable. If sound is important to the concept being presented, the user should be able to direct it to an external connection rather than to the computer's built-in speaker, to permit the use of headphones.

Learning theorists stress the importance of graphic representation as a means of simplifying complex interactions of verbal and nonverbal communication. A picture contributes an image to be stored in memory for later retrieval. This function is critical to learning.

Graphics included in computer-assisted instruction have the same impact on the student. In a review of visual research, Francis Dwyer (1978) concluded that a moderate amount of realism in a visual results in the maximum amount of learning. Too little realism may not offer enough visual clues, and too much may distract the viewer. Graphics in software are often used to focus student attention. Studies have shown, however, that visual stimuli used to attract attention may not be the most effective in sustaining attention (Dwyer, 1978). High-resolution computer graphics offering a moderate degree of realism have the potential to maximize learning. Graphics must support the ideas being communicated without detracting from the instructional objective of the activity. Some very poor programs have been marketed that pair graphic symbols with unrelated text or that animate a concept improperly, making the lesson needlessly confusing. These program flaws must be detected in the evaluation process.

The graphic design of text must be considered in combination with visual presentation. Screen layout and design are important in maintaining student attention and interest. The screen should not be overcrowded and should present only one major idea at a time. Animation extends the descriptive impact of the concept being communicated by showing the logical sequence of development.

In reviewing basic math materials found in products of three large commercial software publishers, Francis Fisher (1982) found examples of terrible graphics design, inappropriate use of sound, and other misapplications of computer technology. Although significant improvements have been made since Fisher's initial research, his findings are still applicable as an element of evaluation.

The program in Figure 1–11 responds to a wrong answer with a confusing screen display. What response is the question "How many are there?" supposed to elicit? The number of empty circles? The number of filled circles? The total number of circles? Is it likely that students who cannot add 7 and 2 in the first place will be able to figure out the intended connection between empty circles and the first number in the problem and filled circles and the second number? Such students can and probably will get the answer faster by counting on their fingers than by puzzling over these complicated, poorly organized instructions.

Figure 1–12 illustrates poor use of the screen area. In the screen to the left, five squirrels have left the box. The two remaining squirrels are located directly above the number 7. The answer box (in which the user is supposed to enter 2) is placed under the five squirrels. The potential confusion here is caused by a designer working against the advantages

Figure 1–11 Confusing screen display

Example of a wrong answer eliciting a confusing response from the computer

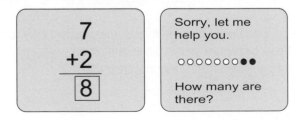

Figure 1–12 **Another confusing screen display**

Example of the poor allocation of screen area

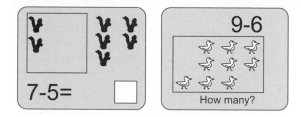

of the medium. Instead of using the screen space to illustrate the subtraction process plainly in terms of numbers and related squirrel symbols, the designer created a visual juxtaposition of actual minuend with the subtrahend symbolized by the two squirrels and the minuend symbolized by the five squirrels with the intended answer. The screen to the right also has a poorly placed, misleading question that appears to be asking how many are in the box. In evaluating software, be alert for such misuses of graphics capability.

An Evaluation Instrument for Educational Software. Having familiarized ourselves with general criteria and guidelines for the evaluation of educational software, we must attempt to develop a process for its evaluation. An effective instrument is at the heart of a successful process. Just as one set of curricular materials is not expected to meet all the needs of all students, one type of software cannot be expected to address all needs. One "standard" list of criteria will not measure all the necessary elements of good educational software in the areas of drill and practice, tutorial, and simulation. A reliable list includes the set of characteristics that make up the events of a good lesson in a particular learning situation. A "best fit" happens when the teacher skillfully matches instructional needs with elements in a software program.

An evaluation instrument must provide for the recording of descriptive information about the software being evaluated as well as a listing of performance criteria. Once the software is described, it must be examined and rated against performance criteria. Reflecting on the general evaluation guidelines previously presented, a criterion section could be developed that would examine some common traits as well as allow for the specific characteristics of drill and practice, tutorial, and simulation software to be analyzed.

There is no single correct way to evaluate educational software. An instrument could be developed that would include only broad guidelines and allow the evaluator considerable leeway in interpreting and applying them. However, an instrument might have a long list of specifics and a complex scoring system, leaving little to the judgment of the evaluator. Think of an evaluation instrument as a communication device that describes and assesses the value of a given software item. It must convey an accurate impression of the software and be easy and convenient to use. A cumbersome evaluation instrument is more trouble than it is worth to potential evaluators and, therefore, will be of little use. A sample form is presented in Figure 1–13. During your study of databases in this course, you may wish to design your own evaluation on a file manager such as AppleWorks or File-Maker® Pro. You will undoubtedly appreciate the inherent advantages of file managers when applied to the task of designing forms and storing the data for later review.

Software Selection

Software that may be effective in one setting may not be useful in another, even if it covers the same concepts. It is important to have a process for determining the quality and content of materials with respect to the needs of the student.

37

Figure 1–13 Software evaluation form

Sample software evaluation instrument

DESCRIPTION

Program Title: _____ OS Requirement: _____

Vendor Name & Address: _____ Program Cost: _____

Content Area: (e.g., Math) _____ Topic: (e.g., Decimals) _____

Grade Level: _____ Supplementary Material Included: _____

Brief Description: _____

_____

_____

EVALUATION

Use the following checklist to refresh your memory regarding important aspects of educational software. Read the entire list first, then check the appropriate items after examining the software. Use the *Summary Evaluation* section to record your impressions of the software.

General Criteria Applicable to All Categories

____ 1. Content is accurate.

____ 2. Content is appropriate to educational goals.

____ 3. Instructions are clear.

____ 4. Program is easy to use.

____ 5. Format is interactive.

____ 6. High level of interest is maintained.

____ 7. User establishes the pace.

____ 8. Progresses in levels of difficulty.

____ 9. Reinforces/rewards user appropriately.

____ 10. Teacher able to modify the content.

____ 11. Keeps record of student progress.

____ 12. No age, gender, or ethnic discrimination.

____ 13. Sound can be controlled.

____ 14. Computer is used effectively.

____ 15. Has suggested off-computer activities.

____ 16. Support materials are effective.

Additional Criteria Specific to Tutorial Programs

____ 1. Variety in presentation

____ 2. Logical, sequential concept development

____ 3. Positive reinforcement

____ 4. Limits frequency of incorrect responses

Additional Criteria Specific to Simulations

____ 1. Clear directions

____ 2. Realistic situation for role playing

____ 3. Results predicated upon user input

____ 4. Promotes problem solving

Summary Evaluation (E = Excellent, VG = Very Good, G = Good, F = Fair, P = Poor)

Appropriateness	E	VG	G	F	P
Performance	E	VG	G	F	P
Documentation	E	VG	G	F	P
Ease of Use	E	VG	G	F	P
Overall Rating	E	VG	G	F	P

Comments: _____

_____

Recommend for purchase? _____

Evaluator's Name: _____ Date: _____

Evaluation is used to assess the quality of the software product. Selection takes evaluation a step further by matching the quality and cost of the software to the specific needs of the school. This can be accomplished in several ways. In the case of an inexpensive or highly specific stand-alone program, the individual making the evaluation may complete the process by recommending purchase. When a more substantial purchase is contemplated or the software under consideration may be applicable in a variety of settings, the collective wisdom, experience, and training of a team of educators may be valuable to better analyze collected evaluations and arrive at a decision regarding selection. Decisions will always take into account costs and budgets, software currently in the collection, equipment that is presently available or that needs to be purchased, the number of machines and the number of students per machine, and the computer literacy of the staff.

The important issue in each case should be the "best fit" between the needs of students and teachers and the features of the software.

Regarding cost impact on budgets, it may be prudent to compare cost on websites that offer discounts to faculty and students as well as volume pricing. At the time of this writing, we identified the following six sites worthy of consideration: *www.academicsuperstore.com, www.sprysoft.com, www.journeyed.com, www.studentdiscounts.com, www.gradware.com,* and *www.ccvsoftware.com.*

Teachers have the final word on instructional use and must use the characteristics of a good learning situation as the criteria to measure the value of the software package. Because district needs and student characteristics vary, professional judgment on what elements are present or missing in relation to an instructional situation is the only feasible standard for evaluation. This judgment also determines what elements need to be supplied in the learning environment or what adaptations need to be made to the software.

Collection development is often the responsibility of the school library media specialist. This person must promote the collection's effective use by teachers and students. This can be done by circulating or posting memos featuring particular software, especially new acquisitions, and short presentations at group, team, department, and school faculty meetings. Bibliographies pertinent to specific topics or events might be posted. One-on-one consulting to meet an individual's need is, perhaps, the most effective way of ensuring good use of the collection.

LET'S REVIEW

According to behaviorist theory, the teacher is the manipulator of an environment that is experienced by the learner. The techniques used reflect a belief that, by tightly structuring the environment, the student's behavior can be shaped to achieve learning. According to constructivist theory, learning is an active and highly individualized process in which learners must construct new knowledge based on their own individual experiences and understandings. Knowledge is produced by the individual learner rather than processed from information received from an external source.

To maximize access to information and the development of knowledge, students need problem-solving tools and problem-solving skills. Authentic assessment techniques enable the teacher and the learner to better emphasize the learning taking place. The use of rubrics for both the learner and the teacher and portfolios enable the student and teacher to measure learning that has taken place.

The digital portfolio is a well-thought-out collection of material designed to show the degree of mastery or achievement a student has attained in working toward a local or national standard. It is a continually updated reflective tool that shows growth over time not only in the mastery of standards but also in the ability of students to evaluate their own learning.

Understanding students as individuals with their different types of intelligence and learning styles allows teachers to make sound and informed decisions when choosing software for their classrooms.

Sensory stimuli are accepted by the learner and given meaning based primarily on past experiences. As perceptions are organized into understanding, the quality of the concrete, visual, and aural stimuli embodied in the software assume significant importance. Examining well-designed software, we find that computer graphics, visuals, and certainly multimedia serve as concrete referents to meaning. Motivation is further heightened when the learner is asked to respond to the program overtly. Communication is enhanced when fields of experience overlap.

Effective software must: (1) stimulate a high degree of interest in the learner; (2) contribute to developmental learning and, thereby, increase the permanence of that learning;

(3) be based in concrete experience to enhance understanding; (4) make optimum use of the visual and, where appropriate, the aural sensory channels to strengthen the reality of the experience.

The software selection process consists of finding sources, product information, and reviews; evaluating the product; and then selecting the product for adoption in a given setting.

An instrument to evaluate software must facilitate the accurate recording of both descriptive and evaluative information and be convenient to use.

LET'S PRACTICE

To complete the specified exercises online, go to the Chapter Exercises Module in Chapter 1 of the Companion Website.

1. Select one piece of software in a curriculum area that is of special interest to you and analyze it in light of Gagné's events of instruction as elements of a good lesson.

2. Design a lesson that you might teach in your class. Do this twice. The first time use a behaviorist approach and the second time use a constructivist approach. Discuss the pros and cons of each approach with reference to your lesson. Which approach would you rather use? Why?

3. Discuss authentic assessment. Do you think that this is a step forward or a step backward for our educational system? Explain. How would you use it in your classroom?

4. Many college and university schools' of education require their students to have their own digital portfolio. If yours does not, outline the topics that you feel would be helpful for you to include in your own digital portfolio. Discuss your answer with others in the class.

5. Search the Web to find a test that would help you find out more about yourself like the MBTI. Take the test and discuss the results. Do the results match how you think of yourself?

6. Review the sample evaluation forms on the Companion Website. Develop your own form for the evaluation of software in the area of drill and practice, tutorial, and simulation. Run a program and evaluate it using your form. Comment on the process of reviewing. Was it frustrating or rewarding? How long did it take you to evaluate the program thoroughly? Would you make any changes in your form now that you have used it?

7. Design a lesson for your classroom in which cooperative learning is stressed. What benefits and hazards might you encounter if you use this lesson with your students? How would you include students with special needs in this lesson? Develop a rubric that would help you and the students evaluate how they did on your lesson.

8. Although there are ideal ways to evaluate and acquire software, what constraints do you believe exist in a school situation that might interfere with performing an evaluation in an optimum way?

9. Determine the evaluation system used by two different magazines or journals that publish software reviews. In each case, who does the reviewing? Is the review based on student use of the program? Describe strengths and shortcomings of both magazines' reviewing systems.

10. Obtain a software catalog from Learning Services (1-800-877-3278 or *www.learningservicesinc.com*). Review their list of the "Top 25 Educator's Choices." Are you surprised with the software in this list? Which software in the list should you learn more about? Review the "Top 10" list for your content area.

PORTFOLIO DEVELOPMENT EXERCISES

To complete this exercise online, go to the Digital Portfolio *Module in Chapter 1 of the Companion Website.*

One NETS•S standard covered in this chapter is "Students practice responsible use of technology systems, information, and software" under *Category 2: Social, ethical, and human issues.* Begin to develop a portfolio of lesson plans that demonstrates your ability to have students reach the NETS•S standards.

1. Design a lesson plan activity for elementary, middle school, or high school students in which they design a software evaluation form that can be used in class. This form must include objective (cost, platform, publisher, date,

and so on) and subjective (overall impression, value in curriculum, and so on) information. Have other students use this form to evaluate several software packages. This lesson should demonstrate that the students have achieved the standard. Be sure to include a system of evaluation for students' understanding and competence to ensure that they have met this standard.

2. Adapt the lesson plan activity you developed in exercise 1 for students to evaluate each others' work.

GLOSSARY

abstract	Symbolizing an object, event, or occurrence that can be observed by the learner
ARCS model	A model designed by Keller to describe the four components of motivation: Attention, Relevance, Confidence, Satisfaction
ASSURE model	A model to aid in the planning and delivery of instruction: **A**nalyze learners; **S**tate objectives; **S**elect methods, media, and materials; **U**tilize media and materials; **R**equire learner participation; **E**valuate and revise
authentic assessment	Consists of assessment tasks that resemble real-world situations
behaviorism	A theory of learning that perceives the teacher as the manipulator of an environment that is experienced by the learner
checklists	Simple ways of observing and categorizing behaviors in a bimodal (observed/not observed) manner
concrete	Actual, direct, purposeful happenings involving the learner as a participant
constructivism	A theory of learning that holds that students interact with the real-life experiences and construct mental structures that provide an understanding of their environment
digital	Electrical current flowing in very discrete units usually depicted as individual packets, 0s and 1s or on/off units
digital portfolio	A portfolio in which all of the components are in a digital format enabling them to be accessed by a computer; often stored on CD-ROMs
electronic portfolio	A portfolio in which all of the components are in an electronic format; items may be in a digital (scanned images, word-processed documents, etc.) and/or analog (videotape, audiotape) format
linear	Proceeding in a step-by-step, sequential manner
noise	Anything that deteriorates the quality of the signal or message
performance-based assessment	See *authentic assessment*
project-based learning	An authentic assessment model for teaching in which projects are used to assess student learning
rating scales	Complex measures where each observation is placed on a scale, usually of numerical values, that measures the degree to which a student completes a task
rubric	A scoring matrix that differentiates the quality of learning using a graduated scale of exemplar behaviors

REFERENCES AND SUGGESTED READINGS

Barrett, H. C. (2000, April). Create your own electronic portfolio using off-the-shelf software to showcase your own or student work. *Leading & Learning with Technology, 27*(7), 14–21.

Bloom, B. (1956). *Taxonomy of educational objectives: The classification of educational goals,* 1st ed. New York: David McKay.

Boettcher, J. (2000, August). Designing for learning: What is meaningful learning? *Syllabus, 14*(1), 54–57.

Bruner, J. (1966). *Studies in cognitive growth.* New York: John Wiley & Sons.

Campbell, L., Campbell, B., & Dickinson, D. (1999). *Teaching and learning through multiple intelligences,* 2nd ed. Boston: Allyn & Bacon.

Collay, M., Dunlap, D., Enloe, W., & Gagnon, G. W. (1998). *Learning circles—creating conditions for professional development.* Thousand Oaks, CA: Corwin Press.

D'Ignazio, F. (1992, August/September). Are you getting your money's worth? *The Computing Teacher,* 54–55.

Dwyer, F. M. (1978). *Strategies for improving visual learning.* State College, PA: Learning Services, pp. 33, 156.

Eichleay, K., & Kilroy, C. (1993–1994, December/January). Hot tips for inclusion with technology. *The Computing Teacher, 21*(4), 38–40.

Fisher, F. D. (1982, Summer). Computer assisted education: What's not happening. *Journal of Computer-Based Instruction, 9*(1), 19–27.

Gagné, R., & Briggs, L. (1974). *Principles of instructional design*. New York: Holt, Rinehart and Winston.

Gagné, R., Briggs, L., & Wager, W. (1992). *Principles of instructional design*. Fort Worth, TX: Harcourt Brace Jovanovich.

Gardner, H. (1983). *Frames of mind*. New York: Basic Books.

Gardner, H. (1993). *Multiple intelligences: The theory in practice*. New York: Basic Books.

Gardner, H. (1999). *Intelligence reframed. Multiple intelligences for the 21st century*. New York: Basic Books.

Guba, E., Wolf, W., DeGroot, S., Kneneyer, M., VanAtta, R., & Light, L. (1964, Winter). Eye movements and TV-viewing in children. *AV Communications Review, 12,* 386–401.

Information Technology in Childhood Education Annual. (1999). The state of children's software evaluation: Yesterday, today, and in the twenty-first century, 220–221.

Johnson, D. W., & Johnson, R. T. (1994). *Learning together and alone. Cooperative, competitive, and individualistic learning,* 4th ed. Edina, MN: Interaction Book Company.

Keller, J. (1987). The systematic process of motivational design. *Performance and Instruction, 26*(9), 1–8.

Merrill, M. D. (2002). First principles of instruction. *Educational Technology Research and Development, 50*(3), 43–59.

Papert, S. (1991). *Constructionism: Research reports and essays, 1985–1991*. Norwood, NJ: Ablex Publishing.

Piaget, J. (1954). *The construction of reality in the child*. New York: Basic Books.

Ross, A., & Olsen, K. (1995). *A vision of the middle school through integrated thematic instruction*. Kent, WA: Books for Educators.

Saunders, W. L. (1992, March). Constructivist perspective: Implications and teaching strategies for science. *School Science and Mathematics, 92*(3), 136–141.

Schlechter, T. (1990). The relative dystructional efficiency of small group computer-based telecommunications for instruction. *Journal of Computer-Based Instruction, 6*(3), 329–341.

Schramm, W. (1954). Procedures and effects of mass communication. In N. B. Henry (Ed.), *Mass media and education, fifty-third yearbook of the National Society for the Study of Education, part II*. Chicago: University of Chicago Press.

Shannon, C. E., & Weaver, W. (1949). *The Mathematical Theory of Communication*. Champaign, IL: University of Illinois Press, 7.

Skinner, B. F. (1974). *About behaviorism*. New York: Knopf.

Wedman, J. F. (1986, November). Making software more useful. *The Computing Teacher, 13*(3) 11–14.

Whitehead, A. N. (1929). *The aims of education*. New York: Macmillan.

Computer Applications in Education

6. What is a typical drill-and-practice lesson format and how can the computer be used in such a lesson?

7. What is a typical simulation lesson format and how can the computer be used in such a lesson?

8. What are the roles of the student and the teacher in the three strategies?

9. What constitutes multimedia and what does it have to offer the learner?

10. What does computer-managed instruction offer you as a teacher?

11. How can the computer enhance your capability as a teacher to design teaching materials?

12. How can the computer be used as an information tool by the student?

13. How is the computer an action research tool?

NETS•T Foundation Standards and Performance Indicators Addressed in this Chapter

I. Technology operations and concepts
   A. demonstrate introductory knowledge, skills, and understanding of concepts related to technology (as described in the ISTE National Education Technology Standards for Students)
   B. demonstrate continual growth in technology knowledge and skills to stay abreast of current and emerging technologies

II. Planning and designing learning environments and experiences
   C. identify and locate technology resources and evaluate them for accuracy and suitability
   D. plan for the management of technology resources within the context of learning activities
   E. plan strategies to manage student learning in a technology-enhanced environment

III. Teaching, learning, and the curriculum
   A. facilitate technology-enhanced experiences that address content standards and student technology standards
   B. use technology to support learner-centered strategies that address the diverse needs of students

IV. Assessment and evaluation
   A. apply technology in assessing student learning of subject matter using a variety of assessment techniques
   C. apply multiple methods of evaluation to determine students' appropriate use of technology resources for learning, communication, and productivity

V. Productivity and professional practice
   B. continually evaluate and reflect on professional practice to make informed decisions regarding the use of technology in support of student learning
   C. apply technology to increase productivity
VI. Social, ethical, legal, and human issues
   B. apply technology resources to enable and empower learners with diverse backgrounds, characteristics, and abilities

▮▮▮▮ LET'S LOOK AT THIS CHAPTER ▮▮▮▮

The title of this book is *The Computer as an Educational Tool: Productivity and Problem Solving.* Too often the term *productivity* has been used with a limited vision. The deeper understanding we seek, however, demonstrates its applicability not only to word processors, graphics, spreadsheets, and database use but also to computer-assisted instruction, computer-enhanced learning, and administrative applications. If we believe that education is in the business of fostering student learning, then computer applications that help students to learn, teachers to teach, and administrators to manage efficiently and effectively should be seen as productivity tools.

Changes are occurring in education, as well as in technology, with school restructuring suggesting a different way of looking at and measuring teacher effectiveness. Pupil learning gains are being included in discussions of productivity. Tutorial instruction, drill and practice, and simulation—all time-tested teaching strategies—are being joined by multimedia instruction and learning. Integrated student records and student portfolios track the progress of students as they gain and construct new knowledge. If computer software implements these strategies in an effective and efficient manner, should not this software be seen as a teacher productivity tool?

This chapter presents an overview and classification of computer applications in education to enable an improved perspective on the breadth of applications and to better understand their relationships. The classification proposed is hierarchical, with divisions made according to function. Classification schemes, no matter how well reasoned, are, by nature, arbitrary. Some applications may not fit neatly in the pigeonholes of the structure, but may cross boundaries and overlap, much as the subjects we teach our students cross boundaries and overlap. We recognizes the importance of multidisciplinary curriculum integration.

▮▮▮▮ COMPUTERS IN EDUCATION

Any classification is an attempt to group like items together in order to study them, noting their similarities and their differences. Early software classifications described **computer-assisted instruction (CAI)** and **computer-managed instruction (CMI).** They, by themselves, are no longer adequate. The software classification model proposed in Figure 2–1 emphasizes function. It places primary emphasis on how software is used.

In this model, the functional use of computers in education has been divided into three categories: management, instruction and learning, and action research. The *management* category includes school and classroom applications in budgeting, accounting, recordkeeping,

Figure 2–1 Computers in education

A classification of computer applications in education

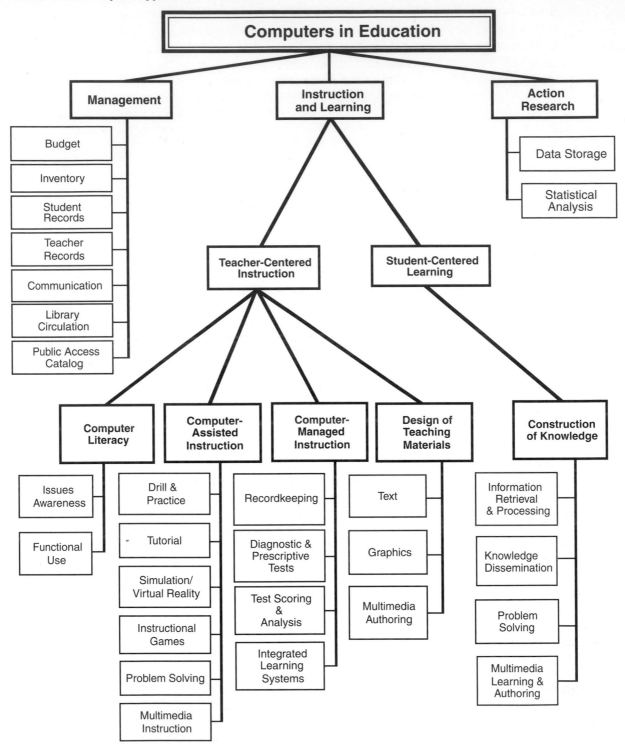

printed and electronic communication, and information retrieval. The category of *instruction and learning* has been subdivided into two areas. *Teacher-centered instruction* includes software functions interacting directly with students under the teacher's control in the design, development, and delivery of instruction. *Student-centered learning* includes recognizing functions that are related to the student involved in constructive activities, which leads to learning. Categories are further subdivided to recognize common computer applications. The *action research* category includes applications in data storage and statistical analysis and must be recognized for the contribution it makes to teaching and learning by placing the teacher in the role of researcher, often examining some aspect of classroom practice. Software classification permits the identification and comparisons of like programs. Organization schemes other than the one proposed in this chapter are, of course, possible and should be encouraged if they will facilitate the study of software and its application. The development and use of classification methods to identify software will facilitate the task of teachers, who ultimately decide which material to use in the classroom. It will promote a better understanding of software selection, evaluation, and collection management. Classification methods can also promote better communication between teachers and publishers. Teachers can more clearly explain their needs to publishers, and publishers can better describe their available products. The software classification must reflect accepted theories and practices in education.

The primary emphasis in this textbook is on the instruction and learning category and then on the management category, although the category of action research is briefly covered as well. The elements of teacher-centered instruction are addressed most thoroughly. Learning theories and the continued evaluation of new technologies are increasingly placing strong emphasis on the growth and development of student-centered learning.

LITERACY AND INSTRUCTION

Before we cover the two categories of instruction, let's look at the concept of literacy. In its broadest sense, literacy has to do with how a person cognitively manipulates a sensory input (i.e., how a person understands, analyzes, evaluates and uses a particular type of input). Several types of literacy have been defined. The ones critical to our discussion are information, media, computer, visual, and integration literacies.

Information literacy means knowing how to find, analyze, and use information. We can easily see the importance of this today with the ever exploding increase of information. Students must learn how to find and gather information from multiple sources, filter out the relevant information, and organize it in a useful format. Such skills as critical thinking and problem solving fit under this category. You are actually using your information literacy skills as you process the information presented in this textbook, on the Companion Website, and while interacting with your instructor.

Media literacy is similar to information literacy in that it includes analyzing, understanding, and evaluating, but broadens to include communication in a variety of forms. You should be able to communicate information in this textbook using oral and written word (word processing, brochures, PowerPoint, web pages), visuals (PowerPoint, web pages, graphics), and data (spreadsheets, databases).

Computer literacy is a vital tool in the modern world. As more students grow up with computers in the home, teachers will spend less time teaching about computers. Classes like this have changed over time to include less "how to use" and more "how to integrate" computers and computer applications. The *digital divide* (U.S. Department of Commerce, 2000) is a term describing the barrier that individuals must overcome if they do not have access to or understand how to use computers and the Internet. (See also expanded discussion on computer literacy later in the chapter.)

Visual literacy describes how individuals are able to interpret and understand visual messages and information, and how to create such information. Visual preferences, developmental stages, prelearning, and culture all affect how individuals interpret and understand visuals. Highway signs, airplane evacuation cards, stock performance charts, and instructions on assembling a child's toy are examples of visuals that should be easy for anyone to interpret. One of the authors recently took a cross-country trip with an international student from Africa. It soon became apparent that he had to stop to teach the student how to read a road map because the student had never used one before. The student was a graduate of engineering. We further discuss this in chapter 6.

Integration literacy is a rather new term used to describe the ability to use a variety of technologies and methods to enhance teaching and learning. As you progress through your educational studies, you are learning and sharpening your integration media skills. You integrate a variety of skills and technologies to appropriately and efficiently match outcomes, goals, and objectives in the classroom.

Forms and traditional definitions of literacy are changing as new media and technologies are developed. It is vital for students to learn new technologies to survive in the twenty-first century (Leu, 2002).

INSTRUCTION AND LEARNING

Since we consider the category of instruction and learning to be the most important, we begin the examination of the model proposed in Figure 2–1 with this category. It is separated into teacher-centered and student-centered instruction. Teacher-centered instruction deals with those functions that directly include the student in either an individual or a group setting and takes into account teacher planning, preparation, and delivery of instruction. Student-centered learning includes the functions that deal with the student involved in constructive activities that lead to learning.

Teacher-Centered Instruction

As seen in Figure 2–2, teacher-centered instruction includes the areas of computer literacy, computer-assisted instruction, computer-managed instruction, and design of teaching materials. Computer literacy acquaints the student with the computer and its functional use. The presentation of information through CAI, under the control of the teacher, and the management of the student's performance and interaction with that information through CMI (though viewed separately for the purpose of functional examination) sometimes overlaps. As a design tool, the computer has become widely used by teachers to create hard copy, as well as projected, instructional materials. Many of these functions are covered in more detail in other chapters.

Computer Literacy as an Element of Teacher-Centered Instruction. As discussed briefly, the subject of computer literacy focuses on the computer as the object of instruction. This topic is not to be confused with computer science instruction, which studies hardware, operating systems, and computer languages. In computer literacy, a scope and a sequence of curriculum goals are usually developed within a school district that specifies what is to be learned about the use of the computer and about its role in society. Computer literacy is not easy to define. It often examines the history of computing, computer awareness, and the functional use of computers. The term also covers the broader role of the computer as it relates to societal issues such as computer access, gender relationships, software copyright, rights of privacy, data security, and information ownership. Many times computer literacy is divided into

Figure 2–2 Teacher-centered instruction
The computer as an instructional tool for the teacher

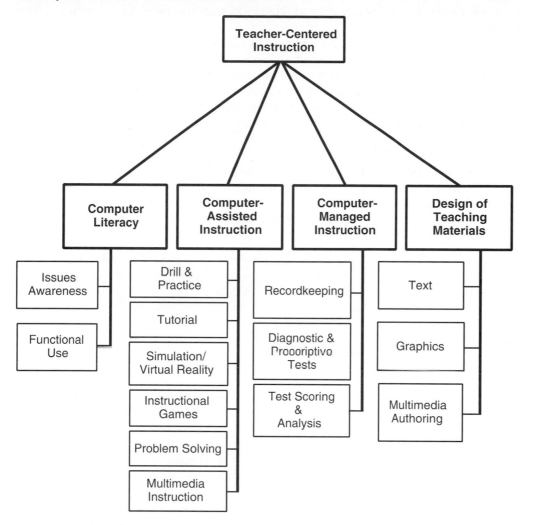

three broad areas: *basic computer skills* such as keyboarding and using various input and output devices, *computers in society* which discusses uses and misuses of computers and the impact of computers on society, and *basic applications skills* such as word processing, databases, and spreadsheets. Some of these issues were already introduced; others are addressed in later chapters. We are using the ISTE/NCATE Foundation Standards and NETS•S as the basis for the definition of computer literacy.

Some educators argue that, as computers become commonplace in homes and schools, the need for computer literacy will be diminished in the curriculum. Some believe that although teaching scope and sequence of skills may no longer be necessary, computer-related issues will remain.

Computer-Assisted Instruction as an Element of Teacher-Centered Instruction. Computer-assisted instruction applies to a teaching and learning situation that involves the direct instructional interaction between computer and student. In this teacher-centered approach, the teacher, ultimately having responsibility for all instruction in the classroom, sets up the learning environment through careful selection and analysis of the instruction material;

ensures that each student has the necessary entry-level knowledge, skills, and attitude to engage in a particular activity; monitors the learning activities, adjusting them according to the students' needs; and follows up with activities designed to promote retention and transfer of learning.

Regardless of the underlying philosophy in the classroom, tutorial instruction, drill and practice, simulation, gaming, and *problem solving* are time-tested instructional strategies. They are strategies that behaviorists can apply in a teacher-centered instructional situation and that constructivists can apply in a student-centered learning environment. These strategies can be used to gain attention, stimulate recall of prior learning, and present new information in ways that approximate real-life situations at a more concrete level than most media used in the classroom.

They are strategies that address the right or the left hemisphere of the brain. They can be tailored to support activities favored by students with concrete-sequential, concrete-random, abstract-sequential, or abstract-random preferred styles. They can be appealing to students with diverse strengths and intelligences. Teachers who understand the individual needs of students will tailor strategies and computer applications to meet those needs. Al Mizell (1997) at Nova Southeastern University states forcefully

> I don't believe enough attention is focused on the value of using computers where they are strongest; e.g., as patient tutors, competent analysts, master presenters of stimulus material, and evaluators of consequences of various decisions made by the student. In other words, they are more valuable for higher level thinking and processing skills than when they are used as electronic page turners. (p. 4)

Tutorial Applications. A **tutorial** program exposes the student to material that is believed not to have been previously taught or learned. A tutorial program often includes a placement test to ensure student readiness and sometimes a pretest on specific objectives to validate the placement test. The computer usually assesses a student's prior learning, determines readiness for the material; and presents material for student observation, note taking, and other interaction. New material is commonly provided in small increments, replete with instructional guidance and appropriate feedback to encourage correct student response.

Tutorial instruction often follows a linear programmed instruction model mainly because it is difficult, time consuming, and, therefore, expensive to write **branching** programs that attempt to remediate incorrect responses. Both linear and branching formats present information and questions that lead toward an identified goal. Linear programs present information in a sequential manner and do not attempt to remediate errors. Tutorials often include initial guidance in the form of prompts to encourage the student to answer correctly, especially at the outset of the lesson.

The diagram in Figure 2–3 illustrates a representation of a linear format often used in tutorial programs. Some programs employ modest branching techniques to provide alternative paths, or branches, for remediation or acceleration. Tutorials must record student responses and allow for teacher analysis of the student's progress to determine whether a goal has been met.

Tutorial programs are often used to help students who have been absent from class. They may also be effective when assigned as independent study to students exhibiting difficulty with specific skills and concepts.

In a behaviorist model, the teacher identifies the proper lesson objectives, selects the appropriate computer program, maintains a reasonably comfortable environment free from unnecessary distractions, and, where needed, provides additional resources and encouragement to the student. The teacher must also monitor student progress by interpreting data collected by the computer program and must be prepared to intervene if necessary. In a constructivist model, the teacher might suggest tutorial software as a way

A typical linear format used in tutorial programs

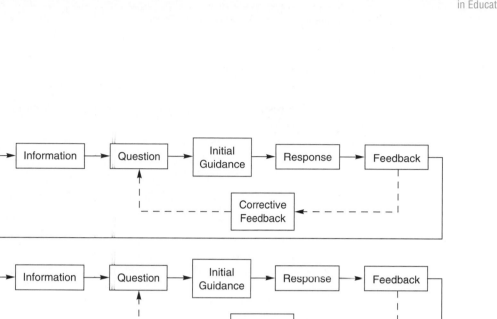

for the student to acquire a particular skill or concept once its value is recognized. The teacher's role is to ascertain readiness on the part of the student, to select the appropriate software, to assess the student's performance as the newly acquired skill or concept is applied to a meaningful task, and to determine whether further practice is required. Working directly at a computer on a tutorial program can provide interest and motivation, if the teacher keeps in mind that it is only one alternative among various strategies to teach specific skills or concepts. Two major complaints leveled at tutorial software are that much of it deals with trivial information and it is not well written. The educational quality of the program must be ascertained and, to maintain its effectiveness, the strategy should not be overused. Many have used tutorial programs that accompany a new piece of software such as Microsoft Word. *Mavis Beacon Teaches Typing!* and *Math Success Deluxe* are wonderful examples of tutorial software.

Drill-and-Practice Applications. **Drill and practice** is a time-honored technique used by teachers to reinforce instruction, by providing the repetition necessary to move acquired skills and concepts into long-term memory. It assumes that the material covered has been previously taught. In the past, teachers used flash cards, worksheets, board games, and verbal

Figure 2–4 Drill and practice

A typical format found in drill and practice programs

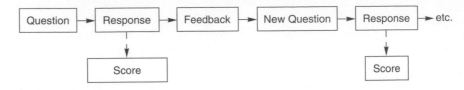

drills to achieve results. Computer programs present an additional and, if used well, more powerful alternative.

Criticism leveled in the past at drill-and-practice software was really aimed at poorly designed software that was boring, that treated all users the same regardless of ability, and that employed undesirable feedback. Teachers tell of students deliberately giving incorrect responses in order to see flashy animated graphics on the screen. The reward offered by that software for making correct responses was the presentation of another boring problem. The diagram in Figure 2–4 illustrates a typical format used in drill-and-practice programs.

When this technique is used, the assumption is made that the topic has already been introduced to the student and that some prior instruction has taken place. In a behaviorist model, the teacher's role, in addition to determining the appropriate lesson objective and delivering the initial instruction, is to select the appropriate software, monitor the student's progress through the material, and assess the student's performance. In a constructivist model, a teacher may suggest drill-and-practice software as a way for the student to refine a particular skill or concept once its value is recognized. The teacher's role, in addition to determining that the student understands and accepts an agreed-on goal, is to ascertain that initial information has been acted on by the student, select the appropriate software, and assess the student's performance as the skill or concept is applied to a meaningful task.

The student must interact with the computer by responding to screen prompts and by providing appropriate keyboard or other input. The student should request teacher or peer assistance if necessary and examine the results of the activity. The computer presents material for student interaction, provides appropriate feedback to student responses, and usually records the rate of success, often displayed as a score or percentage. Effective software requires the student to respond based on deductions and inferences, as well as recall.

A number of factors influence the effectiveness of drill-and-practice software. The teacher must know the program well enough to determine the accuracy of the content and the match between the presentation of the material and an individual student's learning

LET'S GO INTO THE CLASSROOM
Drill-and-Practice Gaming Fun

Many students choose to spend considerable time on the computer performing drill-and-practice writing lessons in a game format. They get immediate feedback on anything they do. It makes learning exciting for them.

Becky Benjamin
Seventh-Grade Language Arts Teacher
Carrollton Junior High
Carrollton, Georgia

style. If the software is to be used in a group setting, should intrinsic gaming strategies be used or can external gaming strategies be used by the teacher? Students must find the material and its presentation interesting enough to be willing to become mentally and emotionally involved. The program's use of basic graphic design, as well as a variety of stimuli such as color, sound, and animation, in both its presentation and feedback screens greatly enhances its effectiveness.

Simulation/Virtual Reality. **Simulation** is another time-honored teaching strategy used to reinforce instruction by the teacher. It can also function effectively in a student-centered environment by providing a climate for discovery learning to take place or for newly acquired skills and concepts to be tested. A simulation can present a sample of a real situation and can offer genuine practice at solving real problems unhampered by danger, distance, time, or cost factors. Simulations require decisions to be made by the student. In the past, teachers used board games, drama, and role-playing to implement the simulation technique. The computer is a useful tool to manage this technique. A sophisticated simulation can present the facts and rules of a situation in a highly realistic manner without the limiting factors of time, distance, safety, and cost and then can adjust these factors to respond to interaction by the student. High levels of cognitive skill are involved in the synthesis of facts, rules, and concepts in solving problems. Simulation permits this synthesis to take place within the classroom.

Consider, for example, the teacher who wants to teach the concept of free elections in a representative democracy. Figure 2–5 suggests a common flow of events in a typical simulation.

A classroom simulation might call for the creation of class offices, including development of a nomination process, establishment of platforms, identification of a polling place, preparation of secret and secure ballots, and agreement on term of office for the successful candidates. This simulation has been conducted for years without a computer. A computer program, however, can increase the sophistication of the simulation and can extend it into a broader context. For instance, it could introduce a number of historical variables that might influence decisions made in the running of a presidential election campaign. In this case, the program could store a wealth of data that can be called on as needed and cross-referenced to demonstrate cause and effect. Simulation software can provide highly realistic practice at solving real problems in the classroom without many of the limiting factors often found in real life.

As in any use of CAI, the role of the teacher is to identify the proper lesson objectives and to select the appropriate computer program. When using simulation software in a

Figure 2–5 Simulation
A typical format found in simulation programs

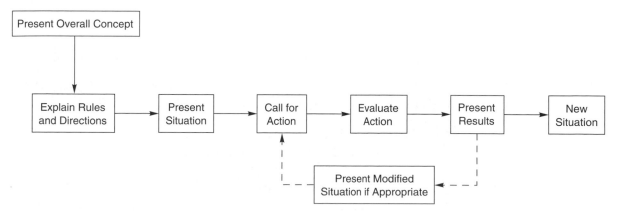

behaviorist model, the teacher often provides background information and may be called on to teach related skills and concepts and to provide additional resources where needed. The teacher must also monitor the progress made by the student or by the group of students and assess their performance. Simulations lending themselves to group use promote social interaction and can often be used as an introductory activity for a unit. In a constructivist model, simulation software may be suggested by the teacher as a way for the student to develop a particular skill or concept in a manner that is close to a real-life situation. The teacher's role is to ascertain readiness on the part of the student, to select the appropriate software, to discuss the student's performance in the simulation, and to suggest a real-world application.

The top screen in Figure 2–6 is from the program *Ballistic*. The user sets initial parameters of initial velocity, angle of projection, and drag medium. By turning on the friction

Figure 2–6 Physics simulation series

Screens from the *Ballistic* and *Potential* programs Developed by Blas Cabrera, Stanford University and published by Intellimation, Santa Barbara, CA. *(Reprinted with permission from Blas Cabrera.)*

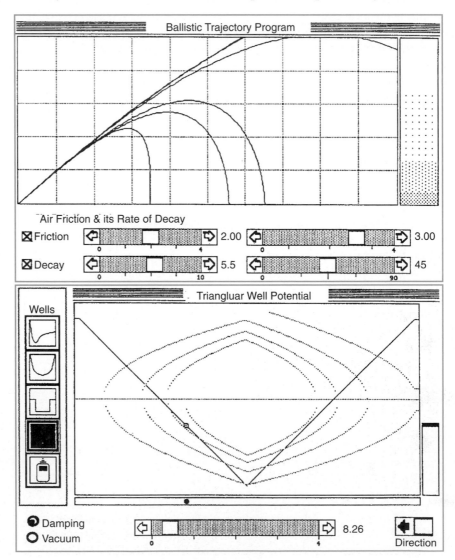

control but leaving the decay control turned off, a medium of constant density is simulated. Turning on the decay control simulates a medium whose density decreases with altitude. Once launched, the projectile leaves a trace in the display window. By varying the parameters of initial velocity, angle of projection, air friction as the drag medium, and altitude-related decay, the user can compare the results of these combined factors as traces in the display window.

The bottom screen in Figure 2–6 is from the program *Potential.* Users choose from four one-dimensional potential wells or create their own. The illustration represents a triangular well: A ball travels downward along the left slope, reaches bottom, rolls a certain distance upward on the right slope, then reverses its direction. This is repeated with diminishing distances until all energy is spent. A damping effect can be employed to observe the effect of various dissipating conditions. Kinetic and potential energies are continually displayed in a column at the right of the screen. Velocity or acceleration can be plotted for each path of the ball.

Both of these examples are intrinsic simulation models that create an artificial environment for the user to explore. In these microworlds, elements of the environment operate according to a regular set of rules. The student manipulates things to learn what their characteristics are within the artificial environment.

In *Oregon Trail,* an award-winning program available with sophisticated graphics on CD-ROM, the user is placed in the position of traveling the 2,000-mile Oregon Trail from Independence, Missouri, to Oregon's Willamette Valley. Having declared an occupation and thereby receiving an allocation of available funds, the user begins preparing for the journey by carefully purchasing supplies.

The screen of Figure 2–7 is a typical one seen as the program progresses. A log, or diary, of the journey appears below the map. Four buttons are arranged at the bottom of the

Figure 2–7 Oregon Trail®

Screen showing choices to be made while traveling the Oregon Trail *(Reprinted with permission of the Learning Company™, Inc.)*

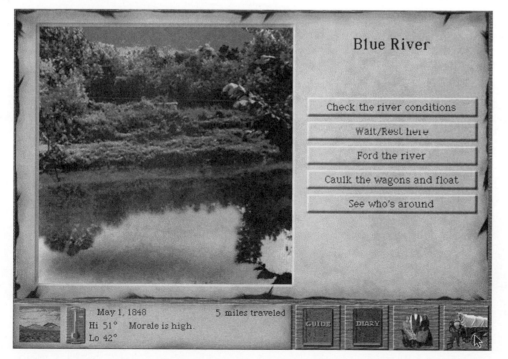

screen, presenting the user with options. The guide button reveals pertinent information about the geography of the region in a separate window. The user is encouraged to keep a diary. The health status of the party can be revealed by pressing the appropriate button. As the journey progresses, the user can change the pace of travel and adjust the rationing of food. "Hunt" calls forth an arcade-type game, allowing the user to collect food. At each stop along the way, the user can see who's around and choose to talk to one or more people, often revealing clues or historical facts.

A Wagon Score is displayed only if the user successfully crosses the trail. A value is placed on the people and supplies that complete the journey. Some occupations receive a smaller allocation of funds than others; some have a more difficult time successfully completing the trip. A mathematical weight is, therefore, assigned depending on the user's chosen occupation.

The program has a management option protected by a password that allows the teacher to clear the List of Legends, adjust the simulation speed and hunting time, and determine network use, if any. A new network version of the program allows a number of users to interact simultaneously with one another on their journey.

The award-winning Carmen Sandiego series of programs (*Where in the USA . . .*, *Where in the World . . .*, *Where in Time . . .*, and so forth) is the all-time, best-selling software in grades K–12. The premise of each program is that, as a detective, you must pick up the trail of one of Carmen's villainous gang members and, following geographic (or historic) clues, deduce the identity of the villain, follow the trail, and ultimately apprehend the culprit (see Figure 2–8).

The program has been so popular for a number of years that it spawned a television program and Carmen Sandiego clubs all over the country. The program simulates actions that might be taken in the real world and requires the user, often working cooperatively with others, to make decisions based on facts gathered. Each program provides an appropriate reference book, such as Fodor's *USA*. The computer's role usually is to create a realistic environment and present material for student interaction, to provide appropriate feedback to

Figure 2–8 Where in the USA is Carmen Sandiego®

A scene from this popular simulation program Image used with permission.™ and © 2006 Riverdeep Interactive Learning Limited, and its licensors. All rights reserved. *www.riverdeep.net, www.broderband.com, www.learningcompany.com*

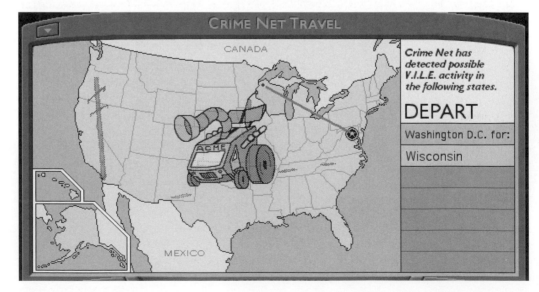

student responses, and, based on decisions made by students, to modify the environment and present new material, allowing the students to witness the results of their decisions.

Students might be asked to trace their travels in the simulation on a map and list the countries through which they travel. Students could be named as "ambassadors" representing each country. They would research the country they represent and present brief reports or hold a mock United Nations meeting and discuss issues of importance to them.

Virtual reality (VR) is a computer-based technology that creates an illusion of reality. Participants interact with, and in fact are immersed in, an artificial environment to the degree that it appears real; it is highly interactive, multisensorial, and vivid enough for the participants almost to think it is reality. Virtual reality, according to Furness (Miller, 1992, p. 14), is "just like you're walking into another world, and you're perceiving it as if it becomes reality itself."

Instructional Games. Though much maligned by some in education, video games and **gaming** segments can be found in all computer-assisted instruction categories. They may be played on a regular computer system or a specially made gaming system such as a PlayStation® or Xbox®. The technique includes a set of rules and a clear contest. Students or groups of students may compete against each other or against the computer or another fixed standard. "Whereas schools largely sequester students from one another and from the outside world, games bring players together—competitively and cooperatively—in the virtual world of the game and in the social community of its players" (Shaffer, Squire, Halveason, & Gee 2005). **Instructional games** may be combined with any number of formats, such as drill and practice, simulations, or problem solving. Most computer games are highly competitive, either with another player or with the computer, and many introduce the elements of speed or time. In most cases they involve some type of fantasy atmosphere. They are usually highly motivational and engage the learner in a situation(s) where the learner is competing for a high score, a prize of some sort, a specific outcome, or a "personal best" effort. Good examples of this type of software include *Dragon in a Wagon, Stickybear, Reading Room Deluxe®*, and *Super Solvers: Gizmos & Gadgets.*

It is possible to first choose one of several levels, such as beginner or mastery level categories, at which to play the game. A popular program in this category is *Zoombinis Logical Journey EEV®* (Figure 2–9).

In this highly entertaining and interactive program, students use pattern recognition and logic to overcome 12 challenges in getting the Zoombinis to their new homeland. There are four levels of difficulty for students in grades 3 through 8. It is designed based on the National Council of Teachers of Mathematics standards 1 through 4. The program contains at least three elements that should be looked for in an instructional game: several levels of mastery, standards or objectives based, and lack of violence or aggressive behavior.

Games can be fun and motivating and many times students are not aware of the learning that is taking place. Some software catalogs have a special section for instructional games under a heading such as "Edutainment."

Video games and gaming are being seen in a new light. Several universities have recently started centers for instructional gaming to study these areas. "Video games have the potential to change the landscape of education as we know it. The answers to the fundamental questions . . . will make it possible to use video games . . . toward a new model of learning through meaningful activity in virtual worlds" (Shaffer et al., 2005).

Problem Solving. When using **problem-solving software**, students use previously mastered skills to solve a challenging problem. This type of software places emphasis on critical thinking, analysis, logic, and reasoning. Students are usually either presented with a problem or have to identify the problem from a given set of data, then state a

Figure 2–9 Zoombinis logical journey EEV®

The Zoombinis must choose the right pizza toppings so they can continue along the road. *(Reprinted with permission of The Learning Company™, Inc.)*

hypothesis, plan strategies, and follow a set of procedures to achieve the final goal or outcome. Students may learn some content as they exercise their higher-order thinking skills.

There are many examples of problem-solving software, even though this category, as with all other categories, blend together. *Zoombinis Logical Journey EEV, Where in the USA Is Carmen Sandiego?* and *Oregon Trail* have been described previously in other categories, but they also fit neatly into problem solving. We usually think that problem-solving software is designed for older children, but this is not necessarily true. Problem-solving software has been developed for children of all age levels. *Reader Rabbit's Playtime for Babies* was developed for children ages 9 through 24 months. It contains 11 activities including a read-along where the child's face and voice can be added. *Arthur's® Kindergarten* along with *Arthur's 1st Grade* and *Arthur's 2nd Grade* cover preK through second grade and include a variety of problem-solving and critical-thinking activities. *Sesame Street Music Maker®* is designed for ages three years and above. It contains eight activities dealing with musical instruments from around the world and actually allows children to compose their own music. *Yoda's Challenge™ Activity* contains six missions, each with four levels of difficulty incorporating critical thinking, geometry, music, map reading, and other skills. We should emphasize that all of these programs may be easily used or adapted for use by students with special needs in higher grades. Other popular problem-solving titles include *ClueFinders Math Adventures, Turtle Math,* and *Widget Workshop™*.

Problem-solving software may be used in a behaviorist-centered classroom but is most often found in one with constructivist learning. In a constructivist environment students would be given little direct training in problem solving; instead, they would be presented with a highly motivating problem and the opportunity and encouragement to solve it on their own or in a group. Constructivists believe that this method of solving problems helps students in a number of ways.

1. Students actually see how information can be used to solve problems in real-life situations.
2. Students find that discovering answers themselves is highly motivating.
3. Properly designed problem-solving software, being both motivational and interesting, will aid students in acquiring and applying content information and research and study skills.

A summary of the teacher, student, and computer roles in computer-assisted instruction is presented for your review in the following table.

	Teacher	Computer	Student
Tutorial	Determines objectives Selects materials appropriate to students Monitors progress Assesses student performance	Presents original material Assesses progress Displays feedback Provides guidance May assess performance Records performance Tests for objectives	Interacts with computer Responds to feedback Controls pace of presentation Examines results
Drill & Practice	Determines objectives Selects materials appropriate to students Teaches original skills or concepts Monitors progress Assesses student performance	Presents material in form of problems or questions Displays feedback May assess performance May record performance	Interacts with computer Responds appropriately Examines results
Simulation	Determines objectives Selects materials appropriate to students Teaches related skills Often prompts students to discover concepts May take an active role in a group Assesses student Performance	Presents a situation Elicits student response Modifies situation May assess performance Demonstrates result of student action	Reacts to situation Refers to external resources if needed Confers with others as needed Makes choices based on information
Instructional Games	Determines objectives Selects materials appropriate to students Sets limits Monitors progress Assesses student performance	Presents situations and materials Competes with student Displays feedback Records performance	Interacts with computer Learns rules Devises strategies Competes with computer Increases skills
Problem Solving	Determines objectives Selects materials appropriate to students Assigns problems Monitors and assists progress Assesses student performance	Presents problem Displays feedback May manipulate data May assess performance	Defines the problem Interacts with the computer Sets up solution Manipulates one or more variables Uses trial and error Increases skills

59

LET'S GO INTO THE CLASSROOM
Kidspiration Learning Experiences

"Kidspiration® (grades K–5) and Inspiration® (grades 3–adult) are digital semantic mapping tools used for graphically expressing ideas. I have found Inspiration and Kidspiration to be excellent vehicles for engaging students in active learning while integrating technology into the curriculum. Using these tools increases my students' comfort level with working in an electronic environment while utilizing critical thinking skills.

This software allows students to organize their ideas in a visual way. Visual maps, also known as graphic organizers, concept maps, and mind maps, can be used for brainstorming, comparing and contrasting, and identifying misconceptions. Both Inspiration and Kidspiration allow the user to show relationships and to present information in linear and nonlinear formats.

Kidspiration and Inspiration not only help students brainstorm and visualize their thinking, but also appeal to students' different learning styles and lend themselves to inquiry-based learning and are a natural component in a web-based learning environment.

Kidspiration was used in the example below to design an appealing, interactive learning experience that would engage students. In this "Cinderella Around the World" activity, students are instructed to answer questions using either words or symbols from the program's symbol palette (seen on left). (Students can also import graphics, play sounds, fill in text, and select fonts and effects.) At the end of this unit, concept maps can be printed out and compared so that students will have a visual representation of the essential question of the unit, that is, how setting and culture affects the elements of a fairy tale.

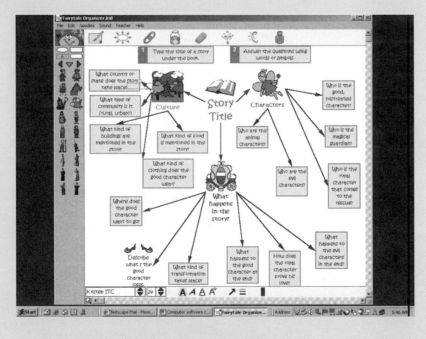

Karen Kliegman
Library Media Specialist
Searingtown School
Albertson, New York

Software to Aid in Problem Solving. The application software used by the authors helped solve the problem of presenting a manuscript to the publisher containing proper spelling, punctuation, and grammar. It was the tool used to solve a specific problem: that of producing a reasonably polished manuscript. Just as this software helped the authors with writing, other software is designed to help people through the problem-solving process.

Think back to some of your own problem-solving experiences. Did you try to picture the problem in your mind or jot things down on paper to organize your thinking, to find relationships, and to come up with a solution(s). Organizing, diagramming, or picturing on paper or on a blackboard are particularly helpful when trying to explain information, problems, or relationships to others. Movie directors use storyboards that picture each scene's actors, set, and camera angle. Chemists use models to help explain difficult chemical reactions. Leonardo da Vinci filled books with diagrams and sketches. This process is called visualization. "A picture is worth a thousand words," so they say. It is true and we can help students save time, energy, and words if we can help them visualize ideas, relationships, and concepts. Many students use the popular *Inspiration*® software, as shown in the example in Figure 2–10, to help organize and visualize those relationships and concepts. You have learned in other education courses that visual learning is a powerful tool in the students' cognitive arsenal.

Figure 2–10 Cultural Research Organizer

A fifth-grade grade project created in Inspiration® *(Courtesy of Karen Kliegman.)*

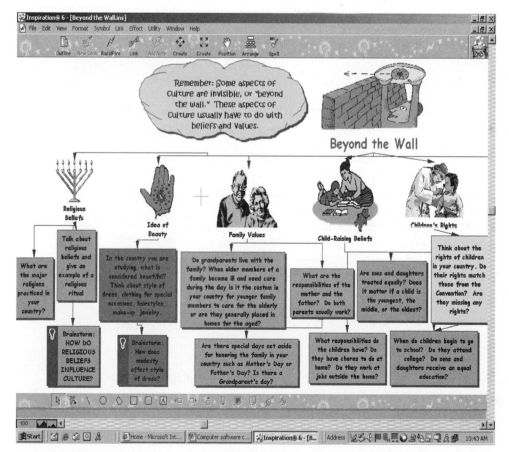

A preview copy of Inspiration and Kidspiration software can be downloaded free from their site *http://inspiration.com*

Computer software can help you visualize a problem. It is easy to make concept maps, webs, and flowcharts using any one of the many drawing programs found in most school computer laboratories. Just as a carpenter might pick a specialized hammer (e.g., framing or tack) to solve the problem of nailing a specific type of nail into a specific medium, we may choose specialized software designed to help us with our problem of making a concept map, web, or flowchart. *Inspiration* for grades 6 to adult and *Kidspiration* for grades K through 5 are examples of specialized software designed to aid in this visualization. They are an easy-to-use, powerful tool that lets the user create pictures of ideas, relationships, and concepts. They allow the user to design, create, and modify concept maps, webs, time lines, outlines, and other graphical organizers at the stroke of a key, the click of the mouse, and/or the drag of an icon. Ideas can be placed on the screen, expanded, rearranged, and organized with ease. Students can quickly grasp visual relationships as these ideas are spread out on the screen or printed on paper. This visualization aids in clarifying thinking, understanding concepts, developing organizational skills, and increasing retention.

Working with Kidspiration®

Two popular software applications used in k–12 classroom, aside from *Microsoft Office® Suite*, are *Inspiration®* and *Kidspiration®*. These wonderful programs allow students to make mind maps and flowcharts, and aid in brainstorming and visualizing ideas and concepts.

   Inspiration® was originally intended for middle school students and above; *Kidspiration®* was intended for the younger grade levels. *Kidspiration®* is more colorful and fun to use and, because of this, has crept into the middle and high school classrooms. Due to its wide acceptance, we will lead you through a brief tutorial showing you how to make a simple concept map using *Kidspiration®*.

LET'S TRY IT!

A copy of this tutorial may be found in the Tutorials folder in the Take-Along CD

In working through the following brief tutorial on **Kidspiration®** you will learn the following:

- How to open the program and choose a picture project on the starter page
- How to change fonts, font sizes, font colors, and styles
- How to make, fill in, and connect information bubbles
- How to add graphics and sounds
- How to add hyperlinks and other features to kidspiration

Once you have downloaded a 30-day trial copy of both *Kidspiration®* and *Inspiration®* from *http://inspiration.com*, or have otherwise accessed the program, open Kidspiration®. Reprinted by permission of Inspiration Software, Inc.

1. OPEN A BLANK PAGE

1.1 Once you open *Kidspiration*, the Kidspiration Starter screen will appear.

Notice the various icons on the Starter screen.

- The New box allows the user to make a new *Kidspiration®* project graphically (Picture) or in outline form (Writing).
- The Open box allows the user to open a *Kidspiration®* project already on the computer.
- The Activities box contains five buttons that contain sample concept maps and projects to give the user ideas or to help the user get started.

1.2 Select Picture from the New box.

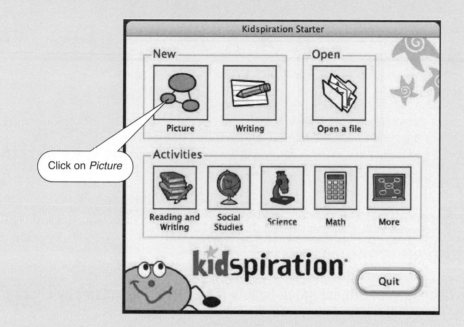

2. DEVELOP YOUR CONCEPT MAP

2.1 Click on the Main Idea box.

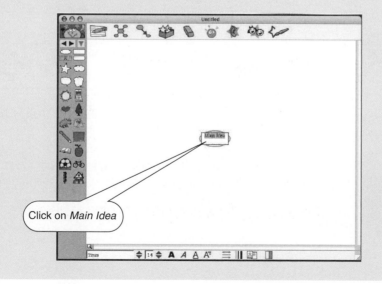

(Continued)

2.2 Place the name of the largest grouping you will use here.

In this tutorial, type *The Animal Kingdom* in this bubble.

2.3 Change the font and font attributes.

Use the font attributes pulldown menus (the two on left for font and size) and buttons (the four letter A's for bold, italics, underline, and font color) at the bottom of the *Kidspiration* screen.

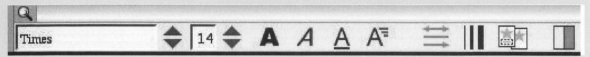

Use the Following: **Times – 18 – Bold** – Text color **BLUE**

Our main idea will not fit correctly using text size 18 but clicking outside of the bubble will enlarge the bubble to the correct size.

3. ADD SUBGROUP BUBBLES

3.1 Choose your largest group bubble (The Animal Kingdom) by clicking on it.

3.2 On the top menu, click on the icon second from the left to add a symbol coming from this bubble. You will see the label "Add Symbol" as you mouse over this tool.

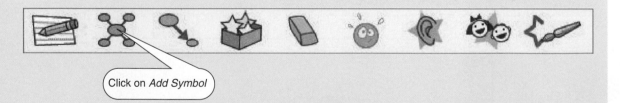

Click on *Add Symbol*

A new bubble will appear each time you click the Add Symbol button. Click it three times. If you do not like where a bubble is placed, just drag it around the screen to the proper location.

3.3 Fill in the subgroup bubbles you need for your concept map with the words *Birds*, *Fish*, and *Mammals*.

3.4 Continue adding other tiers of bubble as in 3.2 and 3.3. Add *Dogs*, *Cats*, and *Mice* to the *Mammals* bubble.

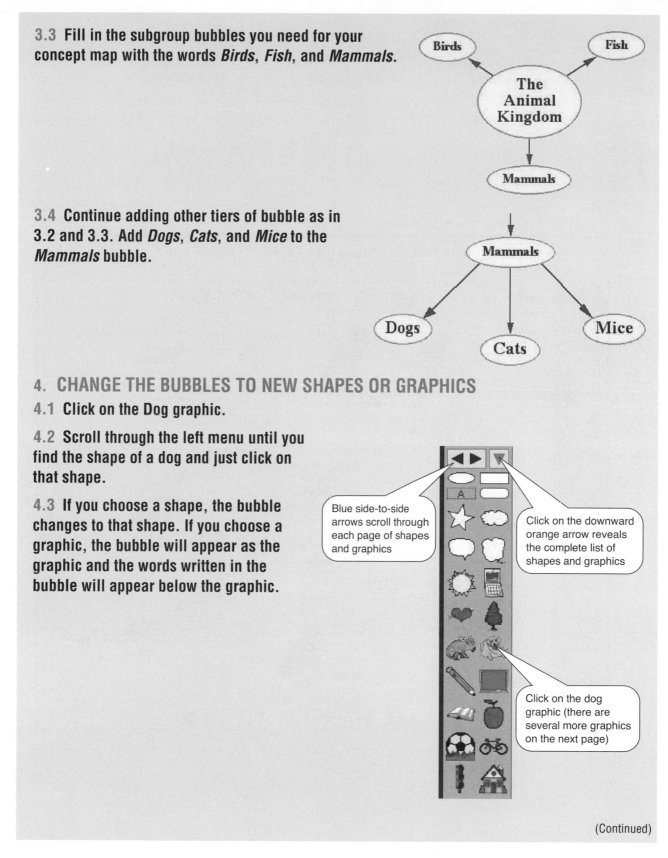

4. CHANGE THE BUBBLES TO NEW SHAPES OR GRAPHICS

4.1 Click on the Dog graphic.

4.2 Scroll through the left menu until you find the shape of a dog and just click on that shape.

4.3 If you choose a shape, the bubble changes to that shape. If you choose a graphic, the bubble will appear as the graphic and the words written in the bubble will appear below the graphic.

Blue side-to-side arrows scroll through each page of shapes and graphics

Click on the downward orange arrow reveals the complete list of shapes and graphics

Click on the dog graphic (there are several more graphics on the next page)

(Continued)

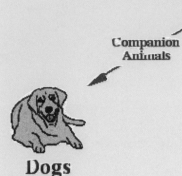

Companion
Animals

Dogs

4.4 Other labels can be added between bubbles by clicking on the arrows and typing the information in the box that appears.

Type *Companion Animal* on the arrow that links the *Mammals* bubble with the *Dog* symbol. (Yes, you cat-lovers, cats are also Companion Animals.)

Keep working on the project until you reach this final Kidspiration.

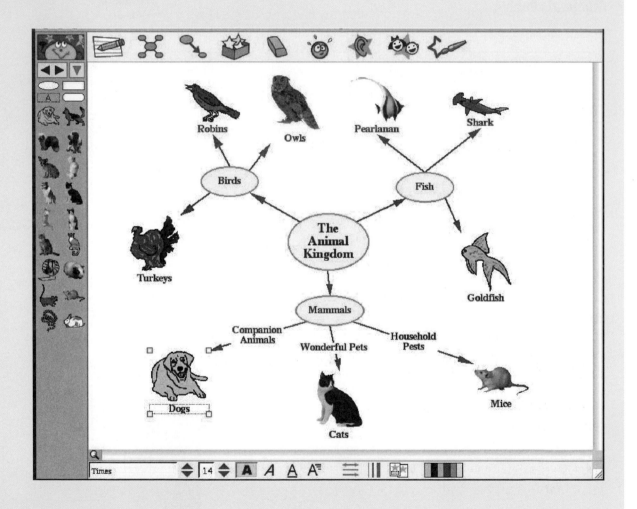

5. OTHER FEATURES TO CUSTOMIZE YOUR CONCEPT MAP

5.1 Change the size, direction, and/or color of the arrow. Click on the arrow and use the three icons on the left side of the bottom menu.

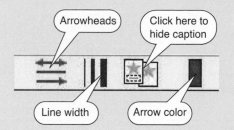

5.2 Change the graphic color by clicking on the graphic (for example, the graphic of the dog) and click on one of the colors that appear.

5.3 Add a graphic to the sheet without having it attached to any bubble.

Simply click on the spot where you want to place the graphic and then click on the desired shape or graphic in the menu.

5.4 Replace a bubble with a graphic of your own.

Just click on the bubble and go to Import a Graphic under the File menu at the top of screen.

5.5 Add a graphic of your own to the sheet.

Click on the spot where you want the graphic to be placed as in step 5.3 and add the graphic as you did in step 5.4.

5.6 Use the Edit menu at the top of the screen to cut, copy, paste, clear, and select all.

Kidspiration 2   File   Edit   Goodies   Sound   Teacher   Help

5.7 Use the Goodies menu to change the background color and to run a spell check.

5.8 Use the Sound menu to record a sound, erase a sound, or change the voice that is heard as you mouse-over words or graphics.

5.9 The Teacher menu allows you to perform many interesting tasks.

We encourage you to experiment with this menu.

(Continued)

5.10 Change your Kidspiration® concept map to outline form by clicking on the Paper and Pencil icon on the top menu.

The Animal Kingdom

Fish

Goldfish

Pearlanan

Shark

Mammals

Mice

Cats

Dogs

The final Kidspiration is now in outline form.

5.11 The top menu bar includes (from left to right):

Outline Form tool, Add Symbol tool, Link Symbols tool, Super Grouper tool, Clear tool, Undo tool, Sound tool, Student Name tool, Create Symbol tool.

Tool	Function
Outline Form	Convert concept map to outline form
Add Symbol	A new bubble appears each time you click this tool
Link Symbols	Adds links and arrows after bubbles are placed on the page
Super Grouper	Allows user to group bubbles on the page
Clear	Allows user to clear a graphic
Undo	Undoes previous keystrokes
Sound	Turns sound on and off
Student Name	Allows students to place their names in a specific location
Create Symbol	Allows users to make their own symbol or graphic

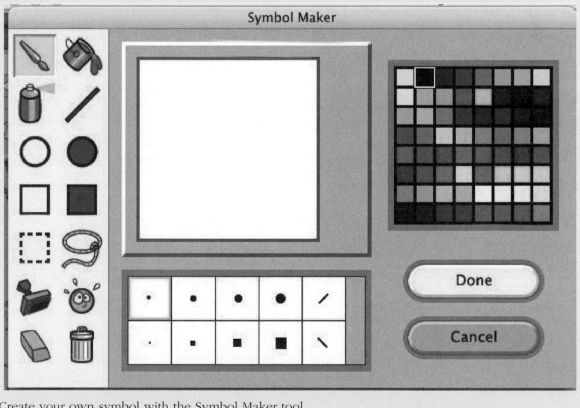

Create your own symbol with the Symbol Maker tool.

LET'S GO INTO THE CLASSROOM
Inspiration® for KWHL Planning

During the past few years, I have used Inspiration® with my kindergarten students to help them develop, investigate, and explore their ideas. Inspiration can be used for a variety of classroom techniques that allow students to explore their ideas visually using graphical organizers. One activity I found especially beneficial—and the students found quite engaging—was using Inspiration® for KWHL planning.

A KWHL chart is a graphical organizer used to gather and illustrate information on any topic: What we **KNOW**, What we **WANT** to know, **HOW** to find out, and, later, What we've **LEARNED**. I have used KWHL charts to brainstorm with my students before we start just about any unit.

Using Inspiration® for KWHL charts is a great way to integrate technology into an everyday classroom activity. With my computer connected to a big screen television, I open up a new Inspiration® document and introduce the topic. Last February, it was Valentine's Day. Prompted by my question—"What do we KNOW about Valentine's Day?"—the students brainstorm and share ideas while I record them into the graphical organizer using Inspiration's® RapidFire™ feature. We then move on to the W and the H parts of the graphical organizer.

When we're done, I print the chart out and post it in a prominent place in the classroom. We refer to the diagram frequently and keep track of our progress in the "What have we learned" category, a great way to help young students begin to develop critical thinking and research skills.

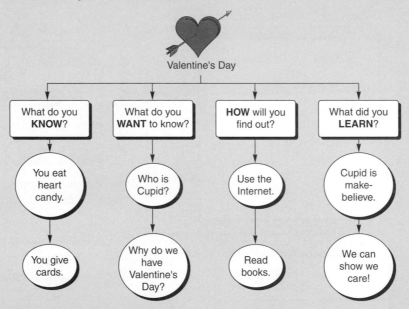

Using Inspiration® with my kindergartners has been fun and engaging. It has also made it easy for me to bring technology into everyday classroom activities with very young students. Using KWHL charts, along with other types of graphical organizers, has helped even the youngest students organize their thoughts, develop critical thinking skills, and even monitor their own learning.

Donna Hall
Kindergarten Teacher
Pinellas County Schools
Pinellas, Florida

Both *Inspiration* and *Kidspiration* present a diagram view that is the visual representation of thoughts, ideas, and concepts; and an outline view that presents the same information in a standard outline form. They both also contain a catalog of over 500 objects, boxes, balloons, and symbols to add interest and drama to the diagram view.

Figure 2–11 is a simple concept map that shows relationships in the development of early civilizations. In it we visually portray the relationship between agriculture and animal husbandry and the dynamics leading the growth of populations and the development of cities.

Figure 2–11 A concept map

A diagram showing relationships between animal husbandry, agriculture, population growth, and city development. (*Courtesy of Inspiration Software, Inc.*)

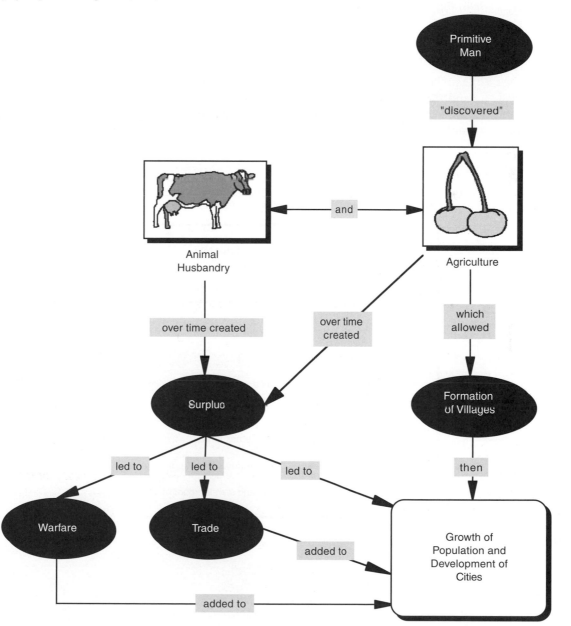

Compare this visual of the information with the outline version of the same information in Figure 2–12. Note that both the diagram and the outline contain the same relative information, but the graphical representation on the concept map seems to show relationships in a clearer manner.

A web is a second type of visual representation showing how different pieces of information relate to each other. There is usually a core concept or main idea in the center with relationships radiating out from the core concept like the spokes of a wheel. Webs are often used to diagram relationships between characters, conflicts, themes, and settings in books and plays. Johnna Solting Horton, a high school media specialist in Minnesota, created Figure 2–13, a web revolving around the play *Romeo and Juliet*. She began with one of the templates included with *Inspiration*. Students viewing this could see at a glance several relationships within the play.

Now compare Figure 2–13 with the outline version of the same information presented in Figure 2–14. Do you find it much more difficult to visualize relationships?

Working with Inspiration®

As mentioned, two popular software applications used in K–12 classrooms are *Inspiration*® and *Kidspiration*®. You have seen how to use *Kidspiration*® in the previous tutorial. Now we will lead you through the creation of a mind map using *Inspiration*®, originally intended for middle school and high school students.

A preview copy of Inspiration® and Kidspiration® software can be downloaded free from their site *http://inspiration.com*

Figure 2–12 An outline

Outline showing relationships between animal husbandry, agriculture, population growth, and city development. *(Courtesy of Inspiration Software, Inc.)*

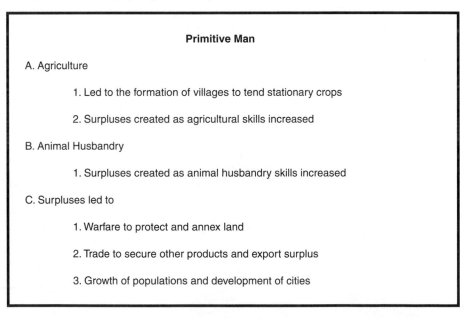

Primitive Man

A. Agriculture

    1. Led to the formation of villages to tend stationary crops

    2. Surpluses created as agricultural skills increased

B. Animal Husbandry

    1. Surpluses created as animal husbandry skills increased

C. Surpluses led to

    1. Warfare to protect and annex land

    2. Trade to secure other products and export surplus

    3. Growth of populations and development of cities

Figure 2–13 A web diagram

A web diagram of *Romeo and Juliet* showing relationships between characters, conflicts, themes, and settings. *(Courtesy of Inspiration Software, Inc.)*

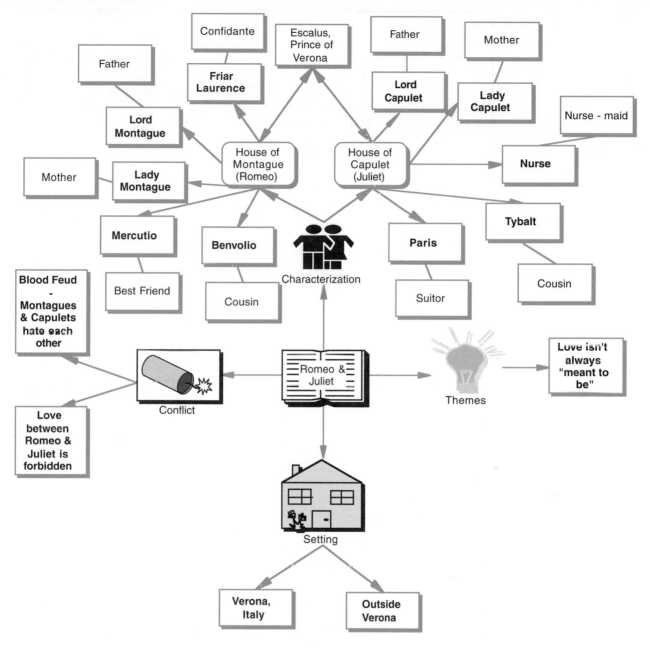

Figure 2–14 A web outline

A web outline of *Romeo and Juliet* showing the same relationships between characters, conflicts, themes, and settings. *(Courtesy of Inspiration Software, Inc.)*

Romeo & Juliet
    I. Setting
        A. Verona, Italy
        B. Outside Verona
    II. Characterization
        A. House of Montague
            1. Friar Laurence
                a. Confidante
            2. Lord Montague
                a. Father
            3. Escalus, Prince of Verona
                a. House of Capulet
                    1. Lord Capulet
                        a. Father
                    2. Lady Capulet
                        a. Mother
                    3. Nurse
                        a. Nurse - maid
                    4. Tybalt
                        a. Cousin
                    5. Paris
                        a. Suitor
            4. Lady Montague
                a. Mother
            5. Mercutio
                a. Best Friend
            6. Benvolio
                a. Cousin
    III. Conflict
        A. Blood Feud -
            Montagues & Capulets hate each other
        B. Love between Romeo & Juliet is forbidden
    IV. Themes
        A. Love isn't always "meant to be"

In working through the following brief tutorial on **Inspiration**® you will learn the following:

- How to open inspiration and choose a picture project on the starter page
- How to change fonts, font sizes, font colors, and styles
- How to make, fill in, and connect information bubbles
- How to add graphics and sounds.

A copy of this tutorial may be found in the Tutorials folder in the Take-along CD

Once you have downloaded a 30-day trial copy of both *Kidspiration*® and *Inspiration*® from *http://inspiration.com*, or have otherwise accessed the program, open *Inspiration*®. Reprinted by permission of Inspiration Software, Inc.

1. OPENING A BLANK PAGE

1.1 Once you open Inspiration, the Inspiration Starter screen will appear.

Notice the various boxes and buttons on the Starter screen.

- The Diagram button allows the user to make a new Inspiration® project graphically (Picture).
- The Outline button allows the user to input an outline (Writing).
- It is possible to alternate between the Diagram and Outline form at any time.
- The Open File button allows the user to open an Inspiration® project already on the computer.
- The Templates button contains sample concept templates and projects to give the user ideas or to help the user get started.
- The Learn To Use button contains examples and helpful information to help you get the most out of the Inspiration program.

1.2 Select Diagram from the Inspiration Starter screen.

(Continued)

2. DEVELOP YOUR CONCEPT MAP

2.1 Click on the Main Idea box.

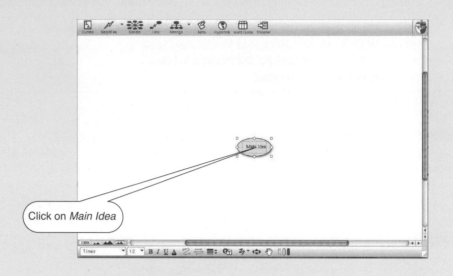

Click on *Main Idea*

2.2 Place the name of the largest grouping you will use in this box.

(For this example, type *The Wizard of Oz* here.)

2.3 Change the font and font attributes.

Use the font attributes pulldown menus (the two on the left for font and size) and buttons (bold, italics, underline, and font color) at the bottom of the *Inspiration*® screen. Fill and line color can be changed using the buttons on the far right of this menu.

Revert   Line color

Font Attributes   Fill color

Change the font to *Size 18* and *Bold*. Our main idea will not fit correctly using text size 18. Clicking outside of the box will resize the bubble to fit the new font size. You could also drag a corner box to make it larger.

You can also change the font attributes using the Text menu at the top of the screen.

Text	Symbol	Link	Ef
Font			▶
Size			▶
Style			▶
Justify			▶
Color			▶
Revert to Style		⇧⌘E	
Fractional Fonts			

3. ADD SUBGROUP BUBBLES USING CREATE

3.1 Choose your largest group bubble by clicking on it.

3.2 Look at the top menu. Click on the icon (tool), third from the left to add a symbol coming from this bubble.

This is labeled "Create". Click on the spoke of the Create tool in the location comparable to the location you would like the new bubble to appear in your concept map. RapidFire will also add bubbles. We will discuss this below.

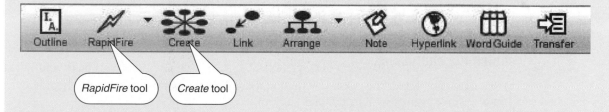

A new bubble will appear each time you click the *Create* button. (We will make two bubbles.) If you do not like where it is placed, just drag it around the screen to the proper location. Fill in the bubble as you did in steps **2.2** and **2.3.**

3.3 Repeat steps 3.1 and 3.2 until you have the subgroups Locations and Movie Stars and changed the fill color and text size.

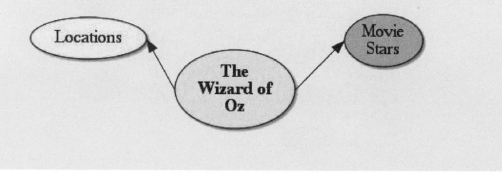

(Continued)

4. ADD SUBGROUP BUBBLES USING RAPIDFIRE

Sometimes you want to rapidly add subcategories to your concept map bubbles, perhaps when your class is brainstorming. This can be done using the RapidFire button.

4.1 Select the Locations bubble to which you want to add subgroups.

4.2 Click the RapidFire button on the top menu.

A red lightning bolt will appear after the title in the bubble you choose.

4.3 Type the word or words you want in the subgroup bubble and either press the RapidFire button or press Return after each word or group of words. An additional bubble will appear each time you do this.

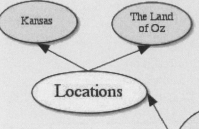

(After clicking on the *Locations* bubble and selecting RapidFire, type *Kansas*. Select Return. Type *The Land of Oz* and select Return. Move the bubbles around as needed for your concept map.)

4.4 Do the same thing for *Movie Stars*.

This time RapidFire Judy Garland, Ray Bolger, Bert Lahr, and Jack Haley.

4.5 Also add the names of the *Characters* in *Kansas* and *The Land of Oz* using RapidFire and change the colors of the bubbles to match the characters.

(Hint: You can change the colors by highlighting all of the boxes of one color [e.g., Ray Bolger, Hank, Scarecrow] and change all of the colors at once.)

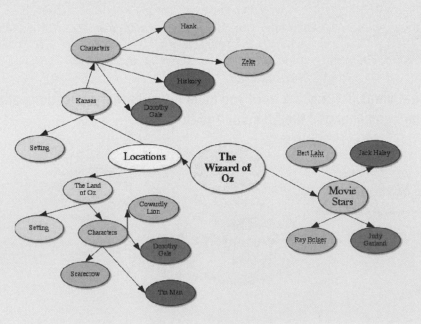

5. CHANGE THE BUBBLES TO NEW SHAPES OR GRAPHICS

5.1 Click on the Cowardly Lion bubble and change it to a picture of a Lion.

5.2 Scroll through the left menu (or click the downward arrow to see the complete list of libraries) until you find a shape or graphic you want to use and just click on that shape or graphic.

Clicking on this arrow will reveal the complete list of shapes and graphics

Symbols

Search / Libraries

Animals 2

Basic
Animals–Plants ►
Arts ►
Everyday ►
Food–Health ►
Fun ►
Geography ►
Math ►
People ►
Process ►
Science ►
Social Studies ►
Technology ►
Work–School ►

New Symbol Library...
Edit Symbol Libraries...

We will use this Lion graphic

Enter search words
√ Photos √ Art Q

These arrows scroll through each page of shapes and graphics

5.3 If you choose a shape, the bubble changes to that shape. If you choose a graphic, the bubble will appear as the graphic and the words written in the bubble will appear below the graphic.

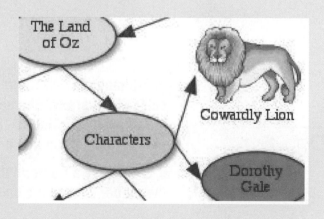

The Land of Oz

Cowardly Lion

Characters

Dorothy Gale

(Continued)

5.4 Other labels can be added between bubbles by clicking on the arrows and typing the information in the box that appears. (In this example, type *Technicolor* and *Black and white*.)

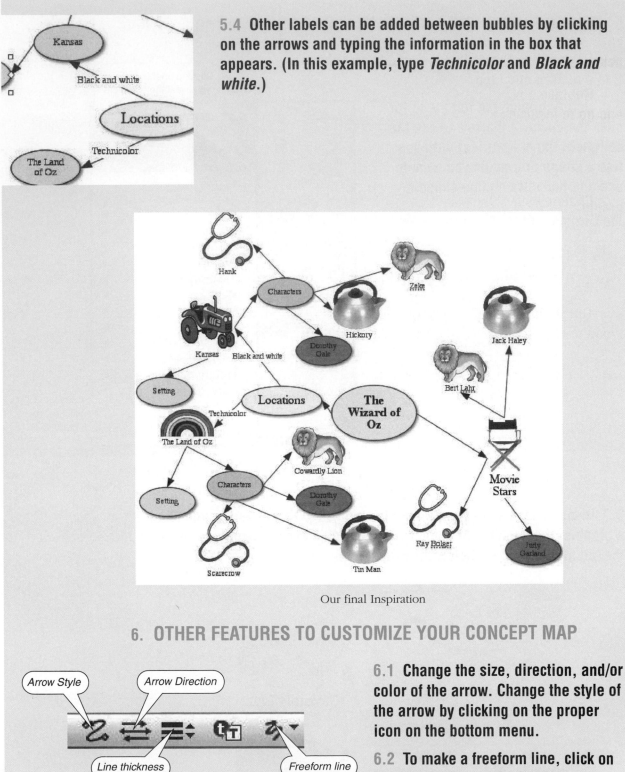

Our final Inspiration

6. OTHER FEATURES TO CUSTOMIZE YOUR CONCEPT MAP

6.1 Change the size, direction, and/or color of the arrow. Change the style of the arrow by clicking on the proper icon on the bottom menu.

6.2 To make a freeform line, click on the proper icon on the bottom menu.

Arrow Style

Arrow Direction

Line thickness

Freeform line

6.3 Add a graphic to the sheet without having it attached to any bubble. Simply click on the spot where you want to place the graphic. Now, just click on the desired shape or graphic in the left menu.

6.4 Replace a bubble with a graphic of your own. Just click on the bubble and go to Insert Graphic under the Edit menu at the top of screen.

6.5 Add a graphic of your own to the sheet. Click on the spot where you want the graphic to be placed and add the graphic as you did in step 6.4.

6.6 Change your Inspiration® concept map to outline form by clicking on the Outline button on the top menu (first one on the left).

6.7 The Outline button changes to Diagram in Outline mode to change the outline back to a diagram.

We hope that you enjoyed this brief tutorial. We have only scratched the surface of the potential of this amazing program. Good luck exploring all of the other parts of the program!

The Wizard of Oz

I. Movie Stars

  A. Judy Garland

  B. Ray Bolger

  C. Bert Lahr

  D. Jack Haley

II. Locations

  A. The Land of Oz

    1. Setting

    2. Characters

      a. Dorothy Gale

      b. Scarecrow

      c. Cowardly Lion

      d. Tin Man

  B. Kansas

    1. Setting

    2. Characters

      a. Dorothy Gale

      b. Zeke

      c. Hickory

      d. Hank

Curriculum Applications of Problem Solving. Rather than attempt to address all of the problem-solving applications (should we call them opportunities?) across the entire curriculum, let's concentrate on information technology, since it is the focus of this textbook. Unlike what has become popular usage in the business world, we define the term *information technology* as the application of a tool to solve problems related to information to be created, received, stored, manipulated, or disseminated. As teachers in an information-rich society, we must strive to encourage students to develop their information skills and to realize that information is power.

Figure 2–15 may be helpful as a lesson-planning tool to develop problem-solving skills in students. Identifying available resources describes the "Given," and specifying the performance indicators establishes the "To Find." The analysis phase is completed. Specifying the need to create, record, access, analyze, and synthesize information suggests

Figure 2–15 A Lesson-Planning Tool
A planning tool to develop problem-solving skills in information technology

Unit of Study: _____

Performance Indicators: _____

_____

_____

Resources Available: _____

_____

_____

Information Needs:

• Creating   (writings, drawings, maps, charts, etc.)

_____

_____

_____

• Recording   (facts, opinions, and impressions for future reference)

_____

_____

_____

• Accessing   (from student or teacher created reports and data files, from bound references, from electronic encyclopedias and atlases, etc.)

_____

_____

_____

• Analyzing   (comparing and contrasting text and numerical and picture data in order to form conclusions)

_____

_____

_____

"Procedure" to solve the problem and completes the synthesis phase of problem solving. The examination of the one or more component parts to the procedure will reveal the information skills that need to be learned by the students. The content becomes the vehicle for the acquisition of the problem-solving skills.

Multimedia Instruction. Few, if any, pieces of software are "pure" drill and practice, tutorial, simulation, instructional game, or problem solving. Some are predominantly one type but embody elements of other approaches. **Multimedia instruction,** more than any other category of software, blurs these lines of distinction. It is also closely related to **multimedia learning.** Refer back to Figure 2–1, and notice that multimedia learning is a subcategory of construction of knowledge under the category of student-centered learning.

Multimedia programs are often used to control the presentation of video information from external sources, such as videotape or DVD, as well as graphic, audio, or textual information from CD-ROM. Although the majority of these programs are designed for individual instruction, they may be adapted for group use by the instructor. Typically, audio and video material (still frames, sounds, or moving images with sound) is presented to the viewer accompanied by computer-generated text in a true multimedia fashion. The instructional designer uses the computer to select the video segment and present it on the screen, often interspersed with computer-generated question frames. Depending on the response to the question, the designer can program the computer to repeat the segment, present another one in a remediation mode, or move on to new information.

Multimedia instruction in CAI format is blossoming rapidly in business and industry as an effective and efficient training tool. It is receiving a good deal of attention at the college and university level and is making some inroads in K–12 education as better software becomes commercially available and as teachers develop increasing confidence and skill in designing their own lessons. In an information tool format, multimedia allows students to create their own visuals and incorporate them into their products or to create their own navigation through existing resources. Because of the breadth of classroom applications possible with this technology, multimedia, hypermedia, and virtual reality are discussed in greater detail in Chapter 10.

Students with Special Needs. When properly used, the software categories we have examined occupy a unique place in the curriculum. Software from each of the categories can be found or adapted for students with special needs. In many cases computers are ideally suited for this task, augmenting, but not replacing, teachers and support personnel. An interesting study of at-risk high school students by Swan and Mitrani (1993) found that there were *more* teacher–student interactions in classrooms where computer-based applications were used than in traditional classrooms. They also found that these interactions were *more* individualized and student centered. Computers can be good teachers and companions for students with special needs, ready to repeat information in a wide variety of ways, patiently waiting for input, and even correcting or channeling input for best results. *Write: OutLoud*® from Don Johnson is an award-winning, talking word-processing program that also contains a talking spell checker. *Co: Write*®, another award winner from Don Johnson, is a user-friendly, word-prediction program that works in conjunction with any word processor. It predicts the completion of partial words that are input, thereby reducing the number of keystrokes needed. Proper use of graphics and sounds can motivate and reinforce students with special needs to further achieve school and personal goals. As stated previously, any of the software programs designed for younger children may be used or modified for use with older students with special needs.

Many different types of special needs devices may be added to a computer to increase the ability of students who have poor coordination or are physically challenged to access

83

and use computers and computer software. These may include such features as a modified keyboard, enlarged monitor, spoken text, and voice recognition.

Curriculum Integration. A danger in examining discrete elements and in categorizing software or computer applications is that we neglect the whole as we examine the separate parts. Much software available today spans more than one category. Tutorial software may well have drill-and-practice components. Simulation software may well introduce new concepts and repeat previously learned material. Classification schemes can become counterproductive if they interfere with an understanding of the potential application of software.

The somewhat arbitrary classification of curriculum during the past decades, especially at the secondary school level, into specific subject matter areas is now breaking down in favor of the integration of disciplines to foster rich learning environments. As we consider computer applications, then, we should keep in mind the concept of integration. The following excerpt by David Thornburg (1991) in his book, *Education, Technology, and Paradigms of Change for the Twenty-First Century*, is an excellent example of classroom application of the computer in an integrated curriculum:

> After exploring California's location on the planet and talking about the geologic upheavals that created some of the spectacular landscape, the students might be encouraged to imagine themselves as members of an ancient tribe of Indians, the Ohlones, for example. Student research on this tribe would allow them to think about the rich civilization these Indians had when the pyramids were being built in Egypt.
>
> As the students learned more about these ancient people, they could learn how to identify animals from their tracks. For this task, students could use *Animal Trackers,* a program from Sunburst Communications that provides clues from which the students must identify a particular animal. Because this program supports databases for grasslands, desert and wooded areas, it can be used all over the country. Each clue provides information of a different sort—habitat, nesting, food, and footprints. After working with this program for a while, students will have learned a lot about native American animals, as well as honing their higher-order thinking skills. This activity provides an opportunity for science to become integrated with social studies.
>
> As the year proceeds, the students might see a new animal through Indian eyes—the strange creatures with two heads and four legs (the Spanish explorers on horseback). At this point some students might want to retain the Indian perspective and others might want to join forces with Portola or Father Junipero Serra as the colonization of California took place.
>
> Later on in the course, the teacher might show the film *Dream West,* showing the life of Fremont as he explored the West and paved the way for the United States to expand its boundaries. At this point, students could use the *Oregon Trail* simulation from MECC to see how well they might fare on their own journey across the country. (pp. 22–23)

Computer-Managed Instruction as an Element of Teacher-Centered Instruction. Although computer-assisted instruction, especially tutorial software, sometimes includes some management and recordkeeping function, its emphasis is on the presentation of information or instruction. Computer-managed instruction, however, stresses the management of student performance in a direct, online approach, with the student working directly at the computer or in an offline approach away from the computer. This category includes programs for keeping student records, diagnostic and prescriptive tests, analyzing test scores, and integrated learning systems.

Most teachers believe in the concept of individualized instruction. With great effort, many succeed. Individualized instruction is not to be confused with independent study. With individualized instruction, a teacher knows all students well on the basis of their personal, cultural, experiential, and academic background; scholastic ability; and learning style. Knowing the students in this manner, the teacher is capable of providing for diversity in the classroom. Given current typical student–teacher ratios, the mainstreaming of students with special needs into the regular classroom and the attendant, legally mandated IEPs, the recordkeeping involved in individualizing instruction is a monumental task. It is, however, a task well suited to the computer. Student progress can finally be tracked effectively and efficiently.

Integrated Learning Systems. Perhaps the pinnacle of computer-assisted instruction is the **integrated learning system (ILS).** A classification system by its very nature is arbitrary. We have chosen to place ILS under computer-managed instruction because of its exhaustive management design. It is really a total learning package spanning both computer-assisted instruction and computer-managed instruction categories. ILSs are powerful and expensive. They usually require their own computer (a file server) to house all of the student software (drill and practice, tutorial, simulation, instructional games, problem solving, and so on) along with software required to individualize instruction, track student progress, store records, and print a variety of reports. Students and teachers gain access to the file server through a network of microcomputers. When a student logs into the file server, the server downloads particular assignments and coursework to the student's computer. It then tracks student progress, tests, and remediates as necessary. Individualized instruction is the major selling point for the ILS. Teachers are able to access student progress notes and tailor the ILS accordingly. Most ILSs contain the entire scope and sequence for a given topic or content area and usually encompass several grade levels of work.

Design of Teaching Materials as an Element of Teacher-Centered Instruction. Many teachers have relied heavily on commercially prepared teaching materials in the form of bulletin boards, overhead transparency masters, printed masters for worksheets, and other handouts. At times this has resulted in an accommodation between the teacher's perceived needs and the materials available that are designed by a third party. This reliance on commercial materials could, at times, be attributed to teachers' lack of confidence in their own creative ability, as well as to the time demands for producing original materials. Teachers are learning that the computer can significantly increase their ability and dramatically decrease production time demands. Much of the information, illustrations, and exercises in this text will help you do just that!

Text. The computer is ideally suited to creating display materials, and users are presented with a wide variety of software from which to choose. A word processor can be used to prepare practice exercises for the student to complete in school or at home. By selecting a large type size, this same program can prepare an overhead transparency master. Color can be used to highlight key words by separating the components of the transparency into two masters and printing them in different colors. Special attention might be paid to programs that facilitate the easy integration of graphics and sound with text.

Graphics. Many individuals do not have a high degree of confidence in their artistic drawing ability. Graphics programs level the playing field. They facilitate the creation of respectable illustrations and often bolster the self-esteem of self-prescribed nonartists. Programs such as *Adobe Illustrator*®, *CorelDRAW*®, *AppleWorks*, *Kid Pix*™, *PC Paint*™, and *Print Shop*® facilitate the creation of bulletin board and display graphics and text. *PowerPoint* allows the creation and projection of a series of images containing text, graphics, sound, and video. Links can also be added to skip to other slides in the series, open web pages, and even open Word documents. Programs such as *AppleWorks*, *DeltaGraph*, *Excel*®, and *Microsoft Works*® generate line graphs, bar graphs, and pie charts from numeric data. Even K–4 students can make graphs, analyze, and compare data with such programs as *Graph Master*®.

Multimedia Authoring. You have noticed in Figure 2–1 that multimedia applications appear as subcategories under teacher-centered instruction, as well as under student-centered learning. Much multimedia software is not procured from commercial sources but created locally by teachers and students. When creating lessons in the multimedia format, the teacher controls audio and video information, as well as text from internal and external sources. Sophisticated yet easy-to-use software such as *ToolBook*®, *mPOWER*®, and *HyperStudio* turn the teacher into a multimedia author. Many teachers fail to realize that a powerful multimedia tool is their old friend *PowerPoint*®.

Programs are available that allow computer screens to be recorded on videotape to serve as titles, credits, animated graphics, and instructional text screens. A variety of scene transitions that allow one image to fade or to merge into another lends sophistication to the recording. Desktop presentation software permits the projection of computer screens by a video projector. Software that supports the design of teaching materials serves as an extension of the creative teacher. Although these materials can be created in other ways, the computer makes it easy and quick, thereby stimulating teachers to maximize their creative efforts.

Student-Centered Learning

Student-centered learning is an approach that views the computer as an information tool for the student to create, access, retrieve, manipulate, and transmit information. One or more students can approach a computer on an as-needed basis in a classroom, school library, or computer lab environment.

When you examine this portion of our classification scheme dealing with student-centered learning, know that many facets referred to under teacher-centered instruction may apply in varying degree to this section as well. The effort here, however, is to focus attention on the student as the user, creator, and disseminator of information and as the builder of knowledge.

Construction of Knowledge. As can be seen in Figure 2–16, student-centered learning encourages students to view the computer as a tool similar to a pencil, brush, or calculator in order to solve a problem. The techniques embodied in student-centered learning are found in subsequent chapters dealing with the computer as a word processing, spreadsheet, database, graphics, or Internet tool. The computer is not only a productivity tool for the teacher but also a tool that enhances the productivity of the student.

The word processor allows the student to express ideas and, with the teacher's guidance, refine the quality of that expression with a reasonable amount of effort in a short period of time. Inquiry strategies can be mapped, content outlines prepared, and detailed reports written. Simple skill-building exercises can become pleasurable. Classroom and school newspapers can be published with word processors and desktop publishing software. Students of all ages can become authors and their books placed in the school library for others to read.

We live in an environment where visual images are constantly bombarding our sense of sight. The advertising industry has made a science of using graphics. Computers have emerged as devices to manipulate visual images and to create forms of video animation. Having recognized the power of visuals to communicate ideas and to persuade viewers, this industry remains at the forefront of computer graphics applications.

Paint and draw programs allow students not only artistic expression but also a powerful nonverbal way to communicate an idea as they prepare signs relating to a co-curricular activity, maps for a social studies project, posters promoting a candidate in a school election, and banners proclaiming significant events. They allow students to explore the spatial relationships of an idea. Graphing programs allow students to examine abstract numeric relationships in a concrete manner.

Figure 2–16 **Student centered learning**
The computer as a learning tool for the student

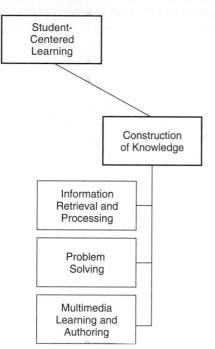

Information Retrieval and Processing. One of the most powerful uses of computer tech-nology is information retrieval. Keyword searching in a library database or on the Web using search engines such as Google® or Yahoo!® allows students to search through millions of pages of information from every corner of the world in just a few milliseconds. In many cases, the problem is not finding the information but finding too much information and, in some cases, finding incorrect information (See city-Mankato, US and Central Park-NY. US for examples.) Web searching will be discussed in greater depth in Chapter 11. Students can also request information from others directly using email. Telecomputing on the Internet, research on the Web, database searching, and spreadsheet forecasting allow a student to investigate information in depth. By developing powerful search strategies, a student can find answers to perplexing questions, connect related facts, and derive new information. By sorting information, a student can examine precedence and develop a better understanding of linear relationships or hierarchical order. By altering variables in a problem, a student can explore cause-and-effect relationships and forecast results of a decision. The computer is indeed a tool that amplifies a person's ability to build knowledge.

Knowledge Dissemination. Computers are the number one source of information dis-semination. One of the authors can remember as a child watching a person set up a page for a local newspaper using old-fashioned type: one letter at a time. Now all printed matter, from this textbook to the date book in our bookbag, are designed on a computer. Students can write essays and produce brochures and signs with the help of computers. This knowl-edge can be disseminated worldwide using the Internet. Information can be sent over email or posted in newsgroups or Blogs. Students as young as third grade can make web pages and post them on the Web. We shall discuss web page construction in Chapter 10.

Problem Solving. The use of the computer as a problem-solving tool is a major focus of this textbook. Problem-solving strategies revolve around having a certain background knowledge, understanding the material at hand, knowing what is expected, developing a solution strategy, and reflecting on its effectiveness. Both linear and nonlinear strategies are considered. The computer can provide background knowledge and act as a tool to explore solution strategies. It can organize and manipulate information, allowing the user to test tentative solutions before adopting the most appropriate one.

Multimedia Learning and Authoring. Multimedia learning gives the student control of powerful tools in the exploration and creation of information. Multimedia tools allow a student to compose a complex message that might include computer-generated sound, graphics, and animation, along with sound and visual forms stored in another medium, such as videotape, DVD, and CD-ROM, or downloaded from a source on the Internet. Multimedia allows the student to explore communication through multiple senses and become the creator, the artist, and the storyteller as vivid mental images are painted. Students learn to access and organize information; display text, graphics, audio, and video information; and present the products as evidence of knowledge they have constructed.

MANAGEMENT

The chart presented as Figure 2–17 suggests that there are several areas in the realm of school and classroom management that are well suited to computer applications. In each area, the computer can be used as a tool to save the user some time, improve the accuracy of information, and allow the user to efficiently handle large amounts of data. Keep in mind that since the focus of this textbook is on the computer as an educational tool, we give a somewhat cursory look at management issues. An entire book could be devoted to the computer as a management tool.

Figure 2–17 Management
The computer as a school and classroom management tool

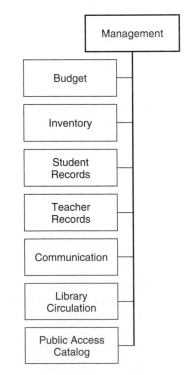

Budget

Budgets must often be built by teachers, department heads, and other administrators to deal with instructional materials, field trip costs, student club activities, personnel, and departmental needs. In preparing a budget, school administrators and teachers depend on records of historical information as a basis for the projection of future needs. It is necessary to understand past practices, allocations, and expenditures. It is equally important to be able to project ahead in areas of school and program enrollment, staffing needs, curriculum changes, and inflation. Computer-based **file managers** and **spreadsheets** are particularly useful tools to accomplish tasks relating to budget preparation and management. On the one hand, they provide the user with current, accurate records in a timely fashion; on the other hand, they provide the ability to reflect changes dynamically as the user manipulates variables to look at projections. Spreadsheets have earned their well-deserved reputation as being "what if" tools. They immediately reflect the results when the user asks, "What if this amount were changed? What impact would this have?"

Inventory

School personnel are accountable for a wide variety of items, ranging from food and janitorial supplies to textbooks, curriculum materials, and instructional equipment. A computer-based file manager can record use, track inventory levels, record the location of items and their condition easily and accurately, and make information available at a moment's notice.

Student Records

A school is required to keep records concerning students. Many of these are ideally suited for electronic storage. Health and immunization records begin in the primary grades. Information about home and parents or guardians is recorded. Attendance is closely followed. Grades are calculated and stored; then grade reports are generated from these electronic grade books. Individual education programs (IEPs) are tracked, and students' growth in ability and performance levels is monitored. Student portfolios may contain numerous artifacts or samples of student work that can be easily stored, organized, and retrieved electronically. Participation in athletics, music programs, programs for the talented and gifted, and co-curricular activities are noted. Well-designed, computer-based systems are efficient and yield more potentially useful information by creating more complete profiles of the students. Integrated student record packages are being used by more and more school districts in the United States and abroad. These packages allow all aspects of a child's education to be stored and accessed through a common interface. They can provide an instantaneous review of specific records regarding a student by teachers, administrators, and special service personnel. Teachers may input and review grades, attendance, and comments right from their desks. Nurses may input and review immunization and medical records from their offices. Guidance counselors may look up attendance and tardy records during a discussion with a parent or student. Administrators may review multiple grouped statistical data that describes student populations to quickly discern past and current trends and projections of future trends.

With the growing trend toward outcome-based education and authentic assessment, the need for software to keep track of, store, and display student achievement has increased. A number of student portfolio development packages have been created to meet this need. Some of these are stand-alone programs and others are add-on programs for *PowerPoint* and *HyperStudio*. Many of these packages link student work to school, district, and national goals as well as objectives and standards. Specific software examples are discussed in Chapter 4.

Teacher Records

Teachers manage information on students, but they also need to manage their own information: syllabi, lesson plans, test banks, evaluation notes, worksheet masters, handouts, and so forth. They can record their participation in professional growth activities that may generate district credit toward advancement. As teachers develop their continuing professional development plans, they may want to use a word processor to keep a reflective teaching journal or use database managers as electronic résumés to store audio or visual artifacts in their own electronic professional teaching portfolios. Many of these activities can now be managed electronically using software described in Chapter 4.

Communication

Parental involvement can increase student achievement and improve the parents' relationship with the school. Written and electronic communication is greatly facilitated by the computer and tends to increase the amount of correspondence between school and home. A **desktop presentation** program allows teachers and administrators to enhance their presentations to students, parents, the school board, and community groups by projecting text, graphics, sound, and video on a screen. Modems and district-wide networks allow schools throughout a district to communicate by exchanging memos, notices of important events, attendance, and other data. Teachers can access lesson plans stored on electronic bulletin boards, websites, or the school or district server. Most schools have home pages, where students and parents can check class assignments, view class and school information, and use email to ask classmates or school-provided tutors questions on homework assignments.

Library Circulation

Manual library circulation systems have existed for a long time in schools and public libraries. A manual system, though acceptable for recording the checkout and return of books and other materials, is time consuming and provides little additional information of benefit to the user. A computerized automated circulation system can record the

Andy Crawford © Dorling Kindersley

checkout and return of materials and can generate lists of the library's holdings. It can record borrowers' transactions quickly and efficiently, generate lists of overdue materials, provide inventory control to a level that was never before possible, and calculate use statistics.

Public Access Catalog

Just as an automated library circulation system can enhance the distribution of materials, an online **public access catalog (PAC)** of a library media center's materials collection can greatly improve access to information. Such a system should allow a user to browse the collection electronically and to perform author, title, subject, and keyword searches.

ACTION RESEARCH

The functional application of the computer to classroom action research, as addressed in Figure 2–18, includes data storage and statistical analysis. Once again the computer is seen as a tool. It is a tool that supports **action research,** placing the teacher in the role of the researcher, often examining some aspect of classroom practice. "Action Research is a fancy way of saying let's study what's happening at our school and decide how to make it a better place" (Calhoun, 1994).

Many researchers divide action research into three forms: the teacher researcher, collaborative research, and schoolwide action research. The first form, teacher researcher, has for its focus classroom teachers trying to solve a problem in their classrooms. The results of this investigation may or may not go beyond the teacher's individual classroom. Many teachers run small studies to make their classrooms run smoother or to discover ways to increase student learning. The second form, collaborative research, usually involves the teacher and other school personnel and is focused on changes in several classrooms, grade levels, or departments. The third form, schoolwide action research, focuses on improvement throughout the school. Many members of the school, from individual teachers through the school leadership and even external groups, may take part in this form of action research (Calhoun, 1993). We are sure that you will be doing action research once you get into the classroom and want to find out why something is happening or how you can improve something. Action research is a wonderful opportunity for you to make a difference. There are many Internet sites that will help get you started.

The state of Oregon has required for several years that student teachers demonstrate their ability to impact pupil learning as a requirement for initial teacher licensing. Faculty at Western Oregon University developed a work sample methodology to address that

Figure 2–18 Action research
The computer as an educator's action research tool

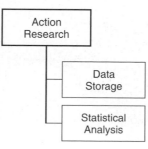

requirement. A number of teacher preparation programs including Western Kentucky University, California State University at Long Beach, Eastern Michigan University, University of Northern Iowa, and the University of Tennessee at Knoxville have adopted this methodology as part of their programs. Work samples are required by the teacher licensing agencies in Louisiana (beginning license) and Oregon (beginning and continuing licenses).

Simply described, the methodology requires student teachers to gather appropriate data to describe their learning environments as fully as possible and to prepare a sample of their work. Community, school setting, grade level, class size, gender ratio, number of exceptional students [talented and gifted youngsters, children with learning disabilities, those for whom IEPs have been written, those with limited English proficiency (LEP), at-risk youth, and so on], and available classroom resources all are described as the context in which instruction and learning take place. A two- to five-week unit of instruction is then designed. Unit goals and objectives are developed based on statewide curriculum goals and district-specific goals. A pretest based on the unit's objectives is developed and administered to the class. Appropriate scoring guides are written for the test items and a **quartile analysis** performed. Lesson plans are written. Following the two- to five-week period of instruction, a posttest is administered. The student teacher is required to compare the test results, analyze the level of learning outcomes, reflect on the instruction given within the described context, and draw conclusions. The personal computer behaves as a number cruncher, providing for the storage and analysis of relevant data in the work sample. Pupil names and pretest scores may be entered in a spreadsheet and sorted in descending order of scores. The teacher may separate the resulting list into four groups and have the spreadsheet calculate the average score for each quartile. Later, individual posttest scores are entered. Once again the spreadsheet can calculate the average score for the previously established quartiles and can calculate the change in quartile averages as well as in individual scores and present the information in graph form based on the data. Reflecting on the demands and support of the teaching context, the teacher can then rate the level of progress toward desired learning outcomes and the equity in the level of progress across the four quartiles.

Anthony Magnacca/Merrill

Data Storage

As in the example on work sample methodology, data storage integrates with other functions dealing with the management of information. Stored data accumulated from various sources can be accessed in the future to examine correlations on SAT scores, GPA, and individual student performance. With the help of a personal computer and appropriate software, teachers and researchers probing a specific topic can analyze data collected on their sample populations and gleaned from student records. Although this certainly could have been done before the advent of the personal computer, now it can be done more easily and cost effectively.

Statistical Analysis

The availability of statistics programs on personal computers allows teachers to analyze data and draw conclusions. This ready access especially encourages the growth of action research at the K–12 level. Numbers entered into spreadsheets can yield simple to complex analyses. Even a simple grade book designed on a spreadsheet can reveal mean, range, and standard deviation of scores. As teachers move toward new product-oriented, criterion-based methods of assessment, they are also attempting to understand and compare student performance through new and different means.

LET'S REVIEW

This chapter examined a framework for software in three major categories: school management, instruction and learning, and educational research.

Instruction and learning was further divided into two major areas, teacher-centered instruction and student-centered learning. Teacher-centered instruction examined the computer as the object of instruction, as well as a tool of instruction and the management of instruction. It was subdivided into the categories of computer literacy, computer-assisted instruction, computer-managed instruction, and design of teaching materials.

Computer literacy was recognized as addressing both issue awareness and functional use. Societal issues related to the computer such as access, copyright, rights of privacy, data security, and information ownership may well continue to command attention in the classroom.

Computer-assisted instruction was subdivided into categories that parallel learning theory. Computer software might take the form of tutorial, drill and practice, simulation, instructional games, problem solving, or interactive multimedia software that combines text, graphics, sound, and animation and that controls live-action video sequences. Drill and practice is a technique used to reinforce previous instruction and newly introduced concepts by providing the repetition necessary to move skills and concepts acquired into long-term memory. A tutorial software program is designed to introduce new information to the student and often includes a placement test to ensure student readiness. Simulation software supports the problem-solving learning that all students must experience to connect concepts into major clusters of knowledge. Instructional gaming software reinforces previous learning using graphics, sounds, and some type of competition format. Problem-solving software introduces students to situations in which they must use new or previously learned information and concepts to state hypotheses, plan strategies, and follow some set of procedures to achieve the final goal or outcome.

Multimedia instruction uses more than one way of conveying information in a multisensory manner.

The distinguishing characteristics that separate the different categories of computer-assisted instruction are beginning to blur, because strategies are being combined to achieve a wider range of objectives.

Computer-managed instruction was discussed as a category of software that helps the teacher track students' progress. If this time-consuming work can be done more efficiently with the aid of the computer, then the teacher will have more time to help students. This alone can make for a more effective learning environment.

The use of computer technology can aid teachers in the design, development, and creation of teaching materials. A vast array of tools are available to the creative teacher to design and produce materials that communicate effectively.

In student-centered learning the computer is a tool for the student to use to create, access, retrieve, manipulate, and transmit information to solve a problem. Understanding the concept of the computer as an information tool relies on accepting the fact that the computer is a productivity tool for the student and teacher alike.

School management was divided by data processing and information retrieval functions into seven functional categories: budget, inventory, student records, teacher records, communication, library circulation, and public access catalog.

Classroom action research includes functions relating to information gathering and processing. The teacher and researcher may examine student performance data in new and revealing ways.

As we consider computer applications, we should keep in mind the concept of curriculum integration.

LET'S PRACTICE

To complete the specified exercises online, go to the Chapter Exercises Module in Chapter 2 of the Companion Website.

1. Create a mock budget for a student activity club in an area of personal interest. List income and expenditures. How could a computer assist you in managing this budget?

2. Identify as many tasks as you can that are included in a school lunch program. Which of these tasks might be facilitated by a computer? Which would not?

3. Describe what we mean by each of these three categories of educational software: school management, instruction and learning, and educational research. Explain how each may be used in the school environment.

4. What is your definition of *computer literacy?* Does it differ from ours? If so, in what ways?

5. Using a subject and a grade level at which you may be teaching, think of a problem or subject that you could use webbing or concept mapping to explain. Diagram this on a sheet of paper. Now do the same using Inspiration or Kidspiration. If neither is available to you, download a trial copy from *inspiration.com* and use it to make the same web or map.

6. Find a school in your area that uses computers for management. Talk to teachers about what they and others in the school think of it. Report your findings to the class.

7. In the library or on the Web, find articles or information discussing and outlining a school's or district's technology plan. Does this school or district give a technology test to new teachers before they are hired? Report your findings to the class.

8. In a small group, discuss the role of computers in all aspects of education. List three reasons why computers can make a teacher's life easier and more interesting, three reasons why school computers can benefit the administration and parents, and three things that may slow the utilization of computers by teachers and administration. Discuss your answers with the class.

9. Think of a problem that you may encounter in your teaching for which you could apply action research to find a solution. Design a small action research study that will help you find the solution.

10. Is there a "best" format (drill and practice, tutorial, and so on) for educational software? Explain your answer.

PORTFOLIO DEVELOPMENT EXERCISES

To complete these exercises online, go to the Digital Portfolio *Module in Chapter 2 of the Companion Website.*

One of the NETS•S standards covered in this chapter was "Students evaluate and select new information resources and technological innovations based on the appropriateness for specific tasks" under Category 5: Technology research tools. Begin to develop your own portfolio of lesson plans that demonstrates your ability to have students reach the NETS•S standards.

1. Design a lesson plan activity for elementary, middle school, or high school students in which they study a career or occupation of an individual or group that you will be studying or someone who is appropriate for your subject area. Using this career or occupation, have students list particular tasks that are performed by members of this occupation and list technology that is available to make workers' tasks in this industry easier. These technologies need not currently be used in the occupation. This lesson should demonstrate that your students have achieved the standard. Be sure to include a system of evaluation for your students' understanding and competence to ensure that they have met this standard.
2. Adapt the lesson plan activity you developed in exercise 1 for students to evaluate each others' work.

GLOSSARY

action research	The teacher as researcher investigates a problem, usually arising from some classroom practice; results are applicable only to the setting in which the research was conducted
branching	A design of some programs that uses techniques to provide multiple alternative paths, or branches, for remediation or acceleration
computer-assisted instruction (CAI)	The direct instructional interaction between computer and student designed to produce the transmission of information
computer literacy	The study of the development and functional use of the computer, as well as related societal issues
computer-managed instruction (CMI)	Use of the computer as a diagnostic, prescriptive, and organizational tool to gather, store, manipulate, analyze, and report information relative to the student and the curriculum
desktop presentation	The display of screens of information stored in a computer often with the use of a video projector
drill and practice	A category of computer software that uses the teaching strategy to reinforce instruction by providing repetition necessary to move acquired skills and concepts into long-term memory
file manager	Software that is designed to create and to manage data files; also called a database manager
gaming	A strategy that includes the elements of a set of rules and competition against others or against a standard
information literacy	The study of how we find, analyze, understand, and use information
instructional games	A category of software that is highly competitive, is intriguing, may include elements of speed or time, and often involves some type of fantasy atmosphere
integrated learning system (ILS)	A hardware and software package designed to present and manage the scope and sequence of one or several content areas; these content areas may encompass several years of instruction
integration literacy	The study of how we use a variety of technologies and methods to enhance teaching and learning
media literacy	The study of how we find, analyze, understand, and use information and how we can communicate this information in a variety of forms
multimedia instruction	The technique of accessing, organizing, and displaying textual, graphic, audio, and video information under the control of a computer, allowing a teacher to convey information in a multisensory manner
multimedia learning	The technique of accessing, organizing, and displaying textual, graphic, audio, and video information under the control of a computer, to meet student needs in conveying information in a multisensory manner
problem-solving software	A category of software that presents students with a problem for which they must state the hypothesis, plan strategies, and follow some set of procedures to achieve a final goal or outcome

public access catalog (PAC)	A computer-based system that provides users access to a library's holdings
quartile analysis	The ranking of performance measures from high to low and the separation of the measures into four groups to study performance by high, medium, and low achievers
simulation	A category of computer software that uses a teaching strategy based on role-playing within structured environments, providing an environment for discovery learning
spreadsheet	Software that accepts data in a matrix of columns and rows, with their intersections called cells; often used with numeric data to forecast results of decisions
tutorial	A category of computer software that uses the teaching strategy in which the student's level of knowledge is first determined before new information is introduced along with learning guidance
virtual reality (VR)	A computer-generated simulated environment with which a user can interact
visual literacy	The study of how we interpret, understand, and create visual messages and information

REFERENCES AND SUGGESTED READINGS

Calhoun, E. (1993). Action research: Three approaches. *Educational Leadership, 51*(2), 62–65.

Calhoun, E. F. (1994). *How to use action research in the self-renewing school.* Alexandria, VA: Association for Supervision and Curriculum Development.

Ertmer, P. A., Addison, P., Lane, M., Ross, E., & Woods, D. (1999, Fall). Examining teachers' beliefs about the role of technology in the elementary classroom. *Journal of Research on Computing in Education, 32*(1), 54–97.

Hill, W. F. (1977). *Learning: A survey of psychological interpretations.* New York: Harper & Row, pp. 214–216.

International Society for Technology in Education. (2000). *National educational standards for teachers.* Eugene, OR: International Society for Technology in Education.

Leu, D. J., (2002). The New Literacies: Research on Reading Instruction with the internet, in Farstrup, A. E., Samuels, S. J. (Eds.) *What Research Says About Reading Instruction*, (3rd ed.) Newark, NJ: International Reading Association, 310–336.

Miller, C. (1992, November). Online Interviews; Dr. Thomas A Furness, III, Virtual Reality Pioneer. *Online, 16*(6) 14–27.

Mizell, A. (1997, July). Unpublished review, Nova Southeastern University, Miami, FL.

Shaffer, W. D., Squire, K. R., Halveason, R., & Gee, J. P. (2005, October). Video Games and the future of learning. PHI Delta Kappen, *87*(2), 104–111 Sosenke, F. (2000, May). World tour. *Learning & Leading with Technology, 27*(5), 32–35.

Swan, K., & Mitrani, M. (1993, Fall). The changing nature of teaching and learning in computer-based classrooms. *Journal of Research on Computing in Education, 26*(1), 40–54.

Thornburg, D. (1991). *Education, technology, and paradigms of change for the twenty-first century.* San Carlos, CA: Starsong Publications.

U.S. Department of Commerce, (2000). *Falling through the not; Defining the Digital Divide.* Retrieved on line April 3, 2006 from *http://www.NTIA.Doc.Gov/NTIA Home/FTTH99/Contents.html*

CHAPTER 3

Impact of the Computer on Education

1. What are computer and technology standards and why are they needed for preservice teachers in today's society?

2. How are shifting paradigms of computer use affecting the classroom?

3. What are the primary processes involved in a computer system (input of data, operations performed on the data, and output of information)?

4. How has computer technology evolved and what is its potential impact on us?

5. What are current and future trends in information technology?

NETS•T Foundation Standards and Performance Indicators Addressed in This Chapter

I. Technology operations and concepts
  A. demonstrate introductory knowledge, skills, and understanding of concepts related to technology (as described in the ISTE National Education Technology Standards for Students)
  B. demonstrate continual growth in technology knowledge and skills to stay abreast of current and emerging technologies
II. Planning and designing learning environments and experiences
  B. apply current research on teaching and learning with technology when planning learning environments and experiences
  D. plan for the management of technology resources within the context of learning activities
  E. plan strategies to manage student learning in a technology-enhanced environment
III. Teaching, learning, and the curriculum
  A. facilitate technology-enhanced experiences that address content standards and student technology standards
  B. use technology to support learner-centered strategies that address the diverse needs of students
IV. Social, ethical, legal, and human issues
  A. apply technology resources to enable and empower learners with diverse backgrounds, characteristics, and abilities
  B. promote safe and healthy use of technology resources
V. Productivity and professional practice
  A. use technology resources to engage in ongoing professional development and lifelong learning
  B. continually evaluate and reflect on professional practice to make informed decisions regarding the use of technology in support of student learning

LET'S LOOK AT THIS CHAPTER

Changes brought about by the computer are occurring in society in general and in education as well. This chapter discusses competencies and performance standards expected of the classroom teacher and explains how they were derived. It then takes a look at national efforts to promote the effective use of technology in schools.

The authors then briefly review significant technology events of the past and present, and predict events in the near future. David Warlick, a noted futurist, and Doug Johnson, an internationally known technologist, join us in examining literacy in a time of rapid change and easing into the integration of technology in the classroom.

COMPUTER COMPETENCIES FOR EDUCATORS

Computers and computer technologies have dramatically changed the face of society as we progress along the twenty-first century. It would be hard to find one corner of our world that has not been changed substantially by them. When used properly, computers and computer technologies allow us to do things that we never could have imagined. We can design and test cars on computers before we even start to build them. We can crash planes on computers to evaluate their design and redesign them when potential problems emerge.

Computers can do more mathematical calculations in a fraction of a second than a person can do in several hundred lifetimes. Most of us use "smart" microwave ovens where you simply put in the food, enter the food type, turn on the microwave, and take out the food perfectly cooked. Sensors read temperature and humidity in the air inside the microwave and feed data into the microwave's computer, and the computer does all the rest. The first astronauts had less computer power in their space capsules than we have in the car parked in our driveway. One of the author's cars is constantly being monitored from space through an OnStar® connection. Computers send email notification to the author if his car has potential problems or needs routine maintenance. It is next to impossible to buy a major appliance whose operation is not governed by an onboard computer. Our cell phone is a miniature handheld computer taking and sending pictures, wirelessly accessing the Internet to surf the Web and send and receive email. It also contains an address book, date book, and all the functions of a Palm® handheld computer.

Just as computers are integrated throughout society, computers should also be integrated throughout the curriculum. This places a special burden on the educator. Fortunately, the burden of integrating computers across the curriculum is far outweighed by the rewards to students and teachers.

Since the first computers arrived in schools in the 1950s and 1960s, much has changed. From the very beginning, computers were tools. They are tools to help students and teachers perform tasks faster and more efficiently. The first computers were big, offsite, and operated by specially trained individuals. Now, computers are small desktop, laptop, or handheld models that can be used with little training.

In the 1960s, educational computing was given a boost because proponents believed that computers could revolutionize education the same way that computers revolutionized business. As the 1970s came to a close, though, it became apparent that this would not be the case. The introduction of microcomputers in schools in 1977 initiated a change in attitude. They brought computer power directly into the classroom. Way back in 1983, the National Commission on Excellence in Education report, *A Nation at Risk*, even recommended that high school students be required to take a computer course.

Over the years, teachers, administrators, school boards, and parents have grappled with the place of computers in the classroom and the curriculum. What computer skills are really necessary for students? What skill level should teachers have? These questions and others have been discussed and addressed by many professional organizations that have published computer competencies for students and teachers. The organization that preservice teachers in any curriculum area or at any level may be most affected by is the National Council for Accreditation of Teacher Education (NCATE). NCATE delineates standards used to measure and accredit teacher education programs throughout the United States. In its "Vision of the Professional Teacher for the 21st Century," NCATE states, "Accredited schools, colleges, and departments of education should . . . prepare candidates who can integrate technology into instruction to enhance student learning. . . . Likewise, the new professional teacher who graduates from a professionally accredited school, college, or department of education should be able to . . . integrate technology into instruction effectively" (NCATE, 2002, p. 4). The International Society for Technology in Education (ISTE) developed computing and technology competencies that have been adopted by NCATE for integration throughout teacher preparation programs (ISTE, 1998).

In the early 1990s, ISTE called together a group of distinguished educators to develop technology standards for teachers. This group, the ISTE Accreditation and Professional Standards Committee, released the very first edition of these standards in 1993, *ISTE Technology Standards for All Teachers*. This first edition contained 13 indicators designed to measure technology competencies of teachers. Because of the fast growth of technology and its spread throughout society, a second edition was published in 1997. This edition contained 18 indicators organized into three broad categories: (1) basic computer/technology operations and concepts, (2) personal and professional use of technology, and (3) application of technology in instruction. Many schools, districts, universities, and states base their current technology standards on this revision. NCATE adopted these standards to measure the effectiveness of technology instruction in teacher education programs it evaluates for accreditation.

The ISTE Accreditation and Professional Standards Committee continued its work and published the National Educational Technology Standards (NETS) for students (NETS•S) in 1998, for teachers (NETS•T) in 2000, and finally for school administrators (TSSA: Technology Standards for School Administrators) in 2001. These standards reflected the results of the NETS project initiated by the ISTE committee and co-sponsored by Apple™ Computer, the Milken Exchange on Education Technology, the National Aeronautics and Space Administration (NASA), and the U.S. Department of Education. "The primary goal of the ISTE/NETS Project is to enable stakeholders in PreK–12 education to develop national standards for educational uses of technology that facilitate school improvement in the United States" (ISTE, 2000A).

As stated, the NETS project features a three-pronged approach: NETS•S, NETS•T, and TSSA. It is important to know and understand these standards. As of this writing, at least 49 of the 51 states have adapted, adopted, and/or referenced at least one of the above sets of standards for certification, licensure, and/or in assessment, curriculum, and/or state technology plans. This includes 37 states for both NETS•S and NETS•T and 36 for TSSA. NETS•S contains 14 performance indicators consolidated into the following categories (ISTE, 2000B).

NETS•S: Technology Foundation Standards for All Students

I. Basic operations and concepts

II. Social, ethical, and human issues

III. Technology productivity tools

IV. Technology communications tools

V. Technology research tools

VI. Technology problem-solving and decision-making tools

NETS•S

Since students are expected to develop and reinforce each of the 14 standards throughout their education, "Profiles for Technology Literate Students" are included in the standards document for grades PreK–2, 3–5, 6–8, and 9–12. These profiles contain performance indicators, curriculum examples, and teaching/learning scenarios to help teachers and students track student learning. It is important that you, as a future teacher, are familiar with these standards and with the "Profiles for Technology Literate Students." As stated, 37 states have either adopted, adapted, aligned, or references the NETS•S standards for students in state technology, curriculum, and/or assessment plans or other state or local documents. To aid in this understanding, the authors have placed a chart in the inside back cover that lists the categories and standards and shows how they align with the information in the individual chapters of this text.

NETS•T

NETS•T contains 23 performance indicators grouped into six categories (ISTE, 2000B).

NETS•T may be particularly important to you since they contain "Technology Performance Profiles for Teacher Preparation" for general, professional, student teaching, and first-year teaching.

TSSA

The Technology Standards for School Administrators contains 31 standards grouped into the following six categories (ISTE, 2002).

Unless you decide to continue your studies in the field of educational administration, you will have little contact with these standards, but knowing that they exist may be important to you.

The use of technology standards allows teachers to strive for a common goal agreed on by a wide variety of fellow educators. Standards allow us to define a product, in this case the competent use of technology and the underlying knowledge that supports that use, and to recognize the evidence of that knowledge and use when we see it. We as teachers use a number of standards of performance and behavior in our classrooms.

The technology standards identify a computer-competent person. We have chosen to focus on the NETS•T standards in this text so that as preservice teachers you will recognize what knowledge, skills, and attitudes will be expected of you as a teacher. You will be preparing citizens of the twenty-first century—citizens who will need to understand and be prepared to deal with serious cultural and ethical issues and who will be expected to extend their capabilities as they create, evaluate, store, and communicate information. The NETS•T standards provide a blueprint to develop the knowledge you will need to help your students and build necessary technology skills. The relevant NETS•T standards are listed at the beginning of each chapter.

> **NETS•T: Educational Technology Standards and Performance Indicators for All Teachers**
>
> I. Technology operations and concepts
>
> II. Planning and designing learning environments and experiences
>
> III. Teaching, learning, and the curriculum
>
> IV. Assessment and evaluation
>
> V. Productivity and professional practice
>
> VI. Social, ethical, legal, and human issues

> **TSSA: Technology Standards for School Administrators**
>
> I. Leadership and vision
>
> II. Learning and teaching
>
> III. Productivity and professional practice
>
> IV. Support, management, and operations
>
> V. Assessment and evaluation
>
> VI. Social, legal, and ethical issues

No Child Left Behind Act

Proper infusion of technology is also a national priority. On January 8, 2002, President Bush signed the No Child Left Behind (NCLB) Act into law. This act affects almost every facet of education as we know it. To improve student achievement through the use of technology, U.S. Secretary of Education Rod Paige announced the new "Enhancing Education

LET'S GO INTO THE CLASSROOM
Technology-Enhanced Lessons Make Learning Fun

"This is a unit where I have my students learn about the states east of the Mississippi River; however, it can easily be adapted to all 50 states or to the region your students are studying. It would be easy to send my students to the library to look this information up in encyclopedias and atlases, but using technology, in this case word processing and the Internet, introduces and reinforces skills that will help them throughout their educational experiences and their life. Technology, when properly used, also seems to make learning more interesting and current and hold the interest of many students who would have been lost or bored just using printed materials.

Students will be involved in an imaginary journey that will take them through the 28 states. They may start in the state of their choice; however, they may not visit any state more than once. The object is to travel to all 28 states in the least number of miles possible. Careful planning is very important. Students will set up a table in Word to help them keep track of their information. Students will also find an interesting "factoids" (small facts) about each state using an Internet site with state information. Once a student has completed his/her trip they will also:

1. Determine how much money would be needed in order to buy gas for the trip (using an average of 23 miles per gallon at $2.89 per gallon. Of course, gas prices may change.).
2. Using 60 miles per hour as an average and driving seven hours per day, they will determine how many days it would take to make the trip.
3. Using the answer to 2, students will determine how much money will be needed for food if breakfast cost $4.50, lunch cost $5.25, and supper cost $7.35 (per person).

The students might present their findings using PowerPoint or HyperStudio, write it up using a word processing application, make a spreadsheet, produce a travel or state brochure or even map out their trip on a bulletin board map with yarn. This is also a great group learning lesson."

Internet Sites

MapQuest: Find the distance from one city to another *http://www.mapquest.com*
Factoids about the states: *http://www.homeschooling.about.com/library/blstateunit.htm*

What Might a Finished Product Look Like?

1. Your **table** will have the following information: (20 points)
   - City to city route with full state name (no abbreviations)
   - Factoid for each state—the factoids will be for the state listed in the "from" column
   - Miles for each city to city entry
2. A **map** of the United States with the following: (10 points)
   - Put a #1 in the "starting" state, #2, #3, etc. until you arrive at your final state (#28)
   - States labeled with their zip code abbreviations
   - Map colored following cartographer's rules
   - Mississippi River marked from its headwaters in Lake Itasca, Minnesota, to the mouth at New Orleans, Louisiana
   - Mississippi River labeled
   - Title

3. A **chart** with your total miles traveled with the following computations completed: (15 points)
   - How much money would be needed in order to buy gas for the trip (using an average of 23 miles per gallon at $2.89 per gallon).
   - Using 60 miles per hour as an average and driving eight hours per day, compute how many days it would take to make the trip.
   - Using the answer to the bullet above, determine how much money was spent on food if breakfast cost $4.50, lunch cost $5.25, and supper was $7.35 (per person).
4. A **cover sheet** with the following information: (95 points)
   - Your name, #, and date
   - Title of project "Trip Through the 28 States East of the Mississippi River" (or other appropriate name)
   - Border

Evaluation

Your finished product will be evaluated on the following (see grading rubric for details):

1. Did you travel to all 28 states without visiting any state more than once?
2. Did you travel to contiguous states?
3. Are computations correct?
4. Did you use correct grammar and punctuation?
5. Are your words spelled correctly?
6. Did you follow the directions for this project?
7. Are all parts of the project included?
8. What is the overall quality and appearance of your final project?

Paula Conley
Skyway Elementary School
Coeur d'Alene, Idaho
A rubric used to grade students for this exercise may be found in Chapter 1.

Through Technology" (ED Tech) initiative shortly after the signing. The goals of ED Tech are to:

- Improve student academic achievement through the use of technology in elementary schools and secondary schools
- Assist students to become technologically literate by the time they finish the eighth grade
- Ensure that teachers are able to integrate technology into the curriculum to improve student achievement (NCLB, 2002)

Title II, Part B, *Enhancing Education Through Technology (E2T2),* of NCLB further consolidates the former Technology Literacy Challenge Fund and local Technology Innovation Challenge Grants into a single state-run ed tech grant program entitled, *Enhancing Education Through Technology.* The primary objectives include:

- Encouraging innovative uses of technology in education
- Full integration of technology into the curriculum
- Broadening access to technology across the community and within the school
- Reaching underserved students and areas
- Establishing a stronger home–school connection
- Increasing staff development including training of administrators

Corbis RF

- Providing ongoing funding and maintenance of technology
- Evidence-based evaluation of the use of technology (T&L Editors, 2002)

The National Education Technology Plan

In the introduction to the report, *Visions 2020 Transforming Education and Training Through Advanced Technologies,* U.S. Secretary of Education Paige wrote, "Indeed. education is the only business still debating the usefulness of technology. Schools remain unchanged for the most part despite numerous reforms and increased investments in computers and networks. The way we organize schools and provide instruction is essentially the same as it was when our Founding Fathers went to school. Put another way, we still educate our students based on an agricultural timetable, in an industrial setting, but tell students they live in a digital age" (U.S. Department of Commerce, 2002).

On January 7, 2005, the National Education Technology Plan titled, *Towards A New Golden Age in American Education,* was officially released. This report was spurred on by the above statement and the No Child Left Behind Act. As we read above, much of NCLB relies upon technology. This plan is meant to aid in motivating and sparking the technology-driven transformation of education. To help school districts and states in this transformation, a set of seven action steps and accompanying recommendations are included in the report. The action steps include:

1. Strengthen Leadership
2. Consider Innovative Budgeting
3. Improve Teacher Training
4. Support E-learning and Virtual Schools
5. Encourage Broadband Access
6. Move Toward Digital Content
7. Integrate Data Systems (U.S. Department of Education, 2006)

The National Education Technology Plan lays the groundwork for states and districts to increase technology utilization in the educational process.

▮▮▮▮ EVOLUTION OF COMPUTER TECHNOLOGY

Rapid changes in computer technology have resulted in greatly improved and expanded applications. As we briefly review significant technology events of the twentieth century, we become aware of a tremendous simplification in computer operation, a vast improvement of the machine and human interface, and a dramatic reduction in equipment size that has taken place. These elements contribute significantly to the expanding computer utilization in society in general and in education in particular. A few milestone historical events are worth noting.

Yesterday

The 1880 census took seven years to process manually and, with a growing population, the 1890 census posed a serious problem. It appeared that it would take more than 10 years to process the census data unless some new method was used. A mammoth computer was invented to process the census data by reading holes punched on cards. The machine also sorted and counted the cards. Because of this new invention, the 1890 census was processed in only three years. The inventor manufactured this device and then merged with another company. The new firm was named International Business Machines (IBM).

Sixty-five years later, the first general-purpose electronic digital computer was introduced in 1945. The ENIAC (Electronic Numerical Integrator and Calculator) occupied 3,000 cubic feet of space, weighed 30 tons, contained more than 18,000 vacuum tubes, and drew 140,000 watts of power when it was running. The light bulb–size **vacuum tube** acted like an electronic switch or gate, passing or blocking an electrical current in a digital circuit. As current was passed or blocked, it was translated into a binary code of 1s (on) and 0s (off). The ENIAC could do only simple addition, subtraction, multiplication, and division operations in a programmed sequence. To change the sequence to address a new problem, the ENIAC had to be rewired by hand. Six years later, in 1951, the first electronic computer to use **transistors** and a stored program entered the market. The half-inch square transistor replaced the vacuum tube, allowing the computer itself to be reduced from building size to room size and then to the size of several large file cabinets.

Programs stored in computers were written in machine language as **binary** code. Think of the vacuum tube for a moment. It can be "on," passing current, or it can be "off," blocking current. This on or off state could be represented by a 1 or by a 0. Zeroes and ones, called **bits,** are often gathered in groups of 8, 16, 32, or more and are referred to as **bytes,** representing an alpha (letter) or a numeric (number) character. Although today's computers still understand only binary code, we fortunately do not have to use this code to communicate with them. Computer languages have been developed that allow us to use English-like words, which are then translated into a binary form. As a side note, around this time in 1969, the U.S. Department of Defense created a network of military computers called ARPAnet (Advanced Research Projects Agency network), which evolved into the present-day **Internet.** It was a Cold War attempt to develop a nonlinear method of linking governmental installations throughout the United States in the hope that such a diffuse network would survive a nuclear attack on the United States. More about the Internet discussed later.

Microcomputers marketed in kit form for hobbyists were introduced in 1975. By 1977, Apple, Commodore™, and RadioShack™ microcomputers were on the market and the microcomputer explosion was under way. The **integrated circuit,** or **chip,** found in those microcomputers was approximately one-quarter-inch square and contained millions of transistors.

Time magazine proclaimed 1982 "The Year of the Computer," because of the significant contributions that personal computers made in complementing human abilities. This is

105

also the year that Microsoft released the MS-DOS operating system for IBM and compatible computers. The term *microcomputer* faded in favor of the term *personal computer.*

Apple Computer introduced the Macintosh computer in 1984. The Mac, as it became known, featured a **graphic user interface (GUI)** that was first developed by Xerox® complete with a mouse, icons, screen windows, and pulldown menus. Until this time, computers had used a text-based interface.

The **World Wide Web (WWW),** an Internet navigation system, was developed at CERN, the European Particle Physics Laboratory in Geneva, Switzerland, in the mid-1980s.

HyperCard®, a program created in 1987 at Apple Computer, is said to have opened the door to multimedia as we know it today. The program has now been supplemented by a number of others, most prominent among them is HyperStudio, a program that works on both the Macintosh and Windows platforms.

After a few setbacks (Windows® 1.0 and 2.0), Microsoft released Windows 3.0, a successful GUI competitor to the Macintosh operating system, in 1990. Windows, in its recent versions, has become the best-selling computer program, or software, of all time and the dominant operating system in almost all market segments.

Unlike the 30-ton ENIAC that occupied 3,000 cubic feet of space, laptops, such as the PowerBook® introduced in 1993, weighed about seven pounds and occupied less than one-seventh of a cubic foot of space. The ENIAC had an internal memory capacity of 12 K, storing about 12,000 characters in its memory. In comparison, laptops introduced in 1993 had a memory expandable to 36 MB (about 36 million bytes), about 3,000 times greater than the ENIAC and 100,000 times more reliable. Today's laptops are smaller, lighter, and significantly more powerful yet.

In 1993, another graphical interface called Mosaic™ was developed. It allowed World Wide Web users almost instantaneous transfer of information in the form of text, graphics, sound, and video through the simple click of the mouse. Applications such as Mosaic used to access the Web are called **browsers.** Mosaic later evolved into the Netscape® Web browser. Internet Explorer™, Safari™, and Firefox™ are now popular Web browsers.

In 1997, Intel Corporation began marketing a supercomputer capable, for the first time, of breaking the trillion-/calculations-a-second barrier. The computer can perform 667 million calculations in the time it takes a bullet to fly one foot.

An accelerating trend since 2000 is the integration of the computer, video, and communications technologies.

Those astonishing developments have taken place in a little more than 50 years. At present, computing power doubles every 18 months! What astounding advances in technology will the next 50 years (or even the next 5 years) bring?

Today

How do learners of today differ from learners of yesterday? It could be argued that the most dramatic changes are the amount of information available and the greatly enhanced access to it. Much of this information is packaged in a visual form and presented in an interactive manner at a rapid rate. Consider how television, magazine, billboard, and radio ads bombard our senses as consumers. As viewers, readers, and listeners, we have adapted to "consume" information differently. We no longer have to communicate in the old ways. We don't have to go to knowledge; it comes to us through electronic fingertip access to databases, libraries, people, and places. We don't have to go to people; they come to us over satellite **web-enhanced cell phones** that allow us to talk with anyone, anywhere; via meeting software that connects several people at different physical locations in a meeting on our computers, be it on a desktop or in a cave in a mountain 5,000 miles from nowhere; and by video over IP, an Internet protocol that moves instructional television and distance learning classes from one point to another through the Internet. Similarly, as the amount of

THE UPGRADE: EASING INTO TECHNOLOGY INTEGRATION
By Doug Johnson

The administrative suggestion that a teacher "integrates technology" into his or her classroom is often met with resistance—resistance caused by the confusion and fear that comes with doing something completely new. If school leaders look only at technology as a tool for "transforming" pedagogy—moving from those practices and activities with which teachers are practiced and comfortable to those which are radically different—it's little wonder they resist.

One study shows that while 70% of teachers are using technology for administrative tasks, only 54% "integrate computers into their daily curriculum." This is not surprising given that most administrative tasks are ones with which teachers are familiar—communicating with parents, keeping grades, and doing attendance. I would argue that "familiarity" is an overlooked variable in the instructional use of technology.

Constructivists say that you can't learn something for which you have no frame of reference. One way to help teachers ease their way into integrating technology into their curricula is to help them take something they already do, and add a technology "upgrade." Find below twelve common activities that classroom teachers may be already doing and some ways technology can be used to "upgrade" the learning process.

Current Activity	Technology Upgrade	Benefits
1. *Teacher lecture*	Computer presentation program (PowerPoint, HyperStudio, Keynote)	Graphics, sounds, movies, and photographs clearly illustrate concepts and heighten student interest. Easier for students to take notes.
2. *Student writing*	Word-processed, desktop published.	Easily edited, spell-checked, handwriting-proof. Added illustrations or graphics. Online peer review and commentary.
3. *Student research*	Use electronic or online resources such an electronic encyclopedia, magazine index, Internet resources.	Quickly accessed. Notes can be copied and pasted into rough draft. Sounds and pictures can be used in multimedia reports. Large number of resources means narrower focus on topic, adding interest.
4. *Book reports*	Use database with fields for title, author, publisher, date, genre, summary and recommendation.	All students contribute to database.
5. *Math problems*	Use a spreadsheet to set up some basic math story problems.	Formulas and operations clearly visible. Charting and graphing capabilities. Data from original surveys converted into understandable information.
6. *Plays, skits, or debates*	Videotape the presentations.	Record for later analysis, sharing with parents. Editing possible. Save as exemplar for future classes.

(Continued)

7. *Create a timeline*	Use Timeliner, Inspiration, or drawing program.	Fast, simple and easy to read. Possible to add graphics and modify time segments.
8. *Student speeches, demonstrations, or lessons*	Videotape. Students use of multimedia to accompany presentations.	Record for later analysis, sharing with parents. Editing possible. Save as exemplar for future classes. Graphics, sounds, movies, and photographs can be used to more clearly illustrate concepts, increase audience attention. Use slides in place of notes.
9. *Drawings to illustrate concepts or accompany writing*	Use drawing or paint program.	Use features of drawing program to create meaningful original illustrations or modify clipart. Edit and use digital camera images or scanned images with writing for improved meaning.
10. *Class syllabus and recommended readings*	Use a web page creator and upload to school web server.	Easily and quickly modified. Direct links to Internet readings. Can be accessed from home by parents.
11. *Class discussion*	Create a class blog with discussion questions.	Students can contribute outside of class time. Shy students might be more likely to contribute. Longer, more thoughtful responses may be given.
12. *Games or simulations*	Use computerized simulations such as SimCity or a title from the Choices, Choices series.	Computer provides more realistic scenarios and visuals in simulations.

The key to a successful upgrade, of course, it that there is *genuine* benefit to using the technology—not just adding for its own sake. From the examples above, some of the key "technology upgrade" benefits include:

1. Helping the teacher address multiple learning styles by allowing extensive use of multimedia in lessons.
2. Motivating reluctant students.
3. Allowing students to add elements of creativity, especially visually to their work.
4. Allowing anytime/anyplace learning and access to information.
5. Allowing student performance to be reviewed and critiqued more easily and by the students themselves.
6. Increasing the audience for student work.
7. Increasing participation by reluctant students.

A final piece of practical advice for "easing into technology integration" is to make sure that technology integration is first implemented in units that are currently less than successful, rather than effective units that students and teachers already enjoy.

An old adage says that the way to eat an elephant is one bite at a time. The technology upgrade can be that first nibble teachers take to successfully and completely integrate technology into their classrooms in positive ways.

Sharma, Dinesh C. (2005, August 29). *Study: Teachers coming to terms with computers.* CNET News: <http://news.com.com/2100-1032_3-5844057.html>.

Doug Johnson
Director of Media and Technology
Mankato Area Public Schools
Mankato, MN
http://www.doug-johnson.com

information available to learners multiplies, the process of learning must evolve. Consequently, schooling is changing dramatically and, with it, the role of the teacher.

Yesterday, learners were generally seen as containers, or vessels, needing to be filled with factual information. Teachers were dispensers of information, and memorization was equated with learning. An "educated person" was well read and knew facts in a variety of fields. With the explosion of information and widespread, immediate access to it, today's learners are faced, like never before, with the need to develop problem-solving skills. Today's educated person knows how to access information efficiently, evaluate it, and apply it effectively as that individual constructs appropriate knowledge.

Centralized information dispensed by the teacher has shifted to individualized information retrieval by the student. The evolution of computer technology has enabled those paradigm shifts as equipment has become smaller, more portable, more affordable, more powerful, and easier to use. As new technology is making vast amounts of information available to teachers and students, a need for highly developed information literacy skills has been recognized. Teachers and students must learn how to conduct effective searches, how to critically evaluate the results of the search, and how to create new knowledge from the information distilled. The American Association of School Librarians (AASL) and the Association for Educational Communications and Technology (AECT) have jointly developed national guidelines for information literacy. Several states have adopted their own in conjunction with the national guidelines.

Change seems to be the hallmark in the twenty-first century. Social and economic struggles of the present have thrust educational and school reform from the theoretical realm of educators into the public arena. Legislators, businesspeople, parents, and other taxpayers are demanding fundamental changes from schools, teachers, and administrators. Each has a unique interpretation of what these changes should be and how they will best occur. Businesses have created, have funded, and are managing for-profit schools, some within the public school system. School choice is an issue that has been the subject of both political rhetoric and informed debate. Some parents advocate more government support of home schooling, whereas others expect help from the school system with childcare, parenting advice, and social services. Taxpayers are dissatisfied with the

Valerie Schultz/Merrill

performance of public schools in relation to the amount of tax money spent. Significant changes in the whole structure of the educational system and our philosophies of education and learning are occurring, a paradigm shift that is discussed in greater detail in the next chapter.

As schools have gradually adopted the use of computers and related technology, they have undergone some degree of instructional change. According to Allan Collins (1991), these trends, identified more than 10 years ago and continuing today, include the following:

1. A change from whole-class to small-group instruction
2. A move from lecture to coaching
3. A move from working with better students to spending more time working with weaker students
4. A shift toward students becoming more engaged in their learning
5. A change to assessment based on products and outcomes
6. A shift from a competitive to a cooperative atmosphere in the classroom
7. A shift from all students attempting to learn the same thing at the same time to different students learning different things at their own rate
8. A move from an emphasis on verbal thinking to the integration of visual and verbal thinking

The computer is an ideal tool shaping and molding these trends. It is convenient, powerful, and small in size. Students and teachers alike are now able to carry with them powerful assistants allowing them to access information from around the world, categorize and assess this information at their own rate and in their own learning style, summarize and encode this information, and deliver it in a variety of ways in audio, video, multimedia, and printed formats through themselves or electronically to any place around the world.

Tomorrow

What the authors talked about as the future as they prepared for the last edition of this text two short years ago is now the present or even the past as we prepare this edition! A computer is no longer just a tool to be used in an educational setting, in a library, or at home, but is turning into an appliance that students carry around in their backpacks like a day planner, a book, or a pen. There are even schools around the country that have opted to replace textbooks with computers, the Internet, "e-books," and CD-ROMS (Associated Press, 2002). We find ourselves in the midst of a powerful information revolution. With the significant restructuring in education occurring in the United States, the way we use computers in the classroom is changing. What role might the computer play in school restructuring? Much will depend on you and teachers like you who recognize the potential of the computer as an intellectual tool. You are in a crucial role. Myron Pincomb, a technology consultant and trainer from Jacksonville, Florida, says that ". . . 95% of educators under-utilize technology. In a lot of schools, the computer is used as a game or a reward—but it has so many other educational uses" (in Hill, 2002, p. 29).

For schools to keep up with the demands of the students, the community, and the government, there will have to be a philosophical shift in the public's perception of education. Often the public's perception is based on the past, on what education was like for them or even how it was like for one of their older children, rather than the reality of what it is like today or its present and future potential. Technology, with its frequent innovations and pervasive influence, provides an impetus for that shift. It also provides the tools educators need to implement change now.

LITERACY: IN A TIME OF RAPID CHANGE
By David Warlick

Most of the readers of this textbook have witnessed two to six decades of the most transformational time in human history. My grandfather, for instance, rode a horse-drawn buggy to his college classes. My daughter takes many of her courses from the convenience of her bedroom, carrying on dynamic discussions with students from around the globe. The technologies that we have invented and integrated into our social, economic, political, and physical endeavors would have shocked any other generation, but for most of us, and certainly our children, rapid change has become a normal part of our experience.

Yet, what remains core in what and how we teach and learn is information, not technology. We learn the skills for accessing, using, and communicating information, so that we can learn from our information and knowledge environment and interact within it, in order to answer our questions, solve our problems, and accomplish our goals. Technology has certainly changed. But perhaps our focus, as educators and learners, should be not so much on how our tools have changed, but how the information environment itself has changed.

Our Changing Information Environment

When I was in school, during the 1950s and 1960s, information was central to my learning. However, when I compare my use of information today, to what and how I learned five decades ago, I see that it has dramatically changed in the following ways.

- What it looks like
- What we look at to view it
- How and where we find it
- What we can do with it
- And how we communicate it

I recently delivered a keynote address at a staff development symposium in New York. During the address, the name of a fairly well-known education researcher slipped my mind. I apologized, and carried on with the presentation. A moment later, a young teacher raised his hand, and, as I acknowledged him, he shared the name of the researcher. He held in his lap, a tablet PC computer, through which he was viewing my web-based online handouts for the presentation. Displayed in another browser tab were the results of a Google search where he had found the name, biography, and a large number of web pages that mentioned the person of note, whose name I had not been able to remember. Several other members of the audience had tablet and laptop computers and were each recording their notes from the presentation in wiki pages that were part of the online handouts. They were, in affect, collaboratively writing a group textbook for the address.

Most of the audio/visual material for the presentation was edited and produced using the same kind of computer that many in the audience were using, and less than $500 worth of cameras (video & still), and audio recording equipment. With one exception, the software used to edit the audio/visuals was free for download from the Internet, or came preinstalled on the computer.

Certainly, technology has changed. But it is the information that we touch with our awareness. As our children spend hours playing video games, is it the machine, the buttons, or the LCD display that they are thinking about? . . . or is it the information that they see on the screen, hear in their headphones, and transmit using their game controllers. It is the information that gives meaning to their experience, and they understand this. It is we, those from my generation, who focus on the machines.

(Continued)

So how, exactly, has the information changed? When we factor all that can be said about today's information environment down to the fundamental characteristics, they are that information is increasingly:

1. Networked
2. Digital
3. Overwhelming
4. It doesn't require a container

If the information you are using did not come to you directly through some sort of network, traveling many feet, or many thousands of miles to reach you, then it has, at some point, existed as electrons. It is increasingly likely that the information you are looking at came to you as ones and zeros—as binary code. It is digital. Again, if it is not appearing to you as expressed by a computing device, rendering the digital code into the information you are reading, viewing, or listening to, then at some point of its existence, it has been digital.

There is no question that we are all inundated by information. We are overwhelmed, and constantly seeking new ways to cope with this avalanche. It is also increasingly likely that some of the information that flows in the information environment was produced by you. You have almost certainly sent email to other people, and perhaps lots of other people, using a mailing list. You may have published a web page, or may be publishing to a weblog. You may be producing and distributing multimedia information, such as a podcast or video blog. In fact, because of various aspects of this new information environment, the chances that you are a published author are astronomically greater than 10 years ago.

If you have produced content that is used by others, then it is likely that that information is digital, and therefore, exists without a container. In the published-print information environment, information was held inside of books, magazines, book shelves, libraries, file cabinets, film, microfiche, photo paper . . . . While information was contained, it could be controlled. Today, information is *out there*. It flows, reshapes itself, is redirected, relinked, associated and reassociated, and copied wildly, and it often happens at the hands of the consumers, not the producers of the information.

Two issues confront us, as educators, as we continue to effectively prepare our students for their future.

1. The first issue addresses directly the changing nature of information, and it manifests itself as a single core question that is central to education. What are the basic skills of a contemporary knowledge environment? What is the emerging definition of literacy?
2. The second issue springs from the first. As we endeavor to understand the new knowledge environment and to redefine the basic skills for interacting productively with that knowledge environment, we must answer the question, "How do these changes affect the methods that we employ in helping students to learn, and to become lifelong learners?"

So the issues break down into **what** (literacy skills) and **how** (lifelong learning skills) students learn.

Inventing and testing new teaching and learning techniques could not happen without a grounding in the new literacies. Making our task much easier is the fact that those four fundamental characteristics of the new knowledge environment align very well with our traditional model of literacy—reading, writing, and numeracy.

What Does it Mean to be a Reader in the New Knowledge Environment?

A majority of the teachers in our classrooms went to school in a time when the information we used was within walking distance. It was a magazine or newspaper on your coffee table, encyclopedia in your bookcase, or a reference book in a library in your town. Today, it's available to us through your personal computer, which more than likely could house more information than most public libraries. Yet, much of the information that we access comes from beyond our computer, through the Internet, a global electronic library of content that is organized in a revolutionary new way—by us.

By most informed speculations, Google currently processes more than a billion searches a day (Battelle). This represents a startling shift in how we use information, especially when we note that Google has only been in existence for less than 10 years. We are increasingly using information to accomplish our goals, large and small, and we are bypassing the traditional gatekeepers of knowledge that my generation took for granted. Very little of the information that we access through our Googlings comes through librarians, teachers, editors, established publishers, peer review, or other filters upon which much of traditional education rests. This suggests two new skills that are necessary for anyone who can effectively use information to accomplish goals.

Finding the Information

Reading is a more essential skill today than at any time in our past. However, the skills involved in finding the information have become much richer and dynamic. A decade ago, being able to use a table of content and index, having a working knowledge of the alphabet, and being able to fake the Dewey Decimal system was all you needed to find the answers to most questions. Today, however, tracking down answers within logical webs of information, constructing an effective and evolving search query, and tapping into the emerging global conversation, called the *blogosphere,* are becoming basic to being a productive information worker.

Not too long ago, I had not even heard of RSS. It is a testament to the rapidly evolving knowledge environment that my RSS aggregator has become central to my personal learning network, which is made up of professional educators, media specialists, philosophers, personal news searches, and access to their digital libraries. Maintaining my personal learning network is a basic skill for me, as I continue to attempt to make a living within the contemporary knowledge environment.

Decoding the Information

As stated above, reading text continues to be a core skill for contemporary literacy. However, today, the amount of multimedia content that we have access to in any moment far outweighs text-based information. The average home with cable or satellite TV has access to 7,000 hours of video and audio programming in a 24-hour period (Gentile). Our news services rely increasingly on real-time news footage, maps, graphs, and animations. Being able to read these alternative and frequently more effective modes of communication is as important today as being able to read text on the page of a book.

Evaluating the Information

When we are so easily able to bypass the traditional knowledge gatekeepers of the Guttenberg era, it becomes essential, a basic skill, for each of us to be our own gatekeeper. Many educators resist, sometimes vehemently, their students use of the Wikipedia as a source of educational information. Yet, this global 700,000+ article encyclopedia that gets its content, editorialship, and management to volunteers from countries around the world, serves as an effective metaphor for the new knowledge environment, where networking has enabled almost anyone to publish almost anything, for almost any reason. When asked to consider content from the Wikipedia for their classrooms, most teachers reject the idea. They ask, "Who wrote this?" or "What is the basis for their expertise?" or "What are their sources?" or other questions. These are the questions that gatekeepers ask. We must now teach our students to ask these questions, because it is a basic skill to be your own effective gatekeeper.

Organizing Information into Personal Digital Libraries

In a published-print knowledge environment, libraries are shared collections of information, compiled and organized by professional librarians, into a collective source of information. Libraries are necessary because information is expensive, or at least the containers that they come in are expensive. Books must be laid out, type set, manufactured, and distributed. Book shelves must be erected and organized, and everything must be labeled, in categories ranging from 0 to 999—as defined by Melvil Dewey in 1876.

(Continued)

However, as information is increasingly networked (ubiquitously accessible), digital (expressible in many mediums), and overwhelming (providing topics from the common to the esoterically obscure), the need arises for more personal digital libraries that follow us around.

We are beginning to accomplish this with our bookmarks. However, any library, community or personal, owes a large degree of its value to its organization. The information is valuable only if we can reliably find the information that helps us solve our problems. We need the technical skills to employ the bookmark features of our browsers, and especially the emerging social bookmark tools and RSS aggregators. But perhaps the more important and lasting skill is the ability to organize information, a skill that librarians are uniquely qualified to teach us.

What Does it Mean to be a Processor of Information in the New Knowledge Environment?

Students in the 1950s and 1960s received, toward the end of each grading period, the class averages up to that point. It was a demanding task for teachers to average, on paper, each student's grades for the period, but not impractical. It became easier for me to average grades with a $19 calculator when I taught. But today, teachers are being asked to use thousands of numbers from ongoing standardized assessments that finely focus us on specific skills that students have mastered or not. Commonly called *Date-Driven Decision Making*, this advance is emblematic of one of two shifts in the world of numeracy.

First is the fact that the problems we attempt to solve with numbers will rarely involve a dozen numbers on a piece of paper, but thousands of numbers, and they will be digital. This does not mean that students need not learn to add, subtract, count, and measure on paper. Understanding the language of numbers is an imperative to contemporary literacy. However, it means that students must gain skills and use appropriate technical tools to answer questions, solve problems, and accomplish goals using thousands of numbers accessed from a variety of sources.

A large portion of the information that confronts us comes as numbers, columns, and rows of data that describe climate, chemicals in the environment, sports, social behaviors and opinions, business practices and results, and almost every other aspect of our society. Being able to select and implement the appropriate tool (spreadsheet program, statistical package, graphing tool, GIS, etc.) to make those numbers tell their story is necessary as we increasingly make our decisions based on large amounts of information. It is equally important to examine the stories produced by the digital work of other people, and then determine the questions that the story answers as well as the questions that it does not answer.

The second shift is more subtle to educators, though many of our children have developed the appropriate literacy skills on their own and for their own reasons. For example, as a family tradition, I have recorded, with a digital video camera, many of the events of our holiday observations. At the end of the season, I would store the video on a VHS tape and label it.

This December, my son attached his recently purchased digital video camera to a tripod and recorded our family decorating the Christmas tree. He then spent an hour cutting the video into individual clips, altering the speed of their play, laying some holiday music under it, and then rearranging and reattaching the clips so that they fit the music. The result was uniquely entertaining.

If we agree that the purpose of arithmetic is to use numbers to solve problems, answer questions, and accomplish goals, then what my son did for us was math. When I was in school, I learned to process numbers. Although I learned some writing, text was for reading, images were for looking at, audio was for listening to, and video was for watching. The second shift that applies to our notions of contemporary literacy is that all information is now made of numbers. Text, images, audio, animation, and video are all made of numbers. As a result, we can use contemporary tools to process text (using a word processor), process images (using graphics software), sound (using audio editors), and animation and video (using animation and video production software).

It is important to note that, in many instances, text, images, sound, and video can be processed for free, depending on the type of computer you are using. Here are some commonly used media editing tools that are conveniently available to information users.

Process	Tool	Available	Computer Type
Word Processing	OpenOffice	Open Source & Free *http://openoffice.org/*	Windows, Linux, & Mac (w/Xwindows)
Image Processing	Gimp	Open Source & Free *http://gimp.org/*	Linux
Audio Processing	Audacity	Open Source & Free *http://audacity.sourceforge.net/*	Windows, Linux, & Mac
Video Editing	iMovie	Preinstalled *http://apple.com/imovie*	Mac OSX
	Movie Maker	Preinstalled *http://microsoft.com/moviemaker/*	Windows XP

This list includes only a few of the easily accessible tools for processing information.

The fact that each of these tools are, in many instances, available for free download from the Internet further illustrates the need for all students to develop skills in processing all forms of information.

What Does it Mean to be a Communicator in the New Knowledge Environment

The third characteristic of contemporary information, mentioned earlier, was the fact that information is overwhelming. We all lament, even if privately, a time when we could keep information at bay behind the covers of books, the pages of our newspapers and magazines, and the walls of our libraries. But we live in a fast-paced and rapidly changing society, and dynamic information is necessary to navigate our world. We should consider, however, that managing all of that information may not be our greatest difficulty, as we seek to work the knowledge environment. More challenging and perhaps more important is learning to get our messages through that storm of information.

We accomplish our goals in collaboration. It may be the collaboration of team members. It may also be the looser collaborations between seller and buyers, political activist and citizens, or teacher and students. Regardless, the success of our endeavors depends on the actions of others, and we influence their actions by communicating. When we feel inundated with information, preparing and delivering a message increases both in importance and difficulty.

Students must learn to write, and to write well. But too often, learning to write becomes a technical endeavor of learning rules, procedures, and structure, independent of becoming an effective communicator. If we can expand our notions of writing instruction toward making our students better communicators, then we must also consider that effective communications will be those that successfully compete for the audience's attention. This will require students to be compelling writers. But it is equally important that they learn to communicate effectively with images, sound, animation, and video.

What are the Emerging Ethical Considerations of the New Knowledge Environment?

In the published-print knowledge environment, information could be contained. It could only exist within containers, on printed paper, within the covers of a book, on the shelves of a book case, within the walls of a library. The information was fenced in, and there was a gate. Gatekeepers controlled the flow of the information, and, in most instances, added value to the information by organizing it in useful ways.

Today, however, the information is digital. The same information can be printed, displayed with light, transmitted, converted to audio, edited, reshaped, and manipulated in any number of ways, by any number of people, simultaneously. The container is gone. The gatekeeper stands watch over their portal, but the information flows freely around them. It takes time for controllers to realize that they have lost control. Yet their power continues, because the questions that the gatekeepers ask, to make decisions on the information they hold, are questions that we must all be taught to ask.

In the published-print knowledge environment, where information was guarded, we were taught to assume the authority of the information that we encounter. We trusted its sources, and assumed that it was reliable. It is what we

(Continued)

were taught and it was the way that we were taught. In a networked digital information environment, we must instead learn to prove the authority. Any consideration or consumption of information must be accompanied by a consideration of its reliability in terms of the goals we are trying to accomplish. The supporting information is as important as the information itself. When information flows free of containers, then it must be tagged with the evidence of its value.

Information Reliability

As a consequence, there is another side to the ethical responsibility to ask gatekeeper questions—the ethical imperative to teach students to ask those questions. It is also our responsibility, as producers of information, to willingly and effectively provide those answers, even before they are asked. It is our responsibility to tag our information products (print, digital, and performed) with the evidence that the information is valuable.

Teachers who do not know the name of the author of their textbook are still teaching their students to assume the authority of the information. If a teacher says to his class, "The world is like this. . .", then they are teaching students to assume authority. If they say, "According to this validated source. . ." or "According to this logic, the world is like this," then they are teaching students to prove the authority.

Information Property

In addition to the ethics of assuring the accuracy, reliability, and validity of information, it is important for each of us to learn and teach that information is property. The lesson plan submitted to an education website is valuable. It is the result of hard work, experience, and knowledge. It also has value to the teachers who use the lesson plan, because it helps them do their job. As we spend time producing information, and as the information we use saves us time, we must understand that the information is property, to no less degree than my car, one of my city's buses, my children's video games, and the school network through which they receive many of their assignments. It is all property to be respected.

To help ourselves learn to appreciate information as property, we must become intellectual property owners. It is incredibly easy to publish today, if only a weblog, for daily or weekly professional reflections. There are many education websites that are accepting lesson plans that are tried and true. Then, teachers' websites should list their publications: the lesson plans they have submitted, where they are available, online and print magazine articles (again, not hard to accomplish), weblogs, and other publications.

Students should also become information owners. First of all, each major student production should be copyrighted, with the ubiquitous

Copyright © 2006 by Johnny Anderson

Then their finished work should be published through the classroom website, a classroom weblog, a school literary magazine, etc. As people become owners of property, they learn to respect the property of others.

Information Infrastructure

There is a third aspect of the new ethical imperatives that desperately needs to be addressed, the information infrastructure. Our information-rich, technology-driven world depends enormously on the wires, routers, web servers, wireless zones, and all the rest of the infrastructure that carries the information. We depend on these digital roadways to no less degree than we do our roads, railroads, bridges, airport, and seaports. We must find a way to integrate the same appreciation and respect for the information infrastructure that we do for our traditional facilities. When kindergarten teachers invite a firefighter into the classroom to talk about community helpers, they should ask, "How do you use the Internet to help you protect property?" "How do you use email to save lives?"

We must understand and deliver the message that planting a virus on a network is no different from planting a bomb under a bridge.

Review

We have sought to expand our notions of what it means to be literate in this information-driven, technology-rich world. The three Rs continue to be at the core of today's basic skills. However, there are larger perspectives that suggest skills that are no less important than being able to read the text in front of you.

Reading Expands into Exposing the Truth

It is essential that all students know how to read. However, in a knowledge environment without gatekeepers, the goal expands from merely being able to read and understand the text, to being able to expose the truth behind the information that you encounter. This includes being able to:

- Find the information that is appropriate to your goal.
- Decode the information, in what ever medium or format.
- Evaluate the information in order to determine its value.
- Organize valuable information into personal digital libraries.

Arithmetic Expands into Employing Information

Our traditional ideas about arithmetic (adding, subtracting, counting, measuring, and calculating) continue to be prerequisites of contemporary literacy. However, as we continue to be confronted by enormous sums of information, new skills with new technologies become essential for people to be able to employ information to accomplish their goals, and these skills are rooted in a working understanding of the language of numbers.

It is equally important to understand that the reason for teaching arithmetic is so that educated people can process and add value to information. As all information is now made of numbers, we must help students learn the math of processing text, images, sound, animation, and video. It's all about processing information. It's all about math.

Writing Expands into Expressing Ideas Compellingly

The only messages that will be successful will be those that successfully compete for their audience's attention. Information must compete for attention in exactly the same way and for the same reasons that products competed for attention on the store shelves. This means that students, in order to be called literate, must not only be able to write well, but they must also be able to communicate effectively with images, sound, animation, and video. This means not only the technical skills, but also the ability to decide which format or medium will best accomplish the goal at hand.

The New Ethics of Information

Edward Bulwer-Lytton, in the nineteenth century, wrote, "The pen is mightier than the sword." In the twenty-first century, the word processor may be mightier than nations. Information is powerful, in ways that we might not have imagined one decade ago. The 2002 economic disaster is one dramatic example, where a handful of corporate executives abused information, and brought the American economy to its knees.

If, while we are teaching our students these prevailing information skills, we are not also teaching them to love and protect the truth, then we will have trouble.

Conclusion

Vinod Khosla, a founding CEO of Sun Microsystems and venture capitalists recently told a story in an interview with John Battelle at the 2005 Web 2.0 Conference in San Francisco. He had been meeting with the principal of his children's school, when their conversation turned to a recent unit on the Hopi Indians that was taught in one of his children's classes.

During their discussion, Vinod took out his Treo mobile phone and conducted a Google search for Hopi Indians. He received links to 460,000 web-based information sources that mentioned *Hopi Indians*. Mr. Khosla said, "There is no longer a need to teach kids the facts. . ." (Khosla)

As teachers read or hear this statement, our natural tendency is to disagree with Vinod, because he does not understand that education is about learning skills and content. But the fact is that Mr. Khosla does get it, because the operant word in his statement is not **facts,** but **teach.**

In this time of rapid change, it is counterproductive to train our children to be teachable. Instead, making our students lifelong learners should become an explicit part of our expressed goals and mission statements and a factor in

(Continued)

every decision that we make as educators. Being a lifelong learner means being literate within one's information environment.

Battelle, John. (2005, December 5, 27). "Didja Know. . . . Updated." John Battelle's Searchblog. <http://battellemedia.com/archives/002093.php>.

Gentile, D. A., & Walsh, D. A. (2002, January 28). A normative study of family media habits. *Applied Developmental Psychology, 23,* 157–178.

Khosla, Vinod. (2005, November 25). "IT Conversations." Vinod Khosla: In Conversations with John Battelle. Web 2.0 Conference, San Francisco, October 5, 2005. Audio Archive. <http://www.itconversations.com/shows/detail796.html>.

David Warlick
Technology Consultant & Author
Raleigh, North Carolina
davidwarlick.com

Technology coordinators help teachers meet their needs

Kathy Schrock, Technology Administrator for Nauset Schools, on Cape Cod, prepares a podcast for her district.

(Photo by Emily Sussman)

The U.S. Department of Education has adopted four national technology goals, and funding is being provided from a variety of sources to help schools install the necessary infrastructure and to train teachers in the use of technology to meet those goals. The goals are as follows:

- All teachers and students will have modern computers in their classrooms.
- Every classroom will be connected to the information superhighway.
- Effective and engaging software and online resources will be an integral part of every school curriculum.
- All teachers will have the training and support they need to help all students learn through computers and through the information superhighway.

Any lasting changes and reforms will need to be preceded by a vision of what future learning environments will be like. What expectations will be placed on the learner? What will be the role of the teacher? What will be the physical structure of the learning environment? How will library media centers fit into this new environment? How will technology affect learning?

The basic curriculum will change as schools focus on information and thinking skills, and as the use of tools such as computers, sophisticated information storage and retrieval systems, holograms, and virtual reality simulations becomes the norm rather than the exception. Teaching methods will change as these tools are incorporated. Instructional materials will reflect the tools being used in learning. Expectations and outcomes will be different for children, teachers, parents, and administrators. The physical structure and internal organization of the school will certainly differ as these changes are assimilated.

In the future, the amount of time children spend in school may well become more flexible as technology provides new tools and inspires new teaching and learning methods. Networking will allow students to work at multiple sites while interacting with the class or the teacher. As students begin taking more responsibility for their own learning, the pace of that learning will have a more natural rhythm dictated by the individual student's needs instead of an imposed district-wide schedule. Some students may choose to work in the early morning, at night, or on weekends. Even young children may choose to work on absorbing projects for extended periods rather than having the day divided into predetermined segments of learning.

Technology will provide students with access to information and the tools to produce substantial work. Each student will have a computer available at school. This may be a personal computer workstation, a shared terminal for database and networking access, a portable, or a handheld computer. The computers will all have wireless networking capabilities and be linked by a network to teachers, parents, homes, databases, electronic bulletin boards, library and information centers, and other people all over the world.

The most exciting use of technology by the students of the future will be an enhancement of their production of authentic, meaningful work. Students will write, illustrate, publish, program, and create models, movies, music, stories, poetry, art, and other products of research and learning. They will use integrated technologies involving CDs and DVDs, computers, multimedia, virtual reality, and holographic imaging. Given access to information and technology, the skills to use them, and the freedom to learn and explore, children will be able to produce work that is barely imaginable to adults today. One of the authors of this text was taught claymation animation by two first graders who later burned their demonstration onto a DVD for him to have with no teachers present as the author looked on in amazement. Reread this last section titled, "Tomorrow." It really is "Today."

Schools are under pressure to provide more than simply a limited-use building with a single mission. Taxpayers complain about expensive buildings and equipment that are virtually deserted for up to a fourth of the year and are available only during school hours during the rest of the year. Teachers find themselves unable to teach academics when children are more in need of a nurse, counselor, social worker, or parent. The school of the future will have to address those needs. A multiple-use neighborhood facility combining education with the traditionally separate fields of childcare, health care, social services, and fitness will more successfully meet the needs of the children and the community. Professionals in each of those fields would staff the facility, working as a team to provide the best possible environment for children and their parents.

In closing this chapter, we want to reemphasize that a computer is a tool. It is a medium between the person and the task to be performed just as a hammer is the medium between the carpenter and the nail to be driven. As the need to fasten something with a nail determines the choice of the hammer as the appropriate tool, the task at hand defines the proper use of the computer, or other medium. Ultimately, the task, the curriculum goal, the objectives, the instructional strategy, and the learning drive the choice of media.

119

LET'S GO INTO THE CLASSROOM
The Networked School

Teachers and students arriving at Lakeville High School walk through the halls casually observing the day's schedule of activities displayed by a presentation program running on video monitors throughout the building. In their classrooms, the teachers sit at their desktop computers that are programmed to automatically boot-up each morning at 7:00 A.M. They are prompted to log in to the server. They retrieve the morning's mail and notices from the email system. Messages may be from the office, colleagues in the building, other employees in the district, and from parents and community members sent via the district-wide area network or the Internet. Next, they check their voice mail and prerecord the day's assignments for absent students on specially programmed phone lines. The teachers are alerted of any important meetings during the day through the use of a scheduling program.

Activity sheets also may need copying before the day begins. Teachers open their files stored on the server and select the pertinent activity sheets. After completing the details of a cover sheet, they send it via the network to the central, networked copier for processing. Before leaving to pick up their copies from the copy center, they may schedule part of the day in one of the school's 12 computer labs. These Macintosh or Windows labs are also networked to the school's server, which enables students to access online materials and retrieve or save their work in their own network files. All of the labs have word processing, spreadsheet, and database programs; Internet access; library access; and specialized programs (e.g., high-end graphics, CAD, world language, music, career resources, writing, business) depending on the function of the particular lab. After working in the labs, some students may move to the video production studio or industrial technology areas and work with computer imaging, three-dimensional modeling, animation, and digital editing to create digital videos or websites for class.

Before classes begin, a teacher may turn to the control panel next to the computer to select a CD-ROM or video for the day's lesson from the centralized video retrieval system. In addition, teachers may bookmark websites to display using the local input connection between the computer and video monitor. Teachers easily switch among commercial/satellite television inputs, presentation programs, videotapes, CD-ROMs, and websites using the system's remote control, while moving around the classroom. When classes begin, teachers take attendance for each student using the online student information system.

Teachers are able to check pertinent student records for various health concerns, test scores, and directory data in the student information system. Teachers use the system to keep track of student attendance, record grades, and track portfolio progress of curriculum standards. At the central office, school district officials are able to check all student and resident data across grade levels. With the help of a geographic information system, district officials quickly assimilate data and display that data on maps. Maps of interest to staff, parents, and community members are then posted on the school and district websites.

Parents are able to access information about their children, school notices, and events via the Internet. Building and district websites provide information on school and district events, courses, schedules, lunch menus, and staff. Individual teachers have course outlines and assessments posted online. When the teachers leave for the day, paperwork doesn't always have to follow them home. Students are able to hand in their work on the network in special folders. Teachers access these folders online in school or at home when needed.

Laurie Quinlan
Communications Instructor
Lakeville High School
Lakeville, Minnesota

Teachers, administrators, school boards, and parents have grappled with the integration of computers into the classroom and the curriculum. The National Council for Accreditation of Teacher Education (NCATE) has adopted technology competencies developed by the International Society for Technology in Education (ISTE) to integrate throughout teacher preparation programs in the United States. These are the technology standards for students (NETS•S), for teachers (NETS•T), and for administrators (TSSA). These were the results of the National Educational Technology Standards (NETS) project.

In the twenty-first century, educational and school reform has been thrust into the public arena. Businesses have created, have funded, and are managing for-profit schools, some within the public school system. For schools to change, there will have to be a philosophical shift in the public's perception of education. Technology provides a turning point for that shift, because its influence pervades so much of our daily lives. Any lasting changes need to be preceded by a vision of what future learning environments will be like. The basic curriculum will change as schools focus on information and thinking skills and as the use of tools such as computers, information storage and retrieval systems, holograms, and virtual reality simulations becomes the norm rather than the exception. Teaching methods will change as these tools are incorporated. Instructional materials will reflect the tools being used in learning.

Rapid changes in computer technology have resulted in greatly improved and expanded applications, as well as a tremendous simplification in operation, a vastly improved user interface, and a dramatic reduction in equipment size. Technology will provide students with access to information and the tools to produce substantial work. Computers will be linked by local and worldwide networks to teachers, parents, homes, schools, databases, electronic bulletin boards, library and information centers, and other people all over the world. The most exciting use of technology by students of the future will be the production of meaningful work. Students will write, illustrate, publish, program, and create models, movies, music, stories, poetry, art, and other products of research and learning. They will use integrated technologies involving optical disks, computers, multimedia, virtual reality, and holographic imaging. This future is now!

LET'S PRACTICE

To complete the specified exercises online, go to the Chapter Exercises Module in Chapter 3 of the Companion Website.

1. Describe your personal use of any tool outside of the educational setting. Now describe how you might use the computer as a tool. Compare your two examples and demonstrate how a tool extends your human capability.

2. Why do you, as a future educator, bear a special responsibility to understand and be able to comfortably use the latest computer technology?

3. It seems that everywhere we look in education we are bombarded by a new set of standards. Why do you think that this is? Do you feel that standards are important? How do they fit into local and national priorities?

4. Review the NETS•S standards (these are for your students) in the appendix of this text. How comfortable are you knowing these and teaching them to your students? In which areas are you weak? Make a list. Review that list again at the end of the semester to see how you have progressed.

5. Review the NETS•T standards (these are for teachers) in the appendix of this text. How comfortable are you with these standards? In which areas are you weak? Make a list. Review that list again at the end of the semester to see how you have progressed.

6. Review the No Child Left Behind (NCLB) Act. How is it impacting the schools in your district? Your state's education system?

7. In the section of the chapter that discusses the *National Education Technology Plan,* U.S. Secretary of Education Paige discusses his view on the present role of technology in education. Do you agree or disagree with his comments? Discuss your reasons for your answer.

8. Did you notice that Secretary Paige called education a "business" in the above noted quote? Do you think that it is? How do you feel about his use of this word? Write a paragraph describing your reaction.

9. Log on to the National Education Technology Plan Website (*http://nationaltedtechplan.org*). Click on The Plan tab at the top of the page. Read over the page that appears (The Plan) and click on the Conclusions link and read that page also. What obstacles do you see in bringing this plan to reality?

10. We have had a short discussion of technology in the past, present, and future. Daydream about your future classroom. How do you think that it will look? What technology would you like in it? Can you think of any technology that is not available today that you would like to have? Discuss your ideal future classroom with the class. Are there differences and similarities between your ideas and the ideas of others?

CW PORTFOLIO DEVELOPMENT EXERCISES

To complete this exercise online, go to the Portfolio Module *in Chapter 3 of the Companion Website.*

One of the NETS•S standards covered in this chapter was "Students use a variety of media and formats to communicate information and ideas effectively to multiple audiences" in Category 4: Technology communications tools. Begin to develop your own portfolio of lesson plans to help your students reach the NETS•S standards.

1. Design a lesson plan activity for elementary, middle school, or high school students encouraging them to work in teams to research one of the issues presented in this chapter (use a variety of media and formats to communicate information and ideas effectively to multiple audiences, and so on) and prepare a word-processed report. This lesson should demonstrate that your students have achieved the standard. Be sure to include a system of evaluation for your students' understanding and competence to ensure that they have met this standard.

2. Adapt the lesson plan activity you developed in exercise 1 for students to evaluate each other's work.

GLOSSARY

binary	Consisting of two parts; limited to two conditions or states of being
bit	The single digit of a binary number, either 0 or 1; derived from the words *b*inary dig*it*
browser	A software program used to access and view sites on the World Wide Web
byte	A grouping of bits (in groups of 8, 16, 32, or more); the code represents one alpha or a numeric character of data
chip	A small piece of silicon housing an integrated circuit that may contain tens of thousands of miniaturized transistors and other electronic components
graphic user interface (GUI)	The on-screen use of pictorial representations (icons) of objects
integrated circuit	An electronic component made up of circuit elements constructed on a single piece of silicon
Internet	A worldwide network of interconnected networks all based on the TCP/IP protocol
transistor	A small electronic device that controls current flow and does not require a vacuum to operate
vacuum tube	A sealed electronic device designed to regulate current flow
web-enhanced cell phones	A cellular telephone able to send and receive data to and from the World Wide Web
World Wide Web (WWW)	An Internet navigation system that allows users, through a graphic browser interface, to access information organized on hypertext-linked screens called pages

REFERENCES AND SUGGESTED READINGS

Associated Press. (2002, October 12). School eliminates textbooks. *The (Mankato Minnesota) Free Press, 119*(162), 7F.

Collins, A. (1991, September). The role of computer technology. *Phi Delta Kappan,* 28–36.

Hill, J. (2002, October). Teaching with technology. *Presentations, 16*(10).

International Society for Technology in Education. (2000A). *National educational technology standards for students: Connecting curriculum and technology.* Eugene, OR: International Society for Technology in Education.

International Society for Technology in Education. (2000B). National educational technology standards for teachers. Retrieved online March 23, 2006, from *http://cnets.iste.org/teachers/t_stands.html.*

International Society for Technology in Education. (2002). Technology standards for school administrators. Retrieved online January 12, 2003, from *http://cnets.iste.org/tssa/.*

International Society for Technology in Education Accreditation Committee. (1998). *Curriculum guidelines for accreditation of educational computing and technology programs.* Eugene, OR: International Society for Technology in Education.

Milken Exchange on Educational Technology. (1999). *Will new teachers be prepared to teach in a digital age? A national survey on information technology in teacher education.* Santa Monica, CA: Milken Exchange on Education Technology.

National Commission on Excellence in Education. (1983). *A nation at risk: The imperative for educational reform.* Washington, DC: U.S. Department of Education.

National Council for the Accreditation of Teacher Education. (2002). *Professional standards for the accreditation of schools, colleges, and departments of education—2002 edition.* Washington, DC: National Council for the Accreditation of Teacher Education.

No Child Left Behind (NCLB). (2002). The facts about . . . 21st-century technology. Retrieved online January 11, 2003, from *http://www.nclb.gov/start/facts/21centtech.html.*

T&L Editors. (2002, September). Trend watch. *Technology and Learning, 23*(2), 8.

Tanner, R. (2000, January). Piloting portfolios: Using portfolios in pre-service teacher education. *ELT Journal, 54*(1), 20–30.

U.S. Department of Commerce. (2002). Visions 2020: Transforming Education and Training through Advanced Technologies. Retrieved online January 14, 2006, from *http://www.technology.gov/reports/TechPolicy/2020Visions.pdf.*

U.S. Department of Education. (2006). National Education Technology Plan. Retrieved online March 23, 2006, from *http://www.nationaltechplan.org.*

Wiebe, J. H., Taylor, H. G., & Thomas, L. G. (2000, Spring). The National Educational Technology Standards for PK–12 Students. Implications for teacher education. *Journal of Computing in Teaching Education, 16*(3), 12–17.

4 CHAPTER

Legal and Ethical Issues

1. How can the computer be modified to accommodate students with special needs?

2. What are some of the laws we must understand in order to help diverse learners in a fair and equitable manner?

3. Do those who have home access to a computer have an unfair advantage over those who do not?

4. Do students who attend schools in affluent neighborhoods have an unfair advantage over those who do not?

5. How should we as teachers strive to promote gender equity in our classrooms? What actions must we take to affirm this goal?

6. How do the copyright laws positively affect both the copyright holder and the user of the copyrighted material?

7. How can teachers and schools limit student exposure to inappropriate sites found on the Internet?

NETS•T Foundation Standards and Performance Indicators Addressed in This Chapter

I. Technology operations and concepts
   A. demonstrate introductory knowledge, skills, and understanding of concepts related to technology (as described in the ISTE National Education Technology Standards for Students)
   B. demonstrate continual growth in technology knowledge and skills to stay abreast of current and emerging technologies
II. Planning and designing learning environments and experiences
   A. design developmentally appropriate learning opportunities that apply technology-enhanced instructional strategies to support the diverse needs of learners
   B. apply current research on teaching and learning with technology when planning learning environments and experiences
   C. identify and locate technology resources and evaluate them for accuracy and suitability
   D. plan for the management of technology resources within the context of learning activities
   E. plan strategies to manage student learning in a technology-enhanced environment
III. Teaching, learning, and the curriculum
   B. use technology to support learner-centered strategies that address the diverse needs of students
   D. manage stduent learning activities in a technology-enhanced environment
IV. Productivity and professional practice
   B. continually evaluate and reflect on professional practice to make informed decisions regarding the use of technology in support of student learning
V. Social, ethical, legal, and human issues
   A. model and teach legal and ethical practice related to technology use
   B. apply technology resources to enable and empower learners with diverse backgrounds, characteristics, and abilities
   C. identify and use technology resources that affirm diversity
   D. promote safe and healthy use of technology resources
   E. facilitate equitable access to technology resources for all students

LET'S LOOK AT THIS CHAPTER

This chapter lays the groundwork for an understanding of the role of computer technology in a diverse society and sets the stage for our further discussions of the computer as an educational tool and a teacher's responsibility concerning ethical technology use. It also raises human issues related to the fair and equitable use of this technology.

Topics covered include computers as helpers for students with special needs (including disabilities, limited English proficiencies, and the talented and gifted), computer access and equity, and a discussion on gender equity. The discussion of students with special needs will also help understand the role that technology tools play to enhance learning and increase productivity.

Copyright and intellectual property along with the safe use and controlling access to the partnering for schools are discussed. This chapter lays the groundwork for ethical technology use and raises human issues related to the fair and equitable use of technology.

SOCIAL CONTEXTS FOR COMPUTERS IN THE CLASSROOM

Today's computer-savvy and X Box–habituated learners have vastly different expectations for their educational experiences than learners of the not-too-distant past. The technoliterate MTV generation is less inclined to sit still and listen to a slow-paced lecture when stimulating, interactive educational and recreational experiences offer other multisensory options. Today's students have a high comfort level with things electronic, digital, and wired. Their level of visual literacy—a result of living in a visually rich and exciting environment—is a distinct factor in how today's students acquire and process information. The challenge remains, however, for the teacher to increase the attention span of this visually literate student beyond instant visual gratification. An approach might be through the development of computer-related, problem-solving techniques.

Because of their versatility and capability for individualization, computers—when they are accessible—can help teachers challenge and educate all students, including those with special needs. Let's take a look at the diversity of learners normally encountered in a typical teaching career and discuss some of the challenges presented.

Students with Special Needs

Students with special needs have often been called "at risk," because many are in danger of dropping out of school. Factors that contribute to this potential risk include "low teacher expectations, lack of motivation, academic difficulty, and lack of meaningful experiences" (Poirot & Canales, 1993–1994, p. 25). Students who are thought of as learning disabled, culturally and linguistically different, or talented and gifted are considered potentially at risk.

As the restructuring of U.S. education progresses, many paradigm shifts are occurring. One such shift is that schools are moving from students with special needs being separated from their regular classmates for instruction to educational programs and practices that have as their aim full inclusion from the child's perspective, that is, where a teacher adapts the learning environment to meet the diverse needs and backgrounds of the children being taught. Many educational theorists also seem to feel that schools will move from being organized on a grade-by-grade and course-by-course basis to being organized to accommodate developmental levels of learners. The computer has a significant role to play in both of these changes.

Students with Disabilities. The Individuals with Disabilities Education Act (IDEA) requires that any student eligible under the law for special education receive specially designed instruction. This includes adapting of content, methodology, or delivery of instruction (Special Education Regulation, 2001). In 2001, 95 percent of schools reported that they had students with learning disabilities, 67 percent had students with physical disabilities, 54 percent with hearing disabilities, and 46 percent with visual disabilities. Computers and technology help to meet the needs of these students. Many times hardware or software modifications will be needed so they may be used by a person with a disability. Currently, more than 50 million Americans have some type of disability requiring certain adaptations to hardware or software just to allow them to use computer technology (Kamp, 1999).

Assistive or adaptive technology devices are defined in The Technology-Related Assistance for Individuals with Disabilities Act as "any item, piece of equipment, or product system, whether acquired commercially or off the shelf, modified or customized, that increases, maintains, or improves functional capabilities of individuals with disabilities" (United States Congress, 1994). This technology includes special keyboards and keyboard software, touch-free switches, touch screens, scanners, monitors and printers, voice recognition and speech synthesizers, and refreshable Braille displays for the blind. Structuring a suitable learning environment for a physically challenged student requires providing the appropriate learning tools to achieve sensory and communication compensation. Research indicates that technology "can be adapted for use by disabled students and can result in higher achievement and improved self-image" (Kober, 1991, p. 17). Assistive devices of all kinds that provide visual, aural, or tactile support greatly extend the capabilities of impaired students to use the computer effectively. The computer-based Kurzweil Reading Machine scans printed documents and converts text into electronic speech. Speech synthesizers, speech recognition devices, image magnifiers, specially designed keyboards with exchangeable overlays, and a variety of switches have made the computer a tool useful to the physically impaired.

Though a good deal of attention has been paid to hardware for special education, software also plays a key role in making the computer accessible. For discussion of speech recognition software, see Descy (2000). The following list, adapted from Karen Armstrong (1995), presents software features that can be helpful to users with disabilities.

- *Easy-to-read screens:* Simple, legible text and menu items are represented in graphics and text.
- *Consistency:* Consistent placement of menus and objects on the screen make programs more intuitive and predictable.
- *Logical labels:* Easily understandable names in lists and menus give a reasonable sense of what will happen when they are selected.
- *Graphics:* Graphics encourage interaction and support nonreaders and beginning readers.
- *Support for inclusion:* Software that appeals to all users promotes inclusion.
- *Documentation:* Instructions are available in large print, Braille, electronic text, or recorded form.
- *Audio/visual cues:* Prompts and feedback provide important support and keep users on track.
- *Built-in access:* Alternative access methods allow users to select appropriate input devices, such as a joystick or touch screen.

A student with a learning disability often harbors feelings of inadequacy. As computers have become increasingly user friendly, they offer that student a chance to be in control and to excel. One day, while visiting a local high school, one of the authors observed a remarkable sight—"exceptional children," working as computer lab assistants, helping the "normal" students as they encountered difficulties. Those lab assistants exhibited a very positive self-concept.

Computers are patient tutors and provide simulated environments in which students with mild physical disabilities and students with learning disabilities can work. Much more information concerning the role of technology and students with disabilities can be found in *Reaching for the Sky: Policy to Support the Achievement of Students with Disabilities* (National Association of State Boards of Education, 1999).

Most computer operating systems (i.e. Macintosh OS and Windows) have many built-in features to make them more user friendly for individuals who are disabled or elderly. Apple designed disability-friendly features in all of their operating systems since the inception of the Macintosh in 1985. Early Windows operating systems were far from disability friendly. Some disability-friendly features now found in both the Mac and Windows OS include:

- *Slow keys:* includes a delay between when a key is pressed and when it is displayed on the screen (This helps prevent unintended multiple keystrokes.)
- *Sticky keys:* allows individuals to press one key at a time instead of pressing a multiple-key command all at once (Instead of pressing Control-Option-7 shortcut at one time, the three keys can be pressed in sequence.)
- *Keyboard navigation:* allows navigation around the desktop and in applications using the keyboard instead of the mouse
- *Speech recognition:* in many operating systems, allows individuals to train the computer to the person's voice (Commands to navigate through menus, control some applications, open and close files, and check buttons and radio buttons are a few of the commands that can be used.)
- *Zoom:* magnifies the text on the screen up to 40 times for easier reading
- *Scalable cursor:* allows the user to greatly increase the size of the cursor
- *VoiceOver:* on the Mac, a built-in screen reader that includes enhanced screen magnification, keyboard control, and spoken English descriptions of what is on the screen
- *Text-to-speech:* allows the computer to speak any alert messages that appear on the screen

There are also many third-party solutions availabe for purchase. Some of the popular ones include a talking word processor called *IntelliTalk*® that combines graphics and speech, *Signing Naturally*® for teaching ASL, *Picture Cues*® containing almost 700 graphics with text and speech to teach life skills to lower functioning students, *Failure Free Reading*® for phonetically deaf and at-risk students, and even a software/hardware combination that turns text into refreshable Braille displays. It's simply impossible to keep up with the newer software and hardware available to aid in accessibility. Two good places to look for information are Microsoft (*http://microsoft.com/enable*) and Apple (*http://apple.com/accessibility*). Both of these sites have up-to-date information on their operating systems and third-party hardware and software, tutorials, and other information of value. The Microsoft OS also contains the Accessibility Wizard, found on the Start menu under All Programs and also Accessibility Options in the Control Panel. In 1998, Congress amended the Rehabilitation Act to require federal agencies to make all of their electronic and information technology accessible to people with disabilities. Even though this does not have to do with you and the classroom, the government site (*http://www.section 508.gov*) also contains a great deal of useful information on hardware and software.

Individual Education Plan (IEP). The Americans with Disabilities Act and Public Law 94-142 requires that each school prepare an individual education plan for each student with special needs. Preparing this without the use of computer technology can be a time-consuming and arduous task. There are several software packages available designed to help educators with IEP preparation. *IEP Power*™ and *IEP Writer Supreme*™ are two popular examples. *IEP Power* is a special education package that includes *Power Planner*™, a program that allows individual teachers to keep track of their daily, weekly, monthly, and yearly activities along with space for their daily lesson plans. Integrated into *IEP Power* is a second program called *IEP Maker*™. The *IEP Power* package contains all of the necessary sections needed to develop an IEP based on national guidelines, right down to data collection, evaluation procedures, and transition services. It also includes space for the recording of all dates, benchmarks, lesson plans, and other information for a complete and permanent electronic record of the student's IEP.

Students with Limited English Proficiency. The computer is a valuable tool in teaching written and spoken communication to students who are from different cultural and linguistic backgrounds than Anglo Americans. The computer's engaging visual feedback can be especially appealing to students with limited English proficiency. Graphics software allows the students to express themselves in ways reflective of their own cultures. The right software transforms the computer into a patient tutor that allows students to make mistakes and to proceed as slowly as necessary. Other software creates a microworld in which a student responds and practices newly acquired language skills. A word processor using a standard typeface or a special typeface, such as Kanji, might allow the students to express themselves in their native language and to teach their classmates a few words and expressions in that language.

Some tutorial, drill and practice, and simulation software is becoming available in non-English-language versions. The most commonly available languages are Spanish, French, and German. Some software allows users to toggle between English and a second language. Many interactive storybooks distributed on CD-ROM allow the user to select the language (English, Spanish, French, or Japanese, for example) in which they would like to read and hear the story. Spell checkers, dictionaries, and thesauruses are commonly available in languages other than English for a number of word processors.

Cooperative learning strategies appear to work well with children who are culturally or linguistically different by integrating them into small groups and then facilitating their integration into the class as a whole. The computer is a tool that lends itself well to a number of cooperative learning strategies.

Students on the Hoopa Indian Reservation spent a year constructing, in their native language, a dictionary of the plants and animals indigenous to their area (Berney & Keyes, 1990). The project proved to be a challenge for them, because their native language is an oral, not a written, language. The computer, with its graphics capability, afforded them a concrete experience.

Students Who Are Talented and Gifted. It is important to acknowledge that even children who are recognized as talented and gifted may be at risk. Boredom, slow pace of instruction, lack of challenge, and lack of recognition of a unique learning style may contribute to the talented and gifted children being at risk for dropping out of school or of not achieving their full potential. Enter the computer, a tool with which to experiment and test hypotheses, analyze information and draw conclusions, express ideas through drawing and writing, and ultimately explore a wide, wide world.

The computer has many times been called the ultimate individualized instruction tool. Children who are disabled and gifted represent the opposite ends of an ability continuum. A case can be built supporting computer use as a means of reaching individual students at either end of the scale. Both types of students will derive satisfaction from constructing a worthwhile product as evidence of their creativity and knowledge.

Most gifted students are inquisitive and academically uninhibited. When introduced to computer programming, they often develop a high degree of problem-solving skills and abilities. These skills allow them mastery in other disciplines. Many talented and gifted children have difficult social adjustments to make, because of their superior intellectual abilities. They are sometimes perceived by other students as uninteresting, overly academic, and having few social skills. They sometimes perceive other students as uninteresting, unchallenging, and flighty. Once again, the computer, used wisely as part of a cooperative learning strategy,

129

LET'S GO INTO THE CLASSROOM
ESL/Home Connection

I teach Beginning ESL (English as a Second Language) to sixth, seventh and eighth grade students in a suburban middle school near Phoenix. Most of the students are recent immigrants from Mexico while some of them are from Asia or Europe. They come with a wide variety of academic experiences but typically they have very limited English skills, some exposure to school, and little or no computer experience. Even the basic mouse movements are awkward for them at first! However, all of them are eager to learn about the computer and anxious to use it.

Due to their limited exposure and need for intensive English instruction, students primarily use the computer for word processing. I have four computers in my room available to students and usually between 15 and 20 students. Giving everyone a chance to finish their work can become a logistics problem especially when you consider that most of the students have never touched a keyboard and use only one or two fingers to type. Also, most of them do not have even basic knowledge of the computer and no understanding of computer terms in either English or their native tongue!

Due to these limitations, I use the writing process in my classroom with only their final copy done on the computer. This serves as a great incentive for them to complete their rough drafts, editing and revising so they can use the computers. They particularly love changing the style, size, and fonts in the text. They also like having a printed copy to take home to their parents.

I have developed a personal narrative unit to strengthen English literacy skills, promote computer skills, and help students make the adjustment to a new culture. In this unit, each student uses the computer to produce a book about themselves. We are using the Easy book program from Sunburst which is a simple book-making program. They have a great time making the pictures on the computer for their books. I also purchased disposable cameras and a scanner with funds from a Chase Active Learning Grant. Students take pictures of their families and friends, and scan pictures from their native countries to illustrate their stories. These books become a link between the school and the home and also a way to introduce the practical uses of technology into their homes. Finally, the goal of ESL is for the students to learn English as soon as possible, to integrate them into the American educational system, and to prepare them to be successful in society. Properly utilized computer technology in the ESL curriculum contributes to the accomplishment of all these goals.

Next year, I plan to create an after-school computer tutorial "club" to train a group of students who can then help the other students master the computer. This idea came about after trying to manage a class of 20, with five on the computer and everybody needing help at the same time. I also plan to make better use of our computer lab and keyboarding programs to build up their typing skills.

Suzanne Sutcliffe
English as a Second Language Teacher
Connolly Middle School
Tempe, Arizona

can provide a positive social experience and help in the development of interpersonal skills. To build interpersonal skills, for example, these students might experiment with telecommunications software, programs that contain interactions with characters in simulations and adventures, programs about social issues, group participation and decision-making programs, and games that involve two or more players.

Computer Access and Equity

What if you gave your students an essay to write and some wrote in pencil, while others used a word processor complete with spell checker, full dictionary, thesaurus, and grammar checker? You would, of course, expect the products to be different regardless of the individual student's skills and aptitudes, because of the tools used. The essays prepared in pencil would probably have some erasures. The essays prepared on the computer, with full control of the elements of the font, may present the best visual appearance. Not only will they appear the best, but they should also be free of typing and spelling errors. They also will probably make the best use of words. Why couldn't the students writing with pencils use a dictionary and thesaurus? They could, of course, but doing so would add a considerable amount of time and effort beyond that spent by the students who used the computers. The conclusion here is that the computer, with its support for easy editing, revision, and text presentation, is a significant tool in the writing process. The student writing an essay on a computer is at a distinct advantage.

It's important to remember, however, that this powerful tool does not relieve the teacher of the responsibility to ascertain that each student learns to spell correctly and learns the proper rules of grammar as they develop their writing skills. If you consider all of the various types of computer software through which the computer can extend the user's capability, you see that the use of this tool has a significant impact. Equal access to that tool is then a serious concern. We currently have a class of "haves" and a class of "have-nots," those with access to computers and those without.

Schools in affluent neighborhoods or those with staff who possess grant-writing expertise are well equipped with computers. They have a reasonably high ratio of computers to students. The computers are located in individual classrooms, in a library media center, and in open computer labs available before, during, and after school hours. Students can search for information, practice skills, learn concepts, and create their own products.

However, because of a scarcity of resources, apathy toward technology, or lack of leadership, other schools have an inadequate number of computers and a poor selection of software. Students at these schools are deprived of the richness of the resources found

Banana Stock Ltd.

LET'S GO INTO THE CLASSROOM
The Goal: Equity; The Approach: Fun, Real Work

How do you get more students of color, particularly girls of color, interested in careers in science and technology? That's a major concern for me as a technology teacher in a low-income urban middle school where a large percentage of the population is English language learners. How I go about ensuring my students' commitment to my class is based on two simple ideas: (1) make the class fun and about what's important to them, and (2) give them depth of content knowledge so they can grab hold of future opportunities, including everything from a computer at home and computer classes to internships and jobs. While I don't expect every student to walk out of my class a computer expert, my goal is to raise my students' confidence in their ability to use computers and persist in the face of new challenges.

Lesson 1: Make it Fun

It seems so simple, but making it fun takes a lot of investigative work on the part of the teacher. In order to understand how to make class compelling, I conduct action research focusing on trying to find out more about my students' interests through questionnaires, observations, and interviews. I propose (and ask students to propose) individual, small group, and whole group projects based on their interest. I also do literature review and artifact collection in the class to understand the myriad ways that my students interact with technology and develop their identities as users and creators of media. Students have many reasons for being in the class and the trick is to amplify whatever reason it was that students chose to come to the class, whether that reason is to learn about technology, hang out with their friends, simply surf the Internet. Regardless of the reason, they will get something out of it that they never expected; and this will help them persist in the face of the demands of the class.

Lesson 2: Give Them Real Work to Do

Again, this seems like a no-brainer, but far too often we fall into the trap of expecting too little of our students and giving them the easy way out. When my class designs a website, we could easily create a PowerPoint and at the click of a button turn it into a website. But why? Doing so would miss a huge opportunity for students to learn. Instead, in my class, we handcode HTML, because learning a basic, user-friendly coding language will help them with a basic conceptual understanding of how the Internet and computers work. And it shows them that they can have some sort of control—by having the power to make it themselves—over the media they are constantly bombarded with. I also have my students engage in projects that have a real audience, such as an eighth grade graduation website, because their desire to live up to the scrutiny of peers and adults makes the work personally meaningful for students. From this experience, I expect my students to walk away with the strategies and practiced persistence to be ready for future opportunities.

What do Students Think about this Approach?

I asked one of my former students, Cindy, why she and others had been so committed to the class, coming day after day, even for meetings outside of the regularly scheduled class. Cindy was a "Youth Facilitator" for two years, helping to build community and inclusion in the class. She said that her personal interest in technology and the opportunity to be a peer leader drew her to the class. Others liked the generally comfortable environment and the opportunity to hang out with friends:

Year after year I found myself looking for classes that had to do with working with computers . . . The only class that had to do with computers and technology was Web Design. So that was the class that I decided to take. Plus, I was a Youth Facilitator for that class, which added a little more responsibility in attending . . . I think that other people just liked the environment [of the class]. All of the people in the class were friends, which made it easier for us to feel comfortable. I think that was what other people in the class liked about the class besides all the new things we were learning in there.

Regardless of the initial reason, Cindy said that students kept coming to class not only because it was fun, but also because the work was compelling. One of the class projects Cindy felt was particularly interesting for students was the graduation website, which publicly celebrated the accomplishments of the graduating eighth grade class. She said that having a project with real-world outcomes helped students to stay committed and enjoy themselves:

For the 8th grade graduation website, I think that's what made us come week after week. Even after the class was over, we felt like we just had to finish the website. We felt like we could not leave the website halfway done, and we had to put a little more effort into finishing it, and having it ready for others to view. Plus, we had already gone through a lot to finish the website.

Cindy continues to use her computer skills in school and professional internships. The more we teachers collectively provide fun and meaningful opportunities to use technology, the greater the probability that all students of color—particularly girls of color like Cindy—will be interested in careers in science and technology and be able to persist in the face of any challenge.

Cassidy Puckett
Web Design and Robotics Teacher
Urban Promise Academy Middle School
Oakland, California
Cassidy_Puckett@hotmail.com.

elsewhere. Although some affluent schools also have lackluster computer-based learning programs, students from these schools usually enjoy supportive, well-educated families who supplement school-based training with home computers. Federal surveys suggest that whites are about three times as likely to have computers at home as blacks or Hispanics; affluent students are nearly four times as likely as poor students.

According to *U.S. News and World Report* ("Digital Divide Hooey," 2000), the 1999 Commerce Department survey, *Falling Through the Net,* found that among American families earning between $15,000 and $35,000, 33 percent of whites owned computers but only 19 percent of blacks did. In 2000, 45 percent of whites were online compared with 35 percent of blacks. However, the percentage of blacks increased almost 50 percent from the prior year. Black families increased spending on personal computers at a rate 14 times faster than white families. In reviewing an October 2000 Pew study, *USA Today* ("Blacks Post Net Gains," 2000) stated that "the Internet's racial divide is closing" (p. 10). This is still not the case though, because the 2006 Pew study found that 74 percent of whites and 61 percent of blacks were now online. Interestingly though, the study also found that a whopping 80 percent of English-speaking Hispanics were online. The 2006 survey did not look at non-English-speaking Hispanics and cautions that most experts believe that this group is not using the Internet in large numbers (Marriot, 2006).

A study by the University of Southern California released in November of 2006 (Jesdanun, 2006) looks at age and Internet use. The study found that 38% of Americans 66 and over were online, 74% of those 19–65, and a whopping 99 of those 18 and under. One reason given for this was Internet access in schools.

133

A common reason given for purchasing a home computer is to assist in the education of children. A recent contact with a leading educational software publisher revealed that the volume of its sales to the home market was significantly greater than that to schools. Unfortunately, some home computers turn into simple game machines, with little software to help children learn. Students with access to a home computer having a word processor and other productivity software constitute an elite group, one with a distinct advantage that more than two-thirds of the student population does not enjoy. This variability of access should influence a teacher's expectation when it comes to the quality of product prepared by the students.

Differences in achievement for students with and without access to home computers exist. Allen and Mountain (1992) reported that, in their study of inner-city black children with access to computers and an online service, one of the primary factors in increased test scores appeared to be whether the children perceived themselves as "haves" or "have-nots." A study by Nichols (1992) suggested that higher achievement scores for students with access to home computers might be the result of those children having an increased desire to succeed. Regardless of the reason—higher self-esteem, higher motivation, or simply more powerful tools with which to work—students with computers tend to achieve higher outcomes.

As stated, computers and technology help to meet the needs of students with disabilities. Unfortunately, special hardware (for example, screen readers, closed-caption television, and special keyboards) for students with disabilities were found in only 47 percent of schools with high minority enrollment as opposed to 61 percent in schools with low enrollment (National Center for Educational Statistics, 2002a).

Fortunately, a survey by the National Center for Educational Statistics (2002c) found that in the fall of 2001, 99 percent of public schools in the United States had Internet access. Having Internet access in schools is not enough though. Students have to have access. In 2001, schools with the highest poverty and minority enrollment had the lowest percent of instructional rooms (classrooms, library/media centers, computer and other labs, and other rooms used for instructional purposes) connected to the Internet (79 percent and 81 percent, respectively), whereas schools with the lowest levels of poverty and minority enrollment had the highest percent of instructional rooms connected (90 percent in each case) (National Center for Educational Statistics, 2002c). If we are going to have all of our citizens thrive in this technological society, we must increase access to computers and technology in schools with high poverty and minority enrollments. Increased access should help drive down the gap between "haves" and "have-nots."

How can access be improved? Teachers in schools with inadequate computer resources should demand access to such an important educational tool. They should make the administration, the school board, and community groups aware of the need. Don't overlook grants and private funding. Many national retail chains (Target, Kmart, Wal-Mart, for example) and local industries and organizations are all places to look for help. Teachers in schools with reasonable computer resources should work toward making the computers available, with an acceptable measure of security and supervision, outside of normal school hours to students, parents, and community groups.

Gender Equity

Gender equity should be a continuing cause of concern to educators. Computer use has suffered from an inherited gender bias that holds that math and science are not "feminine things." Efforts to remedy this bias are in progress. This bias has its roots in the seventeenth century, when inventions in science and technology were made not by aristocrats but in the monastic environment of the universities, which were under the control of the male-dominated political and religious forces of the time. The elite created an aura of a quasi-priesthood of science and technology and erected barriers to keep others, primarily women, out (Noble, 1992). From that point until the mid-twentieth century, women were basically told that math and science were not for them.

It is interesting to note that the person generally recognized as the first computer programmer was a woman, Ada Lovelace (Augusta Ada Byron, Countess of Lovelace), daughter of Lord Byron!

Research shows equal participation of boys and girls in computer literacy and application activities in the elementary and middle-level grades. Girls and boys appear to be equally enthusiastic when it comes to using the computer. As students move into high school, gender differences and, in many cases, unfair stereotypes exert themselves. Girls continue to refine word processing skills and other business (read "clerical") skills, whereas boys overwhelmingly populate the computer science classes. High school girls tend to develop negative attitudes regarding computers (Kirk, 1992). Luckily, this is changing because of the widespread use of the Internet. According to a Pew report, gender parity was reached in Internet usage in 1999 (Pew Research Center, 2000). It appears this parity in usage has increased the comfort level of females and hopefully is carrying over to other computer applications as well.

In a typical school computer lab, computers are available on a first-come, first-serve basis. With more students than computers, the more aggressive students usually get them. Many boys spend countless hours playing video games as preadolescents and gravitate toward the use of computers.

Software itself can contribute to gender inequity. For example, research shows that clip art libraries severely underrepresent women and ethnic minorities, and they reinforce gender stereotypes about sex roles and work (Dyrud, 1996; Milburm, Carmol, & Ramirez, 2001). Additionally, recreational software tends to be loud, flashy, violent, and based on competitive win–lose situations. Even educational software has at times exhibited some of these characteristics. Females tend not to be drawn to this type of software and, therefore, spend less time at the computer as an enjoyable diversion.

Parental encouragement is another factor influencing gender bias. Parents often envision their sons in scientific or technical careers and encourage them to take computer science classes and attend computer camps. Parents are more likely to buy computers for use by their sons than by their daughters. Boys get the message that spending time at a computer is a worthwhile activity.

How should we as teachers strive to promote gender equity in our classrooms? What actions must we take to affirm this goal? We should go out of our way to praise girls' accomplishments on the computer. We must be sure to include them in any special computer-based projects. We can encourage equal access to computers by instituting sign-ups, rotation schedules, and other democratic systems. We should include girls' names in computer examples we give. We must buy and use gender-equitable software and avoid other programs. We should encourage girls to consider careers involving computer use beyond standard clerical applications. We must provide more female role models by inviting women who are computer scientists or who make extensive use of the computer in their professions to speak to our classes. We must continually examine our own behavior and guard against any subtle, even unintentional, actions we might take that would in any way diminish girls' interest or discourage them from interacting with the computer in a meaningful way. More than 200,000 technology-related jobs go unfilled in the United States every year. We cannot afford to let anyone—black or red or brown or white, female or male, rich or poor—be shut out from reaching their full potential because of our unintentional actions.

LET'S GO INTO THE CLASSROOM
Geek is Chic—Integrating Technology into the Lives of Girls

Girls and technology—can the two be successfully integrated? There is a significant body of research that validates what girls in coeducational schools experience on a daily basis, that with regard to technology, girls lag behind boys in use, understanding, and interest on many levels. A growing number of studies indicate that girls are not involved in technology at the level needed to advance the critical-thinking skills that are highly valued in the areas of math, science, and technology careers. Classroom teachers have the power to reverse this trend, if they take into consideration the research recommendations that girls prefer collaborative, rather than isolated, use of technology in education.

How can you, as a future teacher, encourage and support girls in the use of technology within everyday learning experiences? The key is to group girls together, in collaborative, project-based exercises that utilize whatever technology resources are available at your school. We have found that with the wealth of the many project-based resources available on the Internet, that it is not necessary to create innovative projects from scratch. Begin by letting the girls discuss their perceptions of technology. Partner your girls with girls from another school. Let the girls design and control their own projects. Their enthusiasm and inspiration, under your leadership as their teacher, will provide the foundation they need to find that "Geek is Chic!"

Since we began our "Geek is Chic" project, our girls have assumed responsibility for their own learning. They have learned to approach their work as a design team in much the same way a team in the corporate world works—they brainstorm, share, discuss, implement, evaluate, and refine, all traits that are key to successful careers in the math, sciences, and technology fields. As a result of this collaboration, they are now much more confident users of technology. Feeling empowered through a sense of ownership about the technology has been a major key to the success of our project.

One of the key recommendations from an American Association of University Women study is that

computation should be integrated across the curriculum, into such subject areas as art, music and literature as well as engineering and science . . . subjects that already interest girls, as well as promoting critical thinking and lifelong learning.

This recommendation also gives both educators and girls the opportunity to use the technology as designers, rather than being mere consumers. The report also recommends the creation and support of computing clubs and summer school classes for girls, mentoring programs, science fairs and programs that encourage girls to see themselves as capable of careers in technology.

Even though cultural biases and inequities cannot be changed overnight, you, as a classroom teacher, can affect positive change, one girl at a time. Even if the girls decide that a career involving technology is not for them, you will at least have given them the experience they need to make an informed decision. Our model for changing girls' perceptions of, and involvement with, technology might be just what you need to encourage your girls to realize that "Geek is Chic!"

Robyn Treyvaud (Australia)
Curriculum & PYP Coordinator
Junior School, Wesley College
Prahran, Melbourne, Victoria

Lori Rounds (USA)
Director of Technology
The Woods Academy
Bethesda, Maryland

OBLIGATIONS AND EXPECTATIONS IN A COMPUTER LITERATE SOCIETY

Computers have permeated every aspect of our society as we start the twenty-first century. As with all new technologies, we have responsibilities when it comes to using them. Computer technology allows us to do things that we could not easily do before. It is now easy to record some special music onto our computer and send it to our friends. We can copy almost anything on the Internet or in our pocket, and even copy our favorite movie all with just the touch of a few keys and a few mouse clicks. Computer technology is so different from the older print and recording forms. It allows so much to be done by so many that many times regulations and laws can't seem to keep up. Computer technology and the Internet have brought about some of the biggest changes in our ideas about copyright and intellectual property. They have also vastly changed our expectations regarding computer literacy.

Copyright and Intellectual Property

Copyright is a way of protecting intellectual property. **Intellectual property** is something conceived in the mind of an individual and made available to other individuals. This textbook is intellectual property and so is the syllabus for the course you are taking, as well as the computer software you may use. The ownership of intellectual property is defined and protected by copyright law. The first copyright law was passed in the U.S. Congress in 1790.

Quite simply, **copyright** is designed to protect the financial interests of the creators, producers, and distributors of original works of art and information. Without copyright laws there would be little incentive to create or distribute information and works of art. This may sound like a one-sided situation, but it's not if we stop to think about it. Would Microsoft have developed the Windows OS or Microsoft Office®, or would Apple have developed imovie (or would someone have written your favorite book, movie, song, music video, or developed your favorite video game) if there were no financial incentives? Companies and individuals that develop intellectual property win by having their efforts rewarded financially, and we win by having vast amounts of top-notch products available for our use. Copyright is a win–win situation! Upholding copyright laws enriches everyone involved! We must strive to set a good example in all that we do. It is important that we uphold copyright laws in our professional and private lives and that we instill this respect and appreciation for intellectual property and copyright in our students.

Remember, we as teachers and parents are role models. Saying the right thing and doing the wrong thing will reinforce the benefits of doing the wrong thing to our students and our own children. It is not only illegal but also unethical to use or distribute software in ways other than outlined in copyright law. Let's hope that our students will learn as much about upholding copyright law by observing what we do in our classrooms as by listening to what we say. Copyright laws *and their interpretations* are always changing. Part of your professional responsibility is to keep up with the laws that pertain to teaching, learning, and your professional area of expertise. Congress has amended the copyright laws with regard to the fair use of copyrighted computer software.

In addition to copyrighted software, you will probably come into contact with two other types of software. **Freeware** is software that may be copied and distributed free of charge. The author still holds the copyright but has simply given everyone permission to copy and use it. The author of **shareware** has given permission for anyone to try it out and distribute it. The program's opening screen often lists the conditions for its use, usually including a payment made to the author if you continue to use the software. Shareware is usually priced between $10 and $50. There are many sites on the Internet that contain huge archives of freeware and shareware for you to download, install, and enjoy. Check these sites often and take advantage of free email newsletters from many of them. *Cnet.com* and *zdnet.com* are two sites that have links to huge freeware and shareware collections and also have free newsletters containing information on new, favorite, and helpful programs. You may be able to find a program that would be a great help to you or your students at a fraction of the cost of the commercial software equivalent (or it may even be free).

A copy of these guidelines may be found in the Guidelines folder in the Take-Along CD

We May Do the Following

- Install one copy of the software onto our computer hard drive.
- Adapt software to another language as long as it is not available in that language.
- Add features to the software that will help us to better use it.
- Make one archival or backup copy of the software. If the software is copy-protected, we may use utility software to unlock and copy it.

We May Not Do the Following Without the Permission of the Copyright Owner

- Put single-user software on a network.
- Make multiple copies of software for ourselves.
- Make multiple copies of software to give away, loan, lease, sell, or transmit to others.
- Sell our adaptation of the software.

A variation of freeware is Free and Open Source Software (FOSS). FOSS programs are free, customizable, and work on Mac, Windows, and Linux (also FOSS!) operating systems. This software is developed by a person or group and is distributed to anyone who wants it. It is called open source because the computer programming that was used to make the program (called the source code) can be viewed, modified, customized, and improved by anyone who uses the program. Because of this, FOSS software is usually extremely stable and bug free. There are many FOSS programs that are almost identical to commercial versions except, of course, that they are free. The state of New Hampshire is saving millions of dollars by using FOSS instead of purchasing identical commercial programs such as the freely downloadable OpenOffice that is similar to Microsoft Office and the Linux operating system instead of Microsoft Windows. Many schools save thousands of dollars in license fees per year using FOSS. You may be using the Web browser Firefox (*http://www.mozilla.com*) or place calls over the Web using Skype (*http://www.skype.com*), both of which are FOSS programs. Since FOSS programs are open source, you should keep an eye out for updates since users are always improving them. The following table identifies some common FOSS programs.

Commercial	FOSS	Website
Microsoft Office	Open Office	*www.openoffice.org*
Adobe Illustrator	Inkscape	*www.inkscape.org*
KidPix	TuxPaint	*www.newbreedsoftware.com*
Dreamweaver	NVU	*www.nvu.org*
Logo	NetLogo	*ccl.northwestern.edu/netlogo/*
Viseo	Dia	*dia-installer.sourceforge.net/*
Database	MySQL	*dev.mysql.com*
Sound Forge	Audacity	*audacity.sourceforge.net*
Course management	Moodle	*www.moodle.org*
Image editing	GIMP	*www.gimp.org*
Electronic portfolios	Moodle e-portfolio	*portfolio.spdc.org*

More information on FOSS for K–12 schools and personal use can be found at *http://www.netc.org/openoptions/index.html.*

Plagiarism or the representation of someone else's work as one's own has been made simple and quicker with the help of technology. It is now much easier to copy words, paragraphs, and even complete documents. We all know how easy it is to cut and paste. With the help of the Internet, it is now possible to cut and paste our way around the world. How do we, as teachers, combat this? It is not easy. There are sites on the Internet that help you track down articles from phrases or paragraphs, but sometimes it may be as simple to just type a phrase into several search engines and take a fast look at the hits. Unfortunately, there is no easy and sure answer.

Acceptable Use Policies: Protecting Your Students, Your School, and Yourself. Teachers should educate their students in appropriate use of their school's network and the Internet. They should also monitor student usage, because some parts of the Internet contain material not suitable for minors. Many school districts have developed **acceptable use policies (AUPs)** outlining proper Internet use and student responsibilities and require permission forms signed by both parent and student before allowing student access to the Internet. *All* schools using the Internet should have acceptable use policies just as they should have selection policies for library materials. An acceptable use policy for an instructional setting might be thought of as similar to the laboratory safety contract that a science teacher might require. It would include a statement of the responsible behaviors expected of students, with particular attention to potentially unsafe or inappropriate actions, and a set of measured consequences. Acceptable use forms should be signed by the instructor, student, and parent or guardian before the student is allowed online. Parental notification demonstrates that the parents are aware of the instructor's intent and reasonable supervision, to ensure the educationally productive use of classroom resources.

Controlling Access to the Internet. It is not difficult to find or just stumble upon inappropriate materials on the Internet. Under the Children's Internet Protection Act (CIPA) (Public Law 106-554), the validity of which is currently being tested in the courts, no school may receive the e-rate discount to help them pay for Internet access unless the school certifies that it is enforcing a policy of Internet use that includes the use of some sort of blocking or filtering technology (Universal Service Administrative Company, 2002). In 2001, 96 percent of schools with Internet access had in place various procedures and/or technologies to control student access to inappropriate material. Of this number, 98 percent of schools used these procedures or technologies on all Internet-connected computers used by students. These procedures and technologies include monitoring of student use by teachers or staff members (91 percent), blocking or filtering software (87 percent), written contract co-signed by parent (80 percent), written contract signed by student (75 percent), using computer monitoring software (46 percent), honor codes (44 percent), and using only private school intranets (26 percent) (National Center for Educational Statistics, 2002b).

One concern frequently expressed by teachers, school administrators, school boards, and parents is that of the potential for students to access Internet materials that are inappropriate for minors. These materials might be either intentionally or inadvertently located via one of the search engines and may include expressions or descriptions of violence, ethnic hatred, or pornography. As stated previously, it is advisable for the classroom teacher, school building, and school district to have workable acceptable use policies agreed to in writing prior to student use of the Internet. However, even with these in place, many educators are looking to a **web filter,** or blocking program (for example, *Net Nanny*™ or *Cyber Patrol*™), to screen out undesirable content. Filter programs are somewhat effective in looking for key descriptive terms that may reside at Internet locations and thus block student access. However, they may also block an educationally valid search term that

139

possesses meanings other than those appropriate for students of a specific age or ability. None of the blocking programs is perfect and all allow some "undesirable" sites to pass through unblocked. Schools may also be opening themselves to lawsuits if they rely solely on filter programs for protection and these sites pass through unblocked. Whether it is appropriate to use Internet filtering programs has created much controversy in individual classrooms right up through state legislatures. Perhaps the best policy, as with most educational functions, is to provide consistent expectations for student behavior, combined with diligent teacher supervision of student activities during the course of any Internet-based activity.

LET'S GO INTO THE CLASSROOM
Rules of the Road

We require student and parental signatures on the DoDEA Student Computer and Internet Access Agreement at the time a student registers. This general acceptable use agreement sets forth expectations for the student's use of computer resources at school.

We have "rules of the road" on the information superhighway that simplify these expectations in words that are easier for students to remember. Essentially, I view computers and the Internet as instructional resources (like the reference books). Students are not to play games, chat, download without permission, or subscribe to any online offers. Students use gaggle.net for free email pertaining to schoolwork, so they are not allowed to access their personal email on school computers.

Audio files are distracting to other users, so we mute the sound on the computers in the library.

Students have individual accounts on our local area network (LAN); in case of violations, their privileges can be suspended. Our intranet features a "virtual library" page from which students access selected World Wide Web subject directories and search engines as well as recommended sites pertaining to the curriculum. I keep and regularly update a copy on my personal website so that students can access the page from home as well.

Janet Murray
Information Specialist
Yokosuka Middle School
Department of Defense Dependents Schools
Yokosuka, Japan janetm@surfline.ne.jp

LET'S REVIEW

Students with special needs who are sometimes thought of as learning disabled, culturally and linguistically different, or talented and gifted are often at risk of dropping out of school. As the restructuring of U.S. education progresses, educational programs and practices will have as their aim full inclusion from the child's perspective, and schools will be organized to accommodate the developmental levels of learners. Structuring a suitable learning environment for a physically challenged student requires providing the appropriate learning tools to achieve sensory and communication compensation. A student with a learning disability often harbors feelings of inadequacy. As computers have become increasingly user friendly, they offer that student a chance to be in control and to excel. Computers are patient tutors and provide simulated environments in which students with mild physical disabilities and learning disabilities can work.

The computer is a valuable tool in teaching written and spoken communication to students who are culturally and linguistically different. Graphics software allows students to express themselves in ways reflective of their own culture. Other software creates a microworld in which a student responds and practices newly acquired language skills. A word processor might allow students to express themselves in their native language.

Boredom, slow pace of instruction, and lack of challenge may contribute to the talented and gifted child being at risk for dropping out of school. The computer can be used as a tool to test hypotheses, analyze information and draw conclusions, express oneself by drawing and writing, and communicate with others around the world. Talented and gifted children often have difficult social adjustments to make because of their superior intellectual abilities. The computer, used wisely as part of a cooperative learning strategy, can provide a positive social experience and can help in the development of interpersonal skills.

Students using computers are at a distinct advantage because they are using a tool that can extend their capabilities. Some schools are well equipped, with a high ratio of computers to students readily available, and others are not. Whites are about three times as likely to have computers at home as blacks and Hispanics; affluent students are nearly four times more likely than poorer students. Students with access to a home computer having a word processor and other productivity software constitute an elite group with a distinct advantage that more than two-thirds of the student population does not enjoy.

As students move into high school, boys overwhelmingly populate the computer science classes. Parents are more likely to buy computers for their sons than for their daughters and encourage boys to take computer science classes and attend computer camps. Teachers must actively seek out software without gender biases and continually guard against any subtle actions that would in any way diminish girls or discourage them from interacting with the computer in a meaningful way.

Copyright laws are designed to protect the rights and financial interests of the person or people who develop works considered to be intellectual property. Without copyright laws, many incentives would not exist and development of new and improved products and ideas would slow considerably. It is in everyone's best interest to respect the copyright laws.

LET'S PRACTICE

To complete the specified exercises online, go to the Chapter Exercises Module in Chapter 4 of the Companion Website.

1. Do an online bibliographic search in the library on the topic, "Computer Access: In School and at Home." Select only articles written in the past four years. Using a word processor, write a report of at least two double-spaced pages on the issues. Cite references and include a bibliography.

2. Search the Internet to find information on the topic, "Computers and Gender Bias: Cause and Effect." Find four Web pages on the subject posted in the past four years. Using a word processor, write a report of at least two double-spaced pages on the issues. Cite references and include a bibliography.

3. Examine vendor catalogs and locate three programs, in at least two different subject areas, that use a language in addition to English.

4. Locate available graphics software or a word processing program. Make three different 8 1/2-by-11-inch signs to be placed in the computer lab reminding students of copyright laws.

5. Locate several online sources of freeware and software. Can you list any that would be of use when teaching?

6. As our society moves rapidly from an industrial society to an information society, what are the implications of information technology for schooling?

7. What are some of the ways that you will ensure equity for your students when you prepare lessons?

8. Obtain an acceptable use policy from a nearby school district or from the Web. Do you feel that it meets all of the requirements you think are important? What would you add or delete?

9. Research Internet filtering software in the library or on the Web. Write a short paper in which you discuss the pros and cons of Internet filtering. Are you in favor of it or opposed to it? Why? Discuss what you found in class.

10. Research copyright law with respect to education. List and discuss four ways that teachers might unintentionally violate the copyright law.

PORTFOLIO DEVELOPMENT EXERCISES

To complete this exercise online, go to the Digital Portfolio Module in Chapter 4 of the Companion Website.

One of the NETS•S standards covered in this chapter was "Students understand the ethical, cultural, and societal issues related to technology" under *Category 2: Social, ethical, and human issues*. Begin to develop your own portfolio of lesson plans that demonstrates your ability to have your students reach the NETS•S standards.

1. Design a lesson plan activity for elementary, middle school, or high school students encouraging them to work in teams to research one of the issues presented in this chapter (computer access and equity, gender equity, intellectual property, equity laws dealing with education) and have them prepare a presentation for the other students in their classroom. This lesson should demonstrate that your students have achieved the standard. Be sure to include a system of evaluation for your students' understanding and competence to ensure that they have met this standard.

2. Adapt the lesson plan activity you developed in exercise 1 for students to evaluate each others' work.

GLOSSARY

acceptable use policies (AUPs)	Outline proper Internet use and student responsibilities and require permission forms signed by both parent and student before allowing student access to the Internet
copyright	Laws designed to protect the financial interests of the creators, producers, and distributors of original works of art and information
freeware	Software that may be copied and distributed free of charge
intellectual property	Something conceived in the mind of an individual and made available to others
shareware	Software distributed free of charge with conditions that usually include a payment made to the authors if software continues to be used after a trial period
web filter	Blocking program that screens out undesirable content but may also block an educationally valid search term that possesses meanings other than those appropriate for students of a specific age or ability

REFERENCES AND SUGGESTED READINGS

Allen, A. A., & Mountain, L. (1992, November). When inner city black children go online at home. *The Computing Teacher, 20*(3), 35–37.

Armstrong, K. (1995, October). Special software for special kids. *Technology & Learning, 16*(2), 56–61.

Berney, T., & Keyes, J. (1990). *Computer writing skills for limited English proficiency students*. Brooklyn, NY: Report to the New York City Board of Education.

Blacks post net gains. (2000, April 17). *U.S. News and World Report, 128*(15), 45.

Descy, D. (2000, April). "Good morning, HAL-9000". . . "Good morning, Don" . . . A primer on speech recognition software. *TechTrends, 44*(3), 4–6.

Digital divide hooey. (2000, April 17). *U.S. News and World Report, 128*(15), 45.

Drumm, J. E. (1999, April). Teaching information skills to disadvantaged children. *Computers in Libraries, 19*(4), 48–51.

Dyrud, M. (1996, November). *An exploration of gender bias in computer clip art*. Paper presented at the

Association for Business Communication Annual Conference, Chicago, IL.

Grogan, M. (1999, October). Equity/equality issues of gender, race, and class. *Educational Administration Quarterly, 35*(4), 518–536.

Hartshorn, K. (2000, November). Girls take charge of technology. *Leading and Learning with Technology, 23*(3), 18–20.

Jesdanun, A. (2006, November 29) study: 1 from 5 parents say kids online too much, but no effect on or acts either way. New York: Association prog (Retrieved online December 2, 2006 at *https://www.usatoday.com/ tech/news/2006-11-29-number-study-kids-x.htm*

Kamp, S. (1999). How does "fair use" apply to software being used in the schools? *Technology and Learning, 5*(1), 58.

Kirk, D. (1992, April). Gender issues in information technology as found in schools: Authentic/synthetic/fantastic. *Educational Technology, 32*(4), 28–35.

Kober, N. (1991). *What we know about mathematics teaching and learning.* Washington, DC: Council for Educational Development and Research.

LD Online. (2006). LD-Indepth: technology information. Retrieved online June 17, 2006, from *http://www.ldonline.org/ld_indepth/technology/technology.html*

Marriot, M. (2006, March 31). Blacks turn to internet highway, and digital divide starts to close. *The New York Times, CLV*(53,535), A1, A15.

Milburm, S. S., Carney, D. R., Ramirez, A. M. (2001, March). Each by modern media, the picture is still the same account analysis of, lipart. Behavioral science *44*(5–6) 277–294.

National Association of State Boards of Education. (1999). *Reaching for the sky: Policy to support the achievement of students with disabilities.*

National Center for Educational Statistics. (2002a). *Internet access in U.S. public schools and classrooms: 1994–2001 Special hardware and software for students with disabilities.* Retrieved online February 15, 2003, from *http://nces.ed.gov/pubs2002/ internet/6.asp.*

National Center for Educational Statistics. (2002b). *Internet access in U.S. public schools and classrooms: 1994–2001. Technologies and procedures to prevent student access to inappropriate material on the Internet.* Retrieved online February 15, 2003, from *http://nces.ed.gov/ pubs2002/internet/8.asp.*

National Center for Educational Statistics. (2002c). *Internet access in U.S. public schools and classrooms: 1994–2001 School access.* Retrieved online February 15, 2003, from *http://nces.ed.gov/pubs2002/ internet/3.asp.*

Nichols, L. M. (1992, August). Influence of student computer ownership and in-home use on achievement in an elementary school computer programming curriculum. *Journal of Educational Computing Research, 8*(4), 407–421.

Noble, D. E. (1992). *A world without women: The Christian culture of modern science.* New York: Knopf.

Pew Research Center. (2000, May). *Tracking online life: How women use the Internet to cultivate relationships with family and friends.* Retrieved online March 23, 2003, from *http://www.pewinternet.org/ reports/toc.asp.*

Pisano, L. V. (2002, October 2). *What happens when assistive technology doesn't work?* Retrieved online June 19, 2006, from *http://www.ldonline.org/ld_indepth/technology/ assistive_technology_when_it_doesnt_work.html*

Poirot, J. L., & Canales, J. (1993–1994, December/January). Technology and the at-risk—An overview. *The Computing Teacher, 21*(4), 25–26, 55.

Quenneville, J. (2001, Summer). Tech tools for students with learning disabilities: Infusion into inclusive classrooms. *Preventing School Failure, 45*(4), 167–170.

Simpson, C. (1999, September–October). Managing copyright in schools. *Knowledge Quest, 28*(1), 18–22.

Special Education Regulation. (2001). Cited in *Internet access in U.S. public schools and classrooms: 1994–2001.* Retrieved online March 3, 2003, on *http://nces.ed.gov/pubs2002/internet/6.asp.*

Sutherland, S. (2000, March). Accessing technology: How special education can assist. *TechTrends, 44*(2), 29–30.

Timm, J. T. (1999, Summer). Selecting computer programs and interactive multimedia for culturally diverse students: Promising practices. *Multicultural Education, 6*(4), 30–31.

United States Congress. (1994). *Technology-related assistance for individuals with disabilities act of 1988 as amended in 1994.* Retrieved online February 21, 2003, from *http://www.resna.org/taproject/library/ laws/techact94.htm.*

Universal Service Administrative Company. (2002). *Children's internet protection act.* Retrieved online February 21, 2003, from *http://www.sl.universalservice. org/reference/CIPA.asp.*

Webb, B. J. (2000, March/April). Planning and organizing—Assistive technology resources in your school. *Teaching Exceptional Children, 32*(4), 50.

5 CHAPTER

Learning about the Computer

ADVANCE ORGANIZER

1. What are the primary processes involved in a computer system?

2. What typical hardware exists to facilitate entering data?

3. What is a CPU?

4. What are the different types of memory and how do they differ?

5. What typical hardware exists to facilitate extracting information?

6. How has the user interface evolved and what is its impact on you as a user?

7. What is networking's impact on schools?

LET'S LOOK AT THIS CHAPTER

With new or updated computer equipment entering the marketplace constantly, a discussion of hardware can never be truly current. As this is being written, a new product is undoubtedly entering the market; however, this chapter will give you a good basic understanding of computer hardware and establish a firm foundation as you continue to learn about technology and computers during your entire teaching career.

The shift in computer paradigms from centralized institution to interactive and networked becomes apparent as we trace the development of the technology and in particular the development of computer hardware. Now the mobile user employing a personal computer or handheld is able to interconnect with a network of other users in order to exchange information and search a labyrinth of databases to access valuable information. These connections may be through wires or glass fiber, or, more and more, through thin air. Location is no longer a limiting factor.

WHAT IS A COMPUTER?

An understanding of the computer as a tool requires an awareness of its component parts and an appreciation of what each part may contribute as we attempt to use the computer to solve the problems we may encounter. A user must be able to put data into a system, manipulate those data, and retrieve information in an appropriate manner. The user does this by employing a variety of hardware, software, and firmware. Tangible objects such as a monitor, keyboard, mouse, joystick, printer, or disk drive are examples of **hardware.** Not all tangible objects are encompassed by this term, however. For instance, CD-Rs which are tangible objects are generally termed "media" and are considered consumable supplies. Recording a computer program on a CD changes the terminology of the disk to **software.** More precisely, the actual recorded program itself on the medium is the software, but you can see that at some point it becomes difficult to separate the two. A third term, **firmware,** denotes software that is stored permanently in chips usually located on add-on computer cards or printed circuit boards. The *input* is the process of entering data into the computer system. The *operation* is the process of manipulating the data in a predetermined manner by the **central processing unit (CPU)** using instructions defined in the program. The *output* is the process of retrieving the information once the CPU has acted upon it. All hardware other than the computer itself is referred to as peripheral equipment.

Input peripherals such as a keyboard and a mouse allow the user to enter data into the computer system. **Output peripherals** such as a monitor and a printer allow the user to retrieve information from the computer system.

WHAT IS HARDWARE?

Hardware is a term commonly used to designate the equipment components of a computer system. To unravel the confusion related to equipment specification, this chapter is organized according to the three processes of input, operation, and output involved in a computer system (see Figure 5–1). We will examine the hardware and some software related to each. We will also discuss a fourth process, the storage of information.

Before we discuss the actual peripherals, let's take a moment to examine ways to connect peripherals to the computer CPU. Communication must occur between the input peripherals and the CPU as well as between the CPU and the output peripherals. This communication is sometimes referred to as an interface. It is essentially composed of two parts, one built into the peripheral device and the other either software added to the computer or a firmware card that plugs into one of its expansion slots. A cable or wireless device links the computer and its peripherals. Figure 5–2 illustrates the relationship of the various parts. An **extension** is a

Figure 5–1 System components

Three processes in a computer system

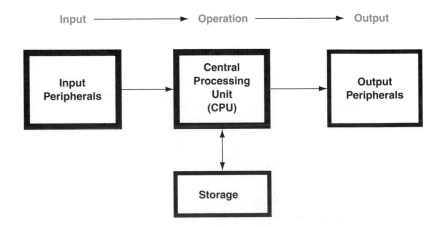

small program that is added to the operating system that allows the application software to interact with the operating system. A device **driver** is another small program that is added to the operating system that allows the operating system to interact with certain hardware peripherals (e.g., a printer). Peripheral devices depend on adequate connections or interfaces to the computer to function well.

The speed of data transfer is an important characteristic of the connections between peripheral devices and the computer. The older *serial* (one data stream at a time) or *parallel* (multiple data streams at a time) interfaces have been replaced by the **Universal Serial Bus (USB)** standard developed by an industry-wide consortium. USB is a high-performance, cross-platform (Windows/Macintosh) technology, yet is simple and user friendly. USB technology can transfer data at a far faster rate than the older serial or parallel connections. Peripheral devices are simple to connect. A device driver, provided by the peripheral's manufacturer, is installed in the computer. The cable is then plugged into the peripheral and the computer. USB connections are **hot-swappable,** meaning that peripherals can be plugged or unplugged from the system without shutting down and restarting the computer.

Digital video and other forms of media have increased the need to transfer vast amounts of data into and out of the CPU. To do this in a time-saving manner, a new standard for connectivity called **FireWire** was developed. FireWire 400 was faster than USB 1.1, hot-swappable, and also platform independent. As with USB, many FireWire peripherals don't need a power cord since they can get their power directly from the computer. Hewlett-Packard, Intel, and other industry leaders jointly developed an even higher speed connection called USB 2.0. Apple Computer then introduced FireWire 800 that has a transfer speed of up to 800 Megabits per second (hence the name) and a theoretical future transfer speed of up to 3,200 Mbps! Many computer manufacturers provide both USB and Firewire interfaces. By the time you read this, there may be an even newer interface. The following table offers a comparison of data transfer speeds.

Serial	=	0.6 Mbps
Parallel	=	3.0 Mbps
USB 1.1	=	12.0 Mbps
FireWire 400	=	400.0 Mbps
USB 2.0	=	480.0 Mbps
FireWire 800	=	800.0 Mbps

Figure 5–2 Communication between components

Computer/peripheral intercommunication in a computer system

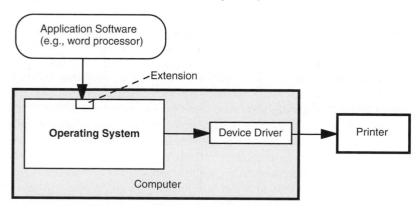

Input Devices

Let's review some hardware components whose function is to enter data into the computer through tactile, audio, video, or electronic means.

The **keyboard** is the primary device through which data are entered into a personal computer system by generating a digital code that can be entered into the computer's memory and be understood by the CPU. We all know that each keyboard contains at least two key configurations, uppercase and lowercase, that can be accessed by using the shift key. Most computer keyboards, however, also contain a third, fourth, or even fifth configuration of keys that can be accessed by pressing combinations of alternative keys simultaneously with the alphanumeric key.

The **mouse** is a small, handheld input device that a user moves on a flat surface such as a desk. Software stored inside the computer moves the cursor on the screen, replicating the motion of the mouse. The software constantly monitors the position of the cursor on the screen. Pressing a button on the mouse results in one of several actions, depending on the program being used.

The **trackpad,** usually found on laptop computers, is a pressure-sensitive pad. By pressing a finger to the pad, the user moves a pointer on the screen.

Printed bar codes similar to the **UPC** (Universal Product Code) found on many products make data entry extremely fast and accurate. The codes are read by devices that sense the sequence of thick and thin lines and their spacing. Two commonly used types of **bar code readers** are handheld wands and stationary readers similar to those commonly employed at grocery checkout counters. The bar code readers generate light, which reflects from the bar code in a light and dark pattern. The reader, sensing the pattern, generates the appropriate matching digital code, thus eliminating the need for time-consuming keyboard entry, with its inherent typing errors.

A school library's automated circulation system is based on a bar code applied to each student's identification card, with appropriate bar codes placed on book spines or card pockets. A bar code reader reads information into a computer and in seconds the checkout procedure is completed.

Graphics tablets similar to that depicted in Figure 5–3 are input devices that allow the user to create or trace figures or drawings of any kind. A student can draw a picture with a stylus provided on the surface of the tablet and see it replicated on the monitor screen. The stylus allows the user far greater control than the mouse in drawing intricate designs. The accompanying software translates the stylus position and displays it as a point on the monitor screen. The series of points are the representation of a straight or curved line segment making up a total picture. You can also fill in solid areas of color, as well as enlarge or reduce the drawing. Again, using the software, the user can select certain shapes, shadings, and line widths or "paintbrush" effects. An art teacher might choose to have students use this device to execute lessons in perspective, line, or contour drawing. With its inherent ability to trace existing material, the graphics tablet is also an excellent device to facilitate the production of maps for a social studies lesson. Keyboards, mice, trackpads, bar code readers, and graphics tablets may be common to the CPU by wires or wirelessly, using radio waves or infrared energy.

Speech recognition devices have been available for a few years to interface with personal computers. Some current applications are part of the operating system and allow words to be spoken into a microphone that conveys the command to the computer. Several voice recognition software packages have entered the market that will allow a computer to enter spoken words into a word processing program. At present, speech recognition software can match spoken word to printed word with about 95 percent accuracy. Voice entry has the advantage of eliminating the need to learn keyboarding skills. It offers speed, ease of use, and the potential for voice recognition security. Voice recognition software will help many physically disabled individuals gain access to a computer who can't access them now. There are a few excellent, yet inexpensive speech recognition products such as IBM's *Via Voice* available for both the Windows and Macintosh platforms. *Dragon Naturally Speaking* and *iListen from Australia* are two others worth considering.

Let's briefly mention photographic and video input devices and look at them more in depth in Chapter 6. These devices greatly facilitate the creation of graphic images in the computer. Still-image **digital cameras** have become popular and more affordable. Most models are easy to use and store a large number of digital images on removable media. **Digital video cameras** along with computer-based video editing systems are making an impact on schools as teachers and students alike become comfortable with the technology. They look and feel like conventional analog video cameras but don't require the student or teacher to learn to use software to convert the analog video signals to digital signals used by a computer. Many schools have now put movie making into their curricula. The Public Broadcasting System (PBS) is developing partnerships with schools in several areas of the country to broadcast video produced by students with digital equipment. Your local public access cable channel might even welcome video productions produced by you or your students. Software and video boards are also available that allow computer screens to be recorded on videotape to serve as titles, credits, animated graphics, or instructional text screens. A variety of wipes and dissolves that allow one image to merge into another lends sophistication to the recording.

Scanners digitize photographs, line drawings, and printed text by reading light reflected from the surface of the object. Some scanners allow the scanning of negatives and color slides by transmitting light through them. The scanner's **resolution** refers to the number of dots per inch (dpi) that a scanner is able to capture. This number is typically expressed by two numbers (1,200 by 2,400, for example). The first number represents the number of dots across the width of the scanning area and the second number represents the number of dots down the length. The important number to remember is the smaller number. This

Valerie Schultz/Merrill

is the limit that the scanner can achieve without using **interpolation,** a process in which the software creates pixels without actually capturing greater detail. The scanner is accompanied by software that allows you to exercise some degree of control over the scanned image's brightness, contrast, resolution, and image size. It is often possible for the user to vary the image's size by **cropping** (adjusting only the outside dimensions) or **scaling** (proportionally enlarging or reducing the entire image) and adjusting brightness and contrast. Flatbed scanners, depending on the model, accept originals with dimensions up to 11-by-14 inches. **Optical character recognition (OCR)** software allows the scanned text to be used in a regular word processing program. Recent software releases have come a long way toward improving the accuracy of the text translation, but there is still some improvement needed.

Output Devices

Output devices are all the hardware items that display information from the computer through audio, video, print, or electronic means. Video monitors and printers are the most common output devices.

The color **video monitor** accepts a computer's digital video signal directly and is the standard for computer applications. Although one or two interconnected large-screen video monitors may suffice when presenting information to a relatively small group of viewers, they are not ideal for large group presentations.

Video projectors such as the one shown in Figure 5–4 are capable of displaying a large (10-foot diagonal or larger) projected image. In a school setting, portable projectors are often housed in a library media center and circulated from there. The brightness of the screen image relates to the projector's output measured in **lumens.** The projected image's lower level of brightness and the presence of ambient room light striking the screen often demand a darkened room to maximize the impact of the projected image.

Printers. For many years, the most popular type of printer in schools was the **dot matrix printer** that prints by pins striking a ribbon and creating an impression on regular bond paper. These printers still persist mostly in commercial applications where multiple part carbon or carbonless forms are generated.

Figure 5–4 Video projector

A video projector used as an output device for group viewing *(Courtesy of InFocus, Inc.)*

Figure 5–5 Ink-jet printer

A schematic showing how an ink-jet printer works

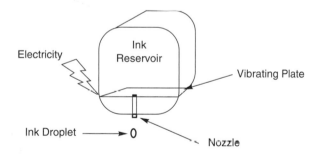

The low-cost **ink-jet printer** prints on regular bond paper or letterhead as well as on photo-finish paper, and is the most popular printer purchased for the home and school. An ink-jet printer has two main components, the *printhead* and the *ink tank*. In the printers commonly found in schools, these two components are usually combined in what is known as the *ink cartridge*. The ink-jet printer's print head squirts ink on the paper (Figure 5–5). An electric current is applied to a plate in the print head causing it to vibrate. This vibration causes dots of quick-drying ink to squirt through precisely controlled nozzles onto the paper. The size of the ink drop can be varied by varying the amount of electricity to the plate and hence the vibration.

Remembering that most print heads are an integral part of the ink cartridge, refilling ink cartridges many times is probably not a good idea since eventually the print head wears out and should be replaced. Ink-jet printers can achieve a resolution of 2400 × 1200 dpi or greater and are sometimes referred to as photo quality. With their low cost, ease of

151

Figure 5–6 Laser printer

A schematic showing how a laser printer works

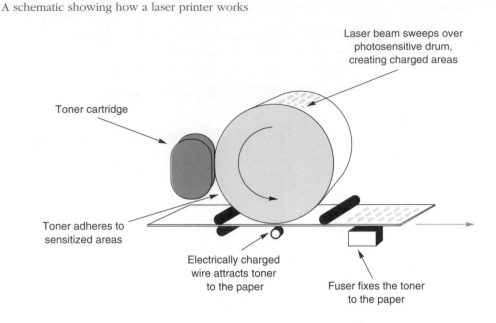

Laser beam sweeps over photosensitive drum, creating charged areas

Toner cartridge

Toner adheres to sensitized areas

Electrically charged wire attracts toner to the paper

Fuser fixes the toner to the paper

maintenance, high resolution, and full-color capability, it's no wonder that they have become so popular for many school, home, and office applications. Multifunction ink-jet printers combining printing, scanning, copying, and faxing, sometimes called "all-in-one" printers, are becoming popular as the choice for home or home office.

Laser printers produce high-quality printing of text and graphics onto plain bond or letterhead paper at a very high resolution, exceeding 1,200 **dots per inch (dpi).** This technology is very similar to the one employed by photocopiers. Laser printers are commonly found in school offices and on networks where several computers can share their use.

A laser printer receives information from a computer and stores it temporarily in its internal memory. It transfers this information as a code that governs the operation of a laser that strikes a photosensitive drum, as illustrated in Figure 5–6, setting up electrical charges on its surface. The drum rotates past a carbon particle toner reservoir, where toner is attracted to the charged areas. A sheet of paper is pressed against this toner-bearing drum and the toner transfers to the paper. Before exiting the printer, the paper passes through a thermal fuser section, which hardens and fixes the toner on the paper.

There are several questions to think about when you purchase a printer. Understanding its primary use will help you to answer the following questions. What is its resolution? How many pages can it print per minute? Would a multifunction printer save money in the long run? Will the printer accept your digital camera's memory card so you can print photos directly from the card? How expensive are the ink/toner cartridges? (Manufacturers make most of their profit on the ink and toner rather than on the printer.) We should caution you, however, to always buy brand-name ink cartridges from a reputable dealer. Over $2 billion in counterfeit ink cartridges are sold each year to unsuspecting individuals. These cartridges can spray ink, leak, clog print mechanisms, void your warranty, and cause permanent damage to your printer.

Modems. The telephone or cable **modem** (*mo*dulator–*dem*odulator) is both an input device and an output device. It translates digital computer information into signals that can be transmitted over telephone or cable lines and then back into a form that can be processed by a computer. The relatively inexpensive modem is a vital link allowing computers to exchange information. So-called "dial-up" modems that operate over normal telephone lines operate at a transmission speed of 56 **Kbps** (56,000 **bps,** bits per second). Modems that operate over cable or specialized phone lines are far faster yet. **Cable modems,** using existing cable television wiring, or **digital subscriber lines (DSLs)** from your phone company are up to 50 times faster than modems using ordinary telephone lines. Proponents of these technologies state that speeds of up to 8 **Mbps** (8,000,000 bps) are theoretically possible with DLS and 30 Mbps (30,000,000 bps) with a cable modem! The following table reviews some of the choices currently available. In reality, however, speeds are considerably slower than that.

Technology	Speed	Comments
Dial-up modem	56 Kbps	Uses phone lines
DSL	128–768 Kbps	Not available everywhere Slower as you get farther from phone company switch
Cable modem	1–7 Mbps	Fastest connection Constant connection The more users, the slower the service

Central Processing Unit

The central processing unit (CPU) is the heart of the computer system through which all instructions and information flow. This term is a throwback to large mainframe jargon, when the CPU was in fact a separate piece of equipment. The CPU is now often referred to as the microprocessor or often just as the "chip." An important consideration of computer CPUs is how fast they can access and carry out instructions and process data. This is known as **clock speed,** or the number of electronic cycles per second that a CPU will process. The more electronic cycles, the faster the CPU carries out instructions. Clock speed is measured in millions of cycles (megahertz or MHz) or billions of cycles (gigahertz or GHz) per second. Speeds exceeding 3.0 GHz are now quite common. Clock speed is not the sole determiner of CPU performance, however. The speed at which data can be transferred from memory to the CPU is also an important factor.

Some new computers employ two or more processor chips and some designs have more than one CPU on the same chip. This not only makes the computer faster but also allows it to run several programs more smoothly and efficiently at the same time.

Internal Memory

Computer manufacturers store instructions that govern the fundamental operations of the computer in a nonvolatile memory called read-only memory **(ROM).** Integrated circuits contain the ROM, which consists of instructions that, once encoded by the manufacturer, cannot be erased, written to, or modified in any way by the user. ROM is called nonvolatile, because it stays on the chip even when the power is turned off. Since the user has no control over the instructions in the ROM, it is often taken for granted. It is, however, responsible for *booting* the computer at start-up and providing important behind-the-scenes control of the computer.

When you load a prepared program, type a letter using a word processor, or enter information into a database management program, you are in fact entering instructions or data and placing them in the computer's random-access memory, or **RAM.** RAM is called **volatile memory,** because it requires a constant source of power to maintain itself. Should power fail for even a brief moment, the contents of RAM are lost forever. This is one reason why it is important to save your work onto the computer's hard disk at least every few minutes. We could write chapters on all of the horror stories we have heard from students about the papers, projects, and assignments that have been lost because of a momentary loss of power or because of a computer that froze and needed to be re-booted again. As careful as we try to be, we have also lost work. No one is immune! Users who are concerned about power outages or interruption usually connect their computer to a battery backup or uninterruptible power supply **(UPS).**

RAM is really only a temporary holding area, where the ideas are manipulated and the data organized before being passed on and stored more permanently on the hard drive or disk. In the case of RAM, bigger is indeed better. The more RAM available, the larger and more sophisticated the application program that can be run on the computer, the more applications can be open at one time, and the larger the file that can be processed. Graphics and digital video files, for instance, can consume a very large amount of RAM. The amount of RAM is measured by counting the potential bytes of information. A byte is usually the amount of memory required to represent one alphabetic or numeric character. The amount of RAM may be expressed in units of 1,000 bytes, represented by the symbol **K,** for **kilobytes,** units of 1 million by the symbol **MB,** for **megabytes,** or in units of 1 billion bytes by the symbol **GB,** for **gigabytes.** Computers today are sold with millions or even billions of bytes of RAM. A minimum of Botway 512 MB to 1 GB is now standard.

External Memory (Fixed Storage)

Auxiliary mass storage of programs and data is very important. Information such as pro-grams can be read by the computer (input), and files can be saved (output) to this media to be later retrieved from it. The most common form of fixed mass memory is the **hard disk.** It is composed of one or more rigid platters coated with a magnetic emulsion. The hard disk is a sealed unit that is usually enclosed in the computer's case and is then referred to as an internal hard disk or drive. Hard disks offer many gigabytes of storage. This amount of memory allows users to place many programs permanently on the hard disk drive.

When a program is read from a disk it is only copied into the computer's internal mem-ory and not removed from the disk. The actual process of searching for and loading a pro-gram is analogous to playing an audio CD. The computer disk and the audio CD are random-access devices with multiple access points. Many different files can be stored on the same disk. Each file has a unique identifier stored in a disk directory or catalog track. When selecting a song to play from an audio CD, you can punch in a code number that will select the beginning of a particular song as the CD is spinning. When you instruct the computer to load a particular file from a disk, the disk rotates while the read-write head scans the surface, looking for the beginning of the file you selected, which it then loads into memory. Combining the two factors of spinning the disk at high speed and quickly moving the read-write head in and out across its surface results in rapid random access to any information on the disk.

As hard disks are used over time, new files are added and old files are erased. Eventually, this causes newly saved files to be scattered, or **fragmented,** in segments at various points of the disk. This fragmentation erodes disk performance and slows down the retrieval of files. Running defragmentation utility software periodically cleans up this storage issue and im-proves disk performance. *Norton Utilities,* as mentioned earlier, will do this for you also.

It is important to remember to save important documents in more than one location, per-haps on a hard disk and on a removable medium as well. The authors of this text store the book chapters on their own desktop computer hard drives and exchange chapters between each other using email attachments and CD-Rs. Remember though, if your hard disk fails and it contains documents that you need, don't panic. There are many utility programs available specifically designed to recover crashed or damaged files or files that have been accidentally erased. It is a good idea to have a copy of a utility program such as *Norton Utilities®* in your school computer lab or media center for just this purpose! It is still a better idea to have multiple copies of all important data and documents.

External Memory (Removable Storage)

The primary type of removable storage in the 1980s and early 1990s was the **floppy disk,** a small wafer of flexible polyester film coated with an emulsion having magnetic properties similar to audio or videotape. It was encased in a 5 1/4-inch square, flexible protective plastic jacket, hence its name. The 3 1/2-inch **microdiskette** format—with its smaller size, improved protection against dirt and physical damage, and far greater storage capacity—replaced the 5 1/4-inch floppy disk in the late 1990s and early 2000s. Though encased in rigid material, it was still referred to as a "floppy." This form of storage has now become a thing of the past, replaced by compact flash media or optical media such as a compact disc, which we will discuss in a moment.

The reasonably priced USB 2.0 **flash drive, pen drive,** or **thumb drive** (Figure 5–7) is a secure and convenient data storage device in an ultra small package. It's about half the size of your thumb and one end of it plugs directly into a USB port on the computer. Holding upwards of 8 gigabytes of storage in a solid-state (no moving parts) memory system, it is a useful medium to transport data to and from school.

Because of the technology used to record and read CD-Audio, Photo-CD, CD-ROM, CD-R, CD-RW, DVD-ROM, and DVD-Video, they are referred to as **optical storage devices.** All of these discs are produced using a specially processed beam of light called a *laser beam* to encode and read information stored in tracks on their surface. The laser beam burns the encoded information into the surface of the disc. As shown in Figure 5–8, another laser beam reads a precise series of tiny depressions (called *pits*) and smooth reflective areas (called *lands*) on the bottom surface of an optical disc. The lands reflect the

Figure 5–7 Flash memory
USB flash memory is also known as a flash drive, pen drive, or thumb drive (©2006 Gateway, Inc., used with permission)

Figure 5–8 Optical disc system
A schematic showing how an optical disc system works

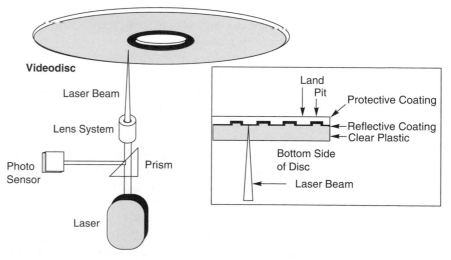

laser beam to a photo sensor and the pits diffract the light beam away from the sensor. This creates a series of on–off pulses, thereby producing a digital signal. The optical disc reader or player decodes the data into the original information that can be displayed on a video screen or printed as hard copy. We use the term *optical* because a laser beam is really a beam of light. Technological developments in laser disc optical storage have greatly facilitated the development of multimedia. Due to the vast amount of information present in multimedia programs, this technology has demanded a great deal of **external memory** storage. Optical disc technology has provided the answer. (You may have noticed that optical storage medium is generally spelled disc—with a *c*.)

CD-Audio. The *CD-audio* (compact disc-audio) digital format, introduced in 1983, has achieved phenomenal success, with millions of players installed all over the world. In only a few years it made record players obsolete. It has supplied the economy of scale and research and development funds that have contributed to the development of CD-ROM and other compact disc formats. Common digital audio formats and file extensions are listed in the following table.

Format	File Extension
AIFF (Mac)	.aif, .aiff
AU (Sun/Next)	.au
MP3	.mp3
Windows Media Audio	.wma
QuickTime	.qt
RealAudio	.ra, .ram
WAV	.wav

CD-ROM. This pervasive medium, the compact disc read-only memory (CD-ROM) was introduced in 1985, two years after the introduction of the CD-audio. This digital format disc measures only 4 3/4 inches but can contain approximately 650 megabytes of data, the equivalent of approximately 300,000 type-written pages of text. Even as far back as 1998, approximately 90 percent of computers manufactured included an internal CD-ROM drive. Although the medium began as a read-only technology, CD-Recordable (CD-R) and CD-Rewriteable (CD-RW) are two recording formats now readily available. The very inexpensive CD-Rs are recordable only once and usually store up to 80 minutes of audio or 700 MB of data. CD-RWs are more expensive, store up to 74 minutes of audio, and 650 MB of data, but are recordable more than once. To add to the complexity of this optical storage issue, you might note that there are CD-R and CD+R as well as CD-RW and CD+RW formats and that they are not compatible with one another.

Drives that can record CD-ROM and/or DVDs (below) are often called **burners** and the process of recording is called burning. Most new computers sold today include either a CD-R, CD-RW, DVD-R, or a combination drive that can record all three formats.

DVDs. Digital Versatile Disc (DVD), also known as Digital Video Disc, is one of the most exciting incarnations of the digital disc medium. DVD players have gained phenomenal acceptance in the home. DVD movie rentals have become the norm. DVD players and recorders are now a popular option on many personal computers. As with CD-ROMs there are many competing and incompatible formats: DVD-R, DVD+R, DVD-R/RW, DVD+R/RW, DVD-RAM, and dual-layer DVD ± RW (+R double layer) to name a few, so it is best to check on compatibility when purchasing a unit. A DVD can be played on either platform's (Windows or Macintosh) operating system. It physically resembles the CD-ROM but, by employing new compression technology, stores much more data (4.7 GB using older red-laser technology and up to 36 GB using the new blue-laser technology) than the CD-ROM. As well as storing vast amounts of data, a DVD can present a feature film containing high-quality video and multiple tracks of surround sound audio channels and 32 tracks of subtitle channels. Due to the DVD's large storage capacity, a film can include a number of different takes of the same scene and multiple endings from which the viewer can choose with the navigation control provided. It is easy to understand why in many areas, video rental stores now rent mostly DVDs and few, if any, videotapes.

The optical disc technologies have gained widespread acceptance as media for classroom instruction. Once a price/performance breakthrough occurs in large video screen, flat screen, and video projection, optical disc technologies will become universally accepted. The film camera is fast becoming an endangered species as digital still camera and DVD technology is improving and becoming more affordable. The following table reviews storage capacities of some common media.

3 1/2" floppy disk	=	1.44 MB
CD-ROM CD-RW	=	650 MB
CD-R	=	700 MB – 4.7 GB
DVD (red laser)	=	4.7 GB (theoretically 17 GB)
DVD (blue laser)	=	23 GB to 100+ GB
Smart Media (SM)	=	32 MB – 128 MB
XD Memory Card (XD)	=	16 MB – 1 GB
Secure Digital Card (SD)	=	32 MB – 2 GB
Mini SD (MiniSD)	=	32 MB – 512 MB
Multimedia Card (MMC)	=	32 MB – 1 GB
Reduced Size Multimedia Card (RS MMC)	=	128 MB – 1 GB
Memory Stick (MS/Duo/Pro)	=	32 MB – 4 GB
Compact Flash Card (CF)	=	128 MB – 8 GB
USB Drive(jump/flash/thumb)	=	16 MB – 8 GB
Microdrive	=	1 GB – 8 GB

USER INTERFACE

The **user interface** can be thought of as the interaction between human and machine. It is receiving a good deal of attention in the design of new **operating systems.** An operating system is a set of programming instructions that sits between the user and the computer. The operating system interprets your actions and executes the desired procedures. Early interfaces progressed from mechanical (throwing switches) to text based (typing command words). Microsoft's MS-DOS (Microsoft-Disk Operating System) used a text-based command line interface that gave the user a great deal of control over the functions of the computer, but it was complex, requiring the memorization of numerous command words.

Apple Computer revolutionized the desktop computer market when it introduced the Macintosh in 1984. It capitalized on research done by Xerox Corporation in the 1970s and was the first commercially successful computer to substitute a **graphical user interface (GUI)** for the text-based command line interface. The computers that run Microsoft Windows and Macintosh computers that you now use all employ GUIs that use icons, pointers, desktops, menus, and windows. OS X (Ten), based on the UNIX operating system, is the most recent Macintosh operating system. Since 1984, graphics have become much more important to the manner in which humans interact with computers. Microsoft introduced a graphic interface for IBM and compatible systems called Windows 1.0 in 1985. It has followed that with many versions through Windows Vista and its current derivative. The Linux operating system can be configured to control IBM compatible computers, Macintoshes, and most other CPUs. Operating systems can be

Figure 5–9 Icons

Various types of icons representing folders, applications, and files

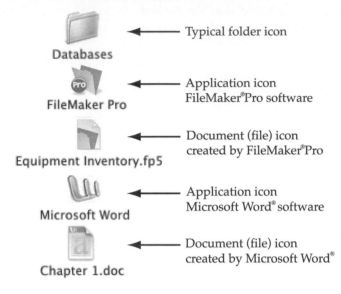

large, complex programs that may take up significant amounts of hard disk space. Presently, 75 percent of school computers and 95 percent of computers worldwide use a Windows operating system.

A third operating system is Linux. It was created by Linus Torvalds in Finland in 1991. Linux is a free, open source system. Because it is open source, users can modify, customize, and improve the OS at will. It is much more stable then either the Mac or Windows operating systems. Linux runs on Apple or PC machines and has saved many schools thousands of dollars in purchasing fees each year. A version of Linux developed especially for the educational environment is called Edubuntu, available from *http://www.ubuntu.com*. Because it is customizable and so stable, it is now the preferred platform for most of the world's critical computer systems.

All major computer operating systems are substituting the use of **icons,** or pictorial representations, for complex verbal commands. Instead of typing a command to retrieve a file from external memory, you might simply move a screen arrow to point to the icon of a file folder and click the mouse button to open the folder. The file can be opened immediately by pointing to it and double-clicking the mouse button. Should you decide later that the file is no longer needed, you can drag its icon to an icon of a trash can or recycle bin, thus "throwing away" or "recycling" the file. Here the screen action replicates kinesthetic behavior associated with everyday occurrences in the work environment.

In examining Figure 5–9, it is easy to see that folder icons look very much like manila file folders used in a filing cabinet. Software publishers design their own unique icons to represent their software and the files or documents created by their software. Program and document icons can be dragged to folder icons in order to store them in that folder. Folders may even be placed inside other folders.

Just as the GUI and pen-based systems have revolutionized the use of the computer, the next generation user interface may take us into brand new territory. The research and development in improving the user interface is focused on making use of the computer as natural and as easy as possible so that the hardware use becomes transparent to the purpose at hand. Rather than being overly conscious of the hardware and concerned with how to perform a computer task, the user should be allowed to concentrate on the content and nature of the problem being addressed.

HANDHELD COMPUTER TECHNOLOGY

Handheld computers, sometimes mistakenly called PDAs (personal digital assistants), palmtops (after the popular Palm® models), or personal PCs, are appearing in schools around the country. Due to the availability of software specifically designed for K–12 schools, increased functionality, and lower costs, many teachers are incorporating them into their classes. These devices use one of two operating systems: Palm OS with about 75 percent of the market and Windows Mobile with most of the rest. Palm OS handhelds are ideal for schools because of their ease of use and school software availability. Windows Mobile is harder to use, crashes more easily, and does not have the school-based software base Palm OS has. Most handhelds contain an address book, notepad, date book, and to-do list and also may come with specially designed versions of Word, Excel, and PowerPoint. Free Web browsing and email software is also available. Handheld computers can be connected to a computer with wires, infrared, and/or wireless technology. A fast Web search for software will find much free and low-cost educational software available for these compact and inexpensive helpers.

Tablet computers (Figure 5–10) are an interesting evolution of the laptop computer. They have been called a cross between a laptop and a personal digital assistant. They are designed to meld the portability and ease of a pad of paper with the computing power and wireless capability of a laptop. Most run on the *Windows XP Tablet PC®* operating system. Many look like and can be used just like ordinary laptops with the following difference. The screen can be swiveled 180 degress and lay flat facing up over the keyboard. It is now possible to write directly on the screen with a supplied stylus. The screen acts like a notepad and not like a touchscreen. Programs allow you to save the handwritten text, equations, and drawings or even automatically convert the handwritten text to typed text. In either case, it is possible to search the handwritten and typed text for words and phrases and synchronize the text with audio clips and presentations and other multimedia files using such applications as *Microsoft Office OneNote®*.

Maria B. Vonada/Merrill

Figure 5–10 Tablet computer

A portable computer smaller than a laptop (© 2006 Gateway, Inc., used with permission)

Figure 5–11 Treo®

The Palm® Treo™ has become a popular smartphone (Courtesy of Palm, Inc.)

Cell phones and **smartphones** provide an incredible array of functions from storing contact information to keeping track of appointments, sending and receiving text messages, surfing the Internet, and even sending and receiving phone messages. Most of us probably have a cell phone tucked away in a pocket or bag. In 2006, Ithaca College in upstate New York hosted the first annual Cellflix Festival, a competition of films shot entirely on mobile phones! A further evolution is the smartphone such as the *Palm® Treo™* (Figure 5–11) and the *Blackberry®*. Smartphones integrate the functionality of a cell phone, a personal digital assistant (PDA), and other information appliances. It has become increasingly difficult to define the functionality of a smartphone or how they differ from cell phones as more gadgets and utilities are added. In the not too distance future, the smartphone may be the all-in-one appliance that we will not be able to be without!

NETWORKING

A cluster of interconnected computers and peripheral devices sharing information is called a **network.** Networks are constructed in order to facilitate the exchange of information and to maximize the use of software and hardware. Networks span the globe. Effective long-distance communications are in fact moving us toward the promised *global village*. As teachers are becoming more comfortable with telecommunications, they are exploring the concept of *global classrooms*. These are composed of computers in classrooms around the world interconnected for the purpose of sharing information, ideas, interests, collaborative projects, and questions. Children and young adults in global classrooms are indeed in the process of becoming citizens of the world.

LET'S GO INTO THE CLASROOM
Learning in Hand

As a fifth-grade teacher, my students and I were pioneers in using Palm handheld computers for learning. Handhelds were very new to educators in 2001, but many were keen to the idea of using inexpensive handheld devices to put computers in the hands of learners. My students and I wanted to use the tiny computers for more than just making appointments, keeping notes, and maintaining checklists. After all, handhelds are tiny computers capable of running a variety of software programs.

There were few Palm software applications written specifically for students when my class and I began handheld computing together. We, therefore, adapted the built-in organizer applications for classroom use. For example, instead of keeping names and numbers in the Palm Address Book, we stored vocabulary words and meanings. Also, the Palm Memo Pad was used for editing practice. I would beam students a paragraph that contained errors and it was their job to find and fix them. It seemed that whatever the activity, students were engaged in their learning because they absolutely enjoyed having their own personal computers.

As more classrooms across the globe embraced handheld computing, more educational software appeared, and much of it was free. For instance, *Quizzler* provided a way for me to make customized multiple-choice quizzes. Students used *Quizzler* to prepare for tests because they appreciated the instant feedback and ease of use. Furthermore, many electronic books became freely available. I was able to make my own eBooks tailored to my curriculum and my students, complete with hypertext, images, and chapters. Students stored these eBooks on their handhelds for an anytime reference. Students could even make bookmarks and take notes inside of their eBooks. Additionally, *MathCard* helped my students practice their multiplication facts in an interactive manner.

Despite scouring the Web for Palm applications, there were certainly things we wanted our handhelds to do, but no software to do it. We posted online our "Palm Software Wishlist" that contained a dozen programs we wanted to see developed for handhelds. Incredibly, programmers volunteered to create these applications and offer them to anyone for free. It was an amazing experience for my students as they were beta testers for software that would eventually find ways onto student handhelds around the world. Programmers from the United States, Canada, and Denmark created applications like *MathAce*, *SpellIt*, and *Dictate*. One of our favorites is *GoneMad*. It's a Palm version of the silly word game Mad Libs. *GoneMad* comes with three sample stories that we wrote. However, the real fun comes from students making their own stories for others to complete. Like paper Mad Libs, *GoneMad* stories elicit giggles and guffaws, all while students practice valuable writing skills.

Currently, as a technology specialist, I coach teachers to integrate technology into their everyday lessons. I help teachers understand that handhelds are not a complete substitute for desktop and laptop computers. However, they can free up some computer lab time, empower students at school and at home, and access an ever-growing library of mostly free software.

Tony Vincent
Technology Integration Specialist
Willowdale Elementary School
Omaha, Nebraska
http://learninginhand.com

Networking offers several important advantages to schools. A network permits resource sharing, that is, the sharing of software and peripheral equipment. Buying network licenses is considerably less expensive than purchasing multiple copies of individual software packages. Without a network, one peripheral device (such as a printer or a scanner) can serve only one computer. A network allows many computers to access connected peripheral devices regardless of where they are physically located.

A network also promotes resource management. Individual users do not have to have every program or file on a disk because those resources can reside on a central network server. Many school networks employ student data management software that provides security and recordkeeping functions. Finally, and most important, a network facilitates information exchange and student collaboration. Students can read files created by a teacher, exchange files among themselves and a teacher, communicate with others by email, or, with the proper software, work simultaneously and interactively on a project. When the network consists of devices that are housed in close proximity to one another such as in one building or on a campus, the network is referred to as a **local area network,** or **LAN.** A network that spans greater distances or covers a wide geographical area is called a **wide area network,** or **WAN.**

Wireless Communications Hardware

Wireless communications is taking the country by storm. In the mid to late 1990s, the telephone industry led the way with cellular and satellite telephones. This revolution paved the way for wireless Internet services and wireless networks now appearing in schools, homes, airports, and even coffee shops. Apple Computer and Lucent Technologies were the first manufacturers to introduce consumer wireless computer networking with their *AirPort*™ feature available on Apple's desktops and laptops in 1999. *AirPorts* can be employed by Windows-based computers as well. The major computer manufacturers such as Dell and Gateway followed soon after. These wireless systems, transmitting data at up to 54 Mbs, include a base station that can transmit and receive data over airwaves thus eliminating the need to wire computers and peripherals together. Most wireless networks use one of the IEEE 802.11 family of standards. You may have heard the term **Wi-Fi,** which is short for Wireless Fidelity, a generic term for any device that uses one of these wireless

Maria B. Vonada/Merrill

LET'S GO INTO THE CLASSROOM
A Wireless Classroom

We've used our wireless laptop lab to complete many lessons. However, one stands out above the rest—our biome project. As a fourth-grade teacher, one skill that needs to be covered in science is creating a food chain, along with expository paragraph writing in language arts, and exploring different regions in social studies. We combined these benchmarks by having our students work in groups to research different regions and biomes.

Each group picked a region to research. Within that region, they found a biome, the plants and animals in that biome, and created a slide show depicting the food chain for that biome. Each food chain was different, because the plants and animals were specific to the chosen biome. Finding good pictures of some animals proved challenging, but each group managed to find exactly what they were looking for on the Internet.

Groups worked in the wireless laptop lab collecting information and graphics to be used in their slide show. The wireless laptops added the mobility to our lesson that we needed. The students could gather in any configuration needed to work on their projects. Also, keeping their information in a folder on the networked drive enable the students to have easy access to their "saved" work. Each day students simply took up where they left off the day before by opening their folder on the networked drive and adding new information to their folder. Once enough information was collected, they were ready to compile this information into a PowerPoint slide show.

The students saved their finished slide shows in two different formats: (1) presentation format and (2) Web page format. The reason we did this was because not all computers have the Microsoft PowerPoint program. Saving the slide show under a Web page format would enable the slide show to be opened with any computer that had access to the Internet. Because the slide shows were also saved on the networked drive, they were easily accessed in all classrooms. Even so, we saved the shows to disks as well to be sure to have access to them no matter where we were for the presentation.

Completed projects were presented to the class and neighboring classes. The students also created a poster-sized food chain, using a word processing program to be displayed outside our classroom. This project was completed in approximately two weeks and the students were so excited about their work that they brought in disks to copy their slide show to show family members.

Vicki Ersek
Fourth-Grade Teacher
Albany Upper Elementary School (Louisiana)

network standards. Wi-Fi devices are appearing all over allowing wireless access in hotels, shops, coffee shops, and even on the street. HomeRF is a wireless standard developed for home use and Bluetooth is a short-range standard that is primarily used to replace cables that connect devices such as a printer or handheld computer to a desktop computer. A summary of several common standards is presented in the following table.

Bluetooth (computer to peripherals)	=	1 MBps (30 feet)
HomeRF (computer to peripherals)	=	2 MBps (150 feet)
802.11b (Wi-Fi)	=	11 MBps (300 feet)
802.11a (Wi-Fi 5)	=	54 MBps (10–30 feet)
802.11g (current standard)	=	54 MBps (500+ feet)
802.11i (under development at publication time)		
802.16 (WiMax)	=	70 MBps (31 miles)

Wireless networking offers all of the advantages of regular networking and one additional benefit—cost. There is no need to map out and run wires between the various pieces of equipment throughout the building. Wiring may be particularly difficult and costly in older school buildings. Many schools are purchasing mobile carts that hold a number of wireless laptops and a wireless receiving hub or access point. These carts are rolled into the classroom, the wireless hub is plugged into the school's network or a telephone line, and the students are able to use their wireless laptops without having to worry about wires to connect them to the network. Mobile wireless computer carts bring the learning right into the classroom. Space is freed up because a separate computer lab is not needed and cost can be reduced because costly wiring is not needed throughout a classroom/computer lab. Students are also freed up to work in comfortable groups as they carry their wireless laptop to special areas of the room and perhaps to the media center if it is within range or it has its own wireless access point. Present radio frequency wireless hardware can send and receive signals up to 300 feet, even through walls, floors, and ceilings. If you set up a wireless network at home or school, make sure it is password protected so others can not use it.

LET'S REVIEW

Viewing the computer as a system of components for input, operation, and output, we discussed several input peripherals such as the mouse, scanner, and digital camera whose function it is to enter data into the computer and make accessing of computer software easier for the user. Output peripherals such as the printer and the digital projector display information from the computer through audio, video, print, and electronic means.

The older parallel or serial connections have been largely replaced by the fast, cross-platform FireWire or USB. External storage devices such as CD-ROMs and DVDs were explained. We also discussed software components of the computer used for its operation such as the computer operating system.

Networking is the interconnecting of computers with each other and with input and output devices to facilitate sharing of information and equipment. We talked about wireless telecommunications and discussed wireless computing in schools as the wave of the present.

You will come in contact with most of the items we discussed. They are all very common; in fact, many of you own most of these right now.

LET'S PRACTICE

To complete the specified exercises online, go to the Chapter Exercises Module in Chapter 3 of the Companion Website.

1. Review a copy of a recent *PCWorld, MacWorld,* or other computer magazine. What are some of the newer computer technologies or programs that they are talking about? How would these advances fit into an educational environment?
2. Research the newest offerings that Windows (PC) and Macintosh manufacture. What pros and cons do you see with each operating system?
3. Describe the difference between RAM and ROM. How much RAM does a modern computer have?

4. We can store data on an internal hard drive, a 3.5-inch floppy, a USB (thumb) drive, and a CD-ROM. What are the pros and cons of each storage medium? How large are the internal hard drives on the computers in your school? How large are typical hard drives on the new models?
5. On which of the storage devices in number 4 do you store your classwork and homework? Why have you chosen this storage medium? Do you back up your work? Is this a good idea? Why or why not?
6. Check some prices and features for the latest printers. Choose one for a lab in the school in

which you may teach. Write a short note to the principal indicating your choice and giving reasons why you chose this particular printer.

7. Research the latest models of digital cameras. Which model would you purchase for home use and which would you purchase for your classroom? Write a short note to the principal indicating your choice and giving reasons why you chose this particular model of digital camera.

8. Discuss the pros and cons of a wired and a wireless classroom. Research some schools in your area. Are they wired or wireless? Why do you think this is the case?

9. Research the different computer models on the market. Which model would you purchase for home use and which would you purchase for your classroom? If these are different models, why did you make this choice? Write a short note to the principal indicating your choice and giving reasons why you chose this particular model of computer.

10. Call a local school library media specialist or computer coordinator. Ask them if you could tour a school computer lab and discuss the type of network it has. Report your results to the class.

PORTFOLIO DEVELOPMENT EXERCISES

To complete this exercise online, go to the Digital Portfolio Module in Chapter 3 of the Companion Website.

One of the NET•S standards covered in this chapter was "Students demonstrate a sound understanding of the nature and operation of technology systems" under *Category 1: Basic operations and concepts.* Begin to develop your own portfolio of lesson plans that demonstrates your ability to have your students reach the NET•S standards.

1. Design a lesson plan activity for elementary, middle school, or high school students in which they design a computer lab. They should be able to give reasons why they decided on the number of computers, the computer operating system, and whether the lab would be wired or wireless. This lesson should demonstrate that your students have achieved the standard. Be sure to include a system of evaluation for your students' understanding and competence to ensure that they have met this standard.

2. Adapt the lesson plan activity you developed in exercise 1 for students to evaluate each other's work.

GLOSSARY

bar code reader	A device that translates the sequence of spaced thick and thin lines to the computer, enabling it to identify an object
bps	A measure of data transmission speed between computers in *bits per second*
burner	A term used to describe a drive that records data onto optical discs such as a CD or a DVD
cable modem	A peripheral device that connects a computer to a television cable system
cell phones	A mobile telephone that can be used over a wide area by connecting to towers scattered through a designated area
central processing unit (CPU)	A chip in the computer where all parts of the system are linked together and where the calculations and manipulation of data take place
clock speed	The number of electronic pulses per second that a CPU will process
cropping	Controlling the size of an image without affecting the size of any of its components
digital camera	A device that captures and stores still images in a digital format
digital subscriber line (DSL)	A service available from some phone companies for fast Internet access
digital video camera	A device that captures and stores moving images in a digital format
dot matrix printer	An impact printer that uses a series of electrically hammered pins to create characters composed of a pattern of dots
dots per inch (dpi)	The number of discrete elements produced by a printer
driver	A small program added to the operating system that allows the operating system to control certain hardware peripherals (e.g., a printer)

extension	A small program added to the operating system that allows the application software to interact with the operating system
external memory	The auxiliary storage of programs and data, often on a removable medium
FireWire	A very-high-speed connection between peripherals and the computer that allows for the transfer of large amounts of data
firmware	Software that is permanently stored on a computer chip
flash drive	An ultra-small, pocket-sized removable memory device
floppy disk	An external storage medium made of flexible polyester film with magnetic properties
fragmented	The dispersal of files stored on disk into segments scattered at various points on the disk
gigabyte (GB)	One thousand megabytes, or one billion bytes, used as a reference to memory storage capacity
graphical user interface (GUI)	The on-screen use of pictorial representations (icons) of objects
graphics tablet	A flat input device on which the user writes
handheld computers	Small handheld devices that can perform most, if not all of the functions of a computer. These functions may include all of the Microsoft Office functions along with Web browsing and email Palm is a manufacturer of handheld computers
hard disk	An external storage medium consisting of a rigid platter coated with a magnetic emulsion and not removable from the disk drive
hardware	Tangible computer parts such as a keyboard, mouse, disk drive, and printer
hot-swappable	The ability to plug or unplug peripherals from the computer system without having to shut down and restart the computer
icon	A pictorial representation of an object
ink-jet printer	A printer that uses a series of electronically controlled nozzles to create characters composed of a pattern of dots squirted onto the paper
input peripherals	Equipment whose function is to enter data into the computer
interpolation	A process in which the scanner software makes up pixels without actually capturing greater detail from the scanned image
kilobyte (K)	One thousand bytes (actually 1,024 in computer terms); used as a reference to memory capacity
Kbps	A measure of a modem's data transmission speed between computers in thousands of bits per second
keyboard	The primary input device for the computer; it generates a digital code that can be understood by the microprocessor
laser printer	A printer that uses a laser beam to create an image on a photosensitive drum and transfers this by means of carbon toner to paper
local area network (LAN)	A network composed of devices located in close proximity to one another
lumens	A measure of a video projector's output affecting the brightness of the screen image
megabyte (MB)	One thousand kilobytes or one million bytes, used as a reference to memory capacity
Mbps	A measure of a modem's data transmission speed between computers in millions of bits per second
microdiskette	A 3 1/2-inch format that houses a magnetic disk in a rigid plastic protective case
modem	A device that translates digital computer information into analog signals that can be transmitted over telephone or cable lines and translates analog signals into a digital form that can be processed by a computer
mouse	A handheld device connected to the input port of a computer, which moves a pointer on the screen
network	The interconnection of computers to allow multiple users to access software and to exchange information
operating system	An operating system enables the central processing unit (CPU) to control and communicate with internal and external devices
optical character recognition (OCR)	Software that allows scanners to digitize text so that it can be used and manipulated as regular text in a word processor
optical storage device	Storage peripherals that are written to and accessed by laser light beams such as CD-ROMs and DVDs
output peripherals	Equipment that displays information from the computer
pen drive	See *flash drive*
pixel	Abbreviation for **pic**ture **el**ement. One pixel is a single point in a graphic image. More pixels in the same area create a sharper image

166

RAM	Random-access memory; volatile internal memory that is erased if power to the computer system is interrupted
resolution	The sharpness of an image. Used to describe output from graphic images, monitors, and printers
ROM	Read-only memory; constant memory contained in an integrated circuit or chip that cannot be modified by the user
scaling	Controlling the size of an image and, in direct proportion, all of its components
scanner	An input peripheral that digitizes photos, line drawings, and text by reflecting light off their surface
smartphone	A mobile (cell) phone that can connect to the Internet allowing it to browse the Web and send and receive email. Most include a camera and software to allow tasks found in a personal digital assistant such as address books, calendars, to do lists, games, and other tasks
software	Information and directions to control the computer; a computer program preserved on a recording medium
speech recognition device	A software program with accompanying microphone that changes the spoken word into text and can be used in a word processing program
tablet computers	A notebook computer capable of storing text and free-hand graphics that are written on the screen with a stylus or may be added using voice or an on-screen keyboard. Once inputted, text can be manipulated as in a word-processing document
thumb drive	See *flash drive*
trackpad	A pressure-sensitive pad, often found on laptop computers, on which the user presses a finger to move a pointer on the screen
Universal Serial Bus (USB)	A powerful, cross-platform communication standard developed to link the computer to external devices
Universal Product Code (UPC)	Universal Product Code; a sequence of thick and thin lines on consumer products spaced to identify a specific item, read by an optical bar code reader
Uninterruptible Power Supply (UPS)	An uninterruptible power supply is a device that provides emergency power from batteries in the event of an AC power failure
user interface	The interaction between human and machine
video monitor	A television set that has been manufactured to accept a video signal
video projector	A device that accepts a video signal and projects an image onto a screen
volatile memory	Internal memory that is available and accessible to the user and requires a constant source of power to maintain itself
wide area network (WAN)	A network that spans great distances or covers a wide geographic area
Wi-Fi	Wireless Fidelity; a generic term for any device that uses one of the IEEE 802.11 wireless transmission standards

REFERENCES AND SUGGESTED READINGS

Dennison, R. F. (2000, May). Don't use a hammer: Appropriate educational uses based upon the characteristics of network tools. *TechTrends, 44*(4), 26–29.

Descy, D. (2000, April). "Good morning, HAL-9000" . . . "Good morning, Don" . . . A primer on speech recognition software. *TechTrends, 44*(3), 4–6.

Joss, M. (2001). Now playing in schools: Digital video. *Technology & Learning, 22*(3), 17–19.

Pownell, D., & Bailey, G. D. (2000, May). The next small thing. *Learning and Leading with Technology, 27*(8), 47–49.

Randall, N. (2000, April 18). Setting up a webcam. *PC Magazine,* 138–140.

Varvel, V. E., & Thurston, C. (2002, Summer). Perceptions of a wireless network. *Journal of Research on Technology in Education, 34*(4), 487–502.

Classroom Applications as Learning Tools

LET'S LOOK AT LEARNING TOOLS

Remember our metaphor that a tool is a medium for completing some work more efficiently and extending the user's ability. We either create a tool or select one from a variety of existing tools and apply it to the task at hand to solve a problem (for example, we use a screwdriver to fasten something, a sewing machine to assemble clothing, an automobile to transport us swiftly and comfortably, and a word processor to record our thoughts in a quick, flexible manner). Accepting this definition of a tool allows us to see its intervention between the user and the information to be created, received, stored, manipulated, or disseminated. The student who locates and downloads information from the Internet, uses a database to search for additional information, then uses a word processor to write a report and a graphics program to draw a map for inclusion in the report is using the computer as a tool to enhance efficiency and effectiveness in response to the problem at hand.

It's time, once again, to check our own perceptions and to ask ourselves the question, "What is technology?" Technicians carry screwdrivers around in their pockets and tinker with hardware, such as a computer. Technologists, however, understand how to use that hardware and related software as problem-solving tools. The tools or equipment—the computer, the DVD player, the camcorder, the ubiquitous overhead projector—all are the "things" of technology. To be most successful as a teacher, these things of technology have to become almost transparent. We don't want to call attention to them but rather, as technologists, focus our efforts on the problems we are trying to solve, the objective we are attempting to reach.

The factory model compared productivity with efficiency, defined it as producing a tangible product, and was often linked to the notion of accomplishing menial, repetitive tasks. A more productive worker built more widgets than a less productive one. All too often, the term *productivity tool* has been used with the limited factory model vision. The constructivist perspective demands a broader understanding. In schools, the term *productivity tool* has been easily understood and readily applied to word processors, graphics, spreadsheets, and databases. A deeper understanding would apply it to learning with computers and would also compare productivity with effectiveness. Rather than limiting our view to developing a product often associated with the performance of clerical or manual tasks, we have begun to see productivity as using tools (such as computers) to maximize or extend our innate capabilities to surmount challenges and solve problems. Productive learners might learn more but they also learn better. Productive writers and artists are not only prolific but, using our definition, have a greater impact on their readers, viewers, and listeners.

Is the computer a productivity tool for the secretary? Absolutely! It enhances the performance of repetitive clerical tasks; but it is also a productivity tool for the administrator to make projections, find information, and communicate effectively. It is a productivity tool for the teacher who selects appropriate hardware or software and adapts it to the instructional, management, or research task at hand. A computer is a productivity tool whenever it is used to assist individuals in solving problems. Students are increasing their productivity by developing sophisticated skills in the creation, access, manipulation, and transmission of information in order to respond to an assignment or solve a problem. We are witnessing the evolution of some time-tested teaching and learning strategies and philosophies as they change to account for new tools and innovations. The computer is a tool that can give students a wider variety of educational experiences than has ever before been offered.

Learning with Still and Motion Graphics Tools

ADVANCE ORGANIZER

1. What are some tools you might use for creating computer graphics?

2. What are bit-mapped graphics?

3. What are vector, or object-oriented, graphics?

4. What is clip art and how can it be used?

5. What is a practical application of computer graphics that you might use as a teacher in designing instructional materials for your classroom?

6. How can you adjust lighting, improve composition, and create layers in Adobe® Photoshop Elements®?

171

NETS•T Foundation Standards and Performance Indicators Addressed in This Chapter

I. Technology operations and concepts
   A. demonstrate introductory knowledge, skills, and understanding of concepts related to technology (as described in the ISTE National Education Technology Standards for Students)
   B. demonstrate continual growth in technology knowledge and skills to stay abreast of current and emerging technologies
II. Planning and designing learning environments and experiences
   A. design developmentally appropriate learning opportunities that apply technology-enhanced instructional strategies to support the diverse needs of learners.
III. Teaching, learning, and the curriculum
   A. facilitate technology-enhanced experiences that address content standards and student technology standards
   B. use technology to support learner-centered strategies that address the diverse needs of students
   C. apply technology to develop students' higher order skills and creativity
   D. manage student learning activities in a technology-enhanced environment
IV. Assessment and evaluation
   B. use technology resources to collect and analyze data, interpret results, and communicate findings to improve instructional practice and maximize student learning
V. Productivity and professional practice
   A. use technology resources to engage in ongoing professional development and lifelong learning
   C. apply technology to increase productivity
   D. use technology to communicate and collaborate with peers, parents, and the larger community in order to nurture student learning
VI. Social, ethical, legal, and human issues
   B. apply technology resources to enable and empower learners with diverse backgrounds, characteristics, and abilities

LET'S LOOK AT THIS CHAPTER

The adage "a picture is worth a thousand words" is an appropriate beginning to any basic discussion about **graphics.** Teachers appreciate the value of this statement because pictorial representations have always been an important means for communicating ideas and concepts to students quickly and accurately. Our earliest ancestors used graphics on the walls of caves or rock outcroppings in Europe, Africa, and Asia, as did Native Americans on skins and bones to record great hunts and other events. Egyptians and Central and South American Indians carved events and rituals on their temples and pyramids. Today, every schoolroom in the country has a map, poster, bulletin board, or other graphic display to brighten the room and inform the students.

Many different graphics tools have been used in instructional situations. The chalkboard, drawings, flowcharts, diagrams, print of different sizes, underlining, and arrows are common tools for enhancing

Liz Moore/Merrill

the communication of ideas to students. Video recorders, overhead projectors, photographs, posters, maps, illustrated textbooks, and television have also added different dimensions to our capabilities in using visuals to affect the learning experience. Each tool expands the user's ability to refine the presentation of ideas and to emphasize key parts through motion, color, size, and blank space. The computer is a visual tool that can present many of these capabilities interactively, adding even more power to graphic communication. Schools have recognized the uniqueness of visual literacy, and many include visual literacy skills training as part of their curriculum.

TOOLS FOR CREATING GRAPHICS

Drawing and painting computer programs have been used by teachers and students alike for decades for three general purposes: (1) to *create* graphics to use for a variety of purposes; (2) to *change* graphics that have been obtained from other sources such as previously created graphics, clip art, scanned images, and images captured by digital cameras; and (3) to *convert* images from one file format to another to make them accessible to other software programs and the Web. Adobe Illustrator®, CorelDRAW, Kid Pix Deluxe, Kid Works Deluxe, Painter™, Canvas™, Photoshop Elements™, and other graphics programs are available for Windows and Macintosh to facilitate the creation of worksheets, newsletters, bulletin boards, and other displays of graphics and text. TuxPaint is a viable alternative to consider. It is a free, open source software program almost identical to Kid Pix. Download a copy from *http://www.newbreedsoftware.com* to save money and licensing fees. TuxPaint has many clip art archives that can also be freely distributed and used. Although these graphics materials can be created in other ways, the computer, along with digital cameras and scanners, makes it easier and less time consuming and thereby stimulates teachers to reach out and maximize their creative efforts.

Digital Cameras

Digital still cameras have become extremely popular and for the most part have replaced film cameras. Most models are easy to use and store a large number of digital images on removable media such as the small postage-stamp-size cards called CompactFlash, Multi-media, Secure Digital, or Memory Stick. The media is sometimes labeled 8×, 12×, 40×, or higher to indicate the transfer rate for the information from the camera's chip to the memory device. The higher the rate, the shorter the interval required between each picture taken. Some cameras can be connected directly to a computer, or its memory card can be placed in a card reader and the images then downloaded to a computer. Once in the computer, the images may be manipulated in a variety of ways by using appropriate software provided by the camera manufacturer, computer manufacturer, or other editing programs and stored as graphic files. In our opinion, Adobe *Photoshop Elements*® is an excellent photo editor and reasonably priced. Other fine programs are Apple's *iPhoto*® and Microsoft's *Picture It*®. They are great tools for preparing photographic images to incorporate into presentations, newsletters, and pamphlets. Many digital cameras can also record short digital video clips as well as sound.

The resolution of input devices such as a digital camera is measured in pixels (*pic*ture e*le*ments). A pixel is a single dot or point in a graphic image. The more pixels in a given area, the higher the resolution or clarity of an image. Image resolution is expressed in **pixels per inch (ppi).** Most digital cameras use a charge-coupled device (CCD) to capture an image. The CCD changes light falling on it into electric energy. The greater the number of pixels on the CCD, the higher the image resolution captured by the camera and the greater the capability to enlarge and print photos without losing detail. The capability of the CCD is expressed in **megapixels** (millions of pixels). It is generally accepted that a 2-megapixel camera is sufficient for printing uncropped 4-by-6-inch photos or displaying web or screen images. A 3-megapixel camera is better for 5-by-7-inch prints, and a 4-megapixel camera is required for 8-by-10-inch prints or for cropping and enlarging of prints. Cameras are now available in 7, 12, and 14 megapixels. The ideal image resolution appears to be between 150 ppi and 360 ppi. Be careful not to confuse this with printer resolution, which is measured in dots per inch (dpi). High printer resolution may be achieved by layering dots one on another, but it may not necessarily mean a higher quality photograph.

Two methods are used to zoom in on the scene being photographed: optical zoom and digital zoom. The optical zoom capability (using a zoom lens like that found on a film camera) actually enlarges the image reaching the camera. The digital zoom only enlarges the pixels already captured by the camera. This process will enlarge the image, making objects in the composition appear closer, but will also lower the image resolution. When

Liz Moore/Merrill

LET'S GO INTO THE CLASSROOM
School/Community Connection

I work in San Fernando High School in North Los Angeles. Many people would write our school off as a lost cause. We have more than 4,000 students in a school designed to hold 1,700 . . . 83 percent score below grade level . . . and many are also struggling with English as a second language. Technology? Only 4 percent of the students have access to any technology at home! We do have a great resource though: our students! My fellow teacher, Veronica Marek, and I decided to use desktop movie production to magnify our students' excitement and passion for learning, hopefully to take them to heights we could only dream of achieving!

Veronica and I decided to have the students take a personal look at immigration and the American dream. We decided rather than talk at great lengths about Ellis Island and the vast waves of European immigrants as many texts do, we would instead focus on real-world, touch-me immigration: the real and personal stories of the students' families, their friends, and themselves.

We had the students gather family photos and documents to design and produce a living, breathing history . . . their history. This assignment preserved their family history and also opened meaningful, personal dialogues between students and parents. Students learned real-world lessons about their families and their heritage. They discovered where they crossed the border and considered their goals and expectations.

Making desktop movies let my students know that they, their families, and their stories are important. They are important to me, important to the school, and important to the community. Videotaping parents and grandparents connected meaningful education to the home. At home and at school and in our student's minds, thinking, writing, and research were all given real-world meaning. With careful planning, actually putting the video, documents, and photographs together on our iMac DVs using the built-in iMovie software was a breeze. The ease with which it was accomplished made the technology practically transparent to the project. They and their projects were one. Going the extra mile to get it "just right" was exciting and fun.

The school and community learning connection did not stop at production time. When it came time to share their movies . . . their lives . . . students asked me to arrange a special evening presentation for the community. The students acted as ushers and even catered the event. Parents and grandparents filled the audience. The video stories were shown with pride and a huge sense of accomplishment . . . and by the end of the evening you could not find a dry eye in the house.

Marco Torres
Social Studies Teacher
Director, San Fernando Education Technology Team
San Fernando High School
San Fernando, California

purchasing a digital camera, the megapixels and the optical zoom numbers are important factors if you plan to enlarge your images. As with film cameras, lens quality and camera body construction play a role in pricing.

Digital video cameras are making an impact on schools. Many computers now have FireWire or USB 2.0 connections and come loaded with video editing software, which makes it possible for very young students with little training to produce professional-looking edited movies. *iMovie*™ from Apple Computer was the first simple digital video editing software. iMovie, along with *iDVD*® allows the user to capture, edit, add titles and special effects, and save movies on DVD. Both are part of Apple's *iLife®* software suite. Similar video editing software such as *Windows Movie Maker®* (also free), *VideoStudio,®* MovieWorks,® and *Pinnacle Studio DV®* are also available for Windows machines. Other popular video editing software are *Avid Express Pro™* and Apple's *Final Cut™.*

CAMERAS AND LITERACY

Cameras can be powerful visual literacy tools as well as tools used to enhance verbal literacy. One of the authors directed a six-week summer writing workshop aimed at middle school students. These students were given a list of topics chosen from their school environment and directed to write about one. The students then signed out inexpensive cameras from school, because they were to use photos to help illustrate their writing. Students learned how to use the cameras and a few simple rules of composition. They were encouraged to let their pictures tell their story. Students were then allowed to experiment and hone their picture-taking skills. While this was happening, the research skills of these young "investigative reporters" were being strengthened as were their basic writing composition skills. Once a week, students wrote a story and incorporated one or more pictures into it.

The cameras proved to be a real motivator for the students. Their measure of progress was a subjective view of the richness of the detail in their stories and of the composition skills exhibited. During the final week of the program, students were assigned the same topic they had initially chosen. An added measure of progress was the comparison of the length of their first and last writing efforts. Their initial output varied from a third of a page to one page in length. The final output was all multiple-page reports.

This summer program experience could be broadened and extended into the regular school curriculum. It could be integrated with social studies by having teams of students collaborate and explore the history and/or geography of their community. By using still or video digital cameras, visual and written documentaries could be developed and old photos scanned to supplement current-day recordings.

Modern Curriculum Press/Pearson Learning

Figure 6–1 **International student media festival**
This is a great place to enter your students' video productions at *http://ismf.net*

Many organizations, most notably Apple computing and AECT (Association for Educational Communications and Technology), have yearly contests for videos in any number of categories produced by students from high school to the lower elementary grades. One popular contest is the International Student Media Festival that AECT has been sponsoring since 1994 Figure 6–1). Producing videos for these contests may be just the thing to highlight a visual literacy unit.

A BRIEF OVERVIEW OF PHOTOGRAPHIC ELEMENTS

To encourage success in the use of a digital camera as a communication tool, a brief review of some photographic elements might be in order. The term *photography* comes from the Greek word *photo,* meaning "light," and the Latin word *graphein,* meaning "to write." Photography, indeed, is writing with light. Befitting to its roots, two of the most important aspects of photography are lighting and composition. These factors will be the focus of the discussion that follows as we take you through the steps of taking great photographs and then manipulating them using a photo editing program such as *Photoshop Elements*®.

Lighting the Shot

When approaching the lighting for any shot, the photographer must consider four elements: the amount of light striking the subject, the color of the light, the quality of the light, and its direction.

Amount of Light	
Too much light	• Washes out subject • Photo is overexposed
Correct amount	• Properly exposed photo • Subject is dark
Too little light	• Photo is underexposed

1. **Amount of light:** A correct exposure requires a correct amount of light. Light that is too strong or too weak must be avoided. Most digital cameras correct for the amount of exposure automatically; however, some allow the photographer to adjust the exposure manually for artistic purposes.

2. **Color of light:** Sunlight exhibits different color qualities at different times of day. Late afternoon sun produces warmer lighting, whereas early morning results in cooler lighting. Warmer lighting is also produced by incandescent lighting. Color film has been manufactured with a color balance of "noon daylight." Digital cameras have built-in "white balance" circuitry designed to eliminate unwanted color casts.

Color of Light	
Warmer lighting	• Emphasizes red end of the spectrum • May create more pleasant skin tones • May give overall reddish cast
Balanced lighting	• Natural look • More accurate color rendition
Cooler Lighting	• Emphasizes blue end of the spectrum • May result in unfavorable skin tones

3. **Quality of light:** Light may be strong and strike the subject from only one angle or diffuse, striking the subject from many directions. Diffuse lighting results in a softer image whereas direct light results in a higher contrast, one with pronounced shadows.

Quality of Light	
Diffuse lighting	• Softer • Lower contrast
Direct lighting	• Sharper relief • Higher contrast of highlights and shadows

4. **Direction of light:** Light coming from directly behind the camera may produce an acceptable photo. Light coming directly toward the camera darkens the subject and may create a difficult situation for the photographer. In this lighting condition, or when dark shadows fall on your subject, it's often advisable to use a fill-in flash from your camera to supplement the available light. In contrast, light coming from the side quartering toward the subject may be the most pleasing while emphasizing surface details in the subject.

Direction of Light	
Light from behind camera	• Flat overall lighting of scene • May result in correct exposure but the subject may lack "sparkle"
Light coming toward camera	• Darkened subject • Silhouettes • Severely underexposed highlights
Quarter lighting	• Very pleasing • Emphasizes surface details

Photographic Composition

Another important aspect of photography is photographic composition. Think of the photo you are about to take as telling a story. While certainly subjective and artistic, photographic composition has a number of agreed upon elements. The following discussion will deal with three of them: the rule of thirds, depth of field, and apparent distance to the subject.

Rule of Thirds. The rule of thirds states that a photograph may be divided into three equal parts or zones vertically and three equal parts horizontally, as shown in Figure 6–2.

Placing the predominant object in the very center of the photograph, as in Figure 6–3, results in a static composition and should usually be avoided.

Placing the object near the edge of the center zone, as in Figure 6–4, tends to draw the viewer more into the composition.

Compare Figure 6–5 and Figure 6–6. In Figure 6–6, notice how the eye is drawn past the foreground, emphasizing a feeling of depth or distance as you look at the birds.

Placing a horizon line in the very middle also results in a less than appealing composition. A horizon line placed near the top

Figure 6–2

Figure 6–3

Figure 6–4

Figure 6–5

Figure 6–6

179

Figure 6–7

Figure 6–8

of the center zone emphasizes the foreground and placed near the bottom of the center zone as in Figure 6–7 emphasizes the background.

Depth of Field. Once you have focused on the subject, depth of field is the area in front of and behind your subject that appears in acceptable focus. As you can see in Figure 6–8, objects outside that range (in this case, beyond) are out of focus or blurred. The easiest way to control depth of field (making it shallower or broader) with a digital camera set to auto exposure is to move closer to the subject, thereby reducing the depth of field or to move farther away, increasing the depth of field. Zooming a lens to restrict the angle of view and increasing the apparent size of the subject also reduces depth of field. By controlling the depth of field you can focus your viewer's attention on what you choose in the composition, throwing unwanted objects out of focus.

Apparent Distance to the Subject. Long shots can establish an overall scene as in Figure 6–9, medium shots can reveal some detail, and close-ups can focus the viewer's attention on important elements of the composition. In photographing people, while distant shots can describe the setting, closer shots increase the involvement with the viewer, as in Figure 6–10. Is Figure 6–9 a photo of a country road? Figure 6–10 is more clearly a photo of a woman walking a dog. Close-ups of faces, even to the extent of cropping part of the head, can be very effective. Besides moving physically closer or farther away from the subject, zooming a lens is the most effective way of framing a shot. An optical zoom involving an actual movement of the lens is preferable to a digital zoom, which is just a magnification of the picture elements on the camera's image sensor. A digital zoom, if overused, can create jagged edges in your image.

Figure 6–9 Long shot
Establishes the overall scene

Figure 6–10 Zooming in
Calls attention to the central elements of the composition

Compare the two figures showing the use of a zoom lens to effect the apparent distance to the subject

Photographic Composition	
The rule of thirds	• Photograph divided into three equal zones vertically and three horizontally
Depth of field	• The area in front of and behind your subject that appears in acceptable focus
Subject motion	• A subject in motion tends to be blurred
Apparent distance to the subject	• *Long shots* can establish an overall scene • *Medium shots* can reveal some detail • *Close-ups* can focus the viewer's attention on important elements of the composition

If you want to sharpen your photographic skills, read "Top 10 Tips" on the Kodak website (*www.kodak.com*). Navigate through the site by choosing Consumer Photography and then Taking Great Pictures. For an excellent book on photography, consider the *National Geographic Field Guide*. You can examine it at *www.nationalgeographic.com/siteindex/photogallery/*.

Of the many photo editing programs available, Adobe *Photoshop Elements*® is a reasonably priced, easy-to-use, yet powerful choice. It has a reduced feature set of the high-end and expensive program, Adobe *Photoshop*®. At the end of this chapter, we will present a brief tutorial to help you improve your photographic editing skills. A more extensive tutorial may be found on the *Take Along CD* accompanying this text.

GRAPHICS TYPES AND PROGRAMS

The two basic types of graphics created by the computer are bit mapped (or raster) and *vector* (or object oriented). Paint programs are used to create **bit-mapped graphics** that rely on direct changes to each dot or pixel that makes up an image. Drawing programs are used to create **vector graphics** that rely on mathematical equations to define the image. Each type of graphic has its own advantages and disadvantages.

Bit-Mapped Graphics (Paint Programs)

For bit-mapped graphics, the computer-generated image is composed of bits, or screen picture elements called pixels. Pretend your monitor screen is a map or grid 600 pixels high by 800 pixels wide. Pixels can be turned on (to appear black or colored) or off (to appear white or clear).

The number of pixels per inch (ppi) affects the resolution of an image. Your computer monitor usually displays images at a resolution of 72 or 96 ppi. A typical printer needs 150 ppi to 300 ppi to display an image accurately.

Many programs that incorporate the name "paint" in their titles produce bit-mapped graphics. This led to the practice of calling bit-mapped programs *paint programs*. Programs such as Kid Pix® (Figures 6–11 and 6–12) and Kid Works Deluxe® often are the user's first introduction to computer graphics. These are highly functional programs with a simple interface that is easily understood by young children. They, as all paint programs, have definite limitations though.

A simplified bit-mapped drawing of the side view of a child's wagon created in a paint program is presented in Figure 6–13, with a dot pattern applied to the body and a solid pattern applied to the wheels.

Figure 6–11 Screen shot from Kid Pix®

Little reading is required. When the top left icon is clicked, pencil thicknesses appear on the lower bar *(Reprinted with permission of The Learning Company™, Inc.)*

Figure 6–12 Another screen shot from Kid Pix®

The menus are also designed for nonreaders *(Reprinted with permission of The Learning Company™, Inc.)*

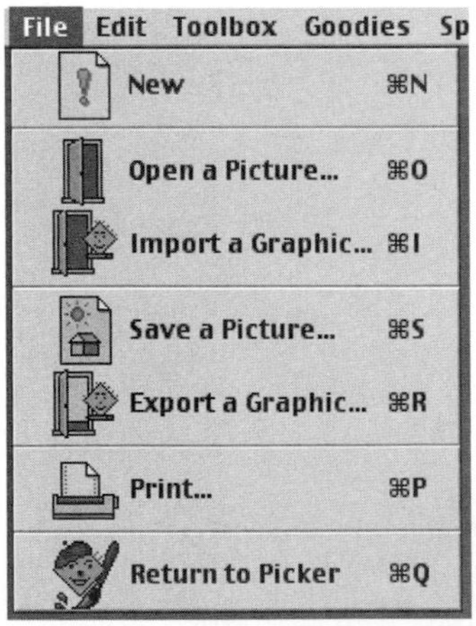

Figure 6–13 Bit-mapped graphic

A wagon composed of simple geometric shapes drawn in a paint program

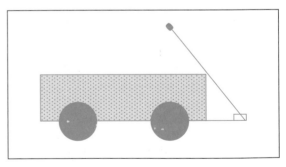

Figure 6–14 shows that same wagon with a section of the drawing enlarged. Horizontal and vertical lines are smooth, but notice the jagged edges of the circle (wheel) and diagonal line (handle shaft). The square shape of the pixel becomes apparent. One of the inherent drawbacks of bit-mapped graphics is that the size of the pixel limits the sharpness, or resolution, of the drawing, regardless of the resolution of the monitor or printer used to display the graphic.

Figure 6–14 Bit-mapped graphic enlarged

Notice the low resolution shown by the jagged edges

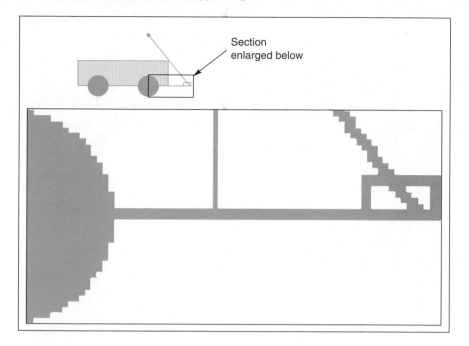

Section
enlarged below

Once a bit-mapped image or lettering is created, it is difficult to change. To modify an existing image in a paint program, the user must turn pixels on and off individually or erase large segments, as shown in Figure 6–15. Notice that the eraser (the white square) is turning bits off; that is, it is turning black or colored pixels white against a white background, virtually making them disappear. Once text is inserted into a "paint" document, typing errors cannot be easily corrected, nor can typefaces, sizes, or styles be changed. When text is inserted, the text itself also becomes a bit-mapped graphic. Think of it as a picture of the words. Once text is fixed in position, it cannot be edited. Pixels composing the letters can be erased like any other graphic element, thereby allowing entire letters and words to be erased. Paint programs allow for some changes in position of the images after they have been created. Unfortunately, it is more along the lines of cutting the image out of a magazine page and pasting it into another position.

Vector Graphics (Drawing Programs)

Instead of being composed of bits or screen pixels that are turned on and off, a vector graphic is determined by mathematical formulas that create discrete objects of a certain size and position. *Adobe Illustrator*®, *Canvas*®, all computer assisted design (CAD) programs, and most programs that incorporate the label "draw" in their titles such as *CorelDRAW*® produce vector graphics. This has led to the practice of calling vector programs *draw programs*. Integrated software packages such as *AppleWorks*® and *Microsoft Works*® *Suite* include a draw program or module.

In Figure 6–16, the front wheel has been moved away from the rest of the drawing. Each picture element is a separate object and can be changed independently. It can be enlarged, reduced, moved, or have its pattern changed. Creating an image in a draw program is conceptually different from creating one in a paint program. Rather than drawing freehand with a pencil or paintbrush, the user of a draw program creates objects of different shapes (e.g., lines, circles, rectangles, and polygons), adjusts line thickness, applies patterns to the objects, then organizes them into new, more complex objects.

183

Figure 6–15 Erasing bits in a paint program

Bits are erased by turning pixels on and off

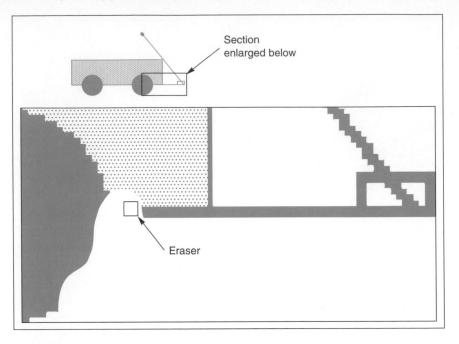

Figure 6–16 Vector graphic

A wagon composed of simple geometric shapes drawn in a draw program

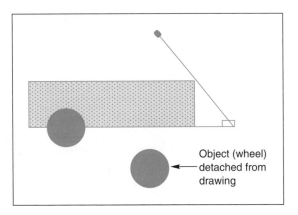

Once objects are created in draw programs, their shape, size, and position can be changed. Two or more objects may be linked or grouped together to form a new object. Text inserted in a drawing remains an editable text object. Typing mistakes can be easily corrected, and typefaces, sizes, and styles can be changed at any time. Being a discrete object, text may also be repositioned at will.

Count the objects making up the wagon in Figure 6–17. There are seven objects: (1) the shaded body of the wagon, (2) the rear wheel, (3) the front wheel, (4) the steering plate, (5) the handle tongue, (6) the handle shaft, and (7) the handle. Because the drawing is composed of independent objects, they may overlap or be layered on top of one another. Notice that, unlike in Figure 6–16, the rear wheel is placed underneath the body of the wagon in Figure 6–17 and that the shading of the body has been changed to a striped pattern. Some graphics programs include both paint and draw layers so that the user can take advantage of what each approach has to offer. Vector graphic files tend to be much smaller than bit-map files.

Figure 6–17 **Vector graphic objects**

Separate objects make up a drawing in a vector graphic

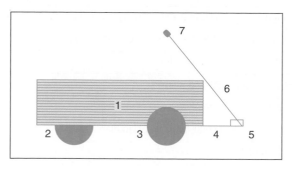

Figure 6–18 **Gradient fill**

A wide variety of gradient fills are available in most programs

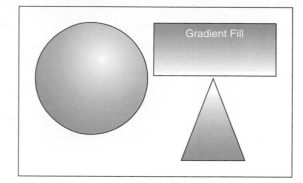

Figure 6–19 **Graphic tools**

Tools commonly found in paint and draw programs

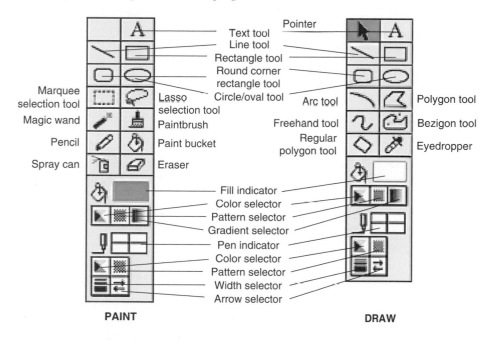

PAINT   DRAW

Many draw programs allow the use of **gradient fill** patterns similar to those shown in Figure 6–18 that begin with a certain density of pattern at a determined point and gradually fade to a less-dense pattern or increase to a denser one. Gradient fills can create the appearance of a third dimension on an object.

The Tools of Paint and Draw Programs

Figure 6–19 illustrates tools that are common to a number of paint and draw programs. As noted previously, high-end graphics programs such as *Painter*® incorporate both paint and draw modes and have many more tools enabling precision control of graphics.

If a paint or draw program is truly to become a productivity tool, the user must become comfortable with the individual program and adept at using it. The following descriptions help to introduce you to these tools.

Paint Tools

Tool	Function
Marquee selection tool	Selects a rectangular area, including any white background present
Lasso selection tool	Selects an irregular shape without any extraneous background
Magic wand	Selects adjacent pixels of the same color
Paintbrush	Paints strokes of various sizes and shapes
Pencil	Paints lines in a freehand manner
Paint bucket	Fills an enclosed shape with color, pattern, or gradient
Spray can	Creates a spray painted effect
Eraser	Erases part of an image pixel by pixel

Draw Tools

Tool	Function
Pointer	Selects, moves, and resizes objects
Arc tool	Draws an arc curving between two points
Polygon tool	Draws closed shapes made up of straight lines and angles
Freehand tool	Draws irregular lines in the manner similar to a pencil
Bezigon tool	Draws shapes, with the user selecting specific points, and draws smooth curves through those points
Regular polygon tool	Draws polygons of equal sides
Eyedropper	Picks up colors, patterns, and gradients from any object drawn

Tools in Common

Tool	Function
Text tool	Inserts text on the screen in a selected font
Line tool	Creates straight lines
Rectangle tool	Creates rectangles and squares
Round corner rectangle	Creates rectangles and squares with round corners
Circle/oval tool	Creates ovals and circles
Color, pattern, and gradient fill selectors	Selects specific color, pattern, or gradient to fill a shape
Color, pattern, width, and arrow pen selectors	Selects specific color, pattern, width, and arrow style for the pen
Fill and pen indicators	Display the specific fill and pen characteristics that have been selected

CLIP ART

For many years, graphic artists subscribed to services that provided them with printed drawings and images. The artists clipped out any illustration that suited their needs and incorporated it into their own original work. This is outdated technology. With the transition to computer graphics, **clip art** files on disk and through the Web are now readily available.

Clip art is a great time-saver for all and an exceptional resource for those of modest or limited artistic skills and talents. Examine the various illustrations found in Figure 6–20. Some files are line drawings, some are detailed illustrations, and others are photographs. Notice the lettering textured with African violets. Among the many sources of clip art, the award-winning *The Big Box of Art* by Hemera Technologies (available for both Windows and Macintosh) is an impressive and reasonably priced standout. It contains approximately a quarter million illustrations and comes on over 20 CDs. Along with a printed volume of images, it includes a search engine that lets you search by graphic type as well as by topic, and displays thumbnails of each illustration indicating which CD to insert once you've chosen your graphic. The textured lettering is accomplished by using the included software called *PhotoFonts*. Most people now get their clip art from one of many image archives on the Web. A quick search will find hundreds of thousands of images in many different file types to download to your computer. A good starting point is *www.awesomeclipartforeducators.com/*

Figure 6–20 Clip art
Samples of various types of clip art *(Courtesy of Hemera Technologies®, Inc.)*

Figure 6–21 **Logo image rendered in *Carved* at cooltext.com**

Other fonts include *Alien Glow, Textured, Old Stone, Starburst,* and *Burning* (an animated font)

Figure 6–22 **Logo image rendered in *Good Dog* at *3dtextmaker.com***

Several hundred fonts can be rendered in color either as stationary images or in 12 animations

Figure 6–23 **Text renderings at *hypergurl.com***

This site offers only six choices but they are all popular

Many websites also let you customize words and fonts, thus enabling you to quickly and easily create graphics in hundreds of different styles, colors, and animations for your web page, Word document, PowerPoint presentation, or any application in which you can insert graphics. Figures 6–21, Figure 6–22, and Figure 6–23 are examples of graphics made at three of these "text rendering" sites.

FILE FORMATS

Once you create a graphics document, you must choose a file format to save the file in order to share the document with others or to open the document in a specific graphics application. Though all these formats can store graphics information, each was designed for a reason. Some are specific to applications, whereas others were designed for sharing among applications.

Graphics files tend to be quite large; therefore, each file format employs a compression technique. One technique examines repeated data patterns and replaces them with a code that describes the pattern and the number of its repetitions. This technique is called **lossless compression,** because, though the file is smaller, no information is lost. This type works well with drawings. The other technique, **lossy compression,** discards information it judges unnecessary, thereby losing some information. It recreates as much of it as possible when the file is opened. The resulting file is much smaller than with a file format employing lossless compression. Color photographs are prime candidates for lossy compression. Any tonal gradations can be identified by the two extremes and intermediate values discarded to be recreated mathematically when the file is opened. Even though it seems difficult to believe that files that are compressed by having data removed are still able to be viewed as though nothing was altered, it does work. A popular video compression standard defined by the Moving Pictures Experts Group is MPEG. Videos compressed using the MPEG method are reduced up to 95 percent in size but still retain near-television quality when viewed. All of the images and movies you see on the Web, in PowerPoints, and most that are printed are saved in a compressed mode.

Though there are many graphics file formats, the following table represents the most common ones used today. Generally speaking, photographs should be saved in JPEG format and color drawings should be saved as a GIF file.

File	Comments	OS	Extension
BMP	Bit-mapped Suitable for drawings	Windows	.BMP
GIF	Graphics Interchange Format Fast transfer over the Internet Supports graphics and animation	Win/Mac	.GIF
JPEG	Joint Photographic Experts Group Efficient storage of photographs Many compression rates Standard for displaying images on the Web	Win/Mac	.JPG
TIFF	Tagged Image File Format Bit-map cross platform and application format Large files	Win/Mac	.TIF

(Continued)

189

EPS	Encapsulated PostScript Used in page layout programs Contains both graphics and text Best used to print on PostScript printers	Win/Mac	.EPS
MPEG	Moving Picture Experts Group Often used for DVDs Supports streaming video over the Web CD quality audio	Win/Mac	.MPG
AVI	Audio-Video Interleaved Limited resolution Cannot support streaming video	Windows	.AVI
WMV	Windows Media Video Small file size but with some loss of quality	Windows	.WMV or .ASF
Quick time	An International Organization for Standardization (ISO) format The most versatile video format	Win/Mac	.QT or .MOV

Size is often an issue when dealing with file storage. It is sometimes easier to comprehend the numbers if we can relate it to something concrete. We have constructed the following table to demonstrate how many JPEG pictures can be stored on common memory devices. The actual number of photos will vary depending on the camera in use, intricacy of the subject, and software in the individual camera.

Potential Number of JPEG Images Stored

Photo Sensor	16 MB	32 MB	64 MB	128 MB	256 MB	512 MB	1 GB
		Memory size					
1 Megapixel	45	9	182	365	731	1462	2925
2 Megapixels	17	35	71	142	284	568	1137
3 Megapixels	13	26	53	106	213	426	853
4 Megapixels	8	16	32	64	128	256	512
5 Megapixels	6	12	25	51	102	204	409
6 Megapixels	5	10	20	40	80	160	320

COPYRIGHT

Purchasing a clip art disk or CD-ROM entitles users to copy images or parts of images to use in their own drawings usually with some restrictions. Be sure to review the copyright statements on the clip art package you use to find out what they are. Some packages allow the purchaser to use the clip art for educational or private home use only. Other packages allow the user to use the clip art for business. Still other packages have no restrictions. It is wise to purchase clip art for school through a source that also sells educational software. These vendors place clip art disks and CD-ROMs in their catalog knowing that they will be used in a school environment.

Ownership of clip art and images found on the Web is sometimes difficult to ascertain. The act of placing something on the Web automatically copyrights it. Therefore, you should think of everything (graphics and text) on the Web as copyrighted. Luckily, there are many sites containing huge archives of clip art and images that are available to use copyright free. Be careful of some sites though. We have found such things as the Nike and Coca-Cola trademarks on some sites. Advertising logos and trademarks are always owned by the company and should never be used without permission. If there is any question, it is a good idea not to use any of the graphics or images found on the site.

With the availability of high-quality, inexpensive scanners, more students and teachers are using graphics and pictures in their newsletters, reports, and web pages. Remember, unless you took the photograph yourself, you probably don't own the copyright. For instance, many people do not realize that unless they specifically bought the rights to their own wedding pictures, they cannot copy them. The copyright for their own wedding pictures is held by the original photographer. All they actually purchased is the set of copies they received, not the permission to make copies. Check the copyright notice written in or on the source of the material. Some material can be copied for noncommercial, educational use.

DESIGN OF INSTRUCTIONAL MATERIALS

In designing any communication, whether it be oral, written, or graphic, the sender of the message must know the anticipated audience that is to receive it and design the communication appropriately. The user must know what will capture the audience's attention and get the information across clearly and convincingly. Many times graphics do just that. Graphics, when properly used, support key points, draw the reader's attention, and add interest to a presentation. Improperly used graphics may be irritating and distracting.

Photographs and line drawings are among the most common type of graphics created on the computer. When preparing line illustrations, consider the following few simple guidelines.

Today, most classroom teachers make overhead transparencies using either the office copy machine or an ink-jet or laser printer. Specially treated clear plastic sheets are used depending on which process (copy machine, ink-jet, or laser printer) will be used. After designing the transparency on a computer, it can be either printed directly onto the special plastic transparency sheet or printed on paper and copied onto a special sheet fed into the office copier.

Designing transparencies in computer graphics is a fairly straightforward task. Using any paint or draw program, create the image you want to project and print it. Using

GUIDELINES FOR PREPARING LINE ILLUSTRATIONS

- Present one topic or main idea per illustration.
- Use thick (bold) lines.
- Keep the use of text to a minimum and use a bold style.

A copy of these rubrics may be found in the Guidelines folder in the Take-Along CD

PowerPoint® as a graphics tool, you could create the entire image to be projected as the finished transparency and save it as a master slide. Print the slide and you have a transparency master. Whether you are projecting an image from your computer or from an overhead projector, if you wish to design a series of images that, when used sequentially, build in an additive nature to a final concept, then open the master slide. Decide what elements of the image should be presented first, delete the rest, and save the result as slide 1. Subsequent steps require you to open the master slide, delete unwanted elements, and save the results as a new slide 2, and so forth. Print each slide as transparencies and reveal them one at a time on the overhead projector.

In examining the process just described, it is apparent that the user, once having acquired a certain degree of skill and comfort level with a computer graphics program, can use it as a tool that extends abilities in a low-tech environment. Other examples include banners that can be created on continuous-form computer paper by programs such as *Print Shop*® in its several versions. Teachers and students can use *Print Shop*® to create banners, calendars, certificates, bookmarks, newsletters, student activity sheets, and much more. Examine the Print Shop® Deluxe menu in Figure 6–24. Students can also design their own websites with this program. Each project is made by following a series of assistant-like steps.

The *Print Shop*® *Deluxe* series contains more than 230,000 graphics and photos; 8,400 project templates; over 100 sound files; 1,300 animations; 30 scalable typefaces; 2,000 quotes and verses, a spell checker; and a thesaurus. School versions include a comprehensive teacher guide containing lesson plans and projects for students in grades 1 through 12. The special Print Shop® website contains more than 25,000 additional images, a design center, a chat group, and more. To help you get comfortable with this versatile

Figure 6–24 Print shop deluxe® menu

This program enables teachers and even very young students to master the production of all types of graphic documents

Figure 6–25 A tiled graphic

This sample tiled graphic prints on 16 sheets of paper

Thanksgiving

program, we present a brief tutorial on using Print Shop® Deluxe to construct a banner toward the end of the chapter.

Some programs take an original (either scanned into the computer or created in a paint program) and allow the user to enlarge it to huge dimensions. The image is printed in segments on four to sixteen (or more) standard 8 1/2-by-11-inch sheets of paper that are tiled, or assembled, into the finished product. The example in Figure 6–25 shows an image printed on sixteen sheets of paper. The sheets are assembled and fastened to each other to form a poster approximately 34 inches by 44 inches. Graphics programs such as these enhance the creative ability of students and teachers and facilitate visual communication.

OTHER GRAPHICS PROGRAMS

As stated throughout the text, computers and computer software are tools to be used to help both teachers and students to be more efficient in their work. Software programs that are particularly helpful and engaging are those devoted to simple graphics and desktop publishing. There are many of these programs on the market today. We have already discussed award-winning *Kid Pix Deluxe*. The handy *Month by Month*® software package that goes along with *Kid Works Deluxe*®, and also found on the accompanying CD-ROM, adds utility by giving the teacher predesigned cross-curricular, theme-based projects to use with students. Another program in the same vein is *Paint, Write & Play*® (Figure 6–26), designed for students in grades K–2.

Productivity tools, such as the graphics programs mentioned in this chapter, really do make time-consuming and difficult projects easy. These tools save time and energy and increase teacher and student efficiency. Technology should be transparent. It should ease difficult tasks. Productivity tools focus on the end product of learning and not on the technology needed to achieve the end product.

193

Figure 6–26 The art studio®

In the program Paint, Write and Play™ *(Courtesy of The Learning Company®, Inc.)*

■■■■ WORKING WITH KID PIX®

As stated earlier in this chapter, teachers and students alike have used graphics programs to create graphics for a variety of purposes. It's one thing to read about paint and draw programs, it's another to work with them. We encourage you to follow along in this introductory tutorial to Kid Pix.® You will see how it allows students to express themselves by writing stories using precreated and user-created backgrounds, pictures, and sounds.

LET'S TRY IT!

A copy of this tutorial may be found in the tutorials folder in the Take-Along CD

In working through the following brief tutorial on creating a picture in *Kid Pix Deluxe 4 for Schools®* you will learn the following:

- How to make a simple picture using Kid Pix
- How to add drawings, paintings, and backgrounds to a Kid Pix document
- How to use several common menu options and features to enhance and customize your Kid Pix picture

KidPix® is one of the most popular creativity tools used in the K–8 environment. A student can create pictures with sounds and animations using painting and drawing tools in the Kid Pix Paint Zone and slide shows in the SlideShow Zone.

1. OPENING AND SETTING DEFAULTS

1.1 Click on the Kid Pix program to open it. You will be asked to type in your name or choose your name from a list of users.

1.2 Select *Controls*

(You will probably only do this the first time that you set up the program for your students, but it is a good idea that you know what is on the Controls menu.)

1.3 Select *Controls* > *Turn Tool Sounds* Off.

You may want to turn the sound off because it can be distracting in the classroom or lab. This tool turns sounds on or off when accessing trays and tools.

1.4 Select *Controls* > *Cambiar a espanol*

To translate menus, tool tips, and Help screens into Spanish.

1.5 Select *Controls* > *Turn Small Kids Mode On.*

When the Small Kids Mode is selected, the user can use all of the art tools and add text to pictures using rubber stamps instead of the keyboard.

1.6 Select *Controls* > *Go to SlideShow.*

This shows the SlideShow screen. SlideShows can be exported as Quicktime movies containing all transition effects.

(Continued)

1.7 Select *Controls > Go to Paint Zone* to Return to the Paint Zone.

Note that two Controls menu items are now highlighted when the screen is in the SlideShow mode:

Turn Text-To-Speech Off: Turns speech in text boxes on or off.
Turn Attached Sounds Off: Turns sounds on or off when a picture is played.

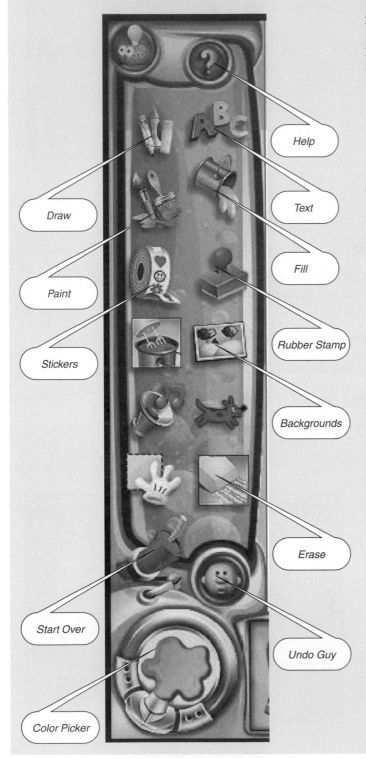

Controls	Help
Turn Tool Sounds Off	
Turn Text-To-Speech Off	
Turn Attached Sound Off	
Cambiar a español...	
Turn Small Kids Mode On	
Turn Manual Advance On	
View Teacher's Note	
Clean Up	
Go to Paint Zone	

2. KID PIX TOOLS

2.1 The Kid Pix Art Tools are found on the left menu. Familiarize yourself with these tools. As a tool is clicked on, the bottom menu usually changes to show options available with that tool.

Common tools are labeled on the right.

196

3. MAKE A SIMPLE DRAWING

3.1 Select *Draw*.

The Draw tools menu will appear at the bottom of the screen.

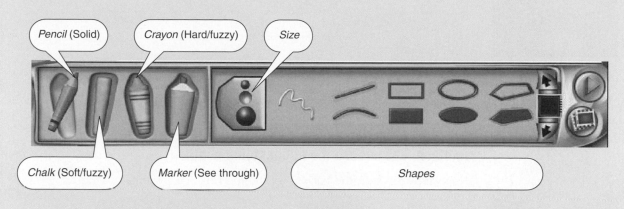

Pencil (Solid) Crayon (Hard/fuzzy) Size

Chalk (Soft/fuzzy) Marker (See through) Shapes

3.2 Select *Color Picker* and choose red.

3.3 Select the unfilled square tool (third from right, top) and draw a rectangle in the middle of the page.

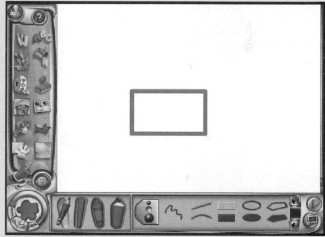

3.4 We don't want this so select Start Over!

3.5 Now select filled rectangle tool (third from right, bottom) and redraw. This time it should be a filled-in red rectangle.

(Continued)

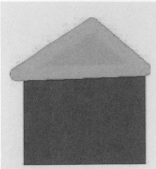

3.6 Now add a green roof using the filled polygon shape (far right, bottom).

4. USING THE LINE AND FILL TOOLS

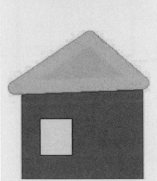

4.1 Select the pencil tool, change the color to black, and choose the thinnest line width.

Now draw a box in the left part of the red box. This will be a window.

4.2 Change the color to white and select the *Fill* tool. Clicking inside the box you drew will fill the box with white.

4.3 Choose the line tool (fourth from right, top) and change the color back to black.

Can you make the cross lines in the window to simulate window panes?

4.4 Dare you add a door?

Remember the *Undo Guy!*

5. USING THE PAINT TOOLS

5.1 Select *Paint*. The *Paint* tools menu will appear at the bottom of the screen.

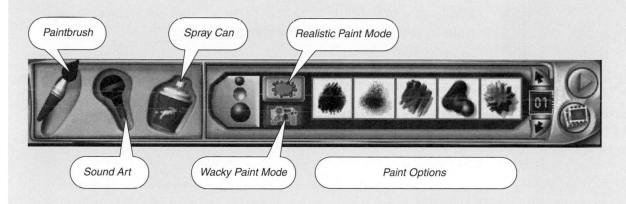

5.2 Now let us draw a tree.

Select *Paintbrush*. Choose the color brown and various Paintbrush *sizes* to draw a tree.

(Continued)

5.3 Select *Paintbrush*, paint option *Spray* and a dark green color to add leaves to your tree.

6. ADD A STICKER

6.1 Select *Stickers* from the side menu and choose an animal to add to your picture from the bottom menu. Use the arrows on the right to see other animals. We chose a skunk.

Our final picture

7. OTHER KID PIX OPTIONS

7.1 A background could have been added at the beginning of the picture process by clicking on the *Backgrounds* tool and choosing one from the bottom menu. Simply drag it onto your blank picture page or import your own picture (select *Add>Import Background*).

Select *Shrink/Stretch to Fit Canvas* to completely fill background. Imported backgrounds can be in BMP, GIF, JPEG, or PICT format. We did not add a background for simplicity of illustration.

7.2 *Animations* are like stickers except that they move like a cartoon when you play them.

Select the *Animations* tool to open the *Animations Library* at the bottom of the page. Scroll through the animations and drag the one you want to your picture.

To play the animation, click on the animation and then on the *Loop* handle (this is the button on the upper right of the animation picture).

7.3 Sounds can be added from the Kid Pix *Sounds Library*, by importing a sound and by recording your own sound.

Select the *Sounds* tool to open the *Sounds Library* at the bottom of the page. Select a folder and a sound you would like. (Click the sound to listen to it.) Drag the sound you would like onto your picture.

Select *Add > Import Sound* and find the file you would like to use on your computer. Windows users should use WAV files and Macintosh users should use AIFF files. To add the sound to the *My Soundslibrary*, select *Addto Library*.

Select the Microphone icon in the Sounds menu at the bottom of the page. Select the left circular red button to start recording and the middle retangular *blue button* to stop recording. Select the *Save button* to save your sound. Name the sound and save it in the *My Sounds* folder.

7.4 You can add digital pictures or pictures from other programs by selecting *Add>Add Graphic*. Graphic may be in BMP, GIF, JPEG, or PICT

(Continued)

format. Choose *Shrink/Stretch to Fit Canvas* if necessary or just click *Open* to add picture and use handles to resize the image.

7.5 Add Quicktime movies by selecting *Add>Add Movie*.

Find the movie file (make sure it is a Quicktime file) on your computer and click on it. Select Open to add the movie. Drag the movie to where you want it in the picture. To play the Quicktime movie, click on the movie and click on the Loop handle (this is the button on the upper right of the movie frame).

Kid Pix comes with a complete 58-page guide in PDF format. Read this to find out many of the other features found in the Kid Pix program.

WORKING WITH PHOTOSHOP ELEMENTS®

As a classroom teacher, we often choose photographs to visualize a concept. Unfortunately, the photographs we take are sometimes in need of improvement if we are to get the most out of them. This is where a basic knowledge of photo editing software becomes useful. We recommended Adobe® Photoshop Elements® earlier in the chapter. Adobe Photoshop® is a $600 program well suited to graphics professionals. Photoshop Elements® with its powerful subset of editing features priced at $100 is for the rest of us. Incidentally, we purchased Photoshop Elements® 4.0 prior to writing the following tutorial for $59.95 with free shipping from *www.academicsuperstore.com*.

If you do not have access to this program, download a trial copy of Photoshop Elements® from the Adobe website *(www.adobe.com/downloads/)* and then copy the *PS Elements Tutorial* folder from the *Take-Along CD* included with the textbook.

An expanded tutorial that will address the editing of color and the removal of "red eye" can be found on the *Take-Along CD*. We suggest you first complete the tutorial in the text, then print the nine-page expanded tutorial from the *Take-Along CD* and practice with it.

LET'S TRY IT!

The extended tutorial may be found in the Tutorials folder in the Take-Along CD

In working through the following brief tutorial on Photoshop Elements, you will learn the following:

- How to adjust the lighting in your photographs
- How to improve composition through cropping
- How to make use of layers in your digital image

1. LAUNCH PHOTOSHOP ELEMENTS

Once you have downloaded a trial version of Photoshop Elements®, or have otherwise accessed the program, and the **PS Elements Tutorial Files** folder containing digital photos has been copied from the **PS Elements Tutorial** folder on the *Take-Along CD* and saved to your computer, open **Photoshop Elements®**.

1.1 Under the File menu, you can choose either Open to go directly to an image file you want to open or choose Browse with Bridge.

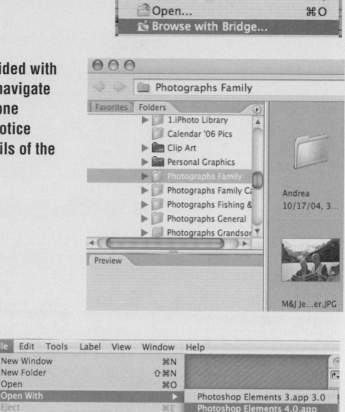

1.2 *Bridge* is a companion program provided with Photoshop Elements® that allows you to navigate through your folders until you locate the one containing the picture you want to edit. Notice that the *Bridge* window displays thumbnails of the photos as well as folders you view.

1.3 Click on the thumbnail of the picture you want to edit and under the *File* menu, choose *Open With* Photoshop Elements 4.0 app.

Retrieve the photo named *1. Rabbit.jpg* from the *PS Elements Tutorial Files* folder.

2. ADJUST THE LIGHTING

The example shown at the right is a high-contrast image where the subject is in deep shadow and appears underexposed. It is difficult to determine what, if anything, is beneath the tree.

2.1 Choose the Brightness/Contrast control following the steps below to correct or improve the lighting in your photographs.

The Brightness slider affects the overall lightness or darkness of the scene. The Contrast slider adjusts the relationship between light and dark.

(Continued)

Experiment with the sliders until you achieve the desired effect.
Hint: Checking the Preview box allows you to see changes as they occur.

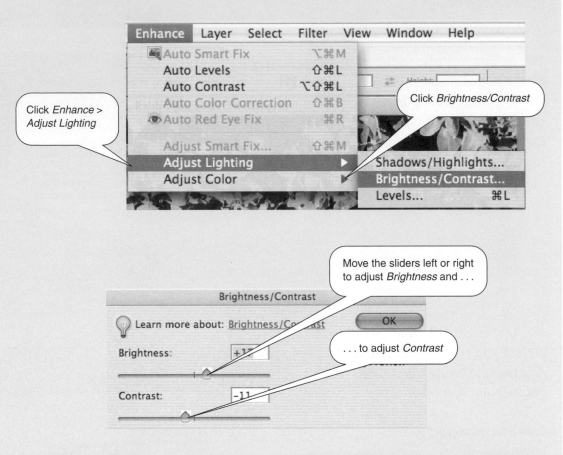

Click *Enhance > Adjust Lighting*

Click *Brightness/Contrast*

Move the sliders left or right to adjust *Brightness* and . . .

. . . to adjust *Contrast*

2.2 Choose the *Levels* submenu for greater control in lighting adjustments. The Levels menu allows you to control the intensity of dark areas, bright areas, and midtones in your image.

Click *Enhance > Adjust Lighting*

Click *Levels . . .*

Levels

Learn more about: Levels

OK

Cancel

Reset

Auto

Channel: Gray

Input Levels: 0   1.00   255

☑ Preview

> Grab one of these three triangles to control *Input Levels*. Notice that the one on the left is black and the one on the right is white.
>
> Slide each one back and forth and watch the impact on your photo.
>
> When satisfied with the appearance of your photo, click on the *OK* button.

Output Levels: 0   255

Compare the two images below that both reveal what is below the tree. Notice that detail was sacrificed in the leaves in the picture on the **left** when it was corrected using the ***Brightness/Contrast*** control in order to brighten the subject. Leaf detail was preserved in the picture on the **right**, however, when it was corrected by using the ***Levels*** control. Both of these, along with the ***Shadows/Highlights*** control, have something to contribute as you adjust the lighting of your photo.

Brightness/Contrast control

Levels control

3. IMPROVE THE COMPOSITION BY CROPPING

Retrieve the photo **2. Summer** *Palace.jpg* from the ***PS Elements Tutorial Files*** folder.

3.1 The example shown at the right is in serious need of improvement.

    a. Someone walked in front of the camera as the picture was taken.

    b. Lighting needs improvement.

(Continued)

c. The horizon is in the middle.

d. The confusing number of objects makes it difficult to focus attention on the distant object in the background.

Before improving the composition, follow the instructions in step **2. Adjust the Lighting** to improve the lighting of the photograph by using the **Levels** submenu, then proceed to crop the image.

3.2 Select the cropping tool and follow the steps below to improve the omposition by cropping the image.

Click on the *Cropping Tool*

3.3 On the cropping tool bar above the image, set the dimensions (proportions) of the image at **12 inches wide by 8 inches high**. Notice that the *Aspect Ratio* window changes from *No Restriction* to *Custom*.

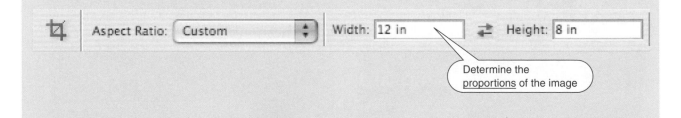

Determine the proportions of the image

3.4 Position the cropping tool at the upper left corner of the image.

Click and hold the mouse button as you drag diagonally across the image. Stop just above the distracting foreground objects.

Leaving the branches showing in the upper right corner will add an interesting framing device contributing to a distance perspective.

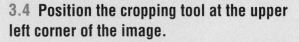

Drag down to this point

3.5 Click on the *Image* menu and select the *Crop* command.

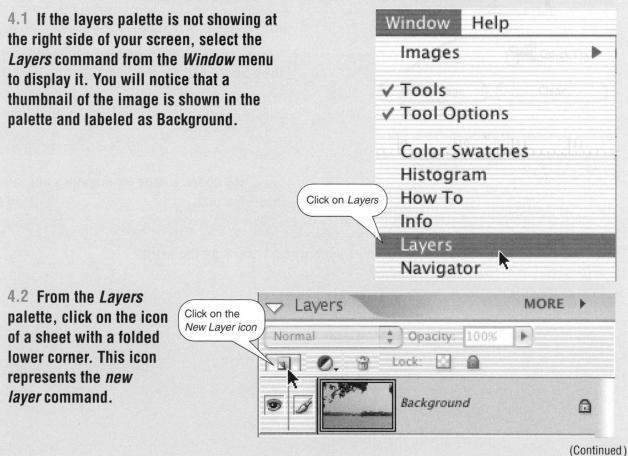

4. ADD INFORMATION BY THE USE OF LAYERS

Photoshop Elements® allows the creation of layers which can be superimposed on the image. Think of these layers as clear plastic overlays containing text or other images that you place over your existing image.

4.1 If the layers palette is not showing at the right side of your screen, select the *Layers* command from the *Window* menu to display it. You will notice that a thumbnail of the image is shown in the palette and labeled as Background.

4.2 From the *Layers* palette, click on the icon of a sheet with a folded lower corner. This icon represents the *new layer* command.

(Continued)

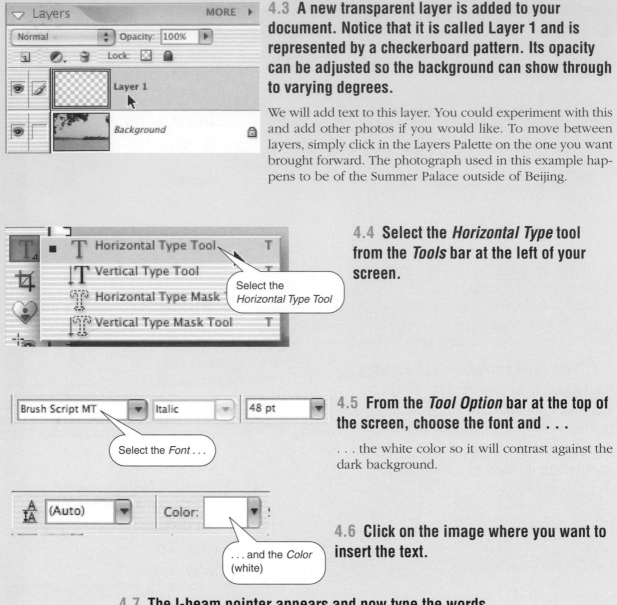

4.3 A new transparent layer is added to your document. Notice that it is called Layer 1 and is represented by a checkerboard pattern. Its opacity can be adjusted so the background can show through to varying degrees.

We will add text to this layer. You could experiment with this and add other photos if you would like. To move between layers, simply click in the Layers Palette on the one you want brought forward. The photograph used in this example happens to be of the Summer Palace outside of Beijing.

4.4 Select the *Horizontal Type* tool from the *Tools* bar at the left of your screen.

4.5 From the *Tool Option* bar at the top of the screen, choose the font and . . .

. . . the white color so it will contrast against the dark background.

4.6 Click on the image where you want to insert the text.

4.7 The I-beam pointer appears and now type the words The Summer Palace.

Notice that your new layer in the Layers pallette has been renamed with the words you typed. Compare the two photographs. The one on the left is the original and the one on the right is the edited photo.

Following this brief tutorial, we suggest that you print the expanded tutorial found in the Photoshop® Elements folder in the *Take-Along CD*. It will review the instructions given above and will demonstrate correcting red-eye as well as color hue and saturation. Make sure you have the trial version of *Photoshop Elements®* (either for the Mac or PC) and the folder entitled "PS Elements Tutorial Files" on your computer so you may put some of these instructions into practice.

▮▮▮ WORKING WITH PRINT SHOP DELUXE®

Teachers and students are in need of a specialized tool that they can use to produce professional-looking printed projects. Teachers may want to produce a pamphlet telling parents about a field trip and students may want to produce one as a handout for a report or project. At other times, calendars for the bulletin board, certificates for a job well done, labels for a class-produced CD, a sign for the hall, or greeting cards may be just the thing for the classroom. One software program that can do all of this and more is *Print Shop® Deluxe*. If you have access to *Print Shop® Deluxe*, you can execute the steps in the following tutorial to create a simple project.

LET'S TRY IT!

In working through the following brief tutorial on Print Shop® Deluxe you will learn the following:

- How to choose a project from the *Select a New Project* menu
- Three different ways that Print Shop® Deluxe helps you through a project
- Text and graphic options available in Print Shop® Deluxe
- How to make a banner using Print Shop® Deluxe

A copy of this tutorial may be found in the Tutorials folder in the Take-Along CD

(Continued)

1. LAUNCH PRINT SHOP DELUXE®

1.1 You can create cards, pamplets, signs, cetificates, and many more graphic objects with Print Shop Deluxe®. As a starting point, we will create a banner for Mrs. Johnson's fifth-grade class. Select the Print Shop Deluxe program either from your hard drive or a CD-ROM. It is best to keep the original CD on hand since many of the files are not transferred to your hard drive when the program is installed. Parts that are not installed will be accessed on the CD if it is still in the CD-ROM drive on your computer.

Where the buttons or commands differ between program version for the Mac or Windows, the second one will appear in parentheses.

2. MAKING A SIMPLE BANNER

2.1 Click on the *Banners* option and click on *Continue* (*Next*). You now have a choice. You can either click the *Quickstart Layout* button if you want to use one of the predefined projects, the *Help Me Design* button if you want less help and more options, or the *Start from Scratch* button if you want to create everything yourself. We will click on *Help Me Design* and then *Continue* (*Next*).

2.2 The *Select a Format* screen will appear.

Select Wide since we are going to make a horizontal banner and choose US Letter as the *Paper Size*.

Don't worry about how long it will be. The program will figure that out after we type in the words.

Click on Continue (*Next*).

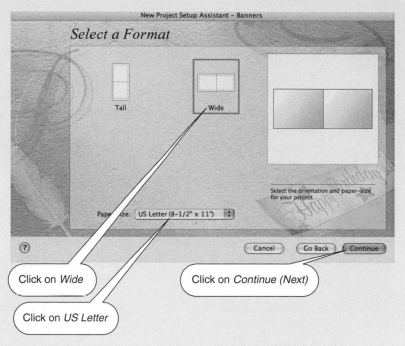

Click on *Wide*

Click on *US Letter*

Click on *Continue (Next)*

2.3 Choose the backdrop you are interested in using from the Select a *Backdrop* window. In this example we are using *Art Deco*. Click on it and click on *Continue* (*Next*).

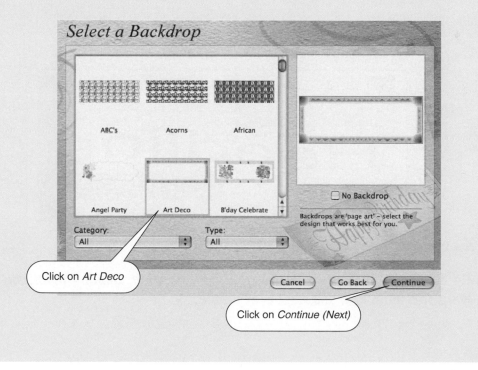

Click on *Art Deco*

Click on *Continue (Next)*

(Continued)

2.4 Choose the layout of the lettering from the *Select a Layout* screen. Don't worry about the pictures on the layout. You can resize or delete them later. Select *Layout 1* then click on *Done.*

You could now click on the two graphics to change their size or even delete them if you wish. We left the two graphics alone. We thought that they would look nice since Mrs. Johnson's school is in an urban location. You can also double click on the text box containing the word **Headline** to change the wording, font, word placement, shape, and/or to use one of the custom graphic fonts provided.

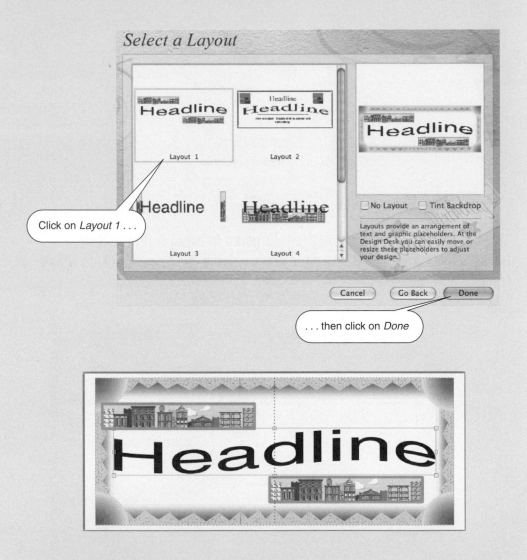

2.5 Click on the *ReadyMade*, *Face*, *Shape*, *Position*, *Depth*, *Proportion*, and *Warp Text* options to see what is available.

We typed "Mrs. Johnson's 5th Grade Class" in the Enter Headline Text Here box.

Create a Headline

Enter Headline Text Here:

Headline

○ ReadyMade   ● Customize

Font: NewZurica

Headline

Type *Mrs. Johnson's 5th Grade Class* in this box.

Face | Shape | Position | Outline | Depth | Proportion

Color

None

☑ Warp Text

Orientation

? | Cancel | OK

Your finished product is shown in Figure 6–27. Though this tutorial has been printed in black and white, you'll enjoy the full color banner from your color printer. Note the way Print Shop changed the two-page banner template to three and a half pages to make room for all of the words.

Even though we didn't have you choose the *Start from Scratch* option, you did see that you had a wide selection of banner backgrounds and font options available. Check out some of the other projects you and your students would be able to make using Print Shop Deluxe®. Programs like this sure make life easier for the teacher and can produce professional-looking graphics for the students and classroom.

Figure 6–27 Finished product
The banner produced in the tutorial on using Photo Shop Deluxe®

LET'S REVIEW

Digital still cameras store a large number of digital images on removable media. Once downloaded to a computer, the images may be manipulated in a variety of ways by using appropriate software and stored as graphic files.

The resolution of input devices such as a digital camera is measured in pixels. The more pixels per inch (ppi), the higher the resolution or clarity of an image. The capability of the camera is expressed in megapixels (millions of pixels).

Two of the most important aspects of photography are lighting and composition. When approaching the lighting for any shot, the photographer must consider four elements: the amount of light striking the subject, the color of the light, the quality of the light, and its direction. Composition includes the following elements: the rule of thirds, depth of field, and apparent distance to the subject.

Some graphics programs facilitate the creation of graphics for bulletin boards and other displays. Some generate drawings; others automatically generate graphs and charts from numeric data.

In bit-mapped graphics, the computer-generated image is composed of pixels that are turned on and off. One of the inherent drawbacks of bit-mapped graphics is that the size of the pixel limits the sharpness, or resolution, of the drawing, regardless of the resolution of the monitor or printer used to display the graphic.

In vector graphics, each picture element is constructed by a mathematical formula that creates a separate object that can be changed independently. Clip art is available as files in paint or draw formats on disk for use in computer graphics programs.

In designing any communication, the sender of the message must know the anticipated audience that is to receive it and design the communication appropriately in order to capture attention and get information across clearly and convincingly.

LET'S PRACTICE

To complete the specified exercises online, go to the Chapter Exercises Module in Chapter 6 of the Companion Website.

1. Discuss the usefulness of two electronic input devices in the creation of graphics.

2. What two computer output devices are essential in a classroom setting? What other device would be useful? Discuss how this other device would be particularly useful to display graphic images.

3. Using a paint program, create a cover page for a report. How does the graphic you created heighten the reader's interest in the report?

4. Write a brief report on a topic of current national interest and use a graphic captured from a scanner to illustrate your report.

5. Using the draw component of an integrated package or a stand-alone draw program, create a set of informational or directional signs for a school lunchroom.

6. Using the same program, create a set of bookmarks that might be placed in a school library to promote books worth reading.

7. Using a paint program, draw the outline map of your state. Add the major cities and other significant geographical features such as rivers and mountains. Print the results as a base cell and two overlays. Explain why you divided the elements the way you did.

8. Using a computer, design a transparency with two overlays. Use one of the methods mentioned in the text to produce a transparency from this. What did you find was the most difficult part of this assignment?

9. Review the copyright notice on disk or CD-ROM clip art. Is it legal to use in a classroom environment? In what instances would it be illegal to use?

10. Search for websites containing educational clip art. Find two or three good sites. Share these sites with your class and instructor.

PORTFOLIO DEVELOPMENT EXERCISES

To complete this exercise online, go to the Digital Portfolio *Module in Chapter 6 of the Companion Website.*

One of the NETS•S standards covered in this chapter was "Students use technology tools to enhance learning, increase productivity, and promote creativity" under *Category 3: Technology productivity tools.* Begin to develop your own portfolio of lesson plans that demonstrates your ability to have students reach the NETS•S standards.

1. Design a lesson plan activity for elementary, middle school, or high school students in which they use a graphics program to produce an outdoor scene. Some examples may include farm, lake, desert, or mountain scenes. Each scene should contain several objects (people, buildings, modes of transportation, vegetation, etc.) along with background, sky, and so on. Try to combine several tools found in the graphics programs. The number that you use should depend on the grade level. Younger students may only use simple tools (background, shapes, etc.). Older students will be required to use more sophisticated tools (patterns, drawing and painting tools). This lesson should demonstrate that your students have achieved the standard. Be sure to include a system of evaluation for your students' understanding and competence to ensure that they have met this standard.

2. Adapt the lesson plan activity you developed in exercise 1 for students to evaluate each others' work.

GLOSSARY

bit-mapped graphics	Computer-generated images composed of bits, or screen pixels, that are turned on (black or colored) and bits that are turned off (white or clear)
clip art	Prepared files of line drawings and images available on disk that are intended to be incorporated into the user's own work
gradient fill	A pattern that begins with a certain opacity or density of pattern at a determined point and gradually fades to one that is less dense or increases to one that is more dense
graphics	Photographic and nonphotographic representations of an object or event
lossless compression	A file compression technique through which no information is lost, though the file is smaller
lossy compression	A file compression technique that discards information it judges unnecessary
megapixel (MP)	One million pixels
pixels per inch (ppi)	The number of *pixels per inch* affects the resolution of an image
vector graphics	Computer-generated images determined by formulas that create discrete objects of a certain size and position

REFERENCES AND SUGGESTED READINGS

Anderson, L. (2005, November). A digital doorway to the world. *T.H.E. Journal, 33*(4), 14–16.

Benedetto, S. (2000, August). DVD Video: A primer for educators. *Syllabus, 14*(1), 46–49.

Burmark, L. (2002). *Visual literacy: Learn to see, see to learn.* Association for Supervision and Curriculum Development.

McInerney, P. (2000, May). Worth 1,000 words. *Learning & Leading with Technology, 27*(8), 10–15.

Setters, P. (1999–2000, December/January). Communicate with pictures: Using still and video photography in science. *Learning & Leading with Technology, 27*(4), 36–39.

Wenderski, G. (2006, January). Smart classroom: camera ready. *T.H.E. Journal, 33*(6), 34–35.

Wilhelm, L. (2005, February). Increasing visual literacy skills with digital imagery. *T.H.E. Journal, 32*(7), 24–28.

Learning with Word Processor Tools

ADVANCE ORGANIZER

1. What is a word processor?

2. What are common features of word processors?

3. What are editing functions found in word processors?

4. Why is lettering important and what are guidelines for its effective use?

5. How might the word processor be a productivity tool for you as a teacher or an administrator?

6. How is the word processor a productivity tool for the student at different grade levels?

NETS•T Foundation Standards and Performance Indicators Addressed in this Chapter

I. Technology operations and concepts
   A. demonstrate introductory knowledge, skills, and understanding of concepts related to technology (as described in ISTE National Education Technology Standards for Students)
   B. demonstrate continual growth in technology knowledge and skills to stay abreast of current and emerging technologies

II. Planning and designing learning environments and experiences
   A. Design developmentally appropriate learning opportunities that apply technology-enhanced instructional strategies to support the diverse needs of learners
   C. identify and locate technology resources and evaluate them for accuracy and suitability

III. Teaching, learning, and the curriculum
   B. facilitate technology-enhanced experiences that address content standards and student technology standards
   C. use technology to support learner-centered strategies that address the diverse needs of students
   D. apply technology to develop students' higher order skills and creativity

IV. Assessment and evaluation
   B. use technology resources to collect and analyze data, interpret results, and communicate findings to improve instructional practice and maximize student learning

V. Productivity and professional practice
   A. use technology resources to engage in ongoing professional development and lifelong learning
   C. apply technology to increase productivity
   D. use technology to communicate and collaborate with peers, parents, and the larger community in order to nurture student learning

VI. Social, ethical, legal, and human issues
   A. model and teach legal and ethical practice related to technology use
   B. apply technology resources to enable and empower learners with diverse backgrounds, characteristics, and abilities

LET'S LOOK AT THIS CHAPTER

Information, techniques, and concepts found in this chapter will help students more fully use word processing as they publish and communicate with individuals. Word processing applications are undoubtedly one of the most important groups of software applications that you and your students will use. It is imperative that you understand the uses and capabilities of this software and are able to pass along this knowledge to your students. As you read the chapter, take some extra time to review and really get to know the word processing software you and your students use. You will be glad you did, because modern word processing applications are no longer simply typing programs but rather have the ability to format, spell and grammar check, and even change case and punctuation on the fly as you type. Word processing applications are some of the most advanced technology communications tools with which you will ever come in contact.

One of the first reasons you probably used a computer as a tool was to write reports and term papers. You have no doubt found the word processor to be a trusted friend. You may have even marveled at the development of word processors over time, especially over the past few years. This friend doesn't simply place your words on paper anymore; it also automatically corrects spelling and grammar and may even place everything in the format that you preset. You could almost say that, to some extent, it is proofing and retyping your paper for you. Just as it has undoubtedly helped you as a student, you will find that the word processor is indispensable to you as a classroom teacher.

Word processing has also become a powerful tool in the hands of students. The use of word processing improves students' attitudes toward writing by making them want to write more and making them feel better about their writing using a larger vocabulary, because they find it easy to correct spelling.

WORD PROCESSORS

The term **word processor** is used to denote a whole category of software whose primary purpose is to facilitate written communication. As indicated in Figure 7–1, word processing is a systematic organization of procedures and equipment to display information efficiently in a written form and to preserve it electronically. Word processing programs usually consist of two basic, interacting parts—a text editor to manipulate text and a print formatter to deliver the text file to the printer. Depending on the individual software, several additional parts such as a spell checker, dictionary, thesaurus, and grammar checker are also present. The **text editor** is the most visible part of the program and is the one that allows the user to manipulate text on a screen display. It is used during the text entry phase as you add, change, and delete text, as well as locate words and phrases and embed the format commands needed to control the print formatter. From the text editor, you can insert the commands to determine the font, margins, line spacing, and so on. The editor also contains the means to save, merge, copy, and insert text from one file to another. All modern word processors display the text on the screen the exact way that it will appear on the printed page. This display is often referred to as **WYSIWYG** (what you see is what you get—pronounced "wizzy wig"). The **print formatter** works behind the scenes to deliver the text file to the printer and ensure that it is printed correctly on paper.

Figure 7–1 Word processing
A schematic illustrating the processes involved

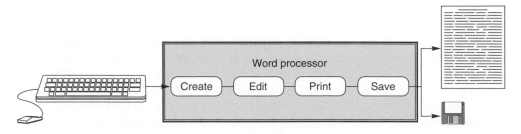

There are several good word processors from which to choose. Selecting the one that is best for you depends on your computer system and on your individual needs. The two most popular word processing programs are Microsoft Word for Windows and Macintosh (found as part of the Microsoft Office suite) and Pages 2, a successor to AppleWorks for the Macintosh. Either program is a good choice, because they have many of the same features. There are also several word processing programs for younger students such as *Read, Write & Type for grades 1 and 2* and *Student Writing Center* for grades 4 through 12. Students with special needs may benefit from *Write:OutLoud*, a talking word processor and speller, and *Co:Writer*, a word prediction program that decreases the number of keystrokes needed to complete each word.

Word Processor Features

Following is a brief list of the features found in word processing programs.

Column Formatting. In addition to specifying top, bottom, and side margins, many word processors allow the user to format a page in more than one column.

Dictionary. This feature provides word definition and syllabication, and allows the user to confirm spelling.

Footer. Similar to a header, a footer is a brief message that may automatically display text or a date, time, or page display that is added to the bottom of each page and can usually be suppressed on a title page.

Footnotes. Some programs allow the user to mark words in the text to be referenced automatically as footnotes at the bottom of the page or as endnotes at the end of the document.

Formatting. Document layout and margins can be applied. Bullets and numbering can be automatically applied to lists; drop caps can begin paragraphs; customized indents and spacing as well as special control over page breaks can be applied to a paragraph; and borders and shading can be applied to sections of text.

Glossary. Often used words and phrases such as a return address or the closing of a letter can be created and stored in a glossary to be called up at any time by a simple keystroke.

Grammar Checking. This feature attempts to identify wordiness, awkward constructions, singular/plural agreement, and the use of passive voice, among other things. Some word processors allow the user to customize the grammar checker by selecting writing styles such as casual, formal, or technical.

Header. This is similar to a footer but is displayed at the top of each page and can usually be suppressed on a title page.

Hyphenation. Because **word wrap** can leave lines of varying lengths, thereby creating a ragged right margin, some word processors allow the user to turn on a hyphenation feature that will generate a hyphen at the most appropriate syllable break in a word at the end of a line.

Indenting. The common first line indent moves the beginning of the first line of a paragraph a predetermined distance from the left margin. A hanging indent begins the first line at the left margin and then moves subsequent lines of the paragraph a predetermined distance from the left margin.

Index. The creation of an index can be greatly facilitated by a feature that allows a user to mark words that are then automatically copied, along with a page reference, to an index at the end of the document.

Insert. Page breaks, page numbers, date and time stamps, autotext (e.g., mailing instructions, salutations, closings, signature), special symbols and characters ( ), ®, ©, etc.), pictures, movies, and hyperlinks can be inserted into your documents.

Mail Merge. An almost indispensable feature—when sending form letters that appear to be personalized with appropriate names, addresses, and even specific content—is the ability to merge data from one data file to another at the proper place in the document.

Orphan/Widow Control. **Orphans** are single lines of text that occur at the bottoms of pages. **Widows** are single lines of text that occur at the tops of pages. Some word processors will not allow these to occur but, instead, will force the appropriate page break so that at least two lines of text appear together.

Outlining. Some of the more powerful word processors have integrated outliners built into them, allowing the user to create an outline of the document and to expand or collapse various levels.

Pagination. Once a user sets the page length of the document by prescribing top and bottom margins on a specified size of paper, this feature allows a word processor to generate page breaks, indicate them on the screen automatically, number pages, and renumber them when editing is performed.

Print Preview. All worthwhile word processors allow the user to see the document on the screen as it will look when printed and closely approach a WYSIWYG state.

Save As. Word processors save the documents created in their native format (e.g., Microsoft Word version "x" saves a document as a Word version "x" file). Most word processors can also save documents in several other file formats. Saving them as a file in a very basic text format allows the documents to be readily transported between word processors. If you want your document to look a bit better, you might want to save it in rich text format (RTF), which is a text format that also keeps a number of the formatting attributes of the original file. Many word processors also allow users to save files as HTML documents for the Web. Before leaving this topic, we must mention another way to save documents. A program called Adobe Acrobat® saves a document in a PDF format (*Portable Document Format*) so it looks like an exact copy of the original document (text, graphics, and all). You must purchase Adobe Acrobat if you want to save documents in this format but Adobe Acrobat Reader®, the program needed to read PDF documents, is free. You should download a copy to your computer if you don't already have it. It is probably possible for you to go to the website for your college or university and download applications and other PDF documents needed at your school. A word to the wise: Get Acrobat Reader and learn how to use it. When you are looking for a job, the employer might just tell you to go to their site and download the application.

Sort. Lists may be sorted alphabetically in ascending or descending order.

Spell Checking. Unlike a dictionary, a spell checker does not display definitions, but compares all words found in the document against its master list. Any word not matching is called to the user's attention and, if possible, a replacement word is suggested. Most allow the user to add frequently used unusual words (proper nouns, acronyms, etc.) to a custom list. We have added the words *Forcier* and *Descy* to ours.

Style Sheet. A style is a set of format characteristics (left aligned, 12 point, Palatino, 0.25 inch first line indent, for example) that can be applied to text. A style sheet is a collection of styles used in a document. Choosing a style for text about to be entered is a timesaving device.

Table of Contents. A feature that facilitates the creation of a table by allowing a user to mark words that are then automatically copied to a table of contents at the beginning of the document.

Thesaurus. This feature soon becomes a writer's favorite tool. A selected word is compared with a list in the thesaurus and a number of synonyms are suggested to avoid undue repetitions or to adjust a subtle nuance in the writing.

Lori Whitley/Merrill

Once you have determined your word processing needs in general, consider the major features that will affect your usage and will minimize the problems you may encounter. If you intend to use a word processor to create a document at home and then wish to print it at school, you will need word processing programs that are able to save and open the same file in a manner that preserves the document's format.

Word Processor Functions

A representative sample of editing functions is presented in Figure 7–2. The user can navigate through the document, adding, deleting, finding, replacing, inserting, and moving information at will.

Many editing features are invoked through pulldown menus and most have keyboard shortcuts or double-key presses so that the program can distinguish a command from a text entry (see Figure 7–3). A double-key press simply means that the user holds down a designated key such as the Command or Alt key and presses a second key. Most word processing programs use similar keyboard shortcuts. Holding down the command key and pressing the "x" key cuts highlighted text, command key and "c" key copies highlighted text into the computer's memory, and command key and "v" key pastes the saved text in Microsoft Word. Learning to use key commands will speed up your word processing.

In addition to the editing commands is a set of commands to determine the format of the printed output. These print commands, of course, are not printed out as text; they are the embedded control commands giving instructions to the printer being used. They allow the user to describe paper size; margins; character typeface, size, and style; right, left, center, or full line justification; and more.

Another way to speed up your word processing is to use the toolbars that come with each word processing program. Most programs automatically display one or two of these. You can display or hide any that you want. The Microsoft Word program that we use has 19 different toolbars we could display. We often use only the *Formatting* toolbar to save space on our monitor screen (Figure 7–4). All 19 toolbars can be turned on and off in the Toolbars option menu found in the View menu.

Figure 7–2 **Editing functions**
Some word processor editing functions

Create a new document	• Select New in the File menu.
Open an existing document	• Select Open in the File menu and choose the document in the dialog window.
Insert text	• Click the mouse where you want to add text and begin typing. Typing spreads apart the existing text to accommodate the new entry. The new material may be as little as a single letter or many paragraphs long.
Word wrap	• After setting the line length for your document, a word that is too long to fit at the end of a line is automatically moved to the following line. Hyphenation can be turned on or off.
Delete text	• With the mouse, highlight the text to be deleted and press the delete key.
Replace text	• With the mouse, highlight the text to be replaced and begin typing. Placing the cursor immediately following a text character and pressing the delete or backspace key erases the character to its immediate left, one character at a time. The remaining text is then automatically rearranged properly, with word wrap and page breaks taken into account.
Move text	• With the mouse, highlight the text to be moved. • Select Cut from the Edit menu to remove the text. (If you wish to duplicate the text, select Copy instead.) • The item is now stored in temporary memory. With the mouse, move the cursor to the point where you want the text to appear and select Paste from the Edit menu.
Find/Replace text	• Select Find from the Edit menu. In the dialog box, type the word or phrase you wish to find and click on Find Next. The cursor will move through the document until it finds your request. • Select Replace from the Edit menu. In the dialog box, type the word or phrase you wish to replace. Type the replacement in the appropriate area and click on Find Next. The cursor will move through the document until it finds your request. You can either replace the item or skip over it by clicking Find Next again.
Undo an edit	• Select Undo from the Edit menu. This command will undo the very last or several of the last keystrokes that you typed. This can be a lifesaver if you hit the wrong keys and something strange happens to the text.
Save your document	• Select Save from the File menu. The first time only that you save a new document you will be asked to name it. It's a good idea to save a document every few minutes. • If you wish to save a different copy of your document, select Save As and give your document a different name.

Figure 7–3 **Shortcuts**
Some keystroke shortcuts in Microsoft® Word® *(Reprinted with permission from Microsoft, Inc.)*

Figure 7–4 **Formatting toolbar**
The formatting toolbar in Microsoft® Word® contains many useful functions. *(Reprinted with permission from Microsoft, Inc.)*

Word Processor Templates

Many word processing programs contain templates that take much of the work out of setting up these tasks. Microsoft Office (which includes Word) presents a Project Gallery, as shown in Figure 7–5, meant to simplify the creation of various documents. Notice the tabs at the top. A number of choices can be made in each tab.

Figure 7–6 shows the Project Gallery again on the left with the *Learn* tab selected. Opening the *Newsletter* template leads the user through a brief tutorial on designing newsletters as shown on the right. Because Microsoft Word is marketed toward the business environment, many of the templates are designed for that audience, but can be readily applied to school and classroom uses.

Figure 7–5 Project gallery

The Project Gallery in Microsoft® Office® contains a variety of templates *(Reprinted with permission from Microsoft, Inc.)*

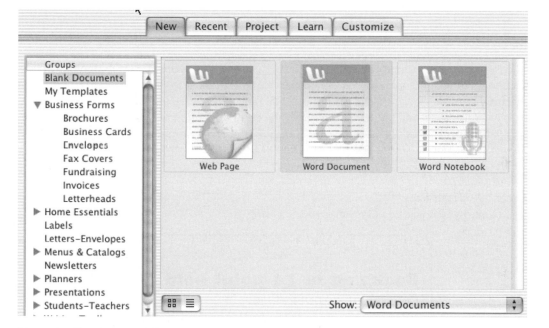

Figure 7–6 Newsletter template

The newsletter template found in the Microsoft® Office® Project Gallery *(Reprinted with permission from Microsoft, Inc.)*

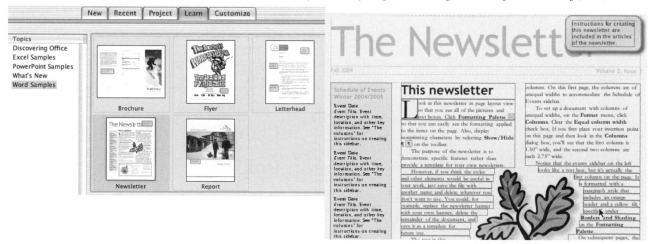

▮▮▮ LETTERING

Word processing has added a new graphic dimension to communicating in print. It's not only what you say and how you say it, but also how it looks on the page. Word processing has placed at our disposal the ability to affect the appearance of the printed word easily yet markedly. Reflecting on the adage "a picture is worth a thousand words," word processing adds somewhat of a "picture" quality to the text medium and requires us to attend to some terms and guidelines concerning the appearance of text.

Font

The collection of characteristics applied to a **typeface** in a particular **size** and **style** is called a **font.** Sample fonts are illustrated in Figure 7–7. Through common usage the term *font* has unfortunately become synonymous with typeface and we commonly refer to the *Courier* or *Times New Roman* fonts.

Size

The height of a letter, expressed in points, is the size. It includes the "x" height as well as ascenders and descenders of lowercase letters. One point was defined as 1/72 of an inch by the inventors of Adobe Postscript. The left side of Figure 7–8 illustrates a progression from 9-point to 24-point type. Different typefaces vary in letter width and thickness of line, sometimes giving the appearance of a variation in size.

Figure 7–7 Sample fonts
Some fonts (a combination of typeface, size, and style)

> **Bookman in 14-point bold**
> *Geneva in 12-point italic*
> Palatino in 18-point plain text

Figure 7–8 Sizes and styles
Sample point sizes on the left and styles on the right

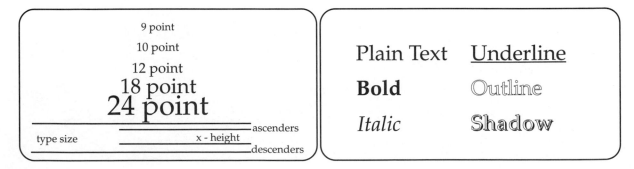

Style

Style refers to the appearance of a particular typeface as visual modifications are applied, as illustrated in the right side of Figure 7–8.

Typeface

A typeface is the design of the letter and the name given to the design. New designs are constantly emerging and are usually copyrighted by the creator. Typefaces affect the feeling imparted by the message, as well as its content. Some have harsh, angular lines; others have soft curves. Some are narrow and condensed; others are round or broad. Some use thick lines and convey a heavy or dark impression to a text, whereas others use thin lines, resulting in a light text. Others are designed for special purposes, such as holidays, flyers, or greeting cards. Serif typefaces such as those illustrated in Figure 7–9 have fine lines that finish the major strokes of the letters. These serve as decorative yet functional connectors that appear to join adjacent letters, thereby helping the reader to perceive groups of letters as words. Therefore, serif typefaces enhance the speed and ease with which text can be read. This textbook is printed in a serif typeface.

Notice that even in plain text some typefaces are darker than others. Also notice that some typefaces occupy more line length in the same point size because of the rounder shape of their letters. The rounder shape of the lowercase letters in Bookman in Figure 7–9 makes this most apparent.

Sans serif typefaces, such as those illustrated in Figure 7–10, usually should not be used in body text. Their clean lines and lack of connectors make them somewhat difficult and tiring to read in body text. Sans serif typefaces should be used primarily in a bold style and large size as headlines and titles. Also notice that different typefaces have thicker or bolder lines, thereby making a stronger statement.

Ornate typefaces, such as those illustrated in Figure 7–11, are certainly attention getting and effective if used sparingly. They are as much graphic as they are text. The message embodied in the ornate design should support the written words.

Every text example shown thus far has been a **proportional-spaced typeface.** That is to say, its design attempts to achieve **optical spacing** by allowing the surface area of the space between each letter to be roughly the same. The distance will, therefore, vary between each letter, depending on its shape. **Monospaced typefaces,** such as Courier or Monaco, are sometimes referred to as having **mechanical spacing.** Their design allows each letter to be equally distant from the next, regardless of the letter

Figure 7–9 Serif typefaces
Notice the connectors in this sample of serif typefaces

Palatino -   An analysis of factors that influence

Bookman - An analysis of factors that influ

Figure 7–10 Sans serif typefaces
Notice the lack of connectors in this sample of sans serif typefaces

Arial -   An analysis of factors that influence

Chicago – An analysis of factors that

Figure 7–11 Ornate typefaces

Notice how the design of the typefaces contributes to their message

Brush Script - Typeface selection

UMBRA - TYPEFACE SELECTION

Snowcap - Typeface selection

Figure 7–12 Proportional and monospaced

This illustrates the difference between optical and mechanical spacing

> **Palatino (proportional)**
>
> An analysis of factors that influence typeface selection must incl
>
> **Courier (monospaced)**
>
> An analysis of factors that influence typeface

LETTERING GUIDELINES

A copy of these guidelines may be found in the Guidelines folder in the Take-Along CD

- Select a suitable typeface to enhance readability and the expression of your words.
- Use sans serif typefaces in a large size for headlines or titles. Used sparingly, they have a simplicity that commands attention. Large amounts in body text are difficult to read.
- Use serif typefaces for body text. The decorations on the letters help to guide the reader's eye movement from one letter to the next, thereby helping the reader to perceive words rather than letters.
- Use ornate text sparingly for special visual effects.
- Avoid mixing typefaces within the same document except for a distinct purpose. Rarely should you mix more than two typefaces in the same document.
- Select a letter size appropriate to the message and its intended impact. Consider that not all output is intended for 8 1/2-by-11-inch paper. Consider the optimum viewing distance and the medium (e.g., a minimum of 18-point size should be used for overhead transparencies and 24 point or larger for presentation slide shows).
- Use style (plain, bold, italic, outline, shadow, underline) for emphasis.
- Allow plenty of white space around a block of text. A block of text takes up space, so be sure to consider it in your overall design.

shape. As you examine Figure 7–12, which illustrates the difference between the two types of spacing, pay particular attention to the lowercase letters *i* and *l* and their adjacent letters.

If you are interested in more information on lettering, including much of the information discussed in this section, review the excellent series of articles found at *http://en. wikipedia.org/wiki/Typeface#Types_of_fonts*.

WORD PROCESSOR APPLICATIONS

Teachers want help in alleviating the paperwork demands made on them. They want help in accomplishing activities that do not involve students directly and are quite often done outside of actual class time. If the time required to perform these tasks could be decreased, teachers would have more time to devote to working with students.

Administrative Applications

Teachers create some written classroom material that changes very little from one year to the next. An exercise sheet or another resource material such as a game or puzzle used once in a unit plan may be used the following year with only slight modification. Material, once designed, can be easily modified to serve a similar purpose in another unit of study. By using a word processor, the teacher could develop a few standard templates and then make appropriate changes as needed.

In addition to the preparation of instructional materials, consider the writing that is expected of a teacher. Ask yourself how a teacher might save time and effort and still accomplish the writing tasks effectively. One example of these writing tasks might be asking parents to allow their child to participate in a school-sponsored field trip. The task might be accomplished by sending home an impersonal request form and asking the parents to fill in the name of their child and sign the form. Using a word processor and merging information from a data file, this process can be personalized, as shown in Figure 7–13. Labels in curly brackets, { }, indicate an item to be inserted from the data file. Microsoft Office® *Help* offers clear instructions on setting up the main document and the data file

Figure 7–13 Form letter

An example of a form letter that can be personalized by merging data

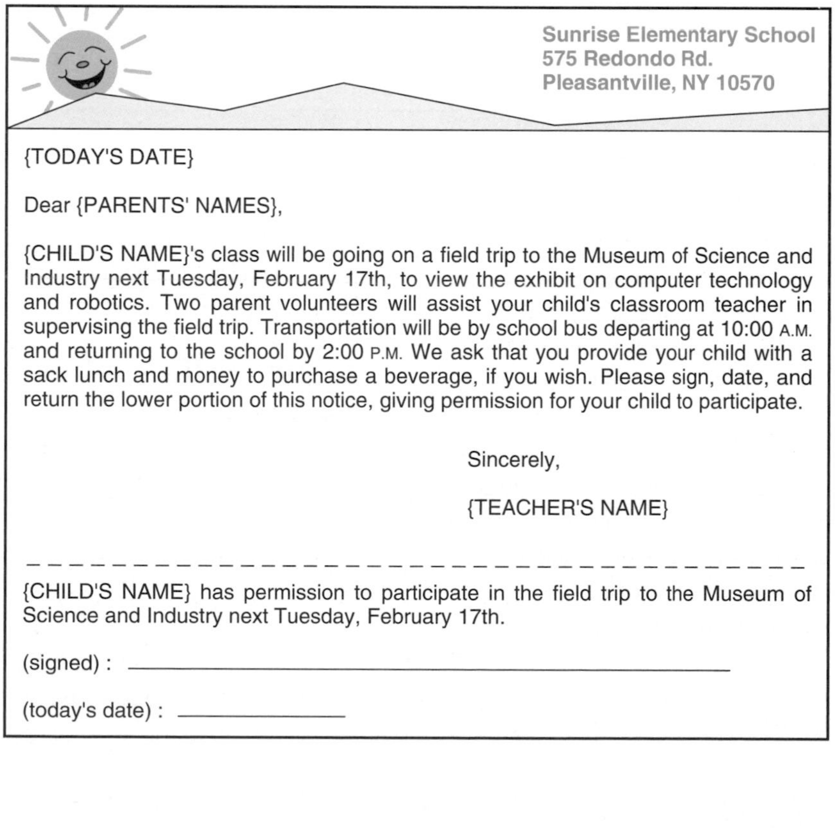

{TODAY'S DATE}

Dear {PARENTS' NAMES},

{CHILD'S NAME}'s class will be going on a field trip to the Museum of Science and Industry next Tuesday, February 17th, to view the exhibit on computer technology and robotics. Two parent volunteers will assist your child's classroom teacher in supervising the field trip. Transportation will be by school bus departing at 10:00 A.M. and returning to the school by 2:00 P.M. We ask that you provide your child with a sack lunch and money to purchase a beverage, if you wish. Please sign, date, and return the lower portion of this notice, giving permission for your child to participate.

Sincerely,

{TEACHER'S NAME}

- -

{CHILD'S NAME} has permission to participate in the field trip to the Museum of Science and Industry next Tuesday, February 17th.

(signed) : _____

(today's date) : _____

227

using Word's Data Manager. Microsoft Word can also retrieve data stored in a spreadsheet or in the popular database manager, FileMaker® Pro. In addition to appearing as a personal communication to the parents, the form letter could be used as a **template** for any other field trip permission form, with a minimum of retyping. **Boilerplate** is a term that comes from the legal profession and signifies material that can be used repeatedly without modification. The term **stationery** is sometimes used as a replacement for template.

Teaching Applications

We often think of a word processor as a tool that enhances an individual's personal productivity, and indeed it is. Collaborative writing, however, is a technique that allows more than one student to engage in a writing activity together. The technique often calls for students to agree on an outline and then to divide the writing tasks among themselves. The written documents are then merged together, and the students edit each other's work and rewrite the composition. If the writing is done in a computer lab, students can brainstorm a story idea and then begin drafting the story on their own computers. After 15 to 20 minutes, students can exchange places and continue writing where the previous student ended. New software allows students sitting at computers on a network to write and to edit each other's documents in real time.

For many years, teachers have promoted the teaching of writing as a process of drafting, revising, editing, and publishing. Teachers need to guide students' composition and provide necessary feedback for revision. The word processor supports writing instruction by making the writing process less tedious, thereby encouraging a far more positive attitude toward writing and motivating students to experiment with language. A study (Raef, 1996) of elementary school students identified as having weak writing skills indicated that the students' motivation to write increased with the use of word processing. Figures 7–14

Figure 7–14 Big book
A big book sample page

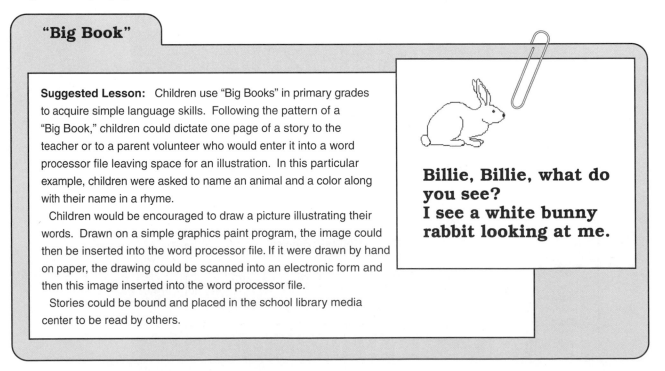

"Big Book"

Suggested Lesson: Children use "Big Books" in primary grades to acquire simple language skills. Following the pattern of a "Big Book," children could dictate one page of a story to the teacher or to a parent volunteer who would enter it into a word processor file leaving space for an illustration. In this particular example, children were asked to name an animal and a color along with their name in a rhyme.

  Children would be encouraged to draw a picture illustrating their words. Drawn on a simple graphics paint program, the image could then be inserted into the word processor file. If it were drawn by hand on paper, the drawing could be scanned into an electronic form and then this image inserted into the word processor file.

  Stories could be bound and placed in the school library media center to be read by others.

Billie, Billie, what do you see?
I see a white bunny rabbit looking at me.

Figure 7–15 Student authors

A big book authored by students

Figure 7–16 Topic sentence

A lesson aimed at topic sentences and getting the main idea of a paragraph

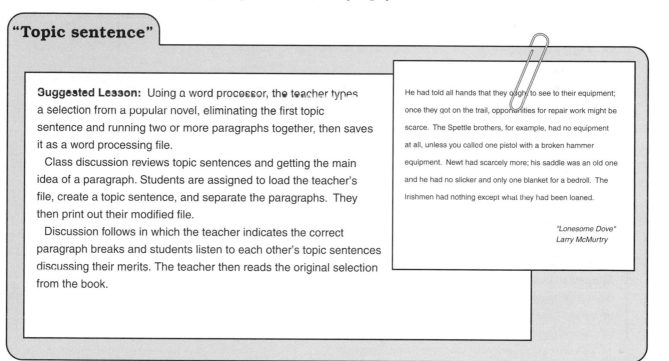

through 7–20 depict lesson activities to illustrate how a word processor might be used as a tool by students to explore creative writing—to write reports, compositions, and poetry. These examples can be modified to serve in a variety of subject areas and grade levels. Word processing objectives, writing objectives, and subject matter objectives often dovetail. If students are to capitalize on the power of the word processor as a tool and use it with confidence, they must develop an understanding of its application and a reasonably high level of skill in its use. Using this tool, they will enhance their written communication as they acquire and construct knowledge in various content areas.

229

Figure 7–17 **Classroom newsletter**

A lesson aimed at guiding students in the publishing of a newsletter

Classroom newsletter

Suggested Lesson: The teacher serves as guide and advisor as students publish a class newspaper. They discuss events of the past week and decide which to report. They focus attention on the importance of the headline and take turns writing the stories. They edit each other's stories for content, spelling, grammar, and creative expression.

An extension of this activity could have the teacher encourage students to interview local business and civic leaders, examine local occupations, or record stories told by old-timers in the community.

Student photographs and drawings could be scanned and inserted in the document. Modest page layout software could eventually replace the word processor and give the publication a more sophisticated look as the students gain skills and experience.

Mrs. Prosser's Classroom News
May 21, 200

School Built on Site of Indian Village

Mr. Gerald Girod showed his collection of arrowheads to Mrs. Prosser's fifth-grade class. He grew up here in Chicopee Falls and started his collection when he was a young boy. He found his first arrowheads in what is now the school playground years before the school was built. He found some small arrowheads that he thinks were used to hunt birds.

Mr. Girod also showed some broken pieces of pottery that he found down on the river bank. The pottery shards, the arrowheads, and pictures of what the playground area looked like before the school was built will be placed in the display case in the school library.

Figure 7–18 **Poem**

A lesson aimed at the discussion of rhyme and meter

Poem

Suggested Lesson: Using a word processor, the teacher types selections from several poems eliminating one line from each poem, then saves the document as a word processor file.

Class discussion reviews rhyme and meter. Students are assigned to load the teacher's file and create the missing line. Each student then prints a copy of the completed poems.

Discussion follows in which the students listen to each other's poems and discuss their merits. The teacher then reads the original selection.

'Twixt optimist and pessimist
_____
The optimist sees the doughnut;
   The pessimist sees the hole.

The pedigree of honey
Does not concern the bee;
A clover, anytime, to him

_____

Dogs in the country have fun.

But in the city this species
Is dragged around on leashes.

Figure 7–19 **Collaboration**

A lesson aimed at fostering collaborative writing

Collaboration

Suggested Lesson: Students agree on a story outline. Using a word processor, they develop some ideas as they write paragraphs into a file. Students merge their separate files into one document.

   This example shows two students' files merged together. Each student then takes a copy of the document and rewrites the entire segment in such a way as the paragraphs take on a coherence and unity of expression.

   Students print their own file when they are finished and exchange papers to compare writing styles. Students are then given the opportunity to modify their own document.

What would the Oregon country be like, she wondered as she gazed at her child burning with fever. Would this interminable trek /ver/end? Would they find the answer to their prayers? Would she, Abner, and their children ever see the green valleys and rushing streams about which they had heard?

The parching heat and blowing dust make every mile seem like 10. The slow creaking of the wagon wheels and plodding of the oxen add to the monotony. The scout says there's a river an hour away where we will make camp for tonight. The thought of water and some rest lift my spirits and give me the energy to keep going.

Figure 7–20 **Writing exercise**

A whole-class exercise in analyzing writing style

Writing exercise

Suggested Lesson: The teacher finds a quotation that illustrates expressive language. Using a word processor, the teacher paraphrases the quotation in a direct style and, after spacing down the page, enters the quotation. Using a large monitor or an overhead display panel, the teacher shows the first section to the class.

   After reading the first section, students rewrite the selection using a more expressive style. They may then read their selection aloud or display it for the class to read. The teacher then displays the original quotation and leads the class in analyzing the style.

   A follow-up activity could have students load each other's files and edit each other's work in an attempt to influence the mood of the selection.

I predict for America, not despair but rather great hope. I believe that anything is possible if people want it badly enough.

I see America, not in the setting sun of a black night of despair ahead of us, I see America in the crimson light of a rising sun fresh from the burning, creative hand of God. I see great days ahead, great days possible to men and women of will and vision . . . .

—Carl Sandburg

231

WORD PROCESSING LESSONS

Commercially published "Big Books" are in a large format that lend themselves to being read and displayed in front of a group of students. They usually contain one story; some have repetition on each page, as illustrated in Figure 7–14.

The example in Figure 7–15 shows a continuous story, with each child responsible for writing and illustrating one page. Books created by children can range over a wide variety of topics and can integrate a number of subject matter disciplines.

Consider the following ideas:

- Write about endangered animals. An illustration and facts about the animals would require some research.
- Use alliteration with names from your hometown or state to foster recognition of place names, cities, towns, rivers, and so on. For example, "Suzy Smith from Seaside sings in the shower" or "Terrific Terry from Troutdale travels along the Trask River."
- Report on a classroom activity: "What I learned about raising quail chicks in school."
- Read a story such as "Alexander and the Magic Pebble" and respond to it: "If I had a magic pebble, I would . . ."
- Engage in wonderful word problems. Write and illustrate math word problems. Place answers to the student-written problems on the last page.

The lessons illustrated in Figures 7–14 through 7–20 are summarized in the following table.

Figure	Lesson Topic
7–14	Creating a "Big Book"
7–15	Creating a "Big Book" authored by students
7–16	Developing the main idea in a paragraph and writing a topic sentence
7–17	Reporting, composition, creative expression, and use of graphics to illustrate writing of a newsletter
7–18	Poetry rhyme and meter
7–19	Collaborative creative expression and writing style
7–20	A whole-class exercise on expressive style

DESKTOP PUBLISHING

The most fully featured extension of the word processing program is the desktop publishing program. The term **desktop publishing** implies the ability to create sophisticated printed documents. Programs in this category contain the most extensive set of commands and include advanced page layout capabilities. These programs may require an investment of time or training to take full advantage of their many features, as well as continual use to maintain skill level. They contain all of the necessary functions for work on full reports, newsletters, brochures, and documents that include **text-wrapped graphics,** as shown in Figure 7–21.

In addition to the features mentioned for standard word processors, desktop publishing programs include the ability to create a master page layout or design that is repeated on every page, to format variable-width columns, to use drop caps at the beginning of paragraphs (as in the first letter of the next paragraph), to import and format graphics, and to wrap lines of text around graphics' irregular edges. Many of these features are being introduced into regular word processing programs as well.

Figure 7–21 Text-wrapped graphics

A graphic may be placed on a page with text wrapped around it

MacGlobe® is a rich database of geographical facts covering every country in the world. It begins with a world map and lets the user choose from regional maps (e.g., continents, political and economic alliances), country maps (e.g., political divisions and elevation), and thematic maps (e.g., population, natural resources, agricultural production, education).

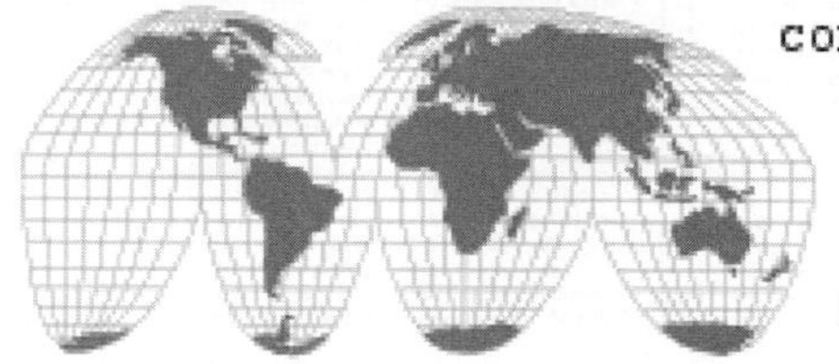

Desktop publishing really takes advantage of the power of the printed page. Embodying all of the features of less powerful word processing programs, it adds to the writer's expressive ability by improving the visual presentation of text and visuals by controlling their juxtaposition. By careful control of the white space on the page, the writer controls the overall appearance of the document and gives added impact to the intended message. A few of the tools used to organize the appearance of text are presented in Figure 7–22. This illustration is presented in what is called a "greeked" fashion. You are not expected to read any text but rather to look at blocks of text as objects.

Headlines grab attention and encourage the viewer to become a reader of the article. To be effective, headlines should be concise and delineated from the body of the text by use of the same or contrasting typeface in a larger size and different style. Boxes can separate parts of a document. They are usually used to isolate specific information, sometimes called sidebars. Horizontal lines or rules can also separate parts of a document. Margins create a white space surrounding the text, which affects a document's feel. Wider margins result in a lighter document. The width of the space between columns, called the gutter, also contributes to the feel of the document. Columns may be of different widths, often with artwork extending across one or more columns. Figure 7–23 is an effort by the authors to compile the most common desktop publishing organization tools into a chart to which you might wish to refer from time to time.

Full-featured desktop publishing, word processing programs can be expensive and quite complex for the average user. Less expensive desktop publishing programs are available with a reduced set of features, making them easier to use. These have found favor with teachers and students who use them to prepare newsletters and bulletins and even to lay out yearbooks. A program such as New Print Shop Deluxe® is a fully featured desktop publishing program aimed at students at all levels from grades 1 through 12. Greeting cards, signs, calendars, banners, certificates, and simple newsletters are some of the projects easily accomplished with this program. Kid Works Deluxe combines a word processor and a paint program and allows Pre-K through fourth graders to produce multimedia books, awards, and other projects. At the other end of the continuum are desktop publishing programs such as PageMaker®. This fully featured professional desktop publishing program can be mastered by students in high school with some practice and effort.

Figure 7–22 Text blocks

This "greeked" illustration shows how text blocks can be publishing tools

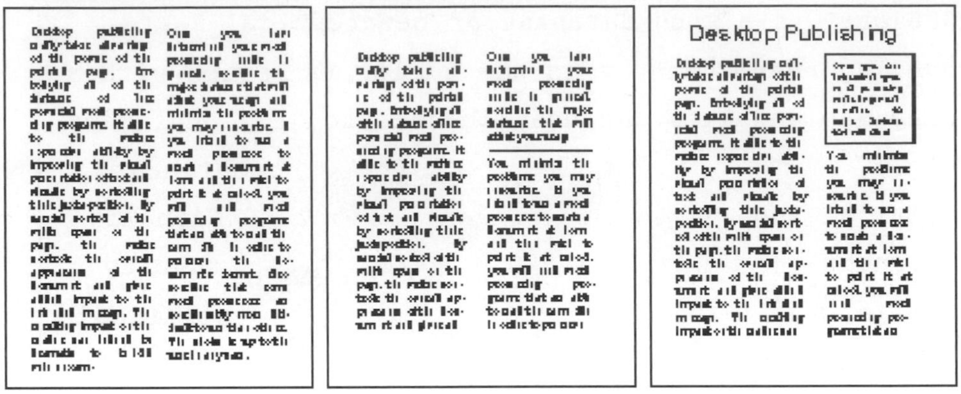

Figure 7–23 Organization tools

Desktop publishing organization tools

DESKTOP PUBLISHING ORGANIZATION TOOLS

Headlines entice people to read an article. They should be designed for impact and should stand out from the text of the article (often by using a contrasting typeface in a larger size). Sans serif bold typefaces are usually used. Avoid long headlines in uppercase type. They are difficult to read.

Captions relate illustrations to the content of the article. They summarize important points. Captions should be treated the same way throughout a publication.

Boxes can highlight parts of a publication. They often contain short, related articles.

Lines are used to separate parts of a publication. Horizontal lines usually separate different topics within the same column. They are often used to draw attention to short sentences ("pull-quotes") that summarize the key points of an article.

Margins determine the relationship of text and graphics. There should always be ample "breathing room" between the content and the page edge. Wide margins promote a "lighter or brighter feel" to the publication.

Columns organize the horizontal placement of content. Text is usually arranged in one or more columns on a page. The space between columns is called the gutter. Narrow gutters often make a publication more difficult to read, because the reader's eye tends to jump between columns.

Column width influences a publication's readability. Readers scan groups of words. Wide columns are more difficult to read because a reader's eyes have to shift several times when reading each line.

Symbols such as bullets and numbers organize lists of items. Use bullets (•) or asterisks (*), or other like symbols (√, °, Δ) when all items in the list are of equal importance. Numbers suggest a linear order.

THE WORD PROCESSOR AS A PRODUCTIVITY TOOL

The computer is a tool, and word processing is one of the most popular and powerful tool uses. Seat work, homework, exercise sheets, lesson plans, bibliographies, class notes, reports, essays, compositions, memos, letters to parents—the list of practical word processing applications goes on and on. It is easy to understand why most people purchasing a personal computer do so primarily to use it as a word processor.

The argument can be built that the word processor and not the computer itself is in fact the productivity tool. Software indeed transforms the hardware. Using the best software appropriate for a given task makes the computer far more effective or productive than using poorly designed or inappropriate software. Once software is loaded into the hardware, perhaps we should no longer refer to it as a computer but, rather, call it a word processor, database manager, or drawing table.

To gauge the word processor value as a productivity tool, the following questions must be answered. Does using the word processor increase my accuracy? Does it ease my task? Does it increase the speed at which I can complete a task? Does it allow me to accomplish something that I might otherwise find impossible? In other words, does it contribute to my efficiency or effectiveness?

LET'S GO INTO THE CLASSROOM
Putting It All Together

Making one-page magazine-style advertisements engages small groups of upper elementary students in a variety of team activities. It leads to high motivation, knowledge and skill sharing, and observable achievements in the language arts, mathematics, and computer literacy.

Collaborative ad-making involves use, sharing, and development of academic and social skills. The task involves "authentic learning," especially when ads are made for actual home and school use, though many students are even more highly motivated when their products or services are fanciful. Students have applied the ad format to making posters for other purposes, for example, to make appeals for emergency relief when natural disasters occur around the world. Many students have expressed interest in doing new ads when they returned to school the following year.

Objectives of the Lesson

1. **To Develop Number Sense:** accurate estimates of costs of common goods and services, correct decimal notations for dollars and cents, and mental calculations of multiples of simple whole or two-place decimal numbers.
2. **To Practice and Expand Desktop Publishing Skills:** keyboarding, selecting fonts and graphics, and designing page layout for clarity and attractiveness.
3. **To Practice and Develop Small-Group Collaborative Decision-Making Skills:** dividing responsibility for individual tasks and combining efforts into a final product.
4. **To Practice Process Writing Skills:** prewriting text elements, keyboarding, reading critically, editing, printing, sharing, and revising.
5. **To Promote Self-Assessment:** students examine products in relation to explicit criteria (clarity, attractiveness, creativity, complexity, accuracy), other groups' work, and exemplary models.

(Continued)

Prerequisite Skills

Students must be familiar with the basic operation of computers, whether Mac or Windows, and with a word processing program such as The Student Writing Center (second graders may use Kid Pix). Also, they must have previously learned how to work effectively within a small group, recognizing their division of roles and collective responsibilities.

Sequence of Activities

(Daily or one-a-week, 50-minute sessions may be abridged or expanded.)

Session 1: The teacher displays and describes magazine ads and asks students to discuss the characteristics and purposes of the ads. Students select two peers to form small groups to examine sample ads and to make a list of features.

Session 2: The teacher asks students what they recall about purposes and characteristics of ads while sketching an ad on markerboard accordingly. The teacher then challenges them to make ads of their own and clarifies which software is to be used and what components and qualities will be expected (real or imaginary products or services; prices for one, two, or three discounts, etc.). Groups of three or four students begin drafting their own ads, while the teacher provides guidance as needed.

Session 3: Students examine and revise their first drafts. The teacher provides guidance concerning product or service and prices. Members of the group take turns keyboarding text and share in decision making about fonts, colors, graphics, and layout.

Session 4: Students revise according to posted criteria, print in draft mode, share, edit, print in color, take home, share with family and friends, and solicit suggestions.

Session 5: Group members discuss suggestions received, make final revisions, print color version, post on bulletin board, or place in approved locations.

Evaluation

Students examine their draft and final ads in relation to posted criteria—clarity, attractiveness, creativity, complexity, and accuracy. They compare their ads with those of their peers and with exemplary models provided by the teacher. The teacher assesses quality of interactions among students in each group, interest and engagement displayed during production, quality of products, and application of skills acquired to related tasks, transfer of skills to new tasks, and subsequent eagerness to use skills for their own purposes.

Steven Hackbarth
Elementary Computer Specialist Teacher
P.S. 6 and P.S. 116
New York City, New York

LET'S REVIEW

This chapter addressed the value of using a word processor in the classroom as a tool to facilitate written communication. Studies have shown that the use of word processing by students increases their motivation to write and expands their vocabulary.

Features that might be considered when choosing a word processor were examined. The more sophisticated programs are expected to contain a greater number of features. After writing needs are determined, a program can be selected that has an appropriate set of features.

Representative editing functions were examined that allow the user to navigate through the document, adding, deleting, finding, replacing, inserting, and moving information at will. In addition, print commands were acknowledged that allow the user to describe paper size; margins; character typeface, size, and style; and right, left, center, or full line justification. Lettering guidelines were suggested in order to take full advantage of the visual impact of print generated from a word processor.

Teacher applications were explored, using the word processor as a tool to save time and effort and to personalize communications. A process called mail merge integrates information from a data file into a word processed document. Material that is used repeatedly without modification is known as a boilerplate and can be incorporated into documents, thereby saving a good deal of time.

Collaborative writing, a technique that allows more than one student at a time to engage in a writing activity, is greatly facilitated by a word processor. New software allows students sitting at computers on a network to write and to edit each others' documents as they write them.

Examples of student applications were presented in a cross-disciplinary fashion to stimulate the reader's imagination and encourage unique creative applications.

LET'S PRACTICE

To complete the specified exercises online, go to the Chapter Exercises Module in chapter 7 of the Companion Website.

1. Examine computer magazines, journals, and catalogs. List advertisements for at least three of the various entry devices available for the computer. Discuss briefly the features that are being promoted.

2. Many programs in the school setting currently use keyboard input from students. There has been a good deal written in the past several years on the subject of keyboard instruction. Write a two- to three-page paper discussing the issue of typing instruction starting at an early level. At what grade level would you begin teaching keyboarding skills? Defend your position. Check your library to review any research on this subject. Cite your sources.

3. Describe at least five examples of how you might use word processing in your work as a teacher. Develop one as a sample.

4. Many word processors automatically reformat and check spelling and grammar as words are typed into the computer. How does this help your students? How could this be detrimental to your students?

5. Which features found in word processing programs would you find indispensable? What feature would you like companies to add to a word processor?

6. Using a word processor, write a two- to three-page reaction paper to the concept of collaborative writing. Include a bibliography listing at least three sources.

7. Using a word processor, write a few paragraphs about the motivation that is prompting you to enter the teaching profession and save the file. Exchange your file with a friend who has written a similar one. Finish the document you have received by adding a few paragraphs of your own describing what you hope to accomplish as a teacher. Edit the entire document for consistency of style. Once again exchange it with your friend and compare the documents.

8. Pick a partner and together choose a topic on which to write. After agreeing on an outline, divide the writing task between yourselves. After completing your independent writing assignment, merge your files. Edit the entire document for consistency of style.

9. Obtain an educational software catalog that contains software for students with special needs. (Don Johnson is one, among others.) Describe how word processing programs for students with special needs might be used to help students who are physically challenged or learning disabled.

10. How might lack of access to a word processor at school or home affect the education and future prospects of a student from a poorer school district?

PORTFOLIO DEVELOPMENT EXERCISES

To complete this exercise online, go to the Digital Portfolio Module in Chapter 7 of the Companion Website.

One of the NETS•S standards covered in this chapter was "Students are proficient in the use of technology" under Category 1: Basic operations and concepts. Begin to develop your own portfolio of lesson plans that demonstrates your ability to have your students reach the NETS•S standards.

1. Design a lesson plan activity for elementary, middle school, or high school students in which they use a word processing program to write a report on a subject that you will be studying. Try to combine several tools found in word processing programs. The number that you use should depend on the grade level. Younger students may only use simple tools (bold, italics, font change, etc.). Older students will be required to use more sophisticated tools (boxes, numbering or bulleting, hanging indents, paragraph or document formatting). This lesson should demonstrate that your students have achieved the standard. Be sure to include a system of evaluation for your students' understanding and competence to ensure that they have met this standard.

2. Adapt the lesson plan activity you developed in exercise 1 for students to evaluate each others' work.

GLOSSARY

boilerplate	Material, such as paragraphs of text, that can be used repeatedly in many documents without modification
desktop publishing	Usually refers to the use of software that contains an extensive set of text and graphics manipulation commands and includes advanced page layout capabilities
font	The collection of characteristics applied to a typeface in a particular size and style
mechanical spacing	Letter spacing that requires letters within a word to be equally distant from each other regardless of the letter shape
monospaced typeface	See *mechanical spacing*
optical spacing	Letter spacing that requires letters within a word to have equal surface areas in the spaces between each other, thereby taking letter shapes into account
orphans	Single lines of text that occur at the bottoms of pages
print formatter	The part of a word processing program that delivers the text file to the printer and ensures that it is printed correctly on paper
proportional-spaced typeface	See *optical spacing*
size	The height of a letter expressed in points
stationery	Sometimes used as a replacement for template
style	(1) A set of characteristics that can be applied to text in a word processor. (2) When dealing strictly with the appearance of text, style pertains more narrowly to the appearance of a particular typeface
template	Preformatted file design; see also *boilerplate*
text editor	The part of a word processing program that allows the user to manipulate text on a screen display
text-wrapped graphics	The format feature that allows the program to wrap lines of text around the edges of graphics
typeface	The design or appearance of a particular letter type and the name given to that design
widows	Single lines of text that occur at the tops of pages
word processor	Software, with accompanying hardware, used primarily to facilitate the creation, editing, formatting, saving, and printing of information in electronic and hard copy form
word wrap	A process of monitoring the entry of words so that words are not split on the right side of the screen
WYSIWYG	(**W**hat **Y**ou **S**ee **I**s **W**hat **Y**ou **G**et) Pronounced "wizzy wig," the exact screen replication of what will be printed on paper

REFERENCES AND SUGGESTED READINGS

Baugh, I. W. (1999–2000, December/January). To keyboard or not to keyboard. *Learning & Leading with Technology, 27*(4), 28–31.

Bowman, M. (1999, May). Children, word processors and genre. *Scottish Educational Review, 31*(1), 66–83.

Bradley, H. (2000, June). Designer documents: 40 ways to make documents look good. *Australian PC User, 12*(6), 67.

Campbell, G. (2000, July). The future is here: Self-typing text. *PC World, 18*(7), 222.

Hayden K. L., & Norman, K. I. (2002, July). K–12 Instruction in the United States: Integrating National Standards for Science and Writing through emerging technologies. Descriptive report. 12. ERIC NO: ED469626.

Kiefer, K. (2002, March). This isn't where we thought we were going: Revisiting our visions of computer-supported writing instruction. Opinion paper. 12. ERIC NO: 46843.

Levin, M. (1997). *Kids in print: Publishing a school newspaper.* Parsippany, NJ: Good Apple. Electronic Learning, 4.

Raef, C. (1996, April). Improving student writing skills through the use of technology. Master's thesis, St. Xavier University. ERIC NO: ED399537.

Tolly, K. (2002, July). Words matter. *Network World,* 14.

CHAPTER

Learning with Spreadsheet Tools

ADVANCE ORGANIZER

1.   What is a spreadsheet and how does it work?

2.   How are text and values entered in a spreadsheet?

3.   How are formulas created in order to manipulate values?

4.   How can a spreadsheet be used to sort textual information?

5.   How can problem-solving strategies be applied to designing spreadsheets?

6.   How might you as a teacher use a spreadsheet as a productivity tool in multidisciplinary lessons and activities to keep and sort records, calculate numerical data, forecast results of decisions, and analyze information?

7.   How can charts be generated from spreadsheet data?

8.   Following a linear problem-solving approach, how can a grade book system be developed on a spreadsheet?

NETS•T Foundation Standards and Performance Indicators Addressed in this Chapter

I. Technology operations and concepts
   A. demonstrate introductory knowledge, skills, and understanding of concepts related to technology (as described in ISTE National Education Technology Standards for Students)
   B. demonstrate continual growth in technology knowledge and skills to stay abreast of current and emerging technologies
II. Planning and designing learning environments and experiences
   A. design developmentally appropriate learning opportunities that apply technology-enhanced instructional strategies to support the diverse needs of learners
III. Teaching, learning, and the curriculum
   A. facilitate technology-enhanced experiences that address content standards and student technology standards
   B. use technology to support learner-centered strategies that address the diverse needs of students
   C. apply technology to develop students' higher order skills and creativity
   D. manage student learning activities in a technology-enhanced environment
IV. Assessment and evaluation
   A. apply technology in assessing student learning of subject matter using a variety of assessment techniques
   B. use technology resources to collect and analyze data, interpret results, and communicate findings to improve instructional practice and maximize student learning
V. Productivity and professional practice
   A. use technology resources to engage in ongoing professional development and lifelong learning
   B. continually evaluate and reflect on professional practice to make informed decisions regarding the use of technology in support of student learning
   C. apply technology to increase productivity
   D. use technology to communicate and collaborate with peers, parents, and the larger community in order to nurture student learning
VI. Social, ethical, legal, and human issues
   A. model and teach legal and ethical practice related to technology use
   B. apply technology resources to enable and empower learners with diverse backgrounds, characteristics, and abilities

LET'S LOOK AT THIS CHAPTER

Spreadsheets increase productivity and can help you and your students creatively solve problems and produce documents and projects to communicate information and ideas effectively. Students learn about a new tool to aid in problem solving and making decisions and develop strategies for solving problems in the real world. They also learn how spreadsheets can be used as a research tool to process data and report results. As a teacher, you can use spreadsheets to automate and simplify number processing in the form of budget data or student grades. You can incorporate them into your curriculum and student assignments. Spreadsheets are fun and easy to set up and use whenever you or your students are called upon to analyze data and make projections.

The term **spreadsheet** originated in the accounting world to refer to data entered in columns and rows on a wide sheet of paper. The data was "spread" across columns in the same row. This ledger sheet, or spreadsheet, as it became known, was in fact a two-dimensional paper grid of rows and columns. Spreadsheets can be used for a wide variety of activities, but most applications of spreadsheets focus on generating numeric information from other numeric information such as creating budgets and income projections and forecasting needed amounts of equipment or supplies based on a number of factors.

The present-day electronic spreadsheet lets the user enter text and values and create formulas that set up relationships between values, which may be governed by the simple arithmetic operators or by sophisticated functions that are expressions of more complex mathematical and statistical formulas. The spreadsheet automatically recalculates all related values as new data entries are made, thereby revealing relationships instantaneously. *Microsoft Excel*™ is a popular spreadsheet program that is part of the *Microsoft Office* suite and available in both Windows and Mac OS. A newer spreadsheet and graphing program designed especially for students in grades 4 through 12 is Inspire-Data from the makers of Inspiration and Kidspiration. It is specifically designed to develop analytical skills and strengthen critical-thinking skills by allowing students to visualize data that they have collected or from several included data sets using tables, Venn diagrams and plots, and static animated time series graphs and charts. Trial copies can be downloaded from *http://inspiration.com.*

Spreadsheets can be used as preformatted databases where stored data can easily be sorted. This may be useful when you want to examine the entire set of data. It is not as useful when you need to search for or select specific data related to an individual item. Many teachers use spreadsheets in place of grade book programs to track student and class progress and grades. Why would a teacher use a spreadsheet instead of a commercial grade book program? Teachers manage grades in many different ways. All too often, a grade book program forces teachers to change their grading methods to adapt to the grade book program purchased. A spreadsheet, on the other hand, can be custom designed to the teacher's system.

Consider the teacher-made grade book spreadsheet example in Figure 8–1. As the classroom teacher uses this grade book spreadsheet by inputting or changing grades, the spreadsheet program will continually calculate the students' total point accumulation and display a final score in column G. This spreadsheet is also designed to keep the statistics on each class activity, identifying the highest, lowest, and average score on the activity, giving the teacher information by which to assess the activity. Any change in any score will automatically update any of this information linked to that score. The rows may be sorted in alphabetical order by the student names in column A at any time; so, as new students are added, the grade book is sorted once again.

■■■■ USING A SPREADSHEET

The illustrations used in this chapter to explain the operation of spreadsheets are actual screens of *Microsoft Excel*™. It is important to note that most spreadsheets, regardless of program or operating system platform, look and act very much alike. To help understand the capability of a spreadsheet, visualize a spreadsheet as a matrix of lettered columns and numbered rows. Take a moment to examine Figure 8–2 as you consider the following. The intersection of a column and a row is called a **cell,** and is identified by a letter

Figure 8–1 **A grade book**

A teacher-created spreadsheet used as a grade book

	A	B	C	D	E	F	G
1	Name	Lab 1	Lab 2	Test	Midterm	Portfolio	Grade
2		10	10	100	100	100	100
3	Alderson, Kathy	9	7	78	75	80	78
4	Chagnon, Laura	7	8	80	80	80	79
5	Hall, Andrea	10	9	98	90	95	95
6	Hall, Les	9	10	92	80	90	89
7	Heilman, Jacob	8	10	90	80	80	85
8	McKinley, Rich	8	8	82	70	90	81
9	Prosser, Peggy	7	8	80	80	85	81
10	Strasbaugh, Kristin	10	7	98	90	95	93
11	Highest Score	10	10	98	90	95	95
12	Lowest score	7	7	78	70	80	78
13	Average	8.5	8.4	87.3	80.6	86.9	85

Figure 8–2 **Data entry**

Data entered in a cell and displayed in the formula bar

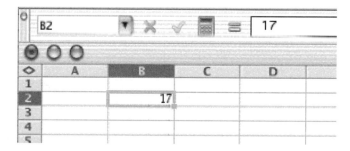

and a number, which is first the column notation (letter) and then the row notation (number) designation. The cursor can be moved around through this grid and positioned in any cell. When you click in a cell, an outline appears around it, indicating that it has been selected as the **active cell.** Notice that the name of the cell also appears in the upper left-hand corner.

When an entry (text or a value) is made from the keyboard, it appears in an area at the top of the screen called the **formula bar.** If you typed the value 17 in cell B2, that cell is identified in the upper left-hand corner of the figure as the active cell; and the value that has been typed in that cell, 17, also appears in the formula bar, the area across the top of the screen. For obvious reasons, this area is sometimes also referred to as the **data entry bar.** Notice the small square at the intersection of B2, B3, C2, and C3. This is called the fill handle and will be discussed later.

A primary task when working with spreadsheets is specifying the relationship between the cells. The data in one cell can be automatically replicated in another by making cells equal to each other. Data in one cell can be added to, subtracted from, and multiplied or divided by data in another cell. Complex mathematical relationships can be expressed in a group of cells. Built-in formulas, called **functions,** may be used or formulas may be created by the user, to express this relationship between cells.

Formulas entered always begin with the *equals* sign and reference cells by their name. In Figure 8–3, the value 17 was entered in cell B2. The formula =B2 was entered in cell A4. This formula will replicate in cell A4 any entry occurring in cell B2.

Figure 8–3 Cell relationships

A formula may relate one cell to another

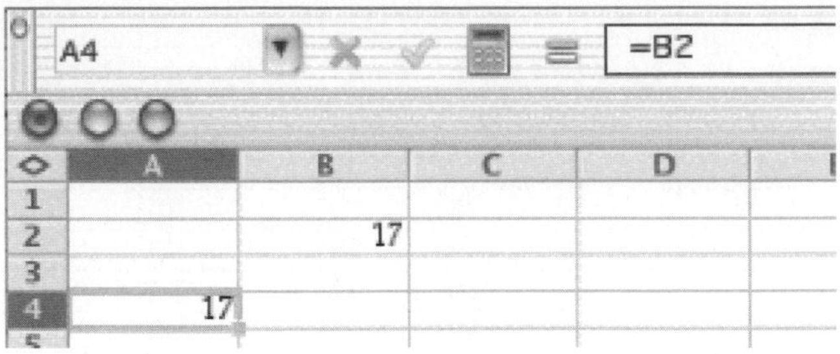

Figure 8–4 Another relationship of cells

A formula acts upon the contents of two other cells

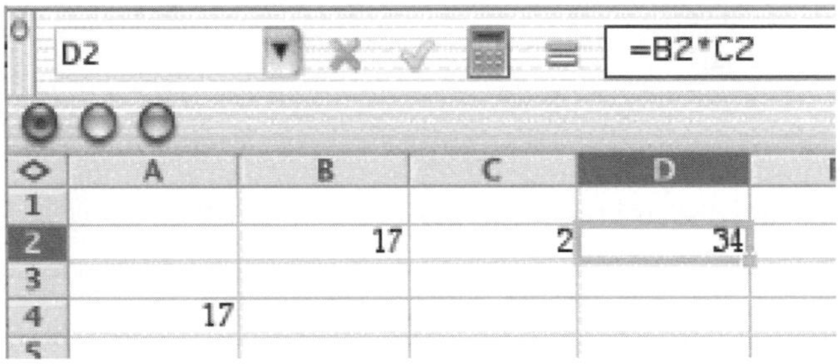

Formulas may contain the arithmetic operations of addition, subtraction, multiplication, division, and exponentiation. These are represented by $+$, $-$, $*$, $/$, and $\wedge$, respectively. The operations are performed in the following order: (1) perform all operations inside parentheses, working from inside out if parentheses are nested within each other; (2) compute exponents; (3) perform all multiplications and divisions in order from left to right; (4) perform all additions and subtractions in order from left to right; and finally, (5) perform order operations ($<$, $>$, and $=$).

Examining Figure 8–4, we see that the value 17 was entered in cell B2 and the value 2 was entered in cell C2. An additional cell, D2, was selected as the active cell and the formula entered in it was $=$B2*C2 [cell B2 (containing the value of 17) * (multiplied by) cell C2 (containing the value of 2)]. Notice that the result of the formula (34) is displayed in cell D2, while the formula itself appears in the formula bar.

In this example, both B2 and C2 are known as relative references in the formula, since they actually relate to cells one position and two positions to the left of the active formula cell, D2. If, on the other hand, the formula is meant to always refer to an exact cell regardless of the placement of the formula cell within the spreadsheet, the reference is called **absolute,** or *fixed*. For example, if the formula must contain a reference to the top cell in the second column, then the cell would be entered into a formula as a fixed reference and in most spreadsheets would be typed as $B$1. The dollar signs indicate that the column and row will not change. Should the formula be cut or copied to any other cell, no matter where it is located in the spreadsheet, the fixed reference would remain to cell B1.

To assist the user, the spreadsheet program contains a wide variety of built-in functions that can be used simply by referencing them in the desired formula, as well as the cells containing the related data. The following are common mathematical functions often used in formulas:

Sum (of values within a group of cells)
Average (of values within a group of cells)

Minimum (lowest of the values within a group of cells)
Maximum (highest of the values within a group of cells)
Standard Deviation (of values within a group of cells)

The group of cells referenced by these functions is designated as a range from the first cell in the group to the last one. Within the formula, the first and last cells in the range are usually separated by a colon or an ellipsis, depending on the particular spreadsheet being used (e.g., F9:F17 or F9 . . . F17), and enclosed in parentheses.

Let's take a brief look at the functions (formulas) that are included in Microsoft Excel™. It is much easier and faster to use these built-in functions than to type in the formula every time. Returning to the grade book example used at the beginning of this chapter in Figure 8–1, to find the average for Lab 1 using the built-in functions, we type the equal sign in cell B13 and then drag from cell B3 to B10 to highlight that range or selection. You can see in Figure 8–5 that we then choose Function . . . from the Insert menu. When the Paste Function menu appears, we select *Statistical* (fewer choices than All) and then the formula for *Average*. Notice that an explanation of the function chosen is presented at the bottom of the dialog box. When a formula is created that has a blank (empty) cell as a divisor, many spreadsheets will generate a *#DIV/O!* message, indicating that they cannot divide by zero. As soon as a value is entered in the divisor cell, the message will disappear.

The Paste Function menu contains many different function categories and function names. Clicking OK in the Paste Function dialog box will cause a window to open to show the formula and cells in use (Figure 8–6 left). We may edit this range of cells if we wish. Clicking OK on this screen will send us back to the spreadsheet now automatically showing the average for Lab 1 (Figure 8–6 right).

Figure 8–5 The built-in function *Average*
Insert menu (left) accesses the *Paste Function* menu (right)

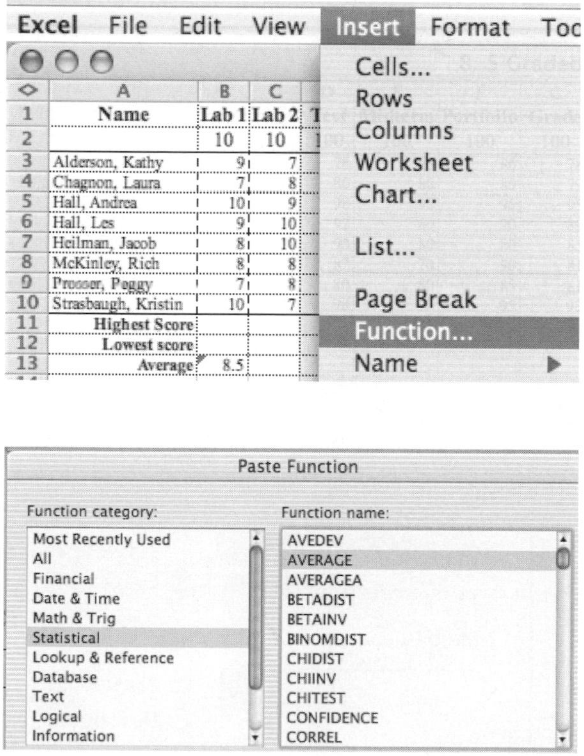

Figure 8–6 Formula and result
Spreadsheet formula (left) and calculated average (right)

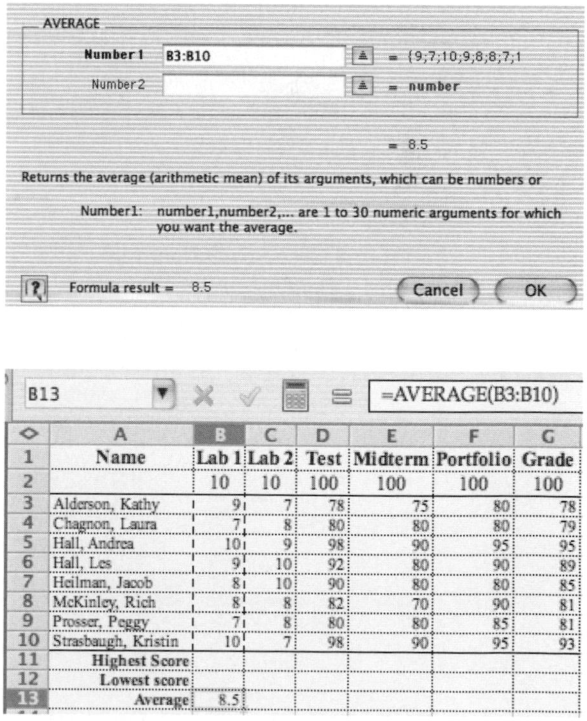

To calculate the students' averages for the remaining categories, grab the *Fill handle*. When you click in a cell, it appears as a small square in the lower right corner where the cell lines intersect. Examine cell B13 in Figure 8–7. Grab the handle and drag across the row highlighting cells C13 through G13 as shown in Figure 8–8. The other averages will be automatically displayed in the appropriate cells.

Replicating the formula can also be achieved by selecting the Fill and Right commands under the Edit menu. Fill Down, Up, and Left are also available commands. The calculation of the highest and lowest scores are also achieved by employing the maximum (MAX) and minimum (MIN) functions built into the spreadsheet and following the procedure just described for using the AVERAGE function.

Data can be sorted in many different ways. Notice that in Figure 8–6 the names in column A are in ascending alphabetic order. To sort by the *Grade* column (G), simply highlight the data you want sorted in columns A through G (drag from A3 to G10—do not include the first two rows nor the last three) and open the Sort window, which is accessed through the Data menu (Figure 8–9 left). Select how you want to sort the data, in this case by column G (Grade) in descending order (Figure 8–9 right) and click OK. The result is displayed in Figure 8–10.

Figure 8–7 Fill handle

A small square appearing in the lower right-hand corner of a selected cell

Figure 8–8 Fill right

Grabbing the *Fill handle* and dragging across the cells replicates the value, in this case, the formula in the selected cells

Figure 8–9 Sorting data

Data menu (left) is used to access the *Sort* menu (right)

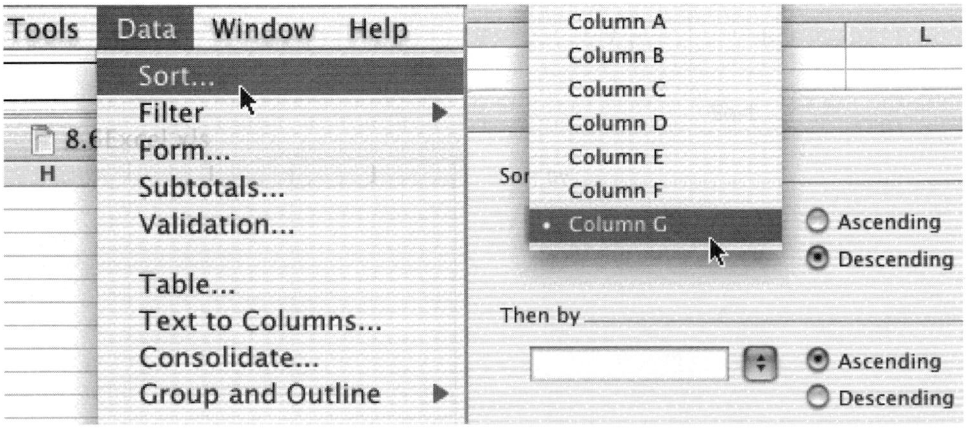

Figure 8–10 **Sorted data**

Spreadsheet is sorted in descending order based on data in column G

◇	A	B	C	D	E	F	G
1	Name	Lab 1	Lab 2	Test	Midterm	Portfolio	Grade
2		10	1	100	100	100	100
3	Hall, Andrea	10	9	98	90	95	95
4	Strasbaugh, Kristin	10	7	98	90	95	93
5	Hall, Les	9	10	92	80	90	89
6	Heilman, Jacob	8	10	90	80	80	85
7	McKinley, Rich	8	8	82	70	90	81
8	Prosser, Peggy	7	8	80	80	85	81
9	Chagnon, Laura	7	8	80	80	80	79
10	Alderson, Kathy	9	7	78	75	80	78
11	Highest Score	10	10	98	90	95	95
12	Lowest score	7	7	78	70	80	78
13	Average	8.5	8.4	87.3	80.6	86.9	84.9

Spreadsheets are in fact highly specialized databases. They can store and manipulate text and numeric values and are sometimes used instead of database managers when their two-dimensional matrix format (columns and rows) lends itself to convenient data entry and when printed report requirements are minimal. The illustration of dinosaur data in Figure 8–11 demonstrates the use of text both as **labels** in row 1 and as data to be manipulated in rows 2 through 6. Spreadsheets are often used as powerful sorting devices to examine information grouped in a variety of ways. Each row in Figure 8–11 contains information about one dinosaur. A multilevel sort has arranged the information by (1) DIET in ascending alphabetical order, then within that first sort by (2) LENGTH in descending numeric order, and then within those two levels of sort by (3) WEIGHT in descending order. This ability to nest one sort within another adds versatility to the spreadsheet. Sorting data allows us to quickly and easily examine relationships. Sorting also allows us to prepare data for generating charts and graphs to visually represent these relationships along a continuum.

An Excel file is referred to as a workbook. An Excel workbook may have multiple pages within a sheet and page breaks will be shown in preview mode. A workbook may also have multiple sheets. Figure 8–12 reveals sheet tabs at the bottom of the workbook screen.

For instance, if you wanted to create a graph of your students' performances based on their grades, you might want to store that graph on a sheet separate from the data. We will show you how to create a sheet in the tutorial at the end of this chapter.

PROBLEM SOLVING WITH SPREADSHEETS

Consider that the process of problem solving might be approached in a nonlinear fashion by an individual with a random learning style. Figure 8–13 illustrates one such approach. "Given" is the information in your possession. "To Find" is the information you are seeking. What are the results you are trying to achieve? "Procedure" is the method you are going to employ to reach your goal. How will you achieve results?

Apply the problem-solving process just reviewed to the following simple word problem: A boy takes home $7.00 an hour from a weekend job. How many hours must he work in order to be able to purchase a $350 bicycle?

Given:	Take-home pay is $7.00 per hour.
	Cost of the bicycle is $350.
To Find:	Number of hours of work required to earn enough to purchase the bicycle.
Procedure:	Divide the cost of the bicycle ($350) by the hourly take-home rate of $7.00.

Figure 8–11 Dinosaurs

Using a spreadsheet to sort text

◇	A	B	C	D
1	**Name**	**Length**	**Weight**	**Diet**
2	Tyrannosaurus	50	8 tons	Carnivorous
3	Allosaurus	25	4.5 tons	Carnivorous
4	Brachiosaurus	70	80 tons	Herbivorous
5	Triceratops	20	7 tons	Herbivorous
6	Stegosaurus	20	4 tons	Herbivorous
7				

Figure 8–12 Sheet tabs

Sheet tabs at the bottom of the worksheet allow navigation between multiple sheets in the same workbook

Figure 8–13 Problem-solving model

A nonlinear approach to problem solving

Given   To Find

Procedure

Figure 8–14 Spreadsheet as a calculator

Using a spreadsheet to calculate and help estimate

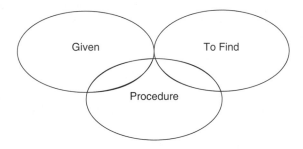

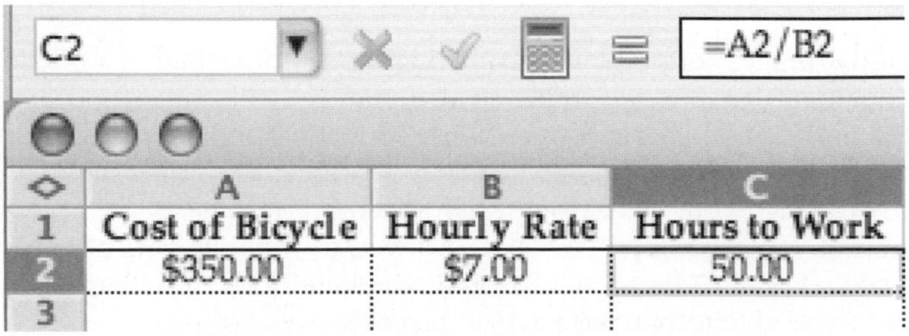

C2   ✕ ✓ 🖩 ≣   =A2/B2

◇	A	B	C
1	**Cost of Bicycle**	**Hourly Rate**	**Hours to Work**
2	$350.00	$7.00	50.00
3			

In Figure 8–14, the cost of the bicycle (350) is entered in cell A2 and the hourly take-home rate (7.00) is entered in cell B2. The formula = A2/B2 (cost divided by hourly rate) is entered in cell C2. Upon completing the formula entry, the formula is displayed in the formula bar, and the value resulting from the formula as hours to work (50) is displayed in the cell.

Having discovered the number of hours necessary to earn the required amount, the boy might now wish to see the effect of moving to a higher-paying job and perhaps purchasing a slightly more expensive bike. He could play "what if" and forecast the results of change.

LET'S GO INTO THE CLASSROOM
Spreadsheet Magic

I work as Computer Coordinator in a K–8 school, working with teachers to integrate technology across the curriculum. Students learn mathematics and other subjects as they use the spreadsheet tool. They are motivated to work on the computer and they take pride in the professional documents they produce. Mistakes can be easily corrected, and assignments can be modified for extension or remediation. Students as young as kindergartners use spreadsheets effectively as they use templates where the formatting of columns, rows, the grid, and print area has been done for them. Initially they learn to move around the spreadsheet, enter text, and duplicate graphics as they count to ten on the grid. Student skills improve gradually as they complete each assignment, and by eighth grade they can do their own formatting. If a template is used at all at this age, it is to save students time so that they can focus on learning and spend less time using the tool.

Students access data on the Internet and they need to interpret this and communicate what they have learned. They use spreadsheets to chart information, and they can then analyze their graphs; for example, they chart their own measurements. The spreadsheet grid provides a structure for organizing data. Students resize the cells to make calendars, multiplication tables, hundreds charts, and flash cards. Borders are selectively shown and hidden, and spreadsheets are used to teach concepts like fractions, decimals, number lines, time lines, and arrays. Learning is enhanced with visual cues as students fill cells with color and pattern, and they count to 100 on the spreadsheet and then fill multiples of threes with color, fives with pattern and see the intersection of the two. Number patterns become evident and they begin to count down rather than across on their hundreds chart. They also insert clip art to make pictographs, or an animal classification table.

Students use spreadsheets to sort data numerically and alphabetically; for example, they enter their spelling words and sort them alphabetically. Formulas are inserted in a template to make calculations for third-grade students, who then focus on solving the problem of spending a target amount at the toy store while the computer does the calculations for them. Older students improve their understanding of abstract algebraic concepts as they make up their own formulas and then generalize them by filling down or filling right; for example, they use formulas to count the number of cells in the entire spreadsheet, or to make a calculator. They explore "What if . . ." type questions as they see how changing one variable affects the numbers that are generated by a formula.

The teachers at our school use spreadsheets as a utility tool: They record grades, make class lists, checklists, rubrics, seating charts. We make "digital worksheets" where students use a template with formulas that check numerical or one-word answers to questions, and gives instant feedback to the students.

I have written a book called *Spreadsheet Magic,* published by ISTE (*http://www.iste.org*). It includes instructions and national standards for 40 spreadsheet lessons for students in grades kindergarten through eighth grade, and a CD-ROM with templates and sample completed assignments. Teachers can access online tutorials for using spreadsheet programs like AppleWorks or Excel, online data sources, and mathematics resources. I have saved a collection of these links at Trackstar, *http://www.digital-lessons.com/* at track 108349.

Pam Lewis
St. Luke School
Brookfield, WI

CURRICULUM APPLICATIONS OF SPREADSHEETS

We have described the spreadsheet as a matrix of interrelated columns and rows and have examined its operation. We understand that it can handle text and values, that it is founded on the ability to relate cells to each other, and that it has powerful built-in formulas. We are also beginning to explore some of the functional uses of spreadsheets to record, organize, and sort data (values and text); to calculate values; and to forecast results. As a recording tool, the spreadsheet allows us to alphabetize lists of names, track expenditures, analyze the performance of players in various sports, and manage a grade book. As a forecasting tool, the spreadsheet allows us to analyze the immediate impact of projected changes. We could, for instance, reveal the impact on a school district's budget of raising teachers' salaries by 5 percent, by 4 percent, by 6 percent, and so on.

The table here illustrates a number of spreadsheet applications in different curriculum areas and at various grade levels shown in Figure 8–15 through Figure 8–21. This table summarizes the functional applications and possible curriculum areas of the lesson examples given.

A copy of each of the Excel files for figures 8–15 through 8–21, as well as one on equipment management, can be found on the **Take-Along CD.** We encourage you to examine the files, manipulate the data, and experiment with these lessons.

Figure	Primary Function(s)	Curriculum Area
8–15	Metric conversion	Mathematics
8–16	Calculation	Mathematics, home economics
8–17	Calculation, analysis	Mathematics, home economics
8–18	Calculation, analysis	Science, social studies
8–19	Recording, analysis	Social studies, mathematics
8–20	Recording, analysis	Athletics
8–21	Forecasting	Mathematics

Figure 8–15 **Metric/English converter**

Using a spreadsheet to convert between two measurement systems

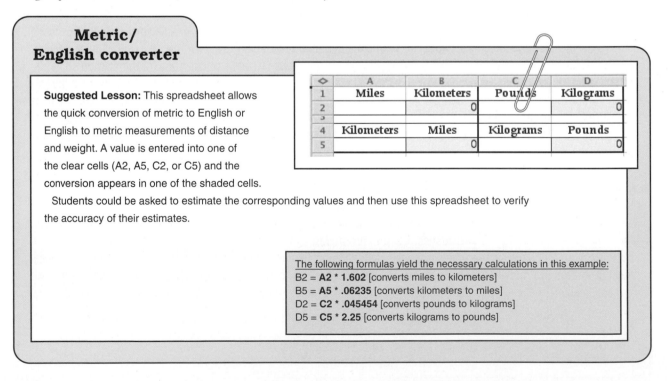

Metric/English converter

Suggested Lesson: This spreadsheet allows the quick conversion of metric to English or English to metric measurements of distance and weight. A value is entered into one of the clear cells (A2, A5, C2, or C5) and the conversion appears in one of the shaded cells.

Students could be asked to estimate the corresponding values and then use this spreadsheet to verify the accuracy of their estimates.

◇	A	B	C	D
1	Miles	Kilometers	Pounds	Kilograms
2		0		0
3				
4	Kilometers	Miles	Kilograms	Pounds
5		0		0

The following formulas yield the necessary calculations in this example:
B2 = **A2 * 1.602** [converts miles to kilometers]
B5 = **A5 * .06235** [converts kilometers to miles]
D2 = **C2 * .045454** [converts pounds to kilograms]
D5 = **C5 * 2.25** [converts kilograms to pounds]

Figure 8–16 **Recipe proportions**
Using a spreadsheet to calculate proportions when modifying a recipe

Recipe proportions

Suggested Lesson: Adapting a recipe to a different number of servings is a common problem faced in preparing a meal. This illustrates how a recipe designed for a set number of servings can be adapted for any number. The example deals with serving sizes of 6, 15, and 24 but in reality any number may be used.

The formula must first calculate the unit measure by dividing the amount by the serving size given in the recipe. In this example, the amount of beef, onions, etc. is divided by 6, the serving size. The formula then multiplies the unit measure derived by the number of servings desired.

◇	A	B	C	D	E
1			\multicolumn{3}{c} Serving Sizes		
2	Ingredients	Measure	6	15	24
3	Lean ground beef	Lbs.	1.5	3.75	6
4	Chopped onion	Cup	0.5	1.25	2
5	Canned corn	Oz.	14	35	56
6	Mashed potatoes	Cup	3	7.5	12
7	Grated cheese	Cup	0.75	1.875	3
8	Salt	tsp.	1	2.5	4
9	Pepper	tsp.	0.5	1.25	2

The following formulas yield the necessary calculations in this example:
D3 = **(C3/$C$2) * D2** [the $ represents an absolute reference]
E3 = **(C3/$C$2) * E2**
Once the formulas are entered in row 3, they can be filled down columns D and E.

Figure 8–17 **Budgeting tool**
Using a spreadsheet to monitor a personal budget

Budgeting tool

Suggested Lesson: A personal finance discussion of budgeting could examine "Where the money goes" in a typical month. This spreadsheet could be used to illustrate some expenses made by a family and to explain the construction of a similar personal spreadsheet for each student.

Students' monthly income would be determined. Expenditure categories could be agreed upon and actual purchases recorded during one month. The proportion of expenses in each category would be revealed in the % row.

◇	A	B	C	D	E
1		Monthly income:	$4,000		
2		\multicolumn{3}{c} Transaction Categories		
3	Date	Food	Clothing	Entertainment	Balance
4	1-Mar	$53.50			$3,946.50
5	3-Mar		$189.00	$98.00	$3,659.50
6	6-Mar	$92.74			$3,566.76
7					
8					
9	Totals:	$146.24	$189.00	$98.00	$433.24
10	%	34%	44%	23%	100%

The following formulas yield the necessary calculations in this example:
E4 = **IF(A4>0,$C$1-SUM(B4:D4),C1)** establishes the initial balance once an entry is made on row 4.
E5 = **IF(A5>0,E4-SUM(B5:D5,"")** calculates a running balance as entries are made on the row. This formula is filled down the column for each row.
B9 = **SUM(B4:B6)** (repeated across columns) totals the amounts in each column.
E9 = **SUM(B9:D9)** this formula, located in column E, adds up the totals.
B10 = **IF(B9>0,B9/$E$9,"")** once an entry appears in the TOTAL cell above it, this formula divides that total by the sum of totals in column E. This formula is repeated for each column.

Figure 8–18 **Climate analysis**
Using a spreadsheet to calculate sums and averages in a cross-disciplinary science and social studies context

Climate analysis

Suggested Lesson: Students enter high and low temperatures and any amount of precipitation each day. The spreadsheet performs all of the calculations. This information might be used in a science unit on weather or might be part of a social studies unit on climate as a component of geography. Data might be recorded from a number of different cities around the world with comparisons made and results analyzed. It's easy to see that it would lend itself readily to multidisiplinary unit.

	A	B	C	D	E	F
1				City: Melbourne, Australia		
2	Date	High	Low	Mean	Amount	Days of
3		Temp	Temp	Temp	Precipitation	Precipitation
4	4/1/04	67	46	57	0.55	1
5	4/2/04	69	50	60	1	1
6	4/3/04	61	46	54	0.33	1
32	4/30/04	76	55	66	0	
33	High Temp	76				
34	Low Temp		46			
35	Average	68	49	59		
36	Amt. Precip.				1.88	
37	Days Precip.					3

The following formulas yield the necessary calculations in this example:
E4 = **IF(E4>0,1,"")**   This formula generates a "1" if an entry appears in column E.
                        It is repeated in each row.
B33 = **MAX(B4:B32)** [column B] returns the highest value in the column.
B35 = **AVERAGE(B4:B32)** [column B] returns the average of the values in the column.
C34 = **MIN(C4:C32)** [column C] returns the lowest value in the column.
C35 = **AVERAGE(C4:C32)** [column C] returns the average of the values in the column.
D35 = **AVERAGE(C4:C32)** [column D] returns the average of the values in the column.
E36 = **SUM(E4:E32)** [column E] adds the values in the column to generate a total.
F37 = **SUM(F4:F32)** [column F] adds the values in the column to generate a total.

CHARTS AND GRAPHS

Abstract numerical data can be presented in a concrete, clear, and interesting manner by line or bar graphs, pie charts, and other pictorial means. Prompted in part by the significant increase in graphs in the popular media (newspapers, magazines, and television news), graphing is now being introduced to students at a much earlier age. Graphs can display relationships that would be more difficult to convey in a text or verbal mode. As visuals, they capture attention and promote greater retention of information.

For a copy of the guidelines for charts and graphs go to the Supplemental Information module in Chapter 8 on the Companion Website, *www.prenhall.com/ forcier*

Although graphs can certainly be informative, they have the potential of expressing a bias by the manipulation of scale. Thus, the analysis and interpretation of graphs has become an important subject in the K–12 curriculum. Students can be presented data and led through exercises designed to promote an understanding of those data. They can then be asked to select the most informative and accurate presentation of the data. They may discover that, depending on the data, numeric tables show the most accurate, but also the most abstract and difficult to understand, relationships.

Line graphs, as shown in the upper left section of Figure 8–22, are ideal for displaying a continuous event or trends over time (e.g., growth or decline over time). Notice the steady increase in sales over the first four weeks portrayed on this graph. The rise and fall of the line on a graph easily portrays the fluctuations in value. Multiple trends can be

Figure 8–19 **Cemetery data analysis**
Exploring data in a local cemetery in a math and history lesson

Cemetery data analysis

Suggested Lesson: In exploring local history, students could be made aware of the value of a local cemetery as a primary resource. Data gathered from headstones could help the understanding of events and conditions prevalent in the local area. Students could first discuss the type of data available in which they might have an interest and formulate relevant questions. They might ask, for example, "How much longer did women live than men? Was there a period of unusually high mortality? How did life expectancy change over time?" and several other questions. Once prepared with data collection sheets and reminded of expected behavior in such a setting, teams of students could visit a local cemetery and gather data by tallying gender, age, and year of death of the deceased. Students would then enter data into a spreadsheet and search for trends and anomalies. The resulting information might generate additional questions requiring further research.

	A	B	C	D	E	F	G	H	I	J	K
1			Total # Died during the years					Total # Died during the years			
2	Age	Men	...–'75	'74–'50	'49–'25	'24–'00	Women	–'75	'74–'50	'49–'25	'24–'00
3	0-10	0					0				
4	11-20	0					0				
5	21-30	0					0				
6	31-40	0					0				
7	41-50	0					0				
8	51-60	0					0				
9	61-70	0					0				
10	71-80	0					0				
11	81-90	0					0				
12	91-100	0					0				
13	Totals	0	0	0	0	0	0	0	0	0	0
14	Percentage										
15	Population*										
16		*population for the midpoint of each quarter century									

The following formulas yield the necessary calculations in this example:
B3 = **SUM(C3:F3)** and G3 = **SUM(H3:K3)** totals the number in columns C through F and H through K. These formulas are repeated in rows 4 through 12.
B13 = **SUM(B3:B12)** totals the values in the column and is repeated in columns C through K.
C15 = **C13/$B$13** and H15 = **H13/$G$13** repeated in the appropriate columns.

compared simultaneously by plotting more than one line on the graph. *Area graphs* are variations of line graphs that are successful at depicting amount or volume. A line is plotted and the area below it is filled in with a selected pattern. Each data set creates a band, with each area being stacked on the preceding one. These graphs can be eye-catching, but, since they show cumulative results, they can, at times, be more difficult to understand.

Column graphs (vertical columns), as shown in the upper right section of Figure 8–22, and *bar graphs* (horizontal bars) present changes in a dependent variable over an independent variable and are excellent ways of comparing multiple variables with a common variable (e.g., different performances during the same time frame) but lack the feeling of continuity displayed by a line graph. Notice how the individual weeks stand out in this graph, making it easy to determine that the first and fourth weeks were the sales leaders. At times, column graphs and line graphs can be combined effectively, as shown in the lower left section of Figure 8–22, to present both discrete and incremental views of the data. More elaborate graphs adding another variable (e.g., different performances at different locations during the same time frame) can be created by stacking the columns/bars.

Pie charts are the ideal way to display part-to-the-whole relationships, or percentages. The size of each slice shows that segment's share of the entire pie. As shown in Figure 8–23, a segment (pie slice) may even be dragged away from the center for emphasis

253

Figure 8–20 **Sports statistics**

Using a spreadsheet to analyze player performance statistics

Sports statistics

Suggested Lesson: Though this example deals with basketball, the recording and statistical analysis of player performance is applicable to all team sports. The coach or an assistant would enter data in columns A (Name), B (Position), C (Minutes played), D (Field Goals Attempted), E (Field Goals Made), G (Free Throws Attempted), H (Free Throws Made), J (Offensive Rebounds), K (Defensive Rebounds), L (Assists), and M (Turnovers) after the game. Formulas in columns F and I would calculate shooting percentages for each player. Additional columns could be added to analyze other facets of

player performance. One or more formulas to calculate the ratio of assists to turnovers taking into account minutes played could focus on the players ball-handling skills.

⬦	A	B	C	D	E	F	G	H	I	J	K	L	M
1	Player	Pos	Min	FGA	FGM	Pct	FTA	FTM	Pct	OR	DR	A	TO
2	Joe	C	30	12	7	58%	8	7	88%	8	14	3	2
3	Rich	C	10	5	3	60%	4	3	75%	3	6	4	1
4	Ryan	G	16	8	5	63%	4	3	75%	1	2	8	0
5	Patrick	G	14	5	3	60%	2	2	100%	2	1	6	0
6	Jake	G	10	3	1	33%	0	0	0%	0	1	4	2
7	Les	F	12	4	1	25%	0	0	0%	2	2	4	3
8	Paul	F	18	14	7	50%	6	2	33%	3	2	5	3
9	Mike	F	10	3	1	33%	0	0	0%	1	1	3	0
10	TEAM			54	28	52%	24	17	71%	20	29	37	11

The following formulas would yield the necessary calculations in this example:
Fn = **En/Dn** calculates field goal percentage [n represents rows 2–10]
In = **Hn/Gn** calculates free throw percentage [n represents rows 2–10]
D10 = **Sum(D2:D9)** calculates the total for the column
A similar formula is used for columns E, G, H, J, K, L, and M

Figure 8–21 **Class fundraiser**

Using a spreadsheet to forecast sales in a class fundraising activity

Class fundraiser

Suggested Lesson: A teacher may at times supervise activity to raise funds through a class project. Before deciding on a specific project, the class may want to consider alternatives with the hope of finding one that will generate the maximum income for effort spent.

⬦	A	B	C	D	E	F
1	Profit	# of	List	Profit	Total Boxes	Boxes per
2	Goal	Students	Price	Margin	To Sell	Student
3	$500	30	$5.00	$2.00	250	8
4	$500	30	$6.00	$2.40	208	7
5	$500	30	$7.00	$2.80	179	6

For example, suppose one of the projects under consideration is the sale of candy. The list price, number of students available, and the target earnings could be set. The spreadsheet would let the class explore the required total sales and the number of units each student would have to sell at the list price. With this spreadsheet, the class could play "what if" and immediately see the results. Selling a more expensive product would reduce the required sales volume and therefore

require a lower sales target per student in order to achieve comparable results.

Initial values are placed in columns A, B, and C. The spreadsheet will calculate the values for columns D, E, and F.

The following formulas would yield the necessary calculations in this example:
D3 = **C3*.40** (assuming 40% profit)
E3 = **A3/D3** [Profit goal divided by the profit margin]
F3 = **E3/B3** [Boxes to sell divided by number of students]
These formulas are filled down each column.

Figure 8–22 **Line and column graphs**

Examples showing how line and column graphs represent data differently

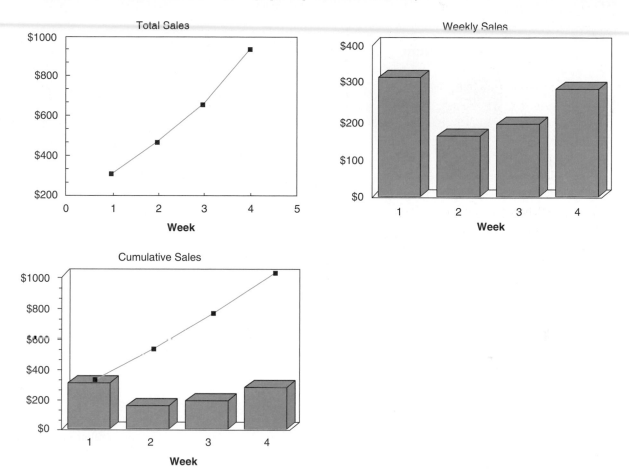

and the chart displayed in three dimensions. Other, more esoteric charts and graphs can be created to display central tendencies, shared variables, and relationships to a common constant.

The following guidelines serve as a brief review.

Several integrated software packages include a built-in graphing function. A number of other computer programs exist that allow a student to enter data directly or input them

GUIDELINES FOR SELECTING THE TYPE OF GRAPH

- Line graphs are ideal for displaying continuous events or trends over time.
- Column graphs and bar graphs present changes in a dependent variable over an independent variable and are excellent ways of comparing multiple variables with a common variable.
- Pie graphs are the ideal way to display part-to-the-whole relationships, or percentages.

A copy of these guidelines may be found in the Guidelines folder in the Take-Along CD.

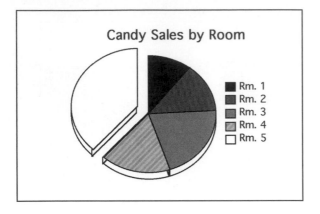

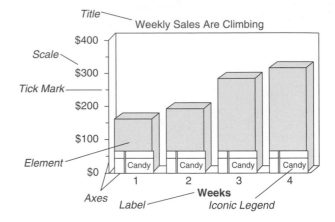

from a text file, determine the appropriate scale, and select the type of graph or chart to be generated by the computer. This allows the student to examine several graphic representations of the same data and choose the most accurate and informative one.

Graph Components

Graphs are composed of certain common basic components. Note the components as they are labeled in the column graph in Figure 8–24. The *title* announces what your graph is all about and often hints at the conclusion you want your viewer to draw. The title "Weekly Sales Are Climbing" is more suggestive of the conclusion you want drawn than would merely titling the graph "Sales."

Data *elements* are the major components of the graph that represent the quantity of the data being portrayed. The elements in Figure 8–24 are columns. As we have seen, elements can also be bars, lines, areas, and wedges.

The *axes* are the vertical and horizontal dimensions of the graph. The horizontal axis is primarily used to display the independent variable such as the *Weeks* shown in this example.

The *scales* located along the axes indicate to the viewer how the data are measured. Scales usually begin at zero at the intersection of the x and y axes. The user can select the range, zero to the maximum amount, and the unit increments within the range. This example uses increments of 100.

Tick marks are short lines located on the axes to serve as visual reference points dividing the axes into evenly spaced units. They may be located on either side of the axis line or may cross through it. They are located at each major unit of scale and evenly distributed between them.

Labels may be applied wherever they are needed to identify other components. The word *Weeks* in Figure 8–24 designates the number of weeks along the horizontal axis.

The *legend* is usually a separate area of the graph that identifies the patterns or textures of columns, bars, or wedges and what they represent. The iconic legend may, however, be used as pictorial elements, similar to the candy boxes used in this example, to strengthen the graph's message.

Figure 8–25 Line and column graphs

Different graph types represent the same data differently

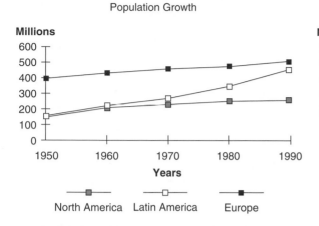

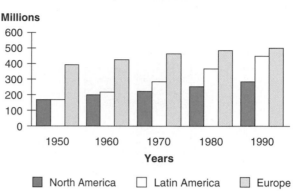

Figure 8–26 Line and area graphs

Different graph types represent the same data differently

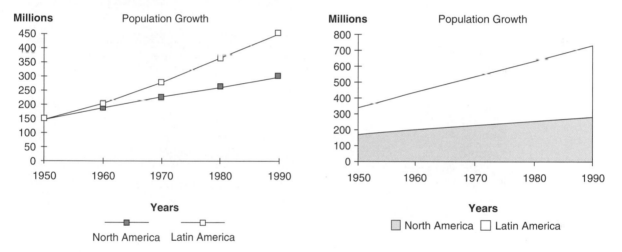

Graphs and How They Communicate

Let's explore graphs in a bit more detail. Figure 8–25 depicts population data in two different graphs, a line graph and a column graph. Both graphs use the same scale, represent data changing over time, and compare three quantities. The line graph clearly shows that population growth is leveling out in North America and in Europe, while it is increasing dramatically in Latin America. The column graph, though depicting the same data, does not show the trend as readily.

In 1950, North America and Latin America each had a population of approximately 165 million. In 1990, North America's population was 278 million and Latin America's was 447 million. Examine the line graph and area graph, shown in Figure 8–26, that portray these changes in population.

The line graph on the left of Figure 8–26 clearly demonstrates the regions' population trends. The area graph on the right effectively displays change in amount, but notice that the top sloping line represents the sum of the population in both regions, and the scale

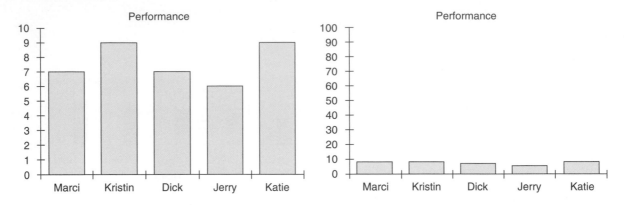

Maria B. Vonada/Merrill

of the graph, therefore, has changed. Does it allow you to better understand the change within each region or is it more difficult to decipher? Which of the two graphs in Figure 8–26 is the most effective at communicating its information at a glance?

An inappropriate choice of scale can be very misleading. Consider the following hypothetical example. Five students received grades on an assignment; a perfect score was 10 points. Bob scored 8 of 10, Kathy 9, Marci 7, Jerry 6, and Kristin 9. The user must decide on the most accurate scale when graphing the data. Examine the two examples presented in Figure 8–27. As demonstrated, selecting the wrong scale may be misleading. Since the perfect score on the assignment was 10, a scale of 0 to 10 was chosen for the graph on the left side of the figure. When this scale is employed, the differences between the students' scores on the assignment are accurately portrayed. It is easy to see at a glance that scores for Kristin and Katie were 50 percent better than Jerry's score. The graph on the right shows the same data on a scale of 0 to 100. Notice how close all scores appear. The scale is too great to show clearly much differentiation and conveys the misleading impression at first glance that all scores were approximately the same.

Figure 8–28 **A linear model**
A linear approach to problem solving

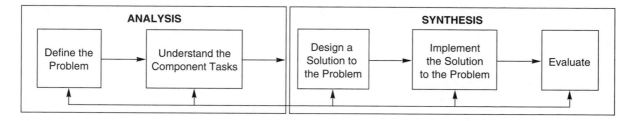

CREATING A GRADE BOOK

Consider the creation of a computerized grade book to report student progress in your classroom. How might we proceed? A linear problem-solving strategy that might appeal more to a sequential learner consists of two phases, the *analysis* phase and the *synthesis* phase. In the analysis phase, we need to clearly examine the problem, define *what* must be done, and clearly identify the specific component tasks that relate to the problem. In the synthesis phase, we plan our strategy and carry out the solution to the problem. Evaluation provides feedback that could modify decisions made in both the analysis and synthesis phases.

In an effort to bring that linear problem-solving process into sharper focus, let's examine the illustration in Figure 8–28 and consider once again the task of recording student progress in a computerized grade book.

Define the Problem

Develop a system to record grades given to student work and then to calculate an equitable and accurate score representative of the student's performance within the class.

Understand the Component Tasks

The following questions must be answered *before* you can sit down at the computer and begin to solve the problem.

- How will student names be entered (last name first)?
- How many different activity types will be allowed for each class (e g , quiz, test, project, portfolio, lab)?
- How many different grades will be entered into each activity type?
- How are grades to be calculated (will they be weighted)?
- How are grades to be reported?
- What information will be calculated concerning class performance?

Design a Solution

The primary purpose of the synthesis phase of problem solving is to help ensure that solutions designed to address the identified tasks are carried out in an effective and efficient manner and that the results are evaluated. Having defined what must be done and having identified tasks, we can now determine how each task can be carried out. The solution to this problem consists of designing labels as identifiers, creating appropriate formulas, and then entering accurate data. Tasks are identified in the following table.

Figure 8–29 **Debugging the grade book**

A linear approach to problem solving

◇	A	B	C	D	E	F	G
1	Name	Lab 1	Lab 2	Test	Midterm	Portfolio	Grade
2		10	10	100	100	100	100
3	Alderson, Kathy	0	0	0	0	0	0
4	Chagnon, Laura	10	10	100	100	100	100
5	Hall, Andrea						0
6	Hall, Les						0
7	Heilman, Jacob						0
8	McKinley, Rich						0
9	Prosser, Peggy						0
10	Strasbaugh, Kristin						0
11	Highest Score	10	10	100	100	100	100
12	Lowest score	0	0	0	0	0	0
13	Average	5.0	5.0	50.0	50.0	50.0	12.5

Identified Tasks to Perform

- Student names will be entered in one column, last name first.
- Grades for two labs, one test, one midterm project, and one cumulative portfolio will be entered.
- Maximum raw scores are established for each activity as follows:
    Labs will have a maximum score of 10.
    The test will have a maximum score of 100.
    The midterm project will have a maximum score of 100.
    Cumulative portfolio will have a maximum score of 100.
- Grades will be weighted as follows:
    Labs will be equally weighted and will together account for 20 percent.
    The test will be weighted 25 percent.
    The midterm project will be weighted 25 percent.
    The cumulative portfolio will be weighted 30 percent.
- The final grade will be reported on a scale of 1 to 100 (a percent).
- The highest and lowest scores will be identified and an average calculated on all activities, as well as on the final grade.

Implement the Solution

At the end of this chapter, a tutorial will lead you through the process of creating a grade book on a spreadsheet using *Microsoft Excel*™. Its design includes the six items just listed in the previous section. Names and grades will be entered; a range of scores established on several measures; a weighting of grades will be determined; a final grade calculated for each student; and, the highest, lowest, and average scores calculated. In addition the tutorial will lead you through creating a simple graph of some of the data.

Evaluate

Debugging is the process of correcting logic and construction errors. An often used debugging procedure is to give the program some test data that will produce known output over the entire range of use. Before entering your students' actual scores into your grade book, you might enter score values that you can compute easily and verify that the computer results are as expected. In Figure 8–29, zero is entered as the score in each item for the first student in cell range B3 to F3, and the maximum (10 or 100) is entered for the second student in cell range B4 to F4. If the results are other than expected, debugging allows you to verify the correctness of your formula, the appropriateness of the functions you employed, and the logic of your design. A look at rows 11, 12, and 13 verifies our expected results.

Documentation that accompanies a computer application provides valuable information for the user. The user of the grade book must clearly understand the intent of the program. Detailed written instructions about how to use the program can better ensure that the program is used effectively. The use of screen shots, such as those commonly found in software manuals, replicating what the user sees at any given point of using the program, is often helpful in illustrating the instructions. The instructions supplied with the grade book must clearly tell the user where and how to enter student names, the maximum scores allowed, where to enter the scores, how the scores will be weighted, and how the final grade will be calculated and reported.

As the classroom teacher uses the grade book/spreadsheet, it will continually calculate the students' total point accumulations and final scores and keep the statistics on each class activity. The rows may be sorted in alphabetical order by the data in column *A* at any time so, as new students are added, the grade book is sorted once again.

The grade book stores data about individual students, but also reveals information about their progress and their comparative performance within the group. The results in Figure 8–30 also reveal that students had a bit more difficulty with the midterm project than either the test or the portfolio.

The grade book **template** (blank form) can be saved after labels and formulas are created but before any names or scores are put into the grade book. By loading the template, naming it with the course name, and resaving it, the teacher may use the same grade book template for many classes.

Space has limited the number of examples given in this chapter. Any calculations that are done regularly are prime candidates for spreadsheet applications. The user needs only to set up a form that replicates the types of calculations that would have to be done by hand and then save the template. Whenever the calculation has to be done again, the template can be loaded and the problem addressed.

COMMERCIALLY AVAILABLE GRADE BOOK SOFTWARE

Now that we have examined the process of building an electronic grade book on a spreadsheet program, it would be worth our while to evaluate commercially available grade book software. The fundamental questions we must ask are: Is the commercial product flexible enough to meet our needs? Can we adapt the software to meet our requirements or will

Figure 8–30 **Grade book spreadsheet**

The completed spreadsheet reveals individual and comparative performance

◇	A	B	C	D	E	F	G
1	**Name**	**Lab 1**	**Lab 2**	**Test**	**Midterm**	**Portfolio**	**Grade**
2		10	10	100	100	100	100
3	Alderson, Kathy	9	7	78	75	80	78
4	Chagnon, Laura	7	8	80	80	80	79
5	Hall, Andrea	10	9	98	90	95	95
6	Hall, Les	9	10	92	80	90	89
7	Heilman, Jacob	8	10	90	80	80	85
8	McKinley, Rich	8	8	82	70	90	81
9	Prosser, Peggy	7	8	80	80	85	81
10	Strasbaugh, Kristin	10	7	98	90	95	93
11	**Highest Score**	10	10	98	90	95	95
12	**Lowest score**	7	7	78	70	80	78
13	**Average**	8.5	8.4	87.3	80.6	86.9	85.1

we have to change our grading system? Does it provide us with information about our students' performance beyond what is available in a grade book that we would create on a spreadsheet?

Whether creating your own personalized grade book or purchasing one that is commercially available, it would serve your interests well to review the analysis phase of the problem-solving process. Clearly define the requisites of your grading system, understand all of its component tasks, and proceed as your grade requirements, time, budget, and personal preferences dictate.

For those choosing a spreadsheet rather than a grade book program, note that there are other spreadsheet programs currently available for use in the classroom in addition to *Microsoft Excel™* and the programs found in *Microsoft Works™ and Appleworks™*. A top-selling one for elementary students in grades 3 and higher is *The Cruncher™*. In addition to the teacher- and student-friendly tutorial programs, this package contains 20 cross-curriculum learning projects and a host of ways to integrate spreadsheets into the curriculum.

WORKING WITH MICROSOFT EXCEL®
TO CREATE A GRADE BOOK

If you have not had much experience using a spreadsheet but found the examples given in Figures 8–15 to 8–21 interesting, we suggest that the following tutorial would help you develop some skills. In addition, should you want to create your own grade book on a spreadsheet, the following tutorial will get you started in personalizing one. We suggest you complete the tutorial from start to finish and then review and modify it to your own needs.

To follow this tutorial, you must have access to Excel®, part of the Microsoft Office® suite. If you do not have ready access to it at your site, you can download a trial version from the *www.Microsoft.com* website.

Maria B. Vonada/Merrill

In working through the following brief tutorial on Microsoft Excel you will review the following items on creating a grade book covered in the textbook tutorial.

- How to enter data (names and raw scores) and formulas (grades)
- How to replicate data and formulas in other cells
- How to create additional sheets in the workbook
- How to replicate data between sheets
- How to create a bar graph based on data in the workbook

A copy of this tutorial may be found in the Tutorials folder in the Take-Along CD.

Once you have acquired a copy of Excel® or downloaded a trial version of it, Open *Microsoft Excel*™ and save the blank workbook as ***Gradebook.***

1. ENTER DATA

1.1 Create labels for each column in rows 1 and 2 and, in this example, in cells A11, A12, and A13 as illustrated.

◇	A	B	C	D	E	F	G
1	Name	Lab 1	Lab 2	Test	Midterm	Portfolio	Grade
2		10	10	100	100	100	100
3							
4							
5							
6							
7		Create labels in rows 1 and 2					
8							
9							
10							
11	Highest Score						
12	Lowest score						
13	Average						
14							

Create labels in cells A11, A12, and A13

1.2 Move the cursor up between two columns. It changes shape to become a double-headed arrow. Hold down the mouse button and move it right or left to change the width of the column to the left.

Based on the font we have chosen, we have set the column widths as follows:
A = 17, **B, C, D** = 5, **E** and **F** = 8, **G** = 6.

(Continued)

			Width: 5.00 (0.49 inches)			
◇	A	B	C	D	E	F	G
1	Name	Lab 1	Lab 2	Test	Midterm	Portfolio	Gra
2		10	10	100	00	100	10
3							
4							

Set column widths by dragging right or left between column headers

1.3 Enter student names in column A, last name first. They may be entered in any order and then later sorted alphabetically by the spreadsheet. Then enter fictitious grades for two labs with a maximum score of 10 each in columns B and C, one test with a maximum score of 100 in column D, *one midterm project* with a maximum score of 100 in column E, and o*ne cumulative portfolio* with a maximum score of 100 in column F. Notice how this is calculated in the formula in Step 2.1.

◇	A	B	C	D	E	F	G
1	Name	Lab 1	Lab 2	Test	Midterm	Portfolio	Grade
2		10	10	100	100	100	100
3	Alderson, Kathy	9	7	78	75	80	
4	Chagnon, Laura	7	8	80	80	80	
5	Hall, Andrea	10	9	98	90	95	
6	Hall, Les	9	10	92	80	90	
7	Heilman, Jacob	8	10	90	80	80	
8	McKinley, Rich	8	8	82	70	90	
9	Prosser, Peggy	7	8	80	80	85	
10	Strasbaugh, Kristin	10	7	98	90	95	
11	Highest Score						
12	Lowest score						
13	Average						

2. ENTER THE FORMULAS

The following weightings have been determined and are reflected in the formula:
The two labs will each have a total score of 10 and weighting of 10 percent of the final grade.
One test will have a total score of 100 and be weighted 25 percent.
One midterm project will have a total score of 100 and a weighting of 25 percent.
One portfolio will have a total score of 100 and a weighting of 30 percent of the final score.
The final grade will be calculated on the basis of 100 in column G.

2.1 In cell G3, enter the formula shown in the formula bar that assigns the weighted value stated above and calculates the final grade.

If you need to refresh your memory concerning the invoking of Functions, review Figures 8–5 and 8–6 in the textbook before proceeding to the next step.

Enter the formula to calculate final Grade.

		C	D	E	F	G
1		Lab 2	Test	Midterm	Portfolio	Grade
2		10	100	100	100	100
3	Alderson, Kathy	9	7	78	75	80	78

Formula bar: =B3+C3+(D3*0.25)+(E3*0.25)+(F3*0.3)

2.2 Place the cursor in the lower right corner of cell G3 and it changes shape. It is called the *Fill handle*. Grab the Fill handle and drag down the G column highlighting cells G4 through G10.

The formula is now repeated down column G as you can see in the illustration on the far right.

Replicating the formula could also be achieved by first highlighting the range of cells in the column
(G3 to G10) and selecting the **Fill** and **Down** commands under the **Edit** menu.

G
Grade
100
78

G
Grade
100
78
79
95
89
85
81
81
93

2.3 Insert the formulas = MAX(B3:B10) in cell B11; = MIN(B3:B10) in cell B12, and = AVERAGE(B3:B10) in cell B13 to calculate the highest and lowest scores and an average of all students' scores on Lab 1. The results of the formulas are shown in the illustration to the right.

These formulas calculating the maximum, minimum, and average scores will then be repeated in columns C through G as shown in the next step.

Formula bar: =AVERAGE(B3:B10)

	A	B	C	D	E	F
1	Name	Lab 1	Lab 2	Test	Midterm	Portf
2		10	10	100	100	10
3	Alderson, Kathy	9	7	78	75	
4	Chagnon, Laura	7	8	80	80	
5	Hall, Andrea	10	9	98	90	
6	Hall, Les	9	10	92	80	
7	Heilman, Jacob	8	10	90	80	
8	McKinley, Rich	8	8	82	70	
9	Prosser, Peggy	7	8	80	80	
10	Strasbaugh, Kristin	10	7	98	90	
11	Highest Score	10				
12	Lowest score	7				
13	Average	8.5				

(Continued)

265

2.4 Grab the Fill handle in the lower right corner of cell B11 and drag across the row highlighting cells C11 through G11.

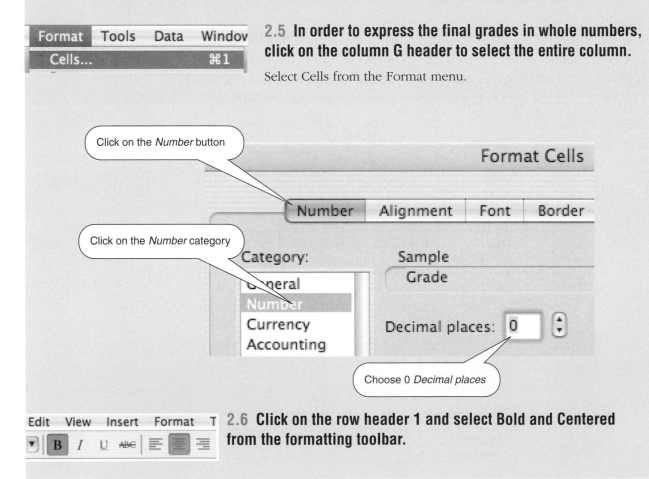

9	Prosser, Peggy	7	8	80	80	85	81
10	Strasbaugh, Kristin	10	7	98	90	95	93
11	Highest Score	10					
12	Lowest score	7					
13	Average	8.5					

Grab the Fill handle in B11
and drag across to G11.
Repeat the process in rows 12 and 13.

Repeat the process in rows 12 and 13.

The other highest scores, lowest scores, and average scores will be automatically displayed in the appropriate cells.

Replicating the formula could also be achieved by first highlighting the range of cells in columns B through G and selecting the Fill and Right commands under the Edit menu.

Format	Tools	Data	Window
Cells...			⌘1

2.5 In order to express the final grades in whole numbers, click on the column G header to select the entire column.

Select Cells from the Format menu.

Click on the *Number* button

Format Cells

| Number | Alignment | Font | Border |

Click on the *Number* category

Category:

Sample

Grade

General

Number

Currency   Decimal places: 0

Accounting

Choose 0 *Decimal places*

| Edit | View | Insert | Format | T |

B *I* U A̶B̶C̶ ≡ ≡ ≡

2.6 Click on the row header 1 and select Bold and Centered from the formatting toolbar.

Click on row header 2 and select Bottom Border from the borders icon on the formatting toolbar.

Select the range of cells (click and drag through) from A11 to A13 and select Bold and Right Aligned from the formatting toolbar.

The completed grade book is shown here.

	A	B	C	D	E	F	G
1	**Name**	**Lab 1**	**Lab 2**	**Test**	**Midterm**	**Portfolio**	**Grade**
2		10	10	100	100	100	100
3	Alderson, Kathy	9	7	78	75	80	78
4	Chagnon, Laura	7	8	80	80	80	79
5	Hall, Andrea	10	9	98	90	95	95
6	Hall, Les	9	10	92	80	90	89
7	Heilman, Jacob	8	10	90	80	80	85
8	McKinley, Rich	8	8	82	70	90	81
9	Prosser, Peggy	7	8	80	80	85	81
10	Strasbaugh, Kristin	10	7	98	90	95	93
11	**Highest Score**	10	10	98	90	95	95
12	**Lowest score**	7	7	78	70	80	78
13	**Average**	8.5	8.4	87.3	80.6	86.9	85

3. CREATE A NEW SHEET

3.1 **To create a new sheet for your workbook, select Worksheet from the Insert menu.**

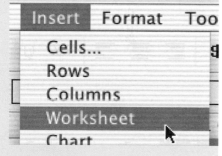

3.2 **A new sheet tab (Sheet2) will appear at the bottom of your worksheet. You can toggle between the two by clicking on the tabs.**

(Continued)

4. REPLICATE DATA ON THE NEW SHEET

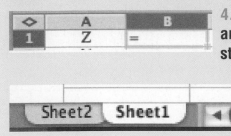

4.1 We will set up this new sheet to present class data anonymously. Begin by typing single letters to represent student names in column A on Sheet2. We chose to use Z though S in inverse alphabetical order.

4.2 On Sheet2, click in cell B1 and type the equal sign (=).

4.3 Click on the tab for Sheet1 bringing it to the foreground.

4.4 Click in cell G3 which represents the final grade for student Kathy Alderson and press the Enter key.

Name	Lab 1	Lab 2	Test	Midterm	Portfolio	Grade
	10	10	100	100	100	100
Alderson, Kathy	9	7	78	75	80	78

That grade is now replicated in cell B1 of Sheet2.

4.5 Remember how you filled in data in other cells in step 2.2? Now you fill down column B by grabbing the bottom right corner of Cell B1 [your cursor changes to a plus sign (+)] and dragging down to Cell B8.

(Or highlight the range of cells B1 to B8 and select Fill > Down from the Edit menu.) The grades now appear throughout the column.

	A	B
1	Z	78
2	Y	
3	X	
4	W	
5	V	
6	U	
7	T	
8	S	

	A	B
1	Z	78
2	Y	79
3	X	95
4	W	89
5	V	85
6	U	81
7	T	81
8	S	93

5. GRAPH SOME OF THE DATA

5.1 To create a bar graph comparing the students' scores anonymously on the Final Grade, select the range of cells from *A1 to B8* on *Sheet2.*

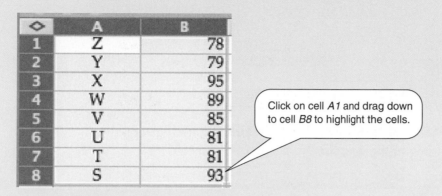

Click on cell *A1* and drag down to cell *B8* to highlight the cells.

5.2 Select the Chart wizard from the Standard Excel toolbar. Once the chart wizard is open, it will guide you step by step in the creation of a graph.

5.3 Select the Column chart type and the *Clustered column* with a 3-D visual effect chart subtype and . . .

. . . click on the *Next >* button at the bottom of the window.

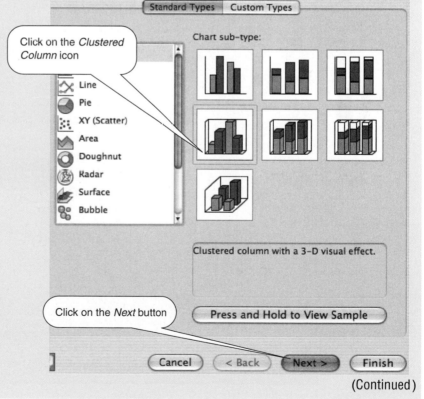

Click on the *Clustered Column* icon

Click on the *Next* button

(Continued)

5.4 The Chart Wizard will display a three-dimensional column graph . . .

. . . and indicate that the data range is the range of cells you just selected in step 1.

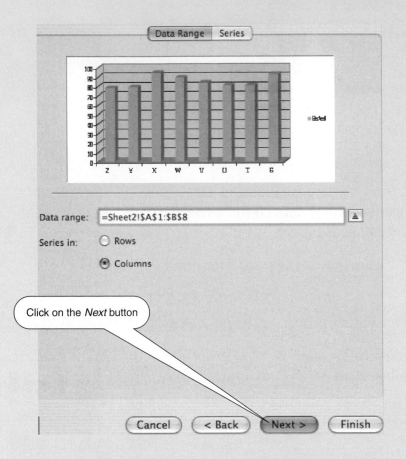

Click on the *Next* button

5.5 Type Final Grade as the Chart title. . .

. . . then click on the Data Labels button.

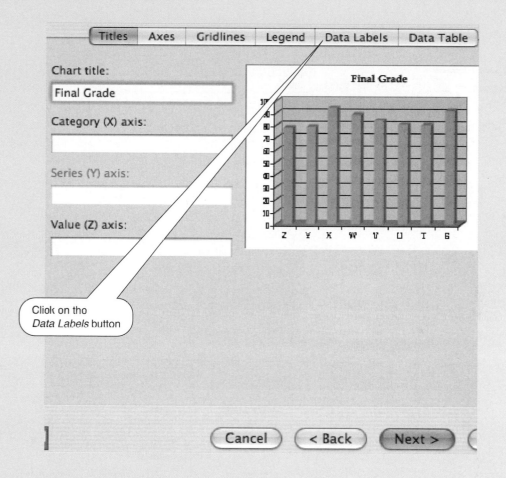

5.6 Click on the Show Value button to have the scores appear as labels on the columns.

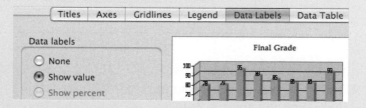

(Continued)

5.7 Click on the button to select the location of the chart as an object in Sheet2.

Chart Wizard – Step 4 of 4 – Chart Location

Place chart:

Click this button

○ As new sheet: `Chart1`

● As object in: `Sheet2` ▼

? Cancel < Back Next > Finish

Click the *Finish* button

You have now completed a column graph for the **Final Grade** as the following figure shows. The final step will be to position it properly on the page.

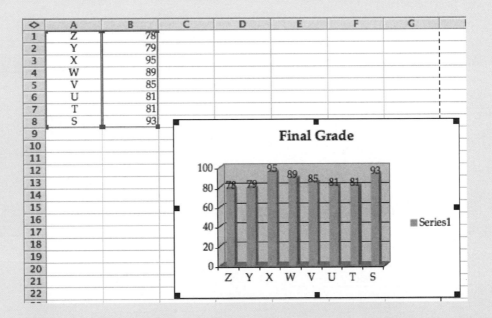

5.8 Click the cursor in the chart area. The cursor changes shape. Hold the mouse button down and drag the chart to the upper left corner of the page. Notice that when the chart is selected, grab handles (dark squares) appear at the corners and side. Grab the bottom right corner handle and drag it so that the chart fills the page side to side.

272

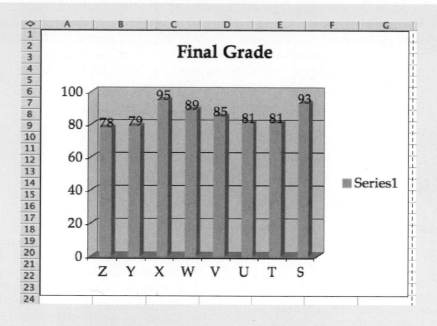

You will discover that by double-clicking on various components of the graph, a window will appear allowing you to alter the appearance of that component. Experiment with the graph until you are satisfied with its appearance.

LET'S REVIEW

An electronic spreadsheet is a two-dimensional matrix of columns and rows. The intersection of a column and row is called a cell. The power of this software lies in the fact that cells relate one to another, allowing the contents of one cell to affect another cell. Cells may contain text, values, or formulas. Complex mathematical, statistical, and logical relationships can be described as formulas. Powerful functions are embedded in the software and can be called up by the user. Since the results of cell relationships are displayed, and changing one cell immediately affects the results of the relationship, spreadsheets are often referred to as "what if" tools and are often used to make projections or forecast results.

Applying a nonlinear problem-solving approach allows us to appreciate that this approach permits divergent-thinking individuals to determine their own pattern without having a hierarchical structure imposed on them. A linear problem-solving strategy that might appeal more to a sequential learner was also examined and applied to the design of a grade book.

A number of examples were given in which a spreadsheet was used to predict results; to promote accuracy of calculations; to generate graphs; to convert metric and English measurements; and, functioning as a database, to sort text.

Graphs can represent abstract numerical data in a concrete, clear, and interesting manner. They can display relationships that would be more difficult to convey in a text or verbal mode. As visuals, they capture attention and promote greater retention of information. The analysis and interpretation of graphs has become an important subject in the K–12 curriculum.

Ideally, a spreadsheet would become a tool for the teacher to examine options and to forecast results. It would be taught to a student, who could use it to answer "what if" questions in any academic discipline in which the act of problem solving dealt with the examination of comparisons. Along with graphics programs, word processors, and database managers, spreadsheets are programs that truly exemplify the concept of using the computer as a tool to extend our human capabilities.

LET'S PRACTICE

To complete the specified exercises online, go to the Chapter Exercises Module in Chapter 8 of the Companion Website.

1. Thinking of the computer as a management tool in education, describe the application of a spreadsheet to three management tasks faced by a teacher on a regular basis.

2. Thinking of the computer as a forecasting tool, describe the application of a spreadsheet to three tasks that a student might face.

3. Design a spreadsheet to record performances on a softball team. Calculate individual and team batting averages and on-base percentages for each game and for the season.

4. Design a spreadsheet to calculate a budget for the first Thanksgiving. From a reference source, identify the food items that were most likely present. Estimate the number of portions needed. Calculate the cost in terms of today's prices.

5. Design a spreadsheet to convert your weight in pounds to kilograms, and your height in feet and inches to centimeters.

6. You are responsible for raising $2,000 in income for each home football game played. Explain your problem-solving strategy and design a spreadsheet to accomplish your goal.

7. Take a poll of your classmates to determine the five cities in which they would prefer to live. Assign a weighting of 5 for their first choice, 4 for their second choice, etc. Design a spreadsheet to record their preferences and identify an overall ranking for the cities chosen.

8. As a variation of exercise 7, design a spreadsheet to record the name and five livability factors for a city (e.g., population size, geographical location, climate, availability of public transit, education level). Rate each factor from one to five. Include a cell that averages these factors. Ask students to rate any five cities. Analyze the class results.

9. Record the gender of each student in your class and the length of time he or she has lived at the current address. Rank order the data from shortest to longest occupancy for each gender. Using the graphing capability of an integrated package or a stand-alone graphing program, create a line graph showing the occupancy ranges for each gender. Describe the results to a classmate.

10. The following problem is derived from an article entitled, "Can You Manage?" (Hastie, 1992). Suppose you are a biologist responsible for managing a healthy, stable deer population in a given area. You must regulate the size of the deer herd according to the habitat that supports it. In other words, you must determine an annual deer harvest so as not to exceed the carrying capacity of the habitat and ultimately destroy it.

- Design a spreadsheet to manage four populations of deer. For Group One, hunters will be allowed to harvest 25 percent of the summer population; Group Two, 50 percent; Group Three, 75 percent; Group Four, 0 percent. Allow all groups to reproduce at a rate of 50 percent (new fawns equal one-half of the number of deer in the group each year).

- For each group, (a) start with 20 deer the first year, (b) for year two, remove number harvested, and (c) add the yearly fawn crop. Continue this process for three more years for a total of five years.

Answer the following questions:

- Which populations decreased in size? Which increased? Which remained the same?

- Suppose you determine the winter carrying capacity of each habitat to be 20 deer. Which harvest rate would allow you to do this and still maintain a reasonably stable population?

- Could you continue to harvest at the same rate each year or would you have to adjust the harvest rate in some years? If so, what rate would you use?

PORTFOLIO DEVELOPMENT EXERCISES

To complete this exercise online, go to the Digital Portfolio Module in Chapter 8 of the Companion Website.

One of the NETS•S standards covered in this chapter was "Students use technology resources for solving problems and making informed decisions" under *Category 6: Technology problem-solving and decision-making tools.* Begin to develop your own portfolio of lesson plans that demonstrates your ability to have your students reach the NETS•S standards.

1. Design a lesson plan activity for elementary, middle school, or high school students in which they use a spreadsheet program to examine and make a decision about a problem. Try to combine several functions found in spreadsheet programs. The number that you use should depend on the grade level. Younger students may only use simple tools (relating cells, simple math functions, etc.). Older students will be required to use more sophisticated tools (multiple functions, formulas, charting, etc.). This lesson should demonstrate that your students have achieved the standard. Be sure to include a system of evaluation for your students' understanding and competence to ensure that they have met this standard.

2. Adapt the lesson plan activity you developed in exercise 1 for students to evaluate each others' work.

GLOSSARY

absolute reference	A formula is meant to always refer to an exact cell regardless of the placement of the formula cell within the spreadsheet
active cell	The cell that is selected and ready for data entry or editing
cell	The intersection of a row and a column in a spreadsheet
data entry bar	See *formula bar*
debugging	The process of removing all logic and construction errors
documentation	Written explanations supporting program maintenance and use
formula bar	The area at the top of the screen that displays the content of the active cell and that can be edited
functions	Built-in mathematical formulas used to calculate cell values
labels	The text descriptors related to adjacent data
spreadsheet	Software that accepts data in a matrix of columns and rows, with their instructions called cells. One cell can relate to any other cell or ranges of cells on the matrix by formula
template	A blank form in a Spreadsheet or File Manager Program

REFERENCES AND SUGGESTED READINGS

Goodwin, A. (2002, March). Using a spreadsheet to explore melting, dissolving and phase diagrams. *School Science Review, 83*(304), 105–8.

Hastie, B. (1992, May–June). Can you manage? *Oregon Wildlife,* 9–10.

Howell, D., Morrow, J., & Summerville, J. (2002). *Using Excel in the classroom.* Thousand Oaks, CA: Corwin Press, Inc.

Johnson, D. R. (2002, September). Use your spreadsheet as a project management tool. *School Business Affairs, 68*(8), 17–20.

Lewis, P. (2002, November). Spreadsheet magic: The basic spreadsheet is a powerful tool for teaching. *Learning and Leading with Technology, 30*(3), 36–41.

Paul, J., & Kaiser, C. (1996, May). Do women live longer than men? Investigating graveyard data with computers. *Learning and Leading with Technology, 23*(8), 13–15.

9 CHAPTER

Learning with Database Tools

1. What is a database?

2. What are its component parts?

3. How do you find information in a database?

4. What is a database manager and how does it work?

5. What are the important concepts related to data storage and retrieval?

6. How can you create and use files with a database manager?

7. How could problem-solving strategies be applied to designing databases?

8. How might you and your students use a database as a productivity tool to store, retrieve, and analyze information?

9. Following a linear problem-solving approach, how can a community resource file be developed in a database?

10. How might you develop a database file to manage your address book?

NETS•T Foundation Standards and Performance Indicators Addressed in this Chapter

I. Technology operations and concepts
   A. demonstrate introductory knowledge, skills, and understanding of concepts related to technology (as described in ISTE National Education Technology Standards for Students)
   B. demonstrate continual growth in technology knowledge and skills to stay abreast of current and emerging technologies
II. Planning and designing learning environments and experiences
   A. design developmentally appropriate learning opportunities that apply technology-enhanced instructional strategies to support the diverse needs of learners
III. Teaching, learning, and the curriculum
   A. facilitate technology-enhanced experiences that address content standards and student technology standards
   B. use technology to support learner-centered strategies that address the diverse needs of students
   C. apply technology to develop students' higher order skills and creativity
   D. manage student learning activities in a technology-enhanced environment
IV. Assessment and evaluation
   B. use technology resources to collect and analyze data, interpret results, and communicate findings to improve instructional practice and maximize student learning
V. Productivity and professional practice
   A. use technology resources to engage in ongoing professional development and lifelong learning
   B. continually evaluate and reflect on professional practice to make informed decisions regarding the use of technology in support of student learning
   C. apply technology to increase productivity
   D. use technology to communicate and collaborate with peers, parents, and the larger community in order to nurture student learning
VI. Social, ethical, legal, and human issues
   A. model and teach legal and ethical practice related to technology use
   B. apply technology resources to enable and empower learners with diverse backgrounds, characteristics, and abilities

LET'S LOOK AT THIS CHAPTER

Databases are wonderful tools you can use in your classroom to enhance learning, increase productivity, and produce creative works. Introduce them to your students as tools to store and manipulate data and incorporate them into your lessons. They can also be used in association with word processing applications to quickly and easily merge data into documents and produce letters and envelopes using the word processor's mail merge feature.

If databases are such an important set of tools for your students to learn and understand, why do they seem so daunting? Perhaps some of us see these tools as belonging in corporate

A tutorial showing how to design an address book in FileMaker Pro may be found in the Tutorials folder in the Take-Along CD.

A FileMaker Pro database for creating and printing true–false and multiple choice test questions may be found in the Lessons and Data Files folder in the Take-Along CD.

America in the realm of massive file servers and legions of technocrats when, in reality, they also belong in the third-grade classroom. Perhaps some of us remember experiences dealing with complex software and elaborate data entry procedures when, in reality, today's database managers are user friendly and easy to operate. If you are among the reluctant to venture into this database world, we encourage you to marshall your determination and examine your world and that of your students. Recognize the ubiquitous data gathering, analysis, and management efforts around you. Step forward with us in this chapter to learn to transform data into information as you build knowledge.

This chapter deals with concepts related to understanding, creating, and using a data file. Some of the examples in this chapter were generated in FileMaker® Pro, a popular and easy-to-use program available for both the Windows and Macintosh platforms. Files created on one platform run seamlessly on the other. In 2004, *Technology & Learning* presented FileMaker® Pro an Award of Excellence as one of the outstanding education products of the year. The concepts described in this chapter also apply to a wide variety of other database managers, including Microsoft Access®. Together we will explore the creation of a database and its application in different areas of the school curriculum. We will discuss Boolean logic and the searching and sorting of data to develop search strategies.

When you finish reading this chapter, we recommend that you download a trial version of Filemaker® Pro from the website (*www.filemaker.com*) and print the tutorial found in the Filemaker® Tutorial folder within the Tutorials folder of the Take-Along CD. It will guide you through the development of an address book. We have also included a database of test questions to help you generate a true–false and multiple choice quiz. It includes 10 sample questions.

▪▪▪ | DATA AND INFORMATION

Information is organized, structured data. Data are everywhere and in themselves, are useless. They are constantly flowing into our minds through our senses. Fortunately, we are very selective in attending to them and we ignore most of them. Our conscious and subconscious minds filter data, accepting some and rejecting the rest. We have the ability to organize the data we accept and give it meaning. Only then do data become information.

Information is power. Information literacy is a survival skill we teach to our students. As they become increasingly information literate, they will understand how data are organized and how to sift through and manipulate the data to access information. Information is purposefully structured data often stored in a database. As Figure 9–1 attempts to conceptualize, a database manager is software designed to structure aural, visual, and textual data and store, organize, access, and correlate it in order to produce information, thereby giving meaning to data.

Database managers not only allow us to input, store, and restructure information but they also give us the ability to pick and choose the parts of our information that we would like to display.

We commonly use databases in our everyday lives. Examples include an inventory sheet of sports equipment in the physical education department, the student records system at your school, and your adress book and holiday or birthday card list at home. One of the most ubiquitous databases is the telephone directory (Figure 9–2). It is a collection of data organized according to a clear structure. To derive useful information from this database, we must understand its structure. Our telephone directory (database) is a collection of facts (data) organized into a series of records that each contain an individual's, family's, or establishment's name, street address, and phone number. The phone number is a unique identifier. Only one person, one family, one institution, or one

Figure 9–1 Data to information

A database manager transforms data into information

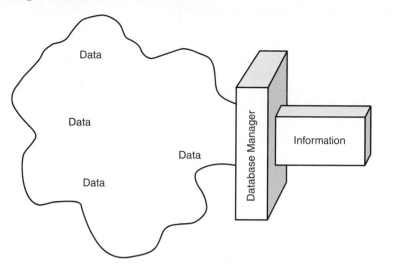

Figure 9–2 Telephone directory

A telephone directory is one of the most common databases (Richard C. Forcier)

business can have that phone number. When we search the phone book, we are usually looking for someone's phone number. Using the alphabetical listing of names as the key, we find the name and corresponding phone number as part of each individual record. The record is composed of all of the data related to that individual entry (i.e., name, address, and phone number). It would be an extremely difficult task to find the phone number in a regular phone book if we knew only the address but not the name. Although the *purpose* of the phone directory is to list the telephone numbers, the *name* is the key to its successful use.

We have defined the concept of a tool as something used to facilitate the performance of a task. A database manager is an appropriate tool in the management of information if it meets one or more of the following guidelines.

We owe it to our students at all grade levels to help them develop data management and information retrieval skills. We are fortunate to have at our disposal easy-to-use database managers designed for the personal computer. Microsoft Access™, FileMaker® Pro, and AppleWorks™ are three commonly used databases.

We have watched third-grade students use a FileMaker® Pro file created by their teacher. This file related to fish that live in the ocean. The students entered data, and then sorted the data and searched the database for specific characteristics such as the depth zone in which certain fish live. Students developed insights as they compared different characteristics. Their interaction provided a testimonial to the user friendliness of this program.

A copy of these guidelines may be found in the Guidelines folder in the Take-Along CD.

GUIDELINES FOR WHEN TO USE A DATABASE MANAGER

- Would a database manager increase the speed of information acquisition?
- Would it increase the ease of information acquisition?
- Would it increase the quality of the information acquired in terms of both accuracy and completeness?
- Would it improve the dissemination of information?

Advantages of Developing and Using Databases

In designing a database, students are engaged in activities that contribute to the development of organizational skills and higher order thinking skills. They refine a specific vocabulary. They research information on a given topic. They verify the accuracy of data, note the similarities and differences among data examined, and explore relationships. They classify information discovered. They consider how information might be communicated effectively to others.

In searching for information in a database, students develop and refine information retrieval skills. They improve their ability to recognize patterns, trends, and other relationships. They are encouraged to think critically by interpreting data and testing hypotheses. All of these skills have real-world applications and contribute to preparing students to take their place as productive members of society.

FILE/DATABASE MANAGERS

A **database** is an organized, structured collection of facts about a particular topic. We studied spreadsheets in Chapter 8, which are also a structured collection of facts. Spreadsheets and databases differ in that spreadsheets are preformatted in columns and rows and are designed to deal mainly, though as we have seen, not exclusively, with numerical data. Spreadsheets also present broad information rather than focus on any individual entry. Databases are much more versatile. They are designed to deal with text, numerical data, visual data, and sound. Unlike spreadsheets, database reports can be formatted in a wide variety of ways. These reports can present data about an individual record, compare records, or summarize information relating to the entire file.

At times, the facts in a database are grouped together in subsets called **files.** A database may consist of a single file or a number of related files. Computer systems for file management are sometimes called **database managers.** The term implies the capability of managing a number of files of data simultaneously or at least in a closely related manner. Programs with this capability are properly called **relational database managers.** Software designed to manage a single file is properly referred to as a **file manager.** Through popular usage, however, distinctions have blurred and the terms have come to be used interchangeably, with file managers now being called database managers or simply databases. We accede to this change in terminology: When reference is made to *database,* we treat it synonymously with *file.*

Database Operation

What is a database manager and how does it actually work? The following table presents the seven major functions of a database manager and indicates that database management software is designed to allow the user to create a structure for the storage, manipulation, and retrieval of data. Once data are entered into the file, the software allows the user to act on those data in a variety of ways. A good **file management** system lets you do four basic tasks.

- Gather related data into a central collection
- Find specific data to meet a particular need
- Reorder those data in various ways
- Retrieve the product of that reordering in a useful form

New data can be created through calculations based on existing data entered into the file. The products of file managers fall into two main categories: the real-time, online search for specific information and the ability to print reports organized in a particular fashion.

File design	Establish structure of file by creating data fields of appropriate type
Form design	Create a layout of fields and where they will appear displayed on the screen or printed on paper
Record editing	Allow data to be entered, altered, and deleted
Record finding	Facilitate the selection of certain records while ignoring others
Record sorting	Organize records according to some field order
Report creating	Find specific records, sort them, and arrange them on a selected form
Report printing	Display the information on the screen or on paper

File Design. The individual data item is the most discrete element of a database and is called a data field, or simply a **field.** In the case of the telephone directory, a phone number is an individual field, as is the address and the name. Fields can contain text, numeric values, dates, pictures, sounds, movies, and even links to websites. Fields can contain calculations that perform mathematical operations on other numeric fields within the record and store the resulting values (e.g., multiplying the contents of two other fields). Fields can also contain summaries of data across a number of records and display the result (calculate the total or the average of specific field values for a group of records). After each field has been defined, this information is saved as the file structure (how the data in each record are stored).

281

Field **labels** are created to assist recognition of fields on the screen or in reports. Figure 9–3 illustrates fields and their labels. Keep in mind that labels simply identify or describe the fields where the data are actually stored.

The data record, or simply **record,** is the building block of the file. A record consists of all the related fields. An individual record in the phone book contains all the data related to that entry (i.e., name, address, and phone number). A file is the aggregation of all the records. The phone book file is the collection of all the records for a city, town, or region. A file, then, consists of individual records that are themselves individual fields.

Form Design. As fields are defined, labels are created and grouped together, creating a **form,** or **layout,** which appears on the screen with areas where data can be entered. It is common to create several layouts for a file, including a columnar one that is referred to as a *List View*. In this layout, a different record is displayed on each line. (This resembles a spreadsheet where a row represents one record and each column represents a different field in that record.) Records can be sorted on the basis of any field and in any order with the results displayed in a convenient way to scan through all or selected records in the file. The white pages of a phone book typically list the name on one line followed by an address and phone number on a second line. The yellow pages often add a picture in a display advertisement to grab attention.

Once data are entered, the layout selected can be thought of as a window through which to examine data in selected fields. Most file managers allow a good deal of freedom in custom designing a layout. Figure 9–4 shows a layout on the left, where fields and their labels are included to facilitate data entry. A second layout on the right contains only the fields to be used as a mailing label (notice that graphics such as the edge trim in this example may be added to a layout). A third layout is in list view. This last layout could be sorted by last name, city, phone, or any other field that would yield useful information. Layouts are created based on the information required by the user. Fields are individually chosen to appear in a layout and their most appropriate position.

Data Entry and Record Editing. During data entry, the file manager displays the field labels on the screen, places the cursor at the first position in the first field, and facilitates the entry of data (e.g., letters, numbers, pictures, or sounds). The user is free to alter or change the

Figure 9–3 Fields and labels

A record showing fields and their corresponding labels

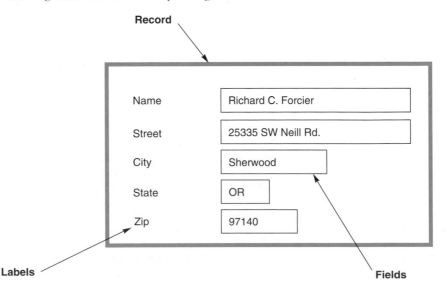

Figure 9–4 Three different layouts

The upper left layout facilitates data entry, the upper right one is a mailing label, and the lower one represents a list view that could be used in an address book

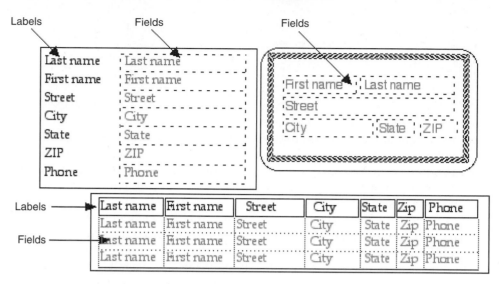

Figure 9–5 Boolean connectors

Boolean connectors facilitate database searches

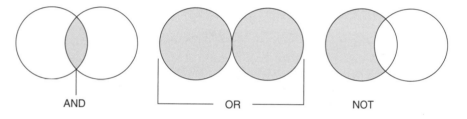

data in any field in any of the records at any time. To edit records, you place the cursor in the appropriate field and type the change.

Record Finding and Sorting. The software allows the user to perform a **logical search,** sometimes called a **query,** to select records based on a wide range of criteria. For example, an *exact match* of a value in a field can be requested (e.g., find field value *equaling* "Francis" = *Francis*). *A match containing a value* in a field can be requested (e.g., find field value *containing* "Francis" = *Francis, Francis*can, San *Francis*co). Many other searches can be performed, including those greater than, less than, or not equal to a value. Searches can be performed on ranges of data by specifying the extremes of the range (i.e., minimum and maximum values). Searches can find all the records except those indicated to be omitted. Compound searches can be constructed to examine data in multiple fields using the **Boolean connectors** illustrated in Figure 9–5. The use of the *AND* connector restricts the search and makes it more specific. The use of the *OR* connector expands the search, making it less specific. The *NOT* connector removes those records having the second search criterion from the set of records otherwise found.

For example, as illustrated in Figure 9–6, one could search a school district's student file by gender and address for all records of girls who live in Springfield, a specific town in the attendance area. The search would be "girls" AND "Springfield." *Both criteria* would

283

Figure 9–6 Selection results using Boolean connectors

Notice that AND is the most restrictive and that OR is the most inclusive

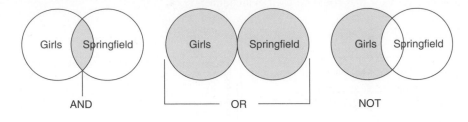

have to be present in the same record in order to select that record; however, one could search the file for records of all girls in the district or records of all students (boys or girls) who live in Springfield. The search would be "girls" OR "Springfield." *Either criterion* would have to be present in a record in order to select that record. All records of girls plus all records of the specified town (both boys and girls) would be selected. A popular way of distinguishing between the two selection connectors is to remember the rhyme that "OR is more." The NOT connector would be used to find all girls who are not living in Springfield.

Data can be sorted or arranged in a prescribed alphabetic, numeric, or chronological order in either ascending (e.g., A–Z, 1–99, 1941–2000) or descending (e.g., Z–A, 99–1, 2000–1941) fashion. This organization of records within the file can be based on any individual field. Most software also allows nested, or multilevel, sorts. For example, one could sort an address book in ascending alphabetical order by last name and then as a second level, by first name. This would create an alphabetic list by last name and then, if any entries shared the same last name, the sort would alphabetize those by first name.

Report Creation and Printing. To develop a report for printing information from the file, the user first selects the appropriate layout, then selects the records to be included in the report (finds the records indicated by the search criteria), and, finally, designates their order (sorts the records found in ascending or descending order in a particular field). For example, to print a list of first names, last names, and birth dates, the user would do the following:

• Designate the size of the page and create column titles that would serve as labels: *First Name, Last Name, Birth Date.*
• Choose the records to be printed: All records? Only those after a certain birth date?
• Define the order: Alphabetic by last name, then first name? Birth date order?

In this example, the list might be sorted by birth date, and, if two or more entries had the same birth date, these names would then be sorted alphabetically. This technique is referred to as a **nested sort,** or **multilevel sort.** Examine Figure 9–7.

A powerful feature of database managers is that data can be entered once, and many reports can be generated simply by instructing the software how to organize the data. You do not have to rework the collected information by hand. Most of your time and energy goes into data entry and maintenance. Very little time is spent generating reports.

Another useful feature of a database is the ability to combine the information it contains with a word processing document using the mail merge feature of the word processing program. The mail merge feature allows specific database fields to be printed in specific areas of the word processing document. Using this feature, it is easy to produce customized letters, reports, and so on. To create a mail merge document in Microsoft Word®, choose Data Merge Manager in the Tools menu as shown in Figure 9–8. Microsoft *Help* is a useful guide in the process.

Figure 9–7 Nested sort in the birth date list

Notice that the last two entries have the same birth date and that Adams is listed first

First Name	Last Name	Birthdate
Fred	Prosser	May 10, 1960
Laura	Gomez	May 26, 1965
Peggy	Prosser	January 8, 1966
Jim	Adams	October 15, 1968
Christina	Garcia	October 15, 1968

Figure 9–8 Data merge manager in Microsoft Word®

Data from a FileMaker® Profile can be merged into a word document

PROBLEM SOLVING WITH DATABASES

Problem Statement. A teacher wishes to make the best use of the local resources in the community.

In an effort to bring the problem-solving process into sharper focus and to understand component tasks, let's consider the management of some resources external to the classroom. Begin by analyzing the required output and formulating questions, such as those that follow, to help determine what is necessary to produce this result.

Understanding Components. What are the resources? How do they align with the curriculum? How might they be accessed by teachers and students?

These items could certainly be further expanded, refined, and organized in outline fashion. An outlining strategy is often helpful in reaching a better understanding of the components.

The outline presented in Figure 9–9 identifies type, curriculum areas, and access as the major headings in response to the preceding questions. It refines each heading using more specific subheadings and, in some instances, even more specific third- and fourth-level subheadings.

Design the Solution. The solution to the information management problem just outlined involves designing a database to store relevant data and to allow easy retrieval of useful information. Figure 9–10 lists data fields derived from the outline presented in Figure 9–9. Notice that a field to store the record entry date is also included so that the information can be examined on a periodic basis to determine its validity or usefulness. We cannot overemphasize the importance of first knowing how the data will be manipulated and reported. Will we be merging this data into a document? If so, should we have had separate fields for last name and first name? Is a title needed (Mr., Ms., Mrs., Dr.)? Will we ever have to sort by city or state?

Error Trapping. Accurate data entry is essential to the production of meaningful information from a database. Error trapping is a process of designing safeguards into your solution. In error trapping, a designer makes sure that the program does not accept entry of incorrect data. If certain values must be excluded when entering data into the file, then a technique must be used to ensure that the unwanted data cannot be entered, thereby preventing potential errors that could cause the program to yield faulty information.

Figure 9–9 Classroom resources

Outlining components of a classroom resources file

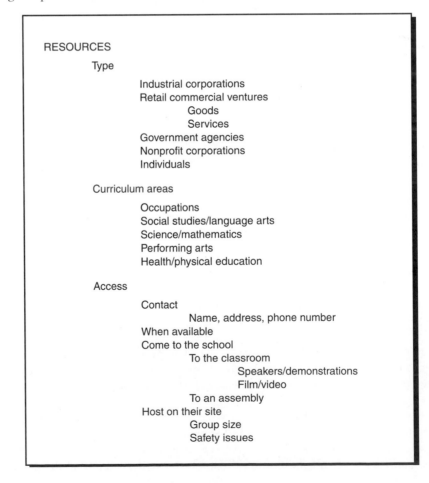

Depending on the capability and sophistication of the software being used, the *Resource type* field in the *Resources file* example could present checkboxes on the screen, as shown in Figure 9–11, representing the available entries rather than depending on input typed from the keyboard.

The *Curriculum areas* field might present the user with a predetermined list from which to make a selection. Checkboxes and predetermined lists also aid in sorting data at a later time by standardizing responses and limiting choices to set options. As illustrated in Figure 9–12, the *Available date* field might be restricted to accept only unique values to prevent double scheduling and to accept only dates that fall between 1/15/07 and 5/15/07. For example, to make sure that the date falls in the correct year. It can prohibit a user from overriding the restriction and display an appropriate message when an attempt is made to enter incorrect data.

Another example of error trapping data entry in a student records database is to designate a range of values from 0 to 4.0 in a field designed to store a numerical equivalent of F to A course grades. Limiting data entry to this range would catch typing errors, such as a double-key press, that might attempt to enter a nonsensical value of 33, for example. Once data is entered into the fields, search strategies should be developed and decisions made on sorting the data to yield the desired information. In more complex applications, **debugging** procedures should be implemented at this time. Debugging is the process of correcting logic and construction errors. It is especially important to verify calculation and summary fields in a database. As we have seen in the preceding chapter, an often-used debugging procedure is to give the program some test data that will produce easily verifiable output. If the results are other than expected, debugging allows you to verify the correctness of your data entry and calculations, the appropriateness of the functions you used, and the logic of your design.

Evaluate. Does using the database produce the anticipated results? Are your information needs satisfactorily met? If not, revisit your design to ensure that the required fields are defined and error trapping procedures are in place.

If you would like to practice the concepts explained in this chapter regarding databases, you might want to follow the tutorial on designing an address book in FileMaker Pro found in the Tutorials folder of the Take-Along CD.

A tutorial giving step-by-step instructions on how to design an address book in FileMaker Pro® may be found in the Tutorials folder in the Take-Along CD.

Figure 9–10 Data fields

Fields defined for the classroom resources file

Resource type	Text
Curriculum areas	Text
Contact name	Text
Contact address	Text
Contact phone number	Text
Available date	Date
Available time	Tme
Location	Text
Presentation type	Text
Group size	Text
Safety issues	Text
Record entry date	Auto enter date

Figure 9–11 Checkboxes

Checkboxes to control data entry and prevent errors

Resource type	
	☐ Industrial
	[X] Retail–Goods
	☐ Retail–Services
	☐ Government
	☐ Nonprofit
	☐ Individual
Curriculum areas	Occupations
Available date	

Figure 9–12 Field validation

Data entry is subject to validation controls in FileMaker® Pro to trap errors

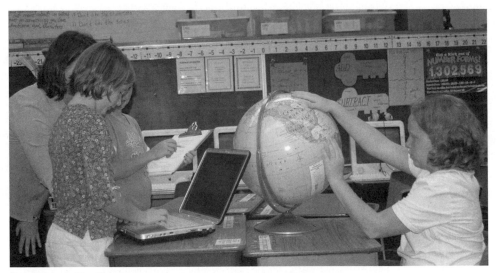

Megan Vonada/Merrill

REVIEW OF DATABASE FEATURES

Following are some features readily found on a number of database managers currently on the market.

- *Accuracy Control.* Database managers should include the ability to restrict or evaluate data entry to ensure its accuracy.
- *Data Entry Automation.* Data, such as a serial number or the date, might be automatically entered when a new record is created. To simplify and control data

entry, a layout might include checkboxes, pop-up lists, or buttons to be clicked with the mouse rather than requiring data always to be entered through the keyboard.

- *Field Definition.* Fields should be able to be defined as text, number (value), date, time, picture, sound, movie, calculation, and summary.
- *Finding Records.* The user should be able to find records using the Boolean connectors of AND, OR, and NOT as well as the operators < (less than), > (greater than), and = (exact match).
- *Layout.* The better database managers allow the user a great deal of control in designing the data layouts (forms or views). Some programs include a number of preformatted layouts along with graphics tools to enhance their appearance.
- *Sorting.* The user should be able to sort the entire file or a found set of records in ascending or descending order. Multiple-level or nested sorts are very useful. They allow records to be sorted first by the contents of one field (e.g., last name) and then by the contents of another field (e.g., first name).

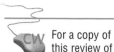

For a copy of this review of database features go to the Supplemental Information module in Chapter 9 on the Companion Website *www.prenhall.com/ forcier*

LET'S GO INTO THE CLASSROOM
Using a Database to Bring Students Together

Why a database? My goal was to come up with a project for my fourth-grade student Travis, who has a hearing impairment, to work on with a hearing peer. I wanted Travis to have the opportunity to learn some new computer skills, do some problem solving with a peer, and practice his communication skills. I needed a problem-solving activity and I've been interested in investigating uses of databases with my elementary students. Learning ways to organize information is always a valuable activity for learners, as is analyzing and evaluating data. A bonus when choosing a database as an analysis tool is the opportunity for the students to grasp the importance of planning the structure of the database and making decisions about its contents before they actually set it up. My plan was to guide Travis and a partner of his choice in developing a class database. This type of project would involve the whole fourth-grade class in which Travis is mainstreamed. Travis and his partner would also serve in the role of mentors who would give their classmates their first exposure to the possibilities inherent with database use. The two mentors would design the database and learn the skills of entering and manipulating the data, and then share those skills with the rest of the class.

Travis chose Richard as his partner and both boys were enthusiastic about jumping right into the project, but this was their first exposure to a database and I wanted to make sure they really understood what a database is and what it can do. Starting with the concrete, I created a "paper database" with note cards to represent fields and labels. I showed Travis and Richard pictures of three children and asked them to tell me about them.

When they told me that one was a boy named Amos who was 8 years old and weighed 63 pounds, I put the information onto my note card "fields" and made a "record" about Amos. We repeated the procedure for Kate and Zoe and discussed number versus text fields. Cards enabled us to sort and find. I showed Richard and Travis a ClarisWorks database centering around Amos, Kate, and Zoe that I had created on the computer, and then the boys "challenged" the computer to find information as quickly and sort cards as accurately as they could. We discussed ascending and descending order and even arranged the fields in Browse and List views. During this activity, everything we did with the computer database, we mirrored with our paper database. It turned out to be a very successful unit!

Susan Monahan
Instructional Technology Facilitator
Austin Independent School District
Austin, Texas

CURRICULUM APPLICATIONS OF DATABASES

Teachers want help in alleviating the paperwork demands made on them. They want help accomplishing activities that do not involve students directly and are quite often done outside of actual class time. If the time required to perform these tasks could be decreased, the teacher would have more time to devote to working with students.

Students need access to increasing amounts of information if they are to construct their own knowledge. Information organization and retrieval skills can be taught using databases. The database is an ideal tool for students to gather and arrange data, examine trends and relationships, and test theories.

We have described a database as an organized, structured collection of facts and have examined its operation. We understand that it can handle text and values, that it is founded on the ability to group data fields into records that can be selected and ordered. We recognize that database managers have powerful built-in formulas. We are also beginning to explore some of the functional uses of databases to record data, organize them according to specific criteria, calculate values, sort data, and print reports.

Several activities are presented to illustrate how a database might be used as a tool by the student or the teacher. The examples present database applications in a variety of subject areas and grade levels and can be easily modified and adapted to individual lessons or units of instruction. If students are to capitalize on the power of the database manager as a tool and use it with confidence, they must develop an understanding of its application and a reasonably high level of skill in its use.

The presidents file shown in Figure 9–13 gathers data relevant to each U.S. president's term of office and provides opportunity to generate interesting information. Many of the reports are in the List View format. Analyses could be made by home state, party affiliation, and prior employment, for example.

The geography file suggested in Figure 9–14 might be set up for all countries of the world or only for countries in a specific geographic region. The process of entering data will require the students to conduct some research to gather the relevant facts. As information about the countries is studied, students could be encouraged to suggest additional fields for the database. Specific inquiries might be made, such as Which country has the largest landmass? Which country has the highest population density? What countries have significant rivers or mountains? Which countries are Spanish-speaking? or What countries have the same ethnic groups? Once information is generated, relationships can be explored. Does the area of the country relate directly to its population density? Is climate related to population density? Referring to a map of the region, do any of the physical features (rivers, mountains, etc.) form political boundaries? Examining countries whose citizens speak the same language, do they share something else in common? Were they part of a political union or an empire? A number of other relationships can be explored based on the students' interest and need for information and the teacher's direction.

A travel agency classroom simulation could be designed to explore existing countries in the database and to determine interests of students. Students could ask to go mountain climbing, spend time in the sun, or go where they could practice a foreign language they are learning. As students reveal a variety of interests, additional fields could be added to the database on that basis.

As an extension of the example illustrated in Figure 9–13, a database could be designed and data entered by students who are using the program "Where in the World Is Carmen Sandiego?" The following fields could be defined: country, city, currency, language, chief products, points of interest, bodies of water, mountains, deserts, and miscellaneous. As students encounter clues, they could search the database and, if results were not achieved,

Copies of the actual working files of the examples used in this chapter (Figures 9–13 to 9–16) are included for your use in the Lessons and Data Files folder on the Take-Along CD.

Figure 9-13 **Presidents file**

Presidents file

Suggested Lesson: The process of entering data into the fields will require the students to conduct some research to gather the relevant facts. Students will be able to print out the following informational tables:

Last Name
First Name
Party
Prior Employment
Vice President
Term of Office
Rank
Home State
Event 1.
Event 2.
Event 3.

  1. Chronological list of presidents

  2. Alphabetical list by last names of presidents to find information pertinent to a specific president

  3. List of presidents sorted by party to examine voting patterns

  4. List of presidents sorted by home state to examine any geographical patterns

  5. List of presidents and events to reveal expressions of party philosophy at the time

  6. Alphabetical list of the prior employment of presidents or a selection of only one employment such as attorney

The following printouts could serve as games, as contests, and for drill and practice.

  1. Leave a blank column for the president's name and print a column of events for a selected date range based on the term of office field. Students must indicate the president who was in office when each event occurred.

  2. Print two lists in alphabetical order, one of the presidents and the other of events, with the objective being to match presidents and events.

  3. Print any of the following reports with a blank column requiring information to be entered.

Possible Reports:

a. Rank	Term dates	First/last name	Party	Vice president
b. Last/first name	Rank	Term dates	Party	Vice president
c. Party	First/last name	Rank	Term dates	
d. Home state	First/last name	Term dates		
e. Last name	Party	Event 1_____		
		Event 2_____		
		Event 3_____		
f. Prior employment	President	Term dates		

they could research the relevant information and create a new record in the database. The database grows more powerful as more clues are encountered, and students refine their information-gathering skills.

The recommended books file suggested in Figure 9–15 would be created by and for students. Unlike the previous examples, it would be used mainly for online searching. It is not intended to replace a library automation system's public access catalog but, rather, to be a file of student opinion regarding books in the school library.

Data would be gathered by students and, for some, might serve as motivation to read. The data could be gathered as part of a school library's reading promotion effort. The data entry itself might be restricted to a few students to control the integrity of the file. An **authority list** (a list of approved headings) might be used for the subject/genre field to facilitate accurate retrieval of information. To accomplish this, the computer could present the user with a predetermined list of entries. A high-to-low numeric rating scale would be devised (e.g., 4–1). The file could be designed to hold multiple reviews and reviewers' names.

Figure 9–14 **Geography file**

Geography file

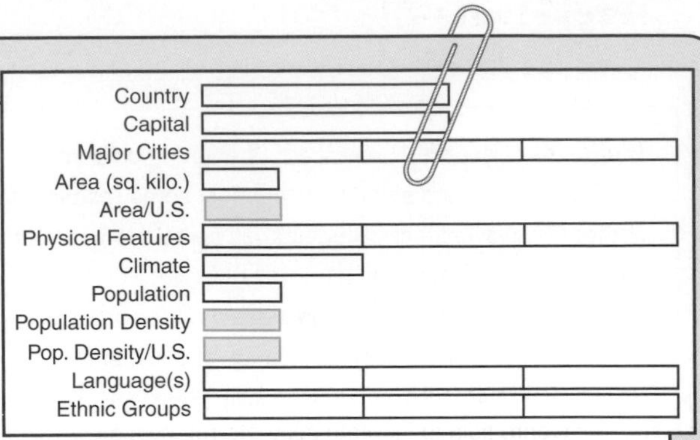

Suggested Lesson: The database contains three calculation fields: Area/U.S. field (Area field/area of the United States expressed as a ratio); Population Density field (Population field/Area field expressed as a ratio); and, Pop. Density/U.S. field (value calculated in the Population Density field/population density of the United States expressed as a ratio). Four fields (Major Cities, Physical Features, Language(s), and Ethnic Groups) are defined to be able to store up to three different values. Students can print out the following informational tables:

1. List by country to find information about cities in a specific country.
2. List by country to find landmass, population, and comparison to the United States
3. List by country to find climate and physical features of a specific country
4. List by country to find ethnic groups and languages in a specific country
5. List by ethnic group to determine countries
6. List by population density to view rank order of countries

Possible Reports:

a. Country	Capital	Major cities			
b. Country	Area	Area/U.S.	Population	Pop. density	Pop density/U.S.
c. Country	Climate	Physical features			
d. Country	Ethnic group(s)	Language(s)			
e. Ethnic group	Country				
f. Pop. density	Country				

Students might query the database by a specific subject/genre, asking for a list of titles at a particular grade level, and then sort the list in descending order by rating scale. They would then be able to find the most popular books in their area of interest.

Once having selected a group of records to examine, students could change to a layout that would let them read a brief description, review, and reviewer name in order to choose a book that appealed to them. The addition of the call number in the layout would help students find the book on the library shelf. A student could search for a favorite author and get a list by title, copyright date, and rating scale to find the most recent and popular work by that author.

A layout that listed the awards (e.g., Caldecott, Newberry, Young Reader's Choice Award), the rating scale, and the reviewer name for each title would allow students to form their own opinion of a reviewer's judgment when compared against a broader measure.

It's easy to see the computer as a creative graphics tool in the visual arts and a composition tool in music, but we should not ignore the fact that the computer is a wonderful manager of information. A database manager, such as suggested in Figure 9–16,

Figure 9–15 **Recommended books file**

Recommended books file

Suggested Lesson: This file created by and for students would be used mainly for on-line searching of student opinions regarding books in the school library. Data could be gathered as part of a school library's reading promotion effort. The data entry itself might be restricted to a few students in order to control the integrity of the file. An authority list (approved headings) might be used for the Subject/Genre field to facilitate accurate retrieval of

| Title |
| Author(s) |
| Subject/Genre |
| Call Number |
| Copyright Date |
| Grade Level(s) |
| Awards |
| Brief Description |
| Review |
| Reviewer |
| Rating Scale |

information. A high-to-low numeric rating scale would be devised (e.g., 4–1). The file could be designed to hold multiple reviews of the same title and reviewers' names. In addition to the on-line use, the following tables could be printed:

1. List of most popular books
2. Descriptions and reviews
3. List by copyright date and rating
4. List of award winning books

Possible Reports:

a. Subject/genre	Title	Grade level(s)	Rating
b. Call number	Title	Reviewer	
Description			

Review

_____

| c. Author | Title | Copyright | Rating |

could be created to store data concerning art and music history. Research could be divided by time period or by medium and assigned to teams of students. Images could be either photographed with a digital camera or scanned into the file. Short excerpts of sound recordings could be imported as well. As data was gathered, it would be entered into the database. Artists working in specific media could be examined. Specific works could be found and examined. Searches could be initiated to examine the art and music of specific time periods and reports prepared. An extension of the example in Figure 9–16 might include a comment field where a teacher's commentary might be stored or students might be encouraged to develop their own comments based on readings done about a particular work.

Databases as Managers of Digital Portfolios

As discussed, teachers have become increasingly interested in authentic assessment measures and techniques, and the portfolio has surfaced as an interesting alternative. Typically, the portfolio is seen as an attempt to gather evidence of a student's performance.

Figure 9–16 **Art and music history file**

Art and music history file

Suggested Lesson: This database file might be used in the study of art history. As the students conduct the research and enter data into this file, they could search the file in a number of different ways. A search by Title would reveal the Artist's Name, the Work, Medium, Style, and Date of one work. A search by Artist's Name could reveal all of the artist's works and their dates. A search by Date could reveal all works across all media to help make comparisons. A search by Medium could focus on just one medium over time.

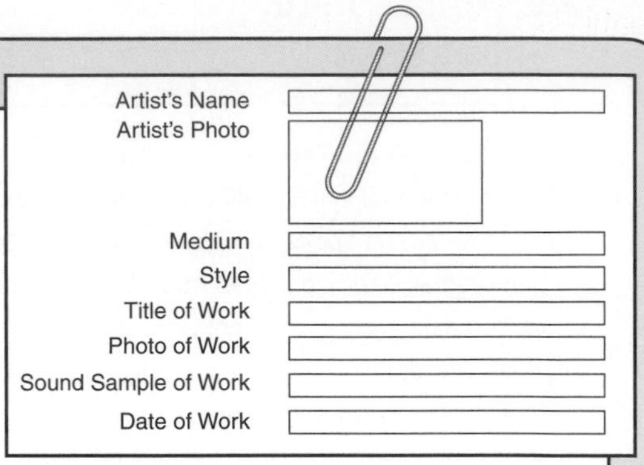

Artist's Name	
Artist's Photo	
Medium	
Style	
Title of Work	
Photo of Work	
Sound Sample of Work	
Date of Work	

The following fields would be defined in the database.

Field Name	Type	Entry Option	
Artist's Name	Text	Required value; Do not allow user to override Indexed	
Artist's Photo	Container		
Medium	Text	Indexed; Value List:	Painting
			Drawing
			Sculpture
			Photography
			Instrumental Music
			Vocal Music
Style	Text		
Title of Work	Text		
Photo of Work	Container		
Sound Sample/Work	Container		
Date of Work	Date		

This evidence can take the form of tests, written assignments, exercises, projects, and audio and video projects completed by the student. By comparing like measures over time, growth can be observed in the individual's performance.

Manual portfolios are difficult to manage and cumbersome to store. As more performance evidence is gathered, portfolio management and the analysis of like measures become increasingly difficult. The shear size of the container for the documentary evidence grows to the point that storage becomes an issue for the teacher and for the school administrator.

Digital portfolios may present an answer to the problems created by manual versions. Written documents and photographs can be scanned into electronic files. Digital pictures can be recorded. Videotaped sequences can be converted to digital formats. Many types of software can be used to tie everything together: HyperStudio, PowerPoint, and Microsoft Word are three examples. A database manager can also provide the management needed to organize the various artifacts collected and can provide efficient analyses of like measures over time. Each student's digital portfolio can be stored on a recordable CD-R or DVD-R.

Commercially Available Databases Related to Curriculum

A number of commercial databases are being marketed to address specific content areas. Databases of scientific facts (e.g., periodic table, scientists, inventions), historical facts (e.g., famous people, events, time lines), and geographic facts (e.g., map locations, climates, migration) are becoming readily available from various publishers of educational software.

The examples that follow as Figures 9–17 through 9–19 are taken from an award-winning program called MacGlobe® (also available as PC Globe™ for Windows), which is a rich database of geographical facts covering every country in the world. It begins with a world map and lets the user choose from regional maps (e.g., continents, political and economic alliances), country maps (e.g., political divisions and elevation), and thematic maps (e.g., population, natural resources, agricultural production, education). The user can paint selected countries or regions in a chosen pattern and return to the world map to observe the results. The program can also display the flag of any country and can display distances, currency conversions, and a number of charts revealing information about each country.

Programs such as this one present the student with a valuable resource of information with which to make comparisons, draw inferences, and construct knowledge. After

Figure 9–17 Map screens from MacGlobe

Maps showing major cities and elevation *(Reprinted with permission of Broderbund Inc.)*

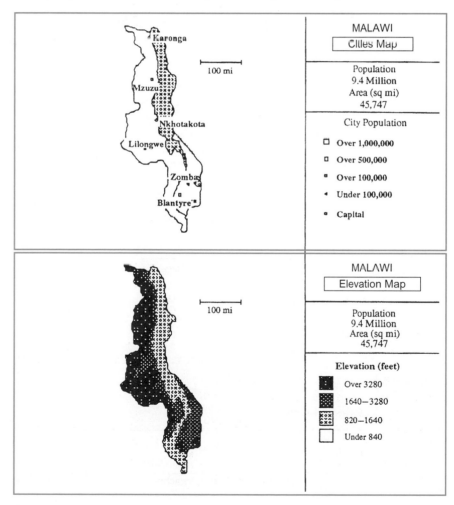

examining Figures 9–17 through 9–19, what would you say in describing Malawi to another student? How is it similar to and how is it different from the United States? What else do you want to know about Malawi?

The top screen in Figure 9–17 shows the location and population of the major cities of the African country of Malawi. The bottom screen shows the elevation of the different regions in the country.

The top screen in Figure 9–18 gives the user a sense of the distance from the West Coast of the United States to the African country of Malawi (distance can be calculated between any two points on the globe). The middle screen reveals time differences between the local point and the distant country. The bottom screen converts currency between the two countries. The three screens in Figure 9–19 reveal statistics about the age, health, and education of the Malawi population.

Figure 9–18 Screens from MacGlobe

Map showing distances and chart comparing currencies *(Reprinted with permission of Broderbund Inc.)*

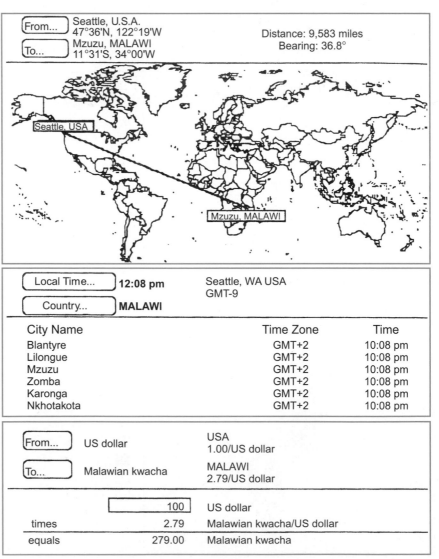

296

Figure 9–19 Statistics screens from MacGlobe

Statistics related to age distribution, health, and education *(Reprinted with permission of Broderbund Inc.)*

MALAWI—Age Distribution

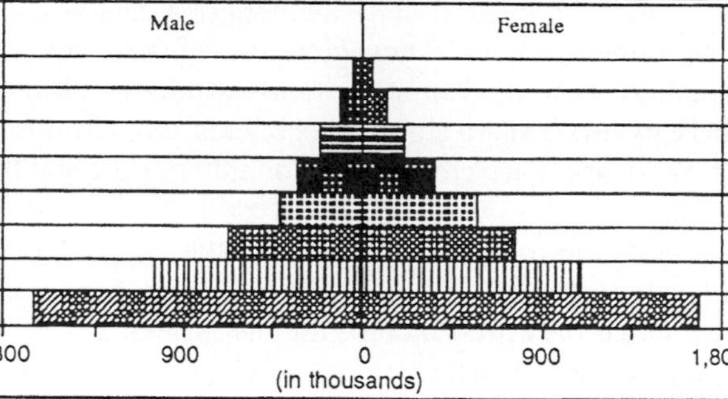

Age	% of Pop'n	Male	Female	% of Pop'n	Age
70+	0.7			0.6	70+
60—69	1.4			1.4	60—69
50—59	2.4			2.4	50—59
40—49	3.5			3.9	40—49
30—39	4.5			6.1	30—39
20—29	7.3			8.1	20—29
10—19	11.1			11.4	10—19
0—9	17.5			17.7	0—9

1,800   900   0   900   1,800
(in thousands)

Total Population: 9,438,000   Life Expectancy (Male):   48 years
Total Male Population: 4,568,000   Life Expectancy (Female): 51 years
Total Female Population: 4,870,000

Health Statistics

Life Expectancy (Male):   48 yrs
Life Expectancy (Female):   51 yrs
Crude Birth Rate: 52/1000
Crude Death Rate: 18/1000
Infant Mortality: 136/1000

	Number	Pop'n per
Hospitals	395	23,894
Hospital Beds	12,617	748
Physicians	262	36,023
Dentists	12	786,500
Pharmacists	12	786,500
Nurses	2,002	4,714

Education Statistics

	Schools	Teachers	Students	Students per Teacher
Primary	2,660	16,885	1,066,642	63
Secondary	91	1,492	30,030	20
Third Level	4	306	2,330	8

GNP for Education	3.3 %
Literacy Rate	22 %

InspireData® is an outstanding new problem-solving tool from the publishers of Inspiration®. It is designed to help students visualize, manipulate, and analyze data to understand the information it reveals. Students can begin experimenting quickly with over 50 curriculum-based databases in science, mathematics, and social studies. The proven strategies of visual learning are applied to the teaching of data literacy. The development of this program was initially funded under a grant from the National Science Foundation.

LET'S REVIEW

A database manager is software designed to structure data to produce information. It is an information management tool with the potential to increase the speed of information acquisition, the ease with which information is acquired, and the quality of the information acquired in terms of both accuracy and completeness. A database may consist of a single file or a number of related files. Database management software is designed to allow the user to create a structure for the storage, manipulation, and retrieval of data. The products of file managers fall into two main categories: the real-time, online searching for specific information and the ability to print reports organized in a particular fashion.

The individual data item is the most discrete element of a database and is called a field. Fields can contain text, numeric values, dates, pictures, sounds, and calculations that perform mathematical operations on other numeric fields within the record and can store the resulting values. Fields can also contain summaries of data across a number of records and can display the result. Field labels are created that identify or describe the fields where the data are actually stored.

The record consists of all the related fields. A file is the aggregation of all the records. As fields are defined, labels are created and grouped together, creating a layout that appears on the screen. Once data are entered, the layout that is selected or created can be thought of as a window through which to examine data in selected fields.

The database manager software allows the user to search for and select records based on a wide range of criteria. Compound searches can be constructed to examine data in multiple fields using the Boolean connectors AND, OR, and NOT. Data can then be sorted or arranged in a prescribed alphabetic, numeric, or chronological order in either ascending or descending fashion based on any individual field. Most software also allows nested, or multilevel, sorts.

To develop a report for printing information from the file, the user first selects the appropriate layout, then selects the records to be included in the report, then designates their order. Data can be entered once, but information can be generated by many varied reports.

Teachers want help in addressing their information needs and alleviating the paperwork demands made on them. Students need access to increasing amounts of information if they are to construct their own knowledge. Information organization and retrieval skills can be taught using databases.

LET'S PRACTICE

To complete the specified exercises online, go to the Let's Practice Module in Chapter 9 of the Companion Website.

1. List at least three database management applications for each of the following and explain how the database addresses a particular productivity need.
    Student
    Teacher
    School administrator

2. Look at your personal tax or budget records. To what areas might you apply a file manager? Do you have records in a paper format that could be stored and manipulated electronically? What would be the advantages and disadvantages of doing this? Would it make you more productive?

3. Develop a file that would include all the information you would need on the students in a given class. Determine the kinds of reports you would need from this file.

4. Determine the kinds of reports you would need if the entire student population of your school were put on a database. What kind of information would have to be placed in the database and how often would this information have to be updated?

5. Using a word processing program, write a letter (holiday, seasonal, how you are doing, family news, job application request, etc.). Leave at least four blank spaces in the letter that will be filled with receiver specific information (person's name, title, location, hobbies, pets, etc.). Develop a database of at least four individual recipients that contains fields for each of the blank spaces. Merge and print the four letters.

6. Select one of the database examples illustrated in Figures 9–13 through 9–16 and create a similar one on paper. Add, delete, or change the fields suggested in order to modify the database to suit your particular needs. Design a series of reports that would address specific information needs.

7. Design a database application for a model digital portfolio. In addition to identification and date fields, include all fields necessary to capture required documentation in text, audio, picture, and video formats. Develop two sample reports that would support comparison of like measures.

8. After examining Figures 9–17 through 9–19 as products of the software MacGlobe, write a brief description of Malawi. Be sure to point out similarities to and differences from the United States. Indicate what else you would like to know about Malawi.

9. List two different database activities that you might use in your future class that would actively involve all of the students. Explain your answer to the class and change ideas if needed.

10. Many times teachers use information gathered from the class to add interest to the database assignments (i.e., age, gender, favorite color). List several types of information that may be too sensitive or objectionable from the students', parents', or administration's view to solicit from your students. Defend the items on your list. Discuss the lists in class.

PORTFOLIO DEVELOPMENT EXERCISES

To complete this exercise online, go to the Digital Portfolio Module in Chapter 9 of the Companion Website.

One of the NETS•S standards covered in this chapter was "Students use technology tools to process data and report results" under *Category 5: Technology research tools.* Begin to develop your own portfolio of lesson plans that demonstrates your ability to have your students reach the NETS•S standards.

1. Design a lesson plan activity for elementary, middle school, or high school students in which they use a database program to assemble and record data and report results. Some examples may include a database of individuals that you might study during the year, a database of teachers in the school, a database of friends and relatives, or a database of something that the students like to collect. Have students sort the data in at least two ways and report their results. Try to combine several tools found in the database programs. The number that you use should depend on the grade level. Younger students may only use simple tools (list function, etc.). Older students will be required to use more sophisticated tools (design multiple layouts, etc.). This lesson should demonstrate that your students have achieved the standard. Be sure to include a system of evaluation for your students' understanding and competence to ensure that they have met this standard.

2. Adapt the lesson plan activity you developed in exercise 1 for students to evaluate each others' work.

GLOSSARY

authority list	A list of approved headings, names, terms, and so on designed to control what is entered into a field
Boolean connectors	Words such as AND, OR, and NOT used to connect search terms
database	The collection of related data records stored and accessed electronically by computer
database manager	Software that is designed to manage electronic data files
debugging	The process of correcting logic and construction errors
field	The group of related characters treated as a unit within a record—for example, the last name of a student; the smallest, most discrete element of a file
file	A collection of related records treated as a unit
file management	A systematic approach to the storage, manipulation, and retrieval of information stored as data items in the form of records in a file
file manager	Software that is designed to create and to manage data files; also now called a database manager
form	See *layout*
label	The descriptor related to a data field

layout	The selection and positioning of fields and their labels for screen or printed use
logical search	The ability to apply logical operators to a search—for example, "Find all words that contain 'th'" or "Find all values greater than 100"
multilevel sort	A series of second, third, and so on levels of sorts performed after a primary one has been performed—for example, sorting a group of students by first name after they were first sorted by last name
nested sort	See *multilevel sort*
query	See *logical search*
record	A group of related fields treated as a unit. For example, in a student file, a record might be all the information stored relating to a given student
relational database manager	Software designed to manage a collection of related electronic data files

REFERENCES AND SUGGESTED READINGS

Arnone, M., & Small, R. (2001, November). *S.O.S. for information literacy: A tool for improving research and information skills instruction.* Paper presented at the National Convention of the Association of Educational Communications and Technology. ERIC NO: ED470194.

Brown, J., Fernlund, P., & White, S. (1998). *Technology tools in the social studies curriculum.* Wilsonville, OR: Franklin, Beedle, & Associates.

Loertscher, D. (2003, June). The digital school library. *Teacher Librarian, 30*(5), 14–25.

Peck, J. K., & Hughes, S. V. (1997, January–February). So much success . . . from a first-grade database project! *Computers in the Schools, 13*(1–2), 109–16.

Repp, R. (1999, March). The World Wide Web: Interfaces, databases, and applications to education. *Learning & Leading with Technology, 26*(6), 40–41.

Sherry, A., & Barlett, A. (2004–2005, December–January). Worth of electronic portfolios to education majors: A "two by four" perspective. *Journal of Educational Technology Systems, 33*(4), 399–419.

Storey, V., Goldstein, R., & Ding, J. (2002, January–March). Common sense reasoning in automated database design. *Journal of Database Management, 13*(1), 3–15.

CHAPTER 10

Learning with Multimedia Tools

1. What is multimedia and how can it be effective?

2. What are hypertext and hypermedia?

3. How could we incorporate multimedia into our teaching and curriculum?

I. Technology operations and concepts
  A. demonstrate introductory knowledge, skills, and understanding of concepts related to technology (as described in ISTE National Education Technology Standards for Students)
  B. demonstrate continual growth in technology knowledge and skills to stay abreast of current and emerging technologies
II. Planning and designing learning environments and experiences
  A. design developmentally appropriate learning opportunities that apply technology-enhanced instructional strategies to support the diverse needs of learners
III. Teaching, learning, and the curriculum
  A. facilitate technology-enhanced experiences that address content standards and student technology standards
  B. use technology to support learner-centered strategies that address the diverse needs of students
  C. apply technology to develop students' higher order skills and creativity
IV. Social, ethical, legal, and human issues
  B. apply technology resources to enable and empower learners with diverse backgrounds, characteristics, and abilities
V. Productivity and professional practice
  C. apply technology to increase productivity

LET'S LOOK AT THIS CHAPTER

The advent of hypertext and hypermedia has changed the way information and ideas are organized and presented. No longer do we have to use complicated and technical tools to infuse various media formats into a presentation.

This chapter deals with multimedia applications that are great productivity tools for you and your students. They help to organize thoughts and ideas and communicate them to others in ways that have never been able to be done before. They enable teachers and students to produce instructional materials, teaching aids, and reports that offer a wide variety of formats enabling it to fit many of the learning styles of students.

MULTIMEDIA: HYPERTEXT AND HYPERMEDIA

Many years ago, Edgar Dale (1969) developed a model for learning that became known as the "cone of experience." This model, as shown in Figure 10–1, illustrates a continuum from direct, purposeful experiences directly involving the learner, located at the base of the cone, to abstract symbols that learners passively observe at the top of the cone. Multimedia was missing when Dale constructed this model in 1946, but it fits neatly in the

Figure 10–1 Dale's cone of experience

(From AUDIO VISUAL METHODS REV @ 1st edition by Dale E. 1954. Reprinted with permission of Wadsworth, a division of Thomson learning: *www.thomsonrights.com*. Fax 800730-2215.)

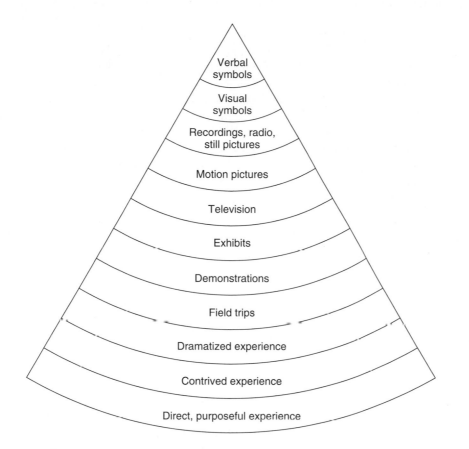

midsection of the cone between exhibits and television. The term *multimedia* surfaced several years later in the 1950s, as educators combined various media in support of each other to heighten the effect on learning.

For more than 50 years, educational researchers have been telling us that people learn better when they are involved in their learning, and that involvement increases as more senses are used by the learner to acquire information. This type of learning increases as we move our students through activities that involve the experiences toward the base of Dale's cone. Thus, multimedia technologies, which can provide stimulating and interactive multisensory experiences to learners, can help teachers improve the quality and the appeal of their instruction.

Many times we hear the terms *multimedia, hypermedia,* and *hypertext* discussed together, often by different people meaning the same thing. Even people in the educational technology field find the words hard to distinguish (Tolhurst, 1995). **Multimedia** simply means a presentation that contains several types of media such as still and moving graphics, text, sounds, and animations used to communicate information. **Hypermedia** refers to linked media. In a hypermedia presentation, it would be possible to move to another place within the presentation and/or from one form of media to another usually through the use of buttons or mouse clicks. **Hypertext** refers to hypermedia links that were at one time textual in nature. This definition is even fuzzier now, because hypertext links found on web pages (textual, images, or buttons) are all referred to as *hypertext links*. We will discuss this in greater detail later.

Multimedia is certainly multidimensional and multisensory, and has great potential for involving the user regardless of learning style. Multimedia has now gone digital! The old "low-tech" slide series accompanied by synchronized audiotapes with perhaps film clips thrown in have given way to personalized "high-tech" experiences of sounds, images, animation, and movies presented to the user on a computer screen or projected in the classroom. The impact of digital technology on multimedia is impressive. Digital multimedia has made it possible for the learner to navigate through combinations of sights and sounds as never before. For educators, the opportunity to involve students so directly in learning and problem solving is one of multimedia's most appealing qualities.

Multimedia software has been developed over the past several years that enable children as young as the first grade to develop multimedia projects with ease. Students can incorporate text, graphics, video, and hyperlinks in reports and projects as never before. *Kid Pix Studio Deluxe*™ and *Kid Works Deluxe*™ allow students to add text and pictures as well as video, sound, music, and animations to projects to help instill a new excitement into learning. *Multimedia Workshop*™ includes photographs, sound effects, music,

LET'S GO INTO THE CLASSROOM
Starting Early with Multimedia

At our small suburban elementary school, we use multimedia software regularly to integrate technology into the curriculum. One of our favorite programs is *Kid Pix Studio Deluxe*.

We use this program in a variety of ways, starting with our kindergarten students. They become acquainted with the drawing tools (usually one or two at a time) until they are comfortable in using them. Teachers introduce these tools and then allow the students to explore, followed by a more directed activity. They use it for graphic arts as well as simple activities such as reinforcing phonics. For example, the students might use the letter stamp and the typing tool to type their "letter of the week" and then find stamps and draw objects that begin with the same sound.

By the time students reach grade one, they are familiar with this program and are ready to try more complex ideas such as building simple slide shows. We have done slide shows in primary grades where each student makes one slide, then it is put together as a class celebration and publication of their learning.

Our students also enjoy creating class books on topics of interest, and this works well because they can use the software to compose their ideas and then use the graphic tools to make accompanying drawings. My students recently finished a science unit on "Rocks and Minerals" and they composed poetry, which was written and illustrated using *Kid Pix*. The laminated covers were coiled together to make a very polished-looking product for our classroom library.

Students in older grades use this program to create more sophisticated multimedia reports with voice-overs, scanned and imported artwork, and graphic arts to share their learning on a particular topic.

By the time our students finish grade six they are comfortable in using graphic and multimedia tools. The tool bars and processes they have been using are very similar to those in other programs such as *HyperStudio* and *PowerPoint*, so these skills will transfer easily to their work in other settings.

Joni Turville
Elementary Teacher and Technology Mentor
Ronald Harvey School
St. Albert, Alberta, Canada

and even *QuickTime*™ movie clips for students to add to their presentations and projects. More sophisticated programs such as *HyperStudio*™ and the versatile *Movieworks Deluxe*™ add even more features such as pop-up text and menus, hypertext links, image, movie, and sound editing as well as easy interface with CD-ROMs, DVDs, and other programs such as *Kid Pix*™ *Studio Deluxe.* Even the new *Microsoft PowerPoint*™ presentation software package contains everything needed to put together a sophisticated multimedia presentation.

Multimedia in its simplest definition means "many media" or "a combination of several media." Something as simple as an old-fashioned slide presentation with taped audio is multimedia. **Digital multimedia,** on the other hand, allows a computer user to combine and control a number of instructional resources in order to present information either within the computer itself or through external sources. Its power lies in its ability to network information resources and to provide ready access to the learner. The real power of multimedia lies in its ability to bring together many forms of media into one presentation as suggested in Figure 10–2. Older multimedia computer programs may be used to control the presentation of video, graphic, audio, and textual information from external sources such as videotape, CD-ROM, or DVD. This audio and video information is presented to the user under the control of the computer. As we will demonstrate later in this chapter, more recent computer programs may be totally self-contained, with all data stored on the internal hard drive, an optical disk (CD-ROM or DVD), or external flash memory (jump or flash drives or flash memory sticks) with all of the information presented to the user through the computer's monitor and speaker.

Multimedia presentations can create multisensory learning experiences for students. Using an instructional program, developed and played on a multimedia computer system, students are able to jump from medium to medium at the will of the developer, utilizing the best medium available to illustrate a particular objective. As a teaching tool, commercially prepared or teacher-designed multimedia programs might include the use of textual, graphic, audio, and video materials to convey information to the user, who would interact with it by reading, listening, observing still and moving images, and navigating through

Figure 10–2 Multimedia equipment

The real power of multimedia is the combining of many different forms of media into one presentation

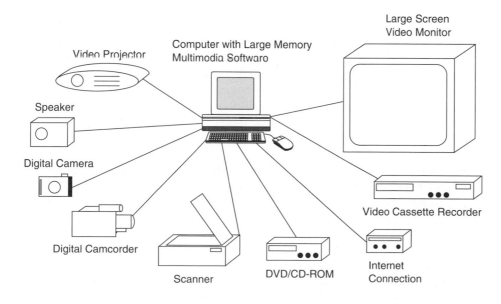

Figure 10–3 Multimedia features

Examine the features found in multimedia programs

Text	Text can be presented in an attention-getting manner. Text may be selected and made into a *button* or *link*.
Graphics	Graphics can be created or imported. Photographs, video still frames, scanned images, and Web images can be imported as well.
Animation	Graphics and text can be animated to illustrate concepts.
Sound	Digitized sounds can be captured from a microphone, audio recorder, audio-CD, and Internet sources. Sounds can be used for an attention-getting effect or to clarify a concept.
Video	Digitized video, a powerful instructional medium, can be captured from a camcorder, VCR, CD-ROM, and other sources.
Data Storage	Database capabilities allow the student to search for information, or they can be used by the teacher to record and analyze a student's performance.
Integration	Integration with audio and video storage devices and with the Internet facilitates direct access to information by the user.
Navigation	The user controls the pace and many times the level of difficulty of the material covered using responses ranging from simple keystrokes or mouse clicks to text entry and evaluation. Links can be established to take the student to other information within the presentation, external information on video and CD-ROM, for example, and information around the world with links to the World Wide Web.

options presented on the screen. As a learning tool, not only can students navigate through this rich medium as they search for information from which to construct knowledge, but they can also express themselves in a number of ways as they author multimedia reports. Features that underlie the power of multimedia as a teaching and learning tool are listed in Figure 10–3.

Multimedia allows students to create their own visuals and incorporate them into their products and to navigate in original and customized ways through existing resources. It gives the student control of powerful tools in the exploration and creation of information. A digital camcorder, digital camera, optical scanner, CD-ROM drive, and DVD and video cassette recorders all become potential information-gathering tools. Multimedia tools allow a student to create a complex statement that might include computer-generated sound, graphics, and animation, along with sound and visual forms stored in another medium such as video cassette, DVD, or CD-ROM.

While normal text written on a page is designed to be read in a linear fashion from beginning to end, hypertext is a nonlinear way of representing text. Because the meaning of the text in this new medium does not depend on sequential ordering, readers can access information according to their own interests and needs, thus giving them much more control in the reading process.

To understand how hypertext works, think of each *information screen* on the computer as a card containing a person's name, address, phone number, and so forth. Cards can be arranged in any order and a user can navigate among the cards in a nonlinear

Prentice Hall School Division

manner, perhaps looking up the phone number for Forcier first, followed by Descy, and finally Stollenwerk. Cards are grouped into logical units, or stacks, and a user can navigate between cards and between stacks in a seamless fashion. "Author" text links on the Descy and Forcier cards could link to each other's card, while "Editor" links on those cards would navigate to the Stollenwerk card. This is exactly the same method of navigation that you have used on the Web. In that case, clicking on an underlined part of the text on a web page, called a hypertext link, transports the user to other information on the same or a distant web server. Navigation in a multimedia presentation, in most instances, is accomplished by clicking on objects called **buttons.** Buttons can be visible objects that look, in fact, like a button or hidden (invisible) objects that could be specific areas of the screen, often covering images or text. Button destinations or **actions,** such as playing a sound or video or moving to another location, can be programmed simply in a matter of seconds using pulldown menus, mouse clicks and/or typing the desired actions, or perhaps just clicking and checking a box listing the desired action. Each screen on a multimedia presentation may be called a **card,** a screen, or a slide and complete groups of these cards or slides are usually called a **stack** or a slide show.

Hypermedia embeds hypertext elements into multimedia. The cards in a hypermedia stack might contain text, graphics, and sounds on their cards, and even animation sequences and digitized video clips. Hypertext buttons can even reach into cyberspace by sending a URL to a web browser such as *Internet Explorer* which will open the web browser and display the page. The term *hypermedia* has largely given way to *multimedia*. Digital multimedia programs contain all the navigation control elements of hypermedia.

To illustrate this concept, imagine that you are using a multimedia geography program and that you are looking at a screen of information about a country. Buttons on that screen may lead you to additional text-based information about that country such as lists of products exported, population statistics, climate conditions, or the definition of a word or phrase. Other buttons could also lead you to graphical information in the form of topographical or political maps, to an audio clip playing a traditional song, or to a digitized video clip either on or downloaded from the Web recorded from yesterday's evening newscast of the country's president delivering a speech to the United Nations Assembly.

APPLICATIONS OF MULTIMEDIA IN EDUCATION

Increasingly more classrooms are acquiring the software and equipment to allow teachers to produce and use multimedia presentations as a method of instruction and to support student development of multimedia projects. Because these technologies are interesting, interactive, multidimensional, and student controlled, they are ideally suited for educational purposes. Learners are engaged by the exciting technology, and they can explore information at their own pace and according to their own interests and needs.

Multimedia authoring can be approached from both the teacher's and student's perspective. The teacher can select and create material, addressing instructional needs ranging from discrete projects aimed at specific facts and concepts to be taught to complete lessons. A chemistry teacher might design a multimedia periodic table of the elements that would allow a user to select an element; identify its atomic number, atomic weight, and discoverer; see an illustration of its atomic structure; and see a picture of the discoverer and read a brief biography. It may also contain interesting information about the uses of the element. An English teacher might create a simple multimedia presentation on Shakespeare that would present the student with lesson objectives, ask specific questions to focus the student's attention, and give the student a brief introduction to the work of Shakespeare being studied. The presentation might contain buttons that allow the students to hear great actors reading or watch short video clips of passages within the work, and a link to the Complete Works of William Shakespeare website (*http://www tech.mit. edu/Shakespeare/*). A teacher of English to speakers of other languages (ESOL) might create a multimedia vocabulary program that would allow a student to see a word and hear it pronounced by a native speaker. An image of an object representing the word might also be displayed along with a written and spoken sentence using the word. At the simplest authoring level, a teacher of any subject at any grade level might create bookmarks to identify sites and return to them easily with the web browser being used. This would allow students to interact with multimedia websites related to current lessons being taught.

From the student's perspective, multimedia authoring presents a rich environment in which to explore information and construct knowledge. Students may do the work individually or in cooperative groups. As an example, students might be assigned the task of developing a multimedia project describing the early settlement and subsequent development of their community. The resulting product might be text gleaned from official records; pictures found in a museum, library, or newspaper archive; and audio clips from live interviews with senior citizens, accompanied by their photographs. Some of the many advantages of multimedia presentations are suggested in the following table.

Advantages of Multimedia Presentations	
Active learning	Creating and using multimedia presentations actively involves the learner
Creativity	A wide variety of input and output mechanisms available as students design their learning activities
Collaboration	Students combine their strengths in developing a single group effort in collaborative projects
Communications	From the initial planning stages through the final presentation, students are able to develop communications skills with each other and the final audience
Control	Students can control the choice of media, the pacing, and in some cases information, to meet their individual learning styles

Feedback	Feedback can easily be built into multimedia presentations
Flexibility	Several paths or learning options may be incorporated to achieve the same outcome
Fun	Students enjoy the process of developing and using multimedia presentations
Individuality	Presentations and responses are able to incorporate many of Gardner's (1993) "intelligences" allowing tailor-made learning activities for each student
Motivation	With proper guidance, students are kept interested by the varied delivery and response methods relieving the boredom so often found in single-medium, single-response presentations
Multisensory	Multimedia presentation can involve text, sounds, static and moving visuals, animations, and movies
Reinforcement	Positive reinforcement can be built in with positive messages, diversions, and explorations of topics in greater depth as the need arises
Remediation	Problems can be caught early and help can be provided for difficult information or concepts on an as-needed basis
Student involvement	Students are able to access a wide variety of knowledge and presentation techniques and construct a learning environment appropriate for themselves and others
Technology	Students apply new and different technologies in an active learning setting application
Thinking skills	The planning, designing, and producing of a multimedia project involves higher order and critical thinking skills as students deconstruct and reconstruct knowledge to meet the project goals and objectives

 ## DISCIPLINE-SPECIFIC MULTIMEDIA IDEAS AND SOFTWARE

The following ideas are meant to stimulate thinking about the application of multimedia presentations in various areas of the curriculum. The challenge to you as a teacher is to take some of these ideas and run with them. How can you adapt them to meet your own individual needs?

- *Art:* What a wonderful place for students of all ages to incorporate multimedia into their studies. Drawing and painting come to mind first, followed by the integration of several forms of media to produce a media-collage on a specific subject. Multimedia tours of great museums, architectural wonders, and tours of artists' home areas add concrete referents to learning.

Recommended Software
Adobe Illustrator™, Adobe Photoshop Elements™, iMovie, iPhoto, Kid Pix Deluxe™, Paint, Write & Play™, The Print Shop Deluxe™, Paint Shop Pro™

- *Creativity:* Creativity with multimedia crosses all disciplines. Creating multimedia presentations involves the senses, critical thinking skills, collaboration, individual and group work, and practice in the ability to bring together material to construct a unique learning situation.

Recommended Software

Inspiration™, Hyper studio™, Imagination Express™, iMovie, iPhoto, Kid Pix Deluxe™, Kidspiration™, The Print Shop Deluxe™, Storybook Weaver Deluxe™, Student Writing Center™

- *Critical Thinking:* Viewing and developing multimedia presentations of all types help students prepare for the future by reinforcing critical thinking skills, logic, memory retention, mind mapping, problem solving, and reasoning.

Recommended Software

Inspiration™, Braincogs™, I Spy™, Strategy Challenges™, Mind Benders™, Thinking Things Collection™, Think Analogies Puzzles™, Thinkology™, Zoombinis™

- *Early Learning:* Add fun and interest to reading, math, science, and social studies. Students interact with the media. Interactive books make stories come alive because students are able to interact with the characters and environment.

Recommended Software

Bailey's Book House™, Clifford the Big Red Dog series, JumpStart series, Kidspiration™, Living Books Library, The Playroom™, McGee Visits Katie's Farm™, Reader Rabbit series, Sammy's Science House™, Stanley's Sticker Stories™, Stickybear series

- *ESL—Foreign Language:* Helps students learn to speak and write English efficiently and effectively.

Recommended Software

English for Kids™, Instant Immersion English™, Jumpstart™, Teacher's Survival Kit: ESL/Bilingual™, The Complete Language Solution™, The Heartsoft Bestsellers ESL™, Usborne's Animated First Thousand Words™, Spanish 1a/Ingles 1a with Phonics con Fonetica™

- *Language Arts:* Students can take just about any topic that they would ordinarily have to write a paper for or present an oral report and make it into a multimedia presentation. Multimedia storybooks, discovery projects, and newsletters all fit here. Students love interactive storybooks.

Recommended Software

The Amazing Writing Machine™, Storybook Weaver Deluxe™, Bailey's Book House™, Clicker series, Reading Blaster™, Student Writing and Research Center™, Reading Explorers™, Writer's Companion™, Ultimate Writing and Creativity Center™, Word Munchers Deluxe™, Clicker™, Phonics Alive™

- *Math:* Many math projects can be presented using a multimedia format. Photos, diagrams, charts, and movies can be added to illustrate mathematical concepts. Skill building and problem solving are easily built in.

Recommended Software

Mighty Math™ (*Astro Algebra, Calculating Crew, Carnival Countdown, Cosmic Geometry, Number Heroes,* and *Zoo Zillions*), Math Blasters™ (*5–7, 6–8, 7–9,* and *9–12*), Logical Journey of the Zoombinis™, Math Concepts™ (*In Motion, One . . . Two . . . Three, Step-by-Step*), Math Munchers, Numeracy Bank series, Stickybear Math Skills

- *Music:* Students are able to learn about composing and actually compose their own music. Musical instruments can be discovered and explored using their sounds and shapes. Rhythm and melody can be explored.

Recommended Software

Apple Garage Band™ , Music Ace™, Juilliard Music Adventure™, Finale™, Making Music™ and Making More Music™, Sibelius™, Sibelius with Photoscore™, Songworks™, Microsoft Musical Instruments™

- *Reading:* Students have fun as they learn to read using interactive story books, phonics games, and vocabulary builders. Self-pacing assures success for even slow readers.

Recommended Software

Let's Go Read™ (*An Island Adventure, An Ocean Adventure*), Reader Rabbit's™ (*Interactive Reading Journey, Kindergarten, Learn to Read, Reading 1, 2, 3*), Reading Blaster™ (*Ages 4–6, Ages 6–9, Ages 9–12, Vocabulary*), Spelling Blaster™, Stickybear's™ (*Phonics I, II, and III, Spelling, Reading Comprehension I and II, Reading Fun Park, Reading Room Deleuxe*), Middleware Reading Comprehension Series™, Phonics Alive Series™

- *Science:* Produce multimedia projects illustrating science concepts bringing in sounds, graphics, and video. Produce interactive lessons on cycles, gravity, motion, the periodic table, and much more. View and interact with information and content safely. Manipulate variables to view outcomes.

Recommended Software

A.D.A.M.™ (*Interactive Anatomy, Essentials, Inside Story*), Learn About Science™ (*Animals, Astronomy, Dinosaurs, Human Body, Matterm Measurement and Mixtures, Plants, Senses, Simple Machines, Weather*), Greatest Discoveries with Bill Nye™, My Amazing Human Body™, Sidewalk Science Series™, Sammy's Science House™, Super Science Shoe™, Thinking Science™, Virtual Labs™ (*Light, Electricity*)

- *Social Studies:* Design interactive field trips using maps, video, and audio with full interactivity. Trace histories of people and places. Produce interactive timelines. Follow the path of explorers. Tour historic sites. Produce newsletters and newspapers.

- *Special Needs:* Multimedia allows students with special needs to master their own world at their own pace using programs designed to meet unique needs and learning styles. The programs are fun and exciting and build knowledge and confidence as students problem solve, increase manual dexterity, and become immersed in their own learning. Satisfaction and self-confidence grow as they make professional-looking presentations with simple tools.

Virtual reality (VR) is a term referring to computer-based technologies ranging from sophisticated three-dimensional simulations to full immersion experiences in which the participants find themselves in a highly interactive, multisensory, artificial environment so vivid that it appears real. It is the ultimate multimedia experience, with elements so carefully and convincingly synchronized that computer-generated audio and visual messages appear to be real. Perhaps you have seen virtual reality games in malls, at carnivals, or outside of a movie theatre.

Multimedia technologies allow users to experience and express information in many ways, including allowing them to interact with this information by creating, or authoring, programs and presentations combining original or ready-made text, graphics, and video clips. Hyper Studio, a multimedia authoring tool, was the most popular single piece of educational software sold to schools in the mid to late 1990s. Unfortunately the company was slow in making it compatable with the Macintosh OS X operating system and, thanks to improvments in Microsoft PowerPoint, it has all but disappeared from schools. Inspiraton and Kidspiration have taken over the number one and two spots respectively. Multimedia technologies give the teacher or student control of powerful tools in the exploration and creation of information. A camcorder, digital camera, optical scanner, CD-ROM drive, and video recorder all become potential information-gathering, composing, and presentation tools. Multimedia tools allow a student or teacher to compose a complex curriculum aide that might include computer-generated sound, graphics, and animation, along with sound and visual forms stored in another medium such as videotape, CD-ROM, or DVD.

Because multimedia involves the combination of more than one medium into a form of communication, there are many different types of multimedia productions. Thus, a variety of programs that help users to create multimedia products and presentations are available.

DESKTOP PRESENTATION AUTHORING TOOLS

Desktop presentation is the design, creation, and display of textual and graphic information under the control of a personal computer and so may be considered a form of multimedia. It has gained favor in boardrooms and business and community meetings, as well as in elementary, secondary, and college classrooms. Desktop presentation is quickly replacing traditional overhead transparencies and photographic slide shows as a medium of projected visual information. To take advantage of this new electronic medium, the user must have access to presentation software that permits the creation or import of text and graphic images and their subsequent organization and display. The medium also requires appropriate hardware such as a computer and projector to display the images to the selected audience. Newer versions of desktop presentation software have become true hypermedia tools. Rather than just a linear display of slides containing multimedia (drawings, images, video, sound, etc.), the developer can easily add hypertext and hyperlinked buttons that allow the user to present the slides in a nonlinear fashion, move between presentations, play audio and video, and open web pages or other programs at will.

Presentation Software

Presentation software such as *Microsoft PowerPoint* provide the user with word processing, outlining, drawing, graphing, presentation management tools, and the ability to move through the presentation in a branching as well as a linear fashion. Any piece of text can be changed into a hypertext link that will move the presentation to any other page in the presentation, or even onto the Internet. Figure 10–4 shows each link as an underlined word. Presentation software also readily accept existing material originally prepared by other word processor, spreadsheet, and graphics programs. In addition, movies, sounds,

Figure 10–4 PowerPoint slide with hypertext links
Each underlined word may take the reader to a new slide, video or audio clip, another file, such as an MS Word® document, or another application, such as Web page on Internet Explorer®

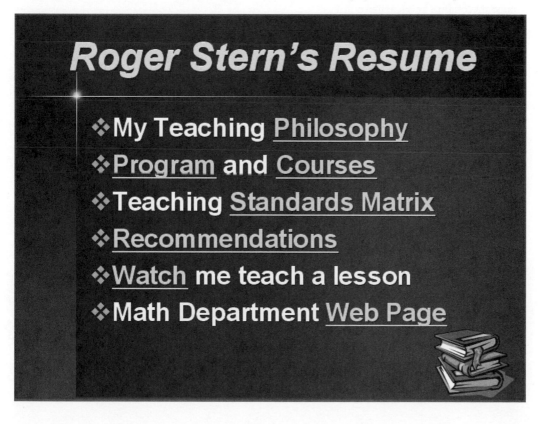

text and graphic animations, hyperlinked buttons, text, and almost anything saved in a digital format can be placed in the presentation making it a truly nonlinear, multimedia presentation. The software also allows the user to print outlines of the presentation, speaker's notes, and handouts.

The software usually allows the user to switch among four different views as the presentation is being created. These views are (1) *normal view* (Figure 10–5), showing the actual slide being developed, the outline to the left, and a window to type teaching notes under the slide; (2) the full presentation in *outline view;* (3) the *slide sorter view* order (Figure 10–6), showing a thumbnail of each slide in order; and (4) the *slide show view* that allows the developer to view the slide on the full screen in the actual presentation mode. Each view can be accessed at any time by clicking the small icons on the bottom bar in the lower left of each screen, shown in Figures 10–5 and 10–6. The illustration of these views were prepared using *Microsoft PowerPoint* and are representative of those created by other desktop presentation programs.

We usually prefer to work in the normal view adding text, graphics, sounds, hyperlinks, and so on, as we deem necessary. The outline view is good for handouts and as a display of the text found on the slides. In the slide sorter view, the order of the slides can be changed by simply clicking on the slide and dragging it to the desired location. Transitions (how one slide changes to another) are also added using this view just by highlighting the desired slide or slides and finding the desired transition on the toolbar directly above the slide sorter view.

PowerPoint allows the user to select transition effects from a wide variety of **wipes** and **dissolves** between visuals. A wipe is a transition effect that allows a second visual to gradually replace the first one being viewed. In a *wipe left* transition, the next visual will enter

Figure 10–5 Normal view
Notice the outline and teacher notes

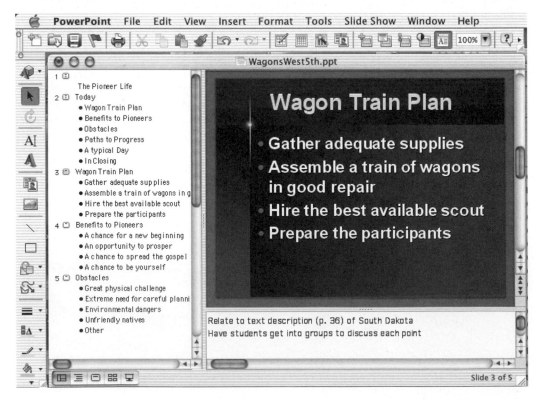

Figure 10–6 Slide sorter view
Notice the transition tool bar

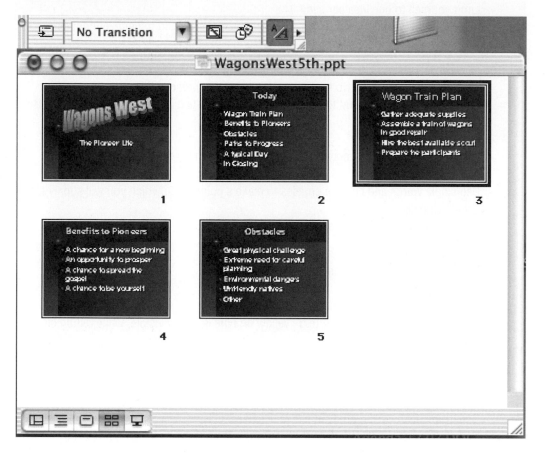

the screen at the right and move leftward across the preceding visual. A dissolve is an effect where one image fades into another.

The following guidelines will ensure a more effective presentation. Remember that the visual dimension is an important part of the presentation, but you as the presenter are the most significant element.

GUIDELINES FOR EFFECTIVE POWERPOINT PRESENTATIONS

General Guidelines

- Begin your presentation with a blank screen to control your audience's focus on your first slide.
- Use an attention-grabbing title screen.
- Use a single background or frame throughout your presentation.
- Avoid a complex background. Keep it simple.
- Place headings at the same location in successive screens.

(Continued)

A copy of these guidelines may be found in the Guidelines folder in the Take-Along CD.

315

- Use generous margins to help focus attention on the content.
- Limit yourself to one idea per slide.
- Select transition effects carefully to create a graceful style and to help your audience follow your train of thought. Avoid mixing transition effects.

Lettering Guidelines

- Limit yourself to one or two typefaces throughout the presentation.
- For maximum visibility and to minimize the amount of text per slide, choose a type size of 24 points or larger.
- Avoid ornate typefaces.
- Use all uppercase letters only in major headings and make them a slightly larger type size.
- Use single words and concise phrases to make a point about which you will supply the details verbally.
- Check carefully to eliminate any spelling/typing errors.

Color Guidelines

- Limit yourself to two or three colors per slide.
- Use the same colors throughout the presentation.
- Use bright colors to emphasize important points.
- Use color contrasts effectively (e.g., yellow on blue is highly visible, while red on black is barely readable).

Graphics Guidelines

- Keep any background graphics or text simple and restrict it to the same screen position.
- Use dingbats (bullets, checkmarks, and other symbols) to organize lists.
- Use drop shadows and gradient fills judiciously.
- Remember that graphics, sounds, and special effects can often distract from the purpose of the presentation. Less is often more!

WORKING WITH MICROSOFT POWERPOINT®

As we have said earlier, desktop presentation software provides the teacher with word processing, outlining, drawing, and graphing tools. Text can be changed into a hypertext link that will navigate to another page in the presentation or even onto the Internet. As you read through the section titled, *"Discipline-Specific Multimedia Ideas and Software,"* you encountered many uses for multimedia presentations and hopefully thought of some additional ones.

We will use *Microsoft PowerPoint*® as an example since it is fun and easy to use, and it is the most popular desktop presentation tool. Macintosh and PC versions of that software have screens and techniques that are almost identical. To follow this tutorial, you must have access to a copy of *PowerPoint*®, part of the Microsoft Office® suite. You can download a trial copy from the *www.microsoft.com* website. We will make a simple presentation you could use in class. We will be choosing a prepared design to streamline this tutorial. We will also add images, links, and other effects to enhance the look and add some multimedia functionality. Upon opening PowerPoint, look at the information available under the Help menu on the menu bar.

A copy of this tutorial may be found in the Tutorials folder in the Take-Along CD.

In working through the following brief tutorial on **Microsoft PowerPoint**™ you will learn the following:

- How to open PowerPoint and choose a project template
- How to format a template
- How to add text and graphics
- How to add hyperlinks
- How to build transitions between slides

1. LAUNCH POWERPOINT

NOTE: Once you have acquired a copy of Microsoft PowerPoint® or have downloaded a trial version of it, open PowerPoint.®

1.1 Open PowerPoint® and view the Project Gallery.

The first screen that you see should look similar to the one shown here.

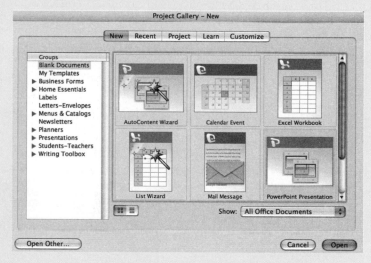

(Some versions of PowerPoint may not open with a Project Gallery. If so, Choose File > New > Form Design Template and proceed to **step 2.**)

1.2 If the Project Gallery does not appear, open it by clicking on Project Gallery found under the File menu.

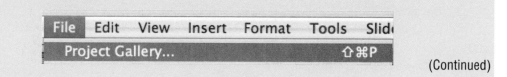

(Continued)

2. CHOOSE A DESIGN TEMPLATE

2.1 Choose Designs under the Presentation menu at the left edge of the screen.

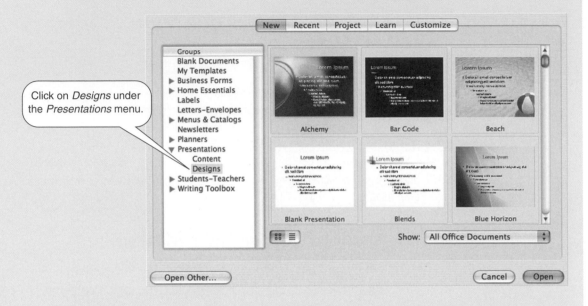

At this point you could take a moment to scroll through and examine the various templates, choosing the one that you would like to use. Keep in mind that it is best to have a solid color background, preferably in a dark color with light text.

2.2 Choose Shimmer, a template with a dark background and click Open.

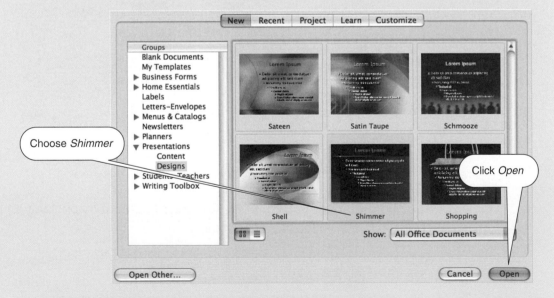

(On some versions of PowerPoint the template names appear as pop-ups as you mouse over them.)

After you have chosen the template, this screen will appear.

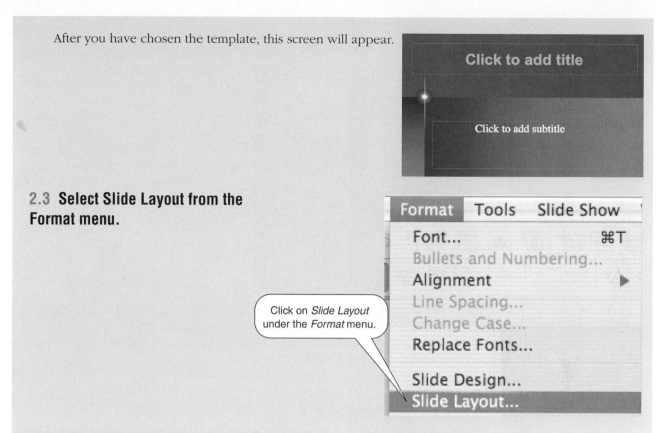

Click to add title

Click to add subtitle

2.3 Select Slide Layout from the Format menu.

Click on *Slide Layout* under the *Format* menu.

Format	Tools	Slide Show
Font...		⌘T
Bullets and Numbering...		
Alignment		▶
Line Spacing...		
Change Case...		
Replace Fonts...		
Slide Design...		
Slide Layout...		

2.4 Choose the Bulleted List layout and then click on the Apply button.

Click on *Bulleted List*

Click on *Apply*

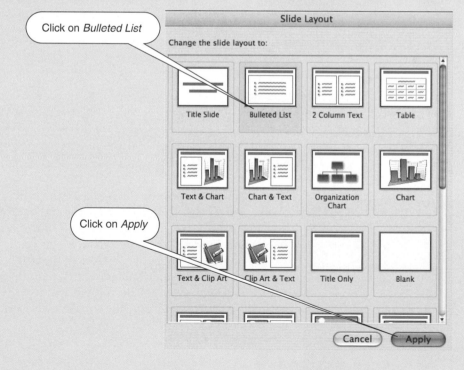

Slide Layout

Change the slide layout to:

Title Slide   Bulleted List   2 Column Text   Table

Text & Chart   Chart & Text   Organization Chart   Chart

Text & Clip Art   Clip Art & Text   Title Only   Blank

Cancel   Apply

(In the future you may want to begin your presentations by choosing Title Slide).

(Continued)

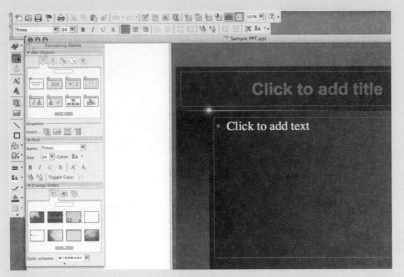

This screen will now appear.

Note all of the different menus in this figure. If all of these horizontal and vertical menus (called *toolbars*) do not appear, access them by selecting Toolbar under the View menu at the top of the screen.

Click on the Standard, Formatting, and Drawing toolbars.

As you drag your pointer over each icon on the toolbars, a brief explanation will appear.

(Toolbars may differ on different versions of PowerPoint.)

WARNING! Before you click in the boxes and add information, you must first reformat the text defaults. A number of *PowerPoint* defaults are not good examples of proper graphic technique! The title color is too dark (not enough contrast with background) and the text box contains a font that is too hard to read. It is (1) too small, (2) not bold, and (3) a serif typeface.

3. FORMAT YOUR TEMPLATE

3.1 From the View menu, move down to Master and over to Slide Master.

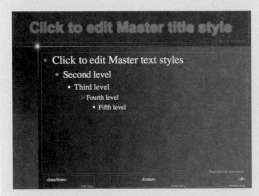

This screen now appears. Changing a format on this slide will change the format (font, font size, font and background color, text location on slide, footer, etc.) **on all of the regular slides using this format** in the presentation except the title slide.

It is quite easy to change the format by treating it as a word processing document. Highlight the words or sections you want to change on the slide master and use the Formatting toolbar, second toolbar from the top (directly over the screen), to make changes.

Make the following changes.

320

3.2 Click on the top line which is the Title box (Click to edit Master title style) and choose the font Arial, 48 point, bold, italic.

To make it really stand out choose a font color of yellow.

3.3 Click on the box below which is the Text box (Click to edit Master text styles…) and choose the font Arial, 36 point, bold.

3.4 While the Text box is selected, choose Format > Bullets and Numbering.

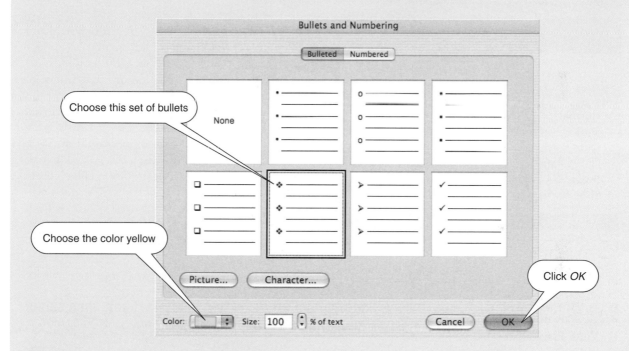

3.5 Choose the fifth set of bullets and choose yellow for the color.

While you are still in the Slide Master, take a look at the three boxes labeled Date Area, Footer Area, and Number Area along the bottom of the window.

If you enter something in these boxes (including an image), it will appear on all the regular slides. If you add an image of your school mascot the "Fighting Bear" to the

(Continued)

Slide Master it will appear on each regular slide except the title slide. If you teach in the "Polar Bear Block," how would you make that appear on all of your slides? You are right if you said that it would be to type "Polar Bear Block" into the footer box.

3.6 **Choose Normal from the View menu.**

3.7 **Click in the Title box and type in the text "Roger Stern's Resume".**

3.8 **Click in the Text box and type in the text "My Teaching Philosophy". Press Return (Enter) between each line and continue to type in the text as in this illustration.**

You have another task to do. You would not want all five bulleted lines of information to appear on the screen at the outset, but would rather have one line of information revealed one at a time with each mouse click. In this manner you control the presentation and only have information disclosed when you are ready to discuss it.

Each one of these bulleted lines of information is often called either a build or a disclosure. Just to confuse the issue, PowerPoint calls them *Animations* or *Animation Schemes!* The most efficient way to add these to your presentation is from the *Slide Master* screen.

Return to the *Slide Master* screen from the View menu

3.9 **First, highlight all of the text in the Text box, then select Custom Animation from the Slide Show menu.**

NOTE: Do not use the selection presented in the Slide Show >> Preset Animations menu. Most of those also have a sound with it that may be distracting to your students.

3.10 A Custom Animation window will open.

Click on Add Effect at the top right of the window.

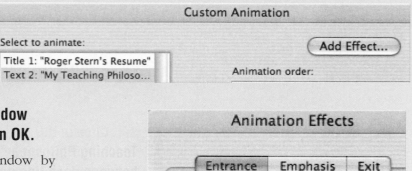

3.11 An Animation Effects window will appear. Click on Fly In then OK.

Close the Custom Animation window by clicking on the OK button.

You may later want to experiment with the various animations. The unusual ones may be fun to look at but they may be distracting to your students.

After completing this first slide, "*Roger Stern's Resume*," you will add six additional slides to your presentation.

Click on *Fly In*

3.12 Return to Normal from the View menu.

3.13 To add a slide, choose the Insert > New Slide menu.

Type "*My Teaching Philosophy*" in the Title box.

Follow the procedure just described to continue adding slides titling, each one according to Roger Stern's Resume:

> Program and Courses
> Teaching Standards Matrix
> Recommendations
> Watch Me Teach a Lesson
> Math Department Web Page

Let's add an image to a slide. You must first be on the slide to which you want to add an image. Return to the first slide, *Roger Stern's Resume*.

3.14 Select Insert >> Picture >> Clip Art . . .

This will open the PowerPoint Clip Art folder. This is usually the same folder as the Microsoft Office Clip Art folder. In the Academic category, choose Classroom, the third item on the top row.

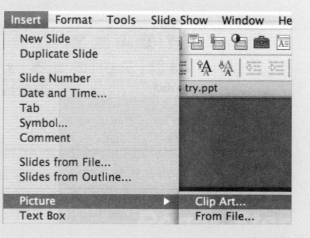

(Continued)

3.15 Click on Classroom and then on the Insert button.

Click on *Classroom*

Click on *Insert*

Now positon and resize the image if necessary on the slide. Make sure it does not conflict with any text.

NOTE: If you have an image that you use often, say the "Fighting Bear" mascot image, you can add it to this clip art folder by using the Import button on the lower left of the Clip Gallery screen. If you have any images (clip art, scanned images, digital photographs, etc.) that are not in the PowerPoint Clip Art folder, you would choose the Insert > Picture > From File . . . option. Use this to locate the image you want on your computer or flash drive. When you find it, select it and press the Insert button.

The title of this chapter is "Learning with Multimedia Tools" and a simple linear presentation is not multimedia. So, let's change this linear presentation into a multimedia one by adding some sounds and movies.

3.16 Return to the Insert menu, move down to Movies and Sounds and select Movie from Gallery ... to add movies stored in the PowerPoint movies folder or Sounds from Gallery . . . to add sounds from the PowerPoint sounds folder.

If you have sounds or movies that are not in this folder, just access them by clicking on the Movie from File . . . or the Sound from File . . . menu item.

IMPORTANT NOTE Movies and sounds DO NOT become parts of the PowerPoint presentation file as an image does. You are simply adding a pointer to the movie or sound file. Because of this, you must always keep your PowerPoint file, sound files, and movie files together. If you just move your PowerPoint file (perhaps to give it to your instructor to correct) and don't move the sounds and movies with it, the pointers will be on your PowerPoint but they will not work because they have nothing to point to!

You have added sounds and movies so you now have a multimedia presentation. Let's turn it into a hypermedia presentation. You do this by changing words or images into true hypermedia links, just like on a web page!

You can have links move us to at least three different locations: (1) You can move to a different slide in the same PowerPoint presentation; (2) you can open up a web page; (3) or you can open up another application (e.g., a document in Microsoft Word).

3.17 **On Roger Stern's Resume, highlight the word Philosophy to make into a link.**

Now choose Insert > Hyperlink.

(Continued)

Insert Hyperlink

Link to: http://mnsu.edu/

Display: Philosophy

ScreenTip...

| Web Page | Document | E-mail Address |

Favorites ▶   History ▶   Launch Web Browser

Enter the Internet address (URL) of the Web page you want to link to. Click Favorites or History to link to a Web page you've visited before or visit frequently.

Anchor:

Locate...

If you want to link to a specific location (anchor) within the Web page, enter the name of the anchor above or click Locate to find it.

Cancel   OK

3.18 Type *http://mnsu.edu/* in the Link to: box and click the OK button.

Now, when you click on the word *Philosophy* in the PowerPoint presentation, your web browser will open and the *http://mnsu.edu* web page will be displayed.

As said earlier, you can also link to another file or another slide in the same presentation. Let us say that you wanted to link the word *Philosophy* to a Microsoft Word document. Highlight the word *Philosophy* and select Insert > Hyperlink. Click on the Remove Link button.

| Web Page | Document | E-mail Address |

Favorites ▶   Select...

3.19 Select Insert >> Hyperlink again but this time click on the Document tab near the middle of the page and click on the Select button.

Now, select the file you want to open. If the Philosophy paper was a Microsoft Word document, you just have to find that and click on the OK button. Now, when you click on the word Philosophy in your presentation, Microsoft Word will open up and display the document!

You can use the same menu to make a link back to another slide in your presentation. Hint: By placing #x. (were x is the PowerPoint slide number) in the Link to: box, you will go directly to the slide you selected.

We have one last thing to do: Put transitions between the slides. Transitions are how one slide moves into another.

3.20 Choose View > Slide Sorter View and select slides 2 through 7.

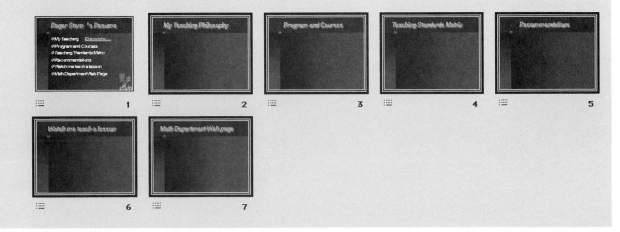

3.21 In the pulldown menu near the top of the screen, replace No Transition with Cover Right-Down.

Select View Show from the Slide Show menu and sit back, relax, and admire your handiwork as you view your presentation.

Now you are on your own!

Remember, if you want to insert something, just click on "Insert" on the top menu bar. PowerPoint is very intuitive and the toolbars are similar to the ones found on Microsoft Word.

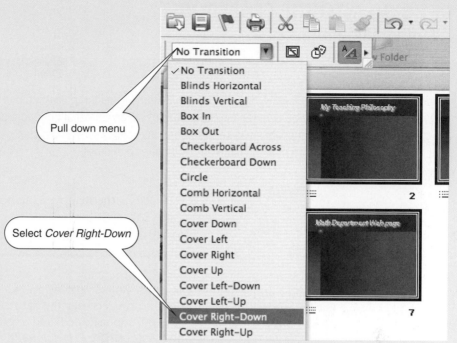

Pull down menu

Select *Cover Right-Down*

Experiment with the Drawing toolbar. See what you can do with the *PowerPoint WordArt*™ feature accessed by clicking the *slanted A* on the drawing toolbar. Have some fun!

DESKTOP PRESENTATION AS A TOOL

Desktop presentation, with its ability to design, create, and display information under the control of a personal computer, is a tool that extends the capability of the user to communicate. This electronic medium requires users to access software that permits them to design and create the message and to use appropriate hardware to display the message effectively. The presentation, once created, may be saved in a single file on disk, making it a portable presentation indeed. It also may be saved as a web presentation able to be accessed from almost any part of the globe. Once again, as we note decreasing equipment size and increasing portability, we see evidence of the paradigm shifts described in Chapter 1. Compare a presenter carrying file folders full of overhead transparencies or carousel trays full of slides to one carrying a floppy disk in a pocket or purse.

Desktop presentation tools can also be utilized in the classroom in a number of different ways. We shall discuss several at the end of the chapter. Teachers with an Internet connection should access the Microsoft website (*http://www.microsoft.com/education/ tutorial.classroom/default.asp*) for a step-by-step tutorial on the use of *PowerPoint.*

HYPERMEDIA AUTHORING TOOLS

HyperCard, a program introduced in 1987 by Apple Computer, is said to have opened the door to multimedia as we know it today. The program has now been surpassed by a number of others, most prominent among them *Hyper Studio,* which works on both the

Macintosh and Windows platforms. Unlike *HyperCard*, which was not an easy program to master, *Hyper Studio* afforded the novice user the satisfaction of creating a multimedia product with ease. Other high-end, sophisticated, and expensive authoring programs such as *Macromedia Director*™ and *Authorware Professional*™ are more useful to experienced and professional multimedia programmers.

Figure 10–7 presents various multimedia applications created in Hyper Studio. The Hyper Studio home stack title page is located at the top center. Top left is a geography stack

Figure 10–7 Hyper studio®

A variety of applications created in Hyper Studio® *(Reprinted with permission from Knowledge Adventure, Inc.)*

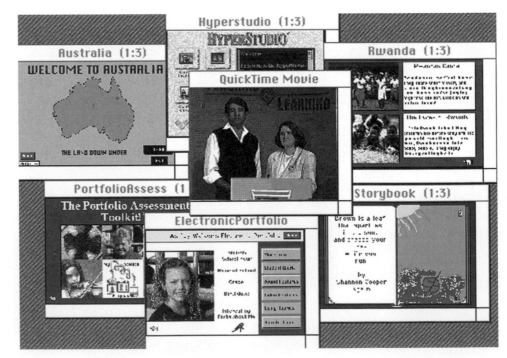

on Australia; top right is a look at the people of Rwanda; bottom left and bottom center are examples of electronic portfolios; bottom right is a storybook created by elementary students that is complete with pictures and text that can be read aloud by the computer; in the center of this collage is a Quicktime™ movie welcoming people to the NECC in Minneapolis. Not only does Hyper Studio allow the user to create buttons that link to the Web through Netscape™, but it is also designed to let users publish their multimedia projects over the Web as well. A Hyper Studio window can be embedded in a web page or the complete Hyper Studio–created display can be an entire Internet document. In many ways, multimedia is a marriage of technologies that allows information to be presented locally to an individual or to groups and globally to anyone accessing the Web.

Even though Hyper Studio is not used as much anymore, it is still in use in a number of locations including the Royal Bank of Scotland, Jimmy Buffett's enhanced music CD, and hundreds of colleges and universities. It is simple enough to allow even first graders to make multimedia presentations with ease. Version updates, project information, training material, and even a free fully functional CD are available through the Hyper Studio website (*http://www.hyperstudio.com*).

LET'S GO INTO THE CLASSROOM
Immunization for PowerPoint Poisoning

Creating Conditions for Powerful Presentations

PowerPoint is such a potent multimedia tool that it is tempting for teachers and students to overuse the program's strong capabilities. The effect may be to distort, undermine, and distract from the real message of the presentation. Here are five practical steps that we tell teachers and students to follow so that they all effectively immunize their presentations against *PowerPoint Poisoning*.

Five Powerful Steps

1. Plan It!
2. Storyboard It!
3. PowerPoint It!
4. Rehearse It!
5. Present It!

The best immunization for PowerPoint Poisoning is to focus upfront attention and energy on planning, organization, and content.

Plan It!

1. Determine who your audience will be.
2. Determine the purpose and content of the presentation.
3. Review, reevaluate, and revise.

Storyboard It!

1. Organize the information in a logical, understandable sequence for your specific audience.
2. Define the major and minor points of the presentation.

(Continued)

3. Write each major point on a sticky note.
4. Storyboard your sticky notes in logical sequence. Reorganize and rearrange as necessary.
5. Review, reevaluate, and revise.

PowerPoint It!
(The authors suggest following the guidelines presented previously in this chapter.)

Rehearse It!

1. Practice—practice—practice.
2. Critically evaluate and adjust your PowerPoint presentation in terms of your purpose.
3. Critically evaluate its effectiveness.

Present It!
The proof is in the presentation. Successfully present the final powerful version of your PowerPoint presentation to an enthusiastic audience in your classroom.

Michael S. Houser, Ed.D.
Educational Technologist (retired)
Heidelberg District Superintendent's Office
Department of Defense Dependents' Schools—Europe
Hanau, Germany

It is importat that you preplan your multimedia presentation. Figure 10–8 lists several steps in this process.

MULTIMEDIA IN A CONSTRUCTIVIST CLASSROOM

Arnold (1996) examined whether using multimedia technology as a tool for accessing information and demonstrating knowledge would improve self-directedness in learners. Her research took place in a suburban elementary school of 14 mixed-age classrooms, with an average of 26 students in each class. Her sample population consisted of 51 students in two fourth-fifth-grade classes. The students were placed in two heterogeneous groups, with consideration given to balancing the variables of grade level and students with special needs.

The groups were assigned a four-week research project on the topic of United States immigration. Group A was taught how to use electronic technology to retrieve information and produce a multimedia report in *Hyper Studio*. Group B was restricted from using electronic technology. At the end of four weeks, the groups were assigned another four-week research project, this time on famous Americans. Group A was restricted from using electronic technology and group B was taught how to use electronic technology to produce a multimedia report. At the end of the eight weeks, the students presented the results of their projects to their peers, teachers, parents, and invited guests.

The analysis of the data focused on differences within each group, not on differences across the two groups. Class mean scores using the Oregon Department of Education Student Self-Directed Learning Scoring Guide showed substantial improvement when students had access to electronic technology. Figure 10–9 summarizes multimedia technology's impact on the students.

Figure 10–8 Planning for multimedia

A number of steps are required in planning a multimedia presentation

---

Overall Considerations

Define intended audience.
Identify size of presentation audience.
Determine time frame for project completion.
Access production materials.
Ascertain size of project group (individual or group).

Preplanning

Determine outline content to be covered.
Develop a card map showing cards and links (make sure that there are no dead ends).
Sketch each card in a storyboard.
List media required for each card.
Make a citation card for each piece of medium not produced by the group.
Sketch each card in detail citing each piece of medium.
List all assignments and responsibilities, due dates, and so on.
Gather materials.

Basic Cards Required

Title card.
Introduction card.
Index or menu card (may be part of Introduction card).
Stack cards
Credits card(s) (citations, acknowledgments, student names, bibliography).

Figure 10–9 Arnold's research

Technology's impact on student self-directedness

	More When Using Technology (%)	More When Not Using Technology (%)
Effective Work Habits		
Focused attention on research	73%	27%
Used time wisely	69	31
Set goals each day	69	31
Had better work habits	67	33
Followed a Work Plan		
Enjoyed researching and gathering materials	57	43
Did a better job finding resources	62	38
Hardest work	65	35
Best-quality work	76	24
Self-Reflection		
Felt responsible for getting work done	72	28
Project that communicated information best	73	27
Project liked doing best	90	10
Proudest of project	79	21

Students took a good deal of pride in the multimedia presentations they had prepared. Students who had been identified as "at risk" were observed being significantly more involved during the electronic technology treatment and exhibiting a higher degree of personal responsibility. Following are the feelings students had about their exposure to multimedia technology, captured in their own words (Arnold, 1996).

> "I really took time to do a good job. I stayed in at breaks to finish it."
> "I worked longer on the technology project and it wasn't just slopped together."
> "It's like it's easier to stick to the project."
> "My tech project shows my hardest work. It looks a heck of a lot better. I worked hard to make it neat, interesting, and fun for the person looking at it."
> "My technology project looks more professional."
> "When I use technology I feel . . . powerful and different. Learning's more fun."
> "I feel privileged because in other generations people were not able to do this. We're lucky!"

Multimedia technology can be a catalyst for change, helping teachers alter their approach to teaching and learning from passive learning to active learning. Roblyer (1999) found that one of the benefits of multimedia is that it gives students a chance to experience and process information through any of several multiple channels. This "may have unique capabilities to facilitate learning because of the parallels between multimedia and the natural way people learn" (Bagui, 1998, p. 4).

Technology can lead teachers to develop more learner-centered environments. Students learned more than was expected and also developed new competencies like the ability to collaborate, to recognize and analyze problems as systems, to acquire and use large amounts of information, and to apply technology to solve real-world problems (Dwyer, 1996).

LET'S REVIEW

Multimedia conveys information in a multisensory manner. Hypermedia uses a nonlinear method of conveying multimedia information.

Multimedia authoring tools allow students and teachers to create and compose desktop presentations, hypertext and hypermedia documents, and other multimedia productions. These creations might include computer-generated sound, graphics, and animation, along with sound and visual forms stored in another medium such as videotape, CD-ROM, or DVD as well as links to websites.

Presentation software makes it possible to index slides, view thumbnail representations in a slide sorter format, and prescribe their subsequent viewing in a specific sequence.

Multimedia technology can be a catalyst for change, helping teachers to alter their approach to teaching and learning from passive learning to active learning. Students take a good deal of pride in preparing multimedia presentations. Students' self-directedness and other study and learning habits may show substantial improvement when they have access to multimedia technology.

LET'S PRACTICE

To complete the specified exercises online, go to the Chapter Exercises Module in Chapter 10 of the Companion Website.

1. Evaluate a multimedia program from your school's software collection. Did it take full advantage of the multimedia format? What were its strengths and

weaknesses? Can you suggest a better way to convey the same information?

2. If your principal told you that you could buy any two multimedia software packages to use in your class, which ones would you choose? Write a short paragraph explaining your choices to the principal.

3. Log on to the Microsoft Education website (*http://microsoft.com/education* at the time of publication). Review the Instructional Resources available on the site. Write a short paragraph telling how this site may be helpful to you in your teaching. What are some of the problems you foresee in trying to add multimedia presentations to your teaching?

4. If you have not already done so, obtain some software catalogs that list software sales such as the one from Learning Services™ (1-800-877-9378). Review the types of software being purchased today. How many of the popular ones do you recognize? How many have you tried firsthand? What conclusions can you make regarding the types of software being purchased?

5. Search AskERIC or another lesson plan archive for lesson plans using multimedia software. Present your findings to the class.

6. Search the electronic database of educational periodicals in your school's library for articles discussing multimedia use and multimedia software. Write a short review of one of the articles. Discuss your review with the class.

7. Ask a student teaching supervisor, mentor teacher, cooperating teacher, and so forth, about the multimedia software found in the schools in your area. What software seems most popular? What obstacles do they see that might inhibit its use in the school? Discuss your findings with the class.

8. Design a multimedia project for the grade level you wish to teach. How many types of media can you incorporate into the project? Discuss your project with the class.

9. Look again at the project that you designed above. Can it be used with handicapped students or students with limited English proficiency? What could you do to make it more accessible?

10. Search the electronic database of educational periodicals in your school's library for the five most recent articles on multimedia in the classroom. What do the authors believe is the apparent impact on education?

PORTFOLIO DEVELOPMENT EXERCISES

To complete this exercise online, go to the Digital Portfolio Module in Chapter 10 of the Companion Website.

One of the NETS• standards covered in this chapter was "Students are proficient in the use of technology" under *Category 1: Basic operations and concepts.* A second one was "Students evaluate and select new information resources and technological innovations based on the appropriateness for specific tasks" under *Category 5: Technology research tools.* Begin to develop your own portfolio of lesson plans that demonstrates your ability to have your students reach these NETS•S standards.

1. Design a lesson plan activity for elementary, middle school, or high school students in which they will work in groups to design and produce a multimedia presentation about your class, a subject they have or will be studying, or their school. They should use a form of HTML editor or PowerPoint. This presentation should be designed to be presented to a group other than their own classmates, such as their parents, religious or community organization, or school board. This lesson should demonstrate that your students have achieved the standard. Be sure to include a system of evaluation for your students' understanding and competence to ensure that they have met this standard.

2. Adapt the lesson plan activity you developed in exercise 1 for students to evaluate each others' work.

GLOSSARY

action	The programmed result of clicking on a hypermedia button
button	A visible object or an invisible area of the screen, often covering images or text, that can be programmed using a scripting language to perform certain actions
card	One screen or frame of a hypermedia presentation
desktop presentation	The design, creation, and display of textual and graphic information under the control of a personal computer often with the use of a video projector

digital multimedia	A multimedia design that allows a computer user to combine and control a number of instructional resources in order to present information
dissolve	Moving from one screen to the next by having one visual fade out as the second fades in
hypermedia	A multimedia presentation that contains links or buttons that will allow the product to be presented in a nonlinear fashion
hypertext	A term synonymous with hypermedia but emphasizes textual links instead of buttons
multimedia	A technique that conveys information in a multisensory manner
stack	A group of cards linked together to form a complete hypermedia presentation
wipe	Moving from one slide to the next by having one slide replace the next by covering it and pushing it off the screen as from left to right or top to bottom

REFERENCES AND SUGGESTED READINGS

Arnold, S. (1996). *Effects of integrative technology on student self-directedness at Mountain View Elementary School.* Unpublished thesis for a Master of Education degree in Information Technology, Western Oregon University.

Bagui, S. (1998). Reasons for increased learning using multimedia. *Journal of Educational Multimedia and Hypermedia, 7*(1), 3–18.

Dale, E. (1969). *Audio-visual methods in teaching* (3rd ed). New York: Holt, Rinehart and Winston, 108.

Dwyer, D. (1996, Winter). Apple classrooms of tomorrow, the first ten years. *Apple Education Digest, http://www.info.apple.com/education/acot.menu.html*

Gardner, H. (1993). *Multiple intelligences: The theory in practice.* New York: Basic Books.

Killmer, K., & George, N. (2002, February). Show and tell in real time: Link a spreadsheet to a PowerPoint slide for up-to-the-minute visuals. *Journal of Accountancy, 193*(2), 57–64.

QED. *Educational technology trends 1997.* Denver: Quality Education Data, 1997.

Roblyer, M. D. (1999). Our multimedia future: Recent research on multimedia's impact on education. *Learning and Leading with Technology, 26*(6), 51–53.

Tolhurst, D. (1995). Hypertext, hypermedia, multimedia defined? Educational Technology, 35(2), 21–26.

CHAPTER 11

Learning with Internet Tools

1. What is the Internet and how did it develop?

2. What kinds of resources are available on the Internet?

3. What are some tools that increase the user's productivity when using the Internet?

4. What is the World Wide Web and how does it relate to the Internet?

5. How does one publish on the Web?

6. How can students evaluate the accuracy of information available on the Web?

7. How are advances in telecommunications affecting the teaching/learning process?

8. How can a user maximize the Web's potential as an information source?

9. What are some styles for citing references to information obtained on the Web?

10. What are some copyright and ownership concerns regarding information, either textual or graphical, obtained from the Internet?

11. What are some benefits and risks encountered when using Internet filtering software?

12. What is an acceptable use policy and why is it important for a school to have one?

13. How can teachers incorporate both directed and exploratory learning styles using the Web?

14. What are some examples of good web-based learning activities?

15. How can instruction be delivered over the Internet?

NETS•T Standards Addressed in this Chapter

I. Technology operations and concepts
   A. demonstrate introductory knowledge, skills, and understanding of concepts related to technology (as described in the ISTE National Educational Technology Standards for Students)
   B. demonstrate continual growth in technology knowledge and skills to stay abreast of current and emerging technologies

II. Planning and designing learning environments and experiences
   A. design developmentally appropriate learning opportunities that apply technology-enhanced instructional strategies to support the diverse needs of learners

III. Teaching, learning, and the curriculum
   A. facilitate technology-enhanced experiences that address content standards and student technology standards
   B. use technology to support learner-centered strategies that address the diverse needs of students
   C. apply technology to develop students' higher order skills and creativity

IV. Assessment and evaluation
   B. use technology resources to collect and analyze data, interpret results, and communicate findings to improve instructional practice and maximize student learning

V. Productivity and professional practice
   A. use technology resources to engage in ongoing professional development and lifelong learning
   C. apply technology to increase productivity
   D. use technology to communicate and collaborate with peers, parents, and the larger community in order to nurture student learning

VI. Social, ethical, legal, and human issues
   A. model and teach legal and ethical practice related to technology use
   B. apply technology resources to enable and empower learners with diverse backgrounds, characteristics, and abilities
   D. promote safe and healthy use of technology resources

▮▮▮▮▮ LET'S LOOK AT THIS CHAPTER ▮▮▮▮▮

This chapter describes the origin of the Internet, traces its development, and explains how it functions. It also explores a number of Internet tools, including the World Wide Web, and their practical application.

Searcing the Web is examined in detail, as is the use of filtered search engines and evaluating Web information. Once information is found on the Internet, the proper way of citing it is explained.

Topics covered in this chapter include the invisible Web, email, discussion groups, chat rooms, instant messaging, blogs, and HTML editors. The chapter ends with tutorials on web page construction.

▮▮▮▮▮ THE INTERNET

It would be impossible, within a single chapter of a textbook, to thoroughly describe the features of a topic so far reaching and as constantly changing as the worldwide collection of computer networks known as the **Internet.** It is without a doubt the best known network today. In reality, though, it is not a single computer network, but a network of computer networks. This supernetwork was first called ARPAnet (Advanced Research Projects Agency network), named for the agency that designed it. Originally, it was a Cold War attempt by the U.S. Department of Defense in the mid-1960s to build a decentralized network linking government installations in the hope that such a network would survive a nuclear attack on the United States. The diffuse nature of the network did not rely on a single pathway to move data, but contained multiple pathways between each point.

The heart of the Internet is a technique called "packet switching," a data transmission method that divides a message into numerous pieces, or packets, each framed by a header and a trailer. The header signals the start of the packet and identifies the sender, receiver, and amount of data the packet contains. A piece of data follows, then the trailer which signals the end of the packet and contains information used by the receiving computer to check for transmission errors. It would be like sending a letter to your best friend, but rather than send it whole in one envelope, you cut it into little pieces, add instructions on how to piece it together, and then send each piece in a different envelope. This packet-switching method transmits each individual packet from point A to point B over the fastest available route. If one route (such as a telephone line or fiber optic cable) is busy or destroyed, packets are simply transmitted over other routes until they all arrive at their destination, where they are reassembled into the complete message.

To continue with the letter paradigm example, rather than place all pieces of your letter into one mail truck to deliver it to your friend, the post office might send each piece in a different truck and each mail truck may take a different route when it leaves the post office depending on road traffic, detours, and so forth. Just before the postal carriers deliver your letter, they piece it all together and place the complete letter in your friend's mailbox.

A set of standards, called **Transmission Control Protocol/Internet Protocol (TCP/IP),** was developed to allow different networks and different types of computers to interconnect. As long as the computer, regardless of operating system (Windows, MacOS, Linux, etc.), runs a version of TCP/IP software, it can send packets to any other computer over the Internet. Over time, tens of thousands of school, business, and government networks became linked in what is now known as the Internet. The commercialization of the Internet in the late 1990s caused such an explosion in interest that the Internet now spans the globe and serves hundreds of millions of users.

Interestingly, the original, decentralized design of the Internet, with no one central hub and no centralized control, has current consequences. The Internet was originally intended to facilitate the free exchange of ideas and information in a military and later an

© Royalty Free/Corbis

academic context. This tradition of free exchange is a major reason why most longtime Internet users resist most forms of regulation or censorship, including governmental regulations governing pornographic sites, taxation of products bought over the Internet, and ownership of audio, video, text, or graphics posted on the Internet.

Now that commercial interests have become such an important part of the Internet, copyright and intellectual property laws have become increasingly important. Because of this, everything on the Internet is owned by the person who placed or contracted to have it placed there. You cannot download text, graphics, movies, anything from the Internet without worrying about the legal implications. It is best to ask before taking information from the Internet. Luckily there are many sites on the Internet that contain huge amounts of free graphics, movies, and sounds for teachers to download and use for education and nonprofit purposes. Just place the words *clipart, free,* and *education* into a search engine and look at the results.

It was not, however, until the advent of the Web—with its graphic user interface supporting text, images, audio, video, and hot links—that the rapid growth in size and popularity of the Internet began. The Internet has expanded from its original national defense and academic functions to a medium for sharing information among educational institutions at all levels, governmental and private agencies, individual users worldwide, and, above all, large and small commercial enterprises. Most people see the Internet as an enormous and immediate source of information. Others see it as an expansive channel for profitable sales of goods and services, while, to still others, it is the source of concern about portions of its content or the social inequities of access to its potential. Regardless of personal viewpoint, the Internet will stand alongside Gutenberg's printing press as one of the greatest change agents in human history.

For educators, the Internet offers opportunities to access an ever-increasing base of knowledge, resources, and people on a global scale. Students may search extensively for information relevant to their lives and aspirations, increase or refine their communication skills, and practice critical evaluation of the information available to them. In addition, the Internet provides a rich environment for students to display, transmit, and discuss the knowledge they have constructed with others outside of their immediate community. It also contains many hazards ranging from fictitious information designed to deceive people (check out *http://city-mankato.us,* for example), to pornography and hate groups not fit for children and young adults. In a survey of teen Internet users, 60 percent said that they have been contacted by strangers (Poftak, 2002). Regardless of the diversity of opinion about its uses, the Internet is rapidly expanding as a dynamic repository for human knowledge and experience; and it will continue to have a profound influence on both the form and the content of human communications.

Students in the classroom will not be strangers to the Internet. Poftak (2002) states that students ages 12 through 17 with Internet access spend an average of 7 hours, 36 minutes online from home; 1 hour, 36 minutes online from school; and 1 hour, 6 minutes online from a friend or relative's home per week. Many of these students have been on the Internet a lifetime, so don't be afraid to ask them for help and assistance!

INTERNET RESOURCES AND APPLICATIONS

As expected with the world at our fingertips, the amount of information available is staggering. Internet software, which was just a few short years ago complicated and difficult to use, has been replaced by user-friendly, almost transparent programs that allow even a novice user to send and receive email, search and surf the Web, and download everything from clip art to software at the click of a mouse. Unfortunately, the old computer axiom, GIGO (i.e., garbage in, garbage out), applies to the Internet as well. Most students and many educators look at the Internet as a vast library of resources. Of teen Internet users, 71 percent say they choose the Internet over going to the library to complete school projects, even though only 51 percent of the students believe that "most or all" of the information on the Web is accurate (Poftak, 2002). Material on the Internet is not filtered for truth, bias, or accuracy as it would be in a real library. Because of this, it is imperative that information found, posted on, or transmitted through the Internet be subject to the same critical evaluation for accuracy and reliability that we might give to any other unfiltered media. This is a wonderful opportunity for us as educators to incorporate training and practice in critical thinking and information evaluation skills within any classroom activity that involves use of the Internet.

Before we discuss how to utilize the Internet in teaching, let us look at the range of applications available. Each application is a tool that has unique features and ways to be used in the curriculum. As stated, good tools, chosen wisely, help us work more efficiently and effectively. Learning should always drive the use of technology; the use of technology should not drive the learning.

Electronic Mail

Electronic mail, or **email,** has become a part of everyday life for many of us. Email allows users to exchange messages with others, whether they're next door or around the globe. All that is needed is an Internet connection, an email program or web browser, and the recipient's email address. Free email accounts are available on the Web from such places as yahoo.com, msn.com, hotmail.com, and even a site called I-love-dogs.com, to name just a few. According to Poftak (2002), a survey of teen Internet users found that 56 percent have two or more email addresses. The number of email messages sent surpassed those sent by regular postal delivery in 1995 and has continued to mushroom since. In 2006, it has been estimated that over 60 billion emails were sent every day by Internet users around the world (Reuters, 2006).

Email has phenomenal holding power. Students eagerly spend time each day reading and writing at the computer. What an opportunity for a teacher to develop language arts skills! Once the novelty and electronic pen pal syndrome wear off, students might see email as a means of accessing information on specific topics and learning about different cultures. A study of college students (Deal, 1995) suggested that an email journal helped students to increase self-assessment skills and synthesize their learning better than traditional journaling.

Let us take a quick look at email addresses. The authors' addresses are *forcier@aol.com* and *don.descy@mnsu.edu*. These addresses consist of two basic parts: the *user ID* (mailbox) and the *domain* and *subdomains* (name and location of the computer). These two parts are separated by the "at" (@) symbol. So an email address is really *mailbox at computer location*. Email addresses are not case specific.

Figure 11–1 identifies the parts of that Internet email address.

Reading the addresses from right to left, ".com" on the Forcier address represents one of the major domains on the Internet and identifies the site as a commercial site. ".edu," on the Descy address, represents another major domain on the Internet and identifies the site as a postsecondary educational one. Some other domains are government agencies (.gov), networks (.net), and organizations (.org). International sites are frequently identified geographically by two characters representing the country in which they are located, for example, Canada (.ca), United Kingdom (.uk), and Australia (.au). Because of the phenomenal volume of new users joining the Internet, the convention of using geographic identifiers within the United States is supplementing the use of .edu and similar domain names. Many public schools in the United States have addresses that include the school, grade level, state, and country. For example, the email address for Pinellas Central Elementary School in Florida is first.lastname@pinellas.k12.fl.us. Each part of an address is separated by a dot (Period).

Again, reading the Forcier address in Figure 11–1 from the right, the next part of the address, "aol," identifies the subdomain name of the commercial provider, sometimes called the **Internet Service Provider (ISP).** "mnsu," on the Descy address, is the subdomain name identifying a computer located at Minnesota State University. The symbol "@" separates the leftmost part of the address, which is the user ID (or mailbox), Forcier or Descy. Now that you know our addresses, we hope to hear your comments and suggestions related to this book. We read them all and many times incorporate them into new editions of the text.

Practice sessions provide the opportunity to stress proper communication rules and mitigate what some believe to be email's negative effect on writing habits and skills because of its informal nature. It is always prudent to keep in mind the safety practices listed in Figure 11–2.

Many email programs now contain spelling and grammar checkers. If this is not the case with the one that your students are using, they might want to compose their communication offline on a word processor, following guidelines for grammar and spelling, then copy and paste their message into the message area of the email program. Figure 11–3 reviews email etiquette (called netiquette!) users should follow.

Email Discussion Groups (LISTSERVs)

Email discussion groups are sometimes called *mailing lists* or **LISTSERVs**™ which is a trademarked brand of email discussion group software that can only be legally used when the email discussion group runs on that software). An email discussion group is an automated mailing list that accepts incoming messages from a person whose email address is on a master mailing list and forwards it to all of the other email addresses on the master list.

The process of adding your email address to an email discussion group is called *subscribing*. Email discussion groups develop around common interests (e.g., Shakespeare,

Figure 11–1 Email addresses
Examine the parts of an Internet e-mail address

rpforcier@aol.com

user id   service provider   commercial
           (subdomain)   (Internet domain)

don.descy@mnsu.edu

user id   university computer   education
          (subdomain)   (Internet domain)

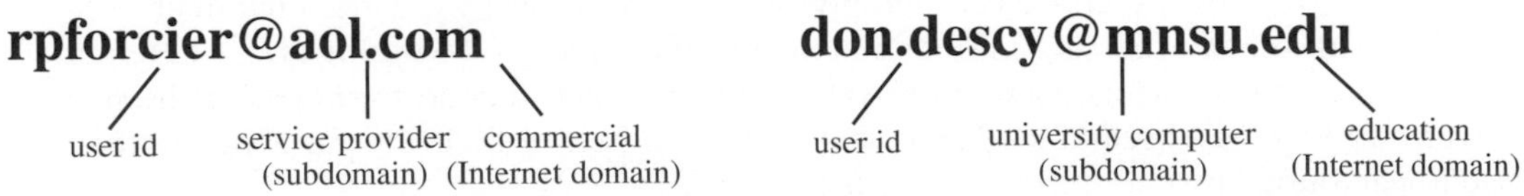

Figure 11–2 Safety practices

Keep in mind these email safety practices

- Email is not private. Write only what you would not mind others reading.

- Email written on school or business computers may be the property of that school or business.

- Many times so-called deleted email is not deleted, but is still on the hard drive or backed up and stored by the network or service provider.

- Place only general information in your email signature. Personal information such as home phone or home address should be avoided.

- If you receive unsolicited advertisements, chain letters, junk mail (called Spam), do not reply to ask to be taken off their mailing list. You are telling the Spamer that your mail account is active and your reply message may lead to even more Spam.

- Choose a password that is easy to remember but difficult to link to you.

- Never give your email password to others.

A copy of these guidelines may be found in the Guidelines folder in the Take-Along CD

Figure 11–3 Netiquette

Some email etiquette

NETIQUETTE

- Compose all but brief messages offline to minimize network traffic.
- Limit each message to one topic and keep it succinct.
- Use subject headings that are descriptive.
- Reply promptly to messages received.
- When replying, restate only enough of the message to clearly identify context.
- Treat email to you as you would a regular mail letter. Do not forward it to others without the writer's permission.
- Delete messages once you have read them.
- Don't be vulgar or offensive.
- Don't attempt to represent yourself as someone you are not.
- Don't criticize ("flame") others on the network.
- Supply clues if you are intending to write using humor, irony, sarcasm, or emotion. Your intent may not be obvious to the reader. Using all uppercase in a word or phrase SHOUTS. Try :-) for a sideways smile or ;-) for a wink.
- Use a signature footer that includes name, school, and email address.
- Practice safe communications. Don't spread viruses! Check downloaded executable files.
- Consider yourself a guest on the system and behave accordingly.

A copy of these guidelines may be found in the Guidelines folder in the Take-Along CD

ESL, English teachers, Bedlington Terriers, or perhaps one for your own class). It is easy to join an email discussion group. In many cases it is just a matter of sending a message such as *subscribe* to the group address. Finding an interesting discussion group is the most difficult part. One large email discussion group directory, containing over 750,000 entries, is Catalist (*http://www.lsoft.com/catalist.html*). Catalist contains specific directions on how to subscribe and write to the discussion group of your choice. Other sites to check are Yahoo (*http://groups.yahoo.com*) and Google (*http://groups.google.com*).

Email discussion groups are usually run by a computer with no human help; therefore, you must follow the *subscribe* and *unsubscribe* procedures and directions on how to send messages and reply directly to others exactly. Many times it is a good idea to just *lurk*—read the messages and not respond—for a few weeks until you feel comfortable with the list and understand its purpose. Lurking is perfectly acceptable and is done by the vast majority of email discussion group members.

Email discussion groups are a wonderful place to gather information, keep current with happenings and news in your field, find answers to questions, and meet people with similar interests. When you ask a question on an email discussion group, you access the brains of hundreds of colleagues from all over the country and perhaps even the world. It is easy to set up your own discussion group for free for your club or organization. One such free site is *yahoogroups.com*.

A word of caution: Email discussion groups can easily generate 40 or 50 messages a day that have to be read, saved to disk, or deleted. You can imagine how many messages might be waiting for you after summer vacation if you don't know how to unsubscribe or temporarily stop your email discussion group mail before you leave. Join an email discussion group of interest, but don't oversubscribe to multiple groups. You will find that they require considerable time just to read or delete the messages.

Information and representative email discussion groups for educators can be found at the Companion Website *http://www.prenhall.com/forcier*

Internet Relay Chat

Internet Relay Chat (IRC) is a real-time public discussion. Individuals log on to a specific site or chat room and watch as others type in messages to other people who are also in the "room." A chat room does not exist as a physical room, but is a metaphor for the specific location on the host computer through which all of the messages for a particular group pass. The individual may join the conversation by typing in messages that will also be displayed on the screen for others in the room to read. It is also possible to hold a private conversation with another individual in the chat room. There are hundreds of chat rooms around the world covering a multitude of interests. Many of you, as college students, know of friends who spend hours in chat rooms every week. Many public schools limit student access to chat rooms, because of the inability to identify who the students are chatting with or what their intended purposes may be. Several screened chat rooms for teenagers can be found at Teen Chat Center (*http://www.teenchatcenter.com/*).

Instant Messaging

Instant messaging is like IRC, but it is carried on between two individuals or a small group using software that each person has on his or her computer. As one person types on the computer, the typing is also displayed on the recipient's computer. Individuals using cell phones and pagers can also join in the "conversation." Many instant messaging programs are available free online from such places as AOL/Netscape, Microsoft, and Yahoo. Along with conversation, photos, audio, and live web cams can be used with most programs. Interactive themed backgrounds are available in a variety of subjects including cartoons, movies, animals, and nature. Many programs allow the typist to take on the appearance or role of one of the characters in the theme. A survey released in November 2002 found that nearly 87 million people in the United States were using instant messaging (Anthony, 2002).

Blogs

A blog (short for weblog) is an online tool that allows an individual to keep an online journal. This journal may take the form of diary-like entries, commentary, poetry, novel, text, or whatever the blogger desires. There are many free sites on the Web where people can start and keep a blog (see, for example, *http://blogger.com* and *http:// blogspot.com*). Registration is easy and even people with a rudimentary knowledge of computers can maintain one. Some blogs allow readers to post questions and comments along with the commentary. They are ideal for discussion and collaboration. Some teachers use blogs to produce news-type programs and others post information and allow students to comment on the same page. Good general discussions about blogs and blogging in education are "Using Blogs to Integrate Technology in the Classroom," found at *http://www.glencoe.com/sec/teachingtoday/ educationupclose.phtml/47*, and "Blogs in Education," at *http://awd.cl.uh.edu/blog.*

WORLD WIDE WEB

Many people confuse the Internet with the **World Wide Web.** The Web can be defined as "a global hypertext system that uses the Internet as its transport mechanism" (Pfaffenberger, 2000). Just as a telephone line can carry conversation, FAX messages, television signals, and computer traffic, the Internet can carry email, instant messages, and web pages.

Before the introduction of the Web, the Internet was a text-based medium. Images and sounds could be transferred over the Internet, but only as separate files requiring special software to access or view them. You could only access words (like a page in a novel), no images of any kind. It was not like the brilliantly colored web pages of today.

Web pages are written in **HyperText Markup Language (HTML),** which tells the receiving computer how to display the page. The HTML code is plain English or English word abbreviations placed between brackets (< and >). Each code is called a tag. HTML code is quite easy to write, as illustrated later in the chapter.

You will notice later that all web page addresses start with "http." **HyperText Transfer Protocol (HTTP)** is the set of rules that govern how web pages are written, transferred, and displayed. HTTP assures web page creators following this protocol that their pages can be accessed, transferred, and displayed by everyone else following the same protocol.

The two pieces of software required to view a web page are web *server* software and web *browser* software. **Web server** software is located on a computer, called the host that contains the web pages. Server software is needed to access the web pages on the host computer and to transmit the web page over the Internet to other computers. Web server software is easy to set up and use. It must be placed on a computer with a permanent Internet address that can be left on at all times. Apache™, Microsoft IIS™, Sun Java System™, and Zeus™ are a few popular web server software packages. A **web browser** is software that runs on the user's machine, translates HTML code received from a remote web server, and displays the web page on the user's machine. Common popular browsers are Internet Explorer™, Netscape Navigator™, Apple Safari™, Firefox®, and Opera®. Web browser software must be on the receiving computer to receive and display the web page.

The World Wide Web consists of many websites, each having a unique address called a **Uniform Resource Locator (URL).** Each website contains at least one web page. The main page of a website is the one usually accessed first and is called its **home page.** A website may have a number of pages, each capable of displaying text, graphics, and dynamic links to other pages, sites, sounds (audio), or movies (video).

Mosaic™ was the first graphic browser. A graphic browser displays pictures, backgrounds, and so forth, along with the text. Netscape Navigator™ was derived from Mosaic™. Microsoft Internet Explorer™ is the most popular web browser in use today.

Apple Safari™, first released in 2003, is designed to make full use of the new Macintosh OS X operating system.

Internet Explorer™ allows users to create a list of **favorites,** to hold sites that are visited frequently. Favorites, in fact, become a personalized directory of favorite web pages. The Favorites file is saved on the computer as an individual file that can be transferred electronically to another computer and then used to call up the website on the new computer. Remember that when we purchase a new computer, you just have to transfer your Favorites file from the old computer to the new one. The Help menu on the browser should explain how to perform this task. In addition, the entire set of favorites for a given computer can be saved as an HTML file that can be opened and viewed as a document in another computer's browser, complete with the individual favorites linked to the URLs. Educators can utilize these capabilities to provide for Internet-based lessons, with students directed to specific Web locations in the order desired by the instructor.

Netscape Navigator™ is another popular web browser. It also allows the user to save favorite sites in a file called **Bookmarks.** Recent versions of Netscape *Navigator*™ include an **HTML editor** to assist the user in creating or modifying web pages, as well as providing annotations for a bookmarks page. The editor is called *Communicator*™ and is accessed through the Window menu at the top of the screen. This is a great free tool for students to learn how to make their own web pages. Versions of the *Explorer*™ and *Netscape*™ browsers are available for both the Windows and Macintosh platforms. Apple released a web browser called *Safari* in 2003 that is claimed to be the fastest browser for the Macintosh.

Features common to most web browsers include the ability to print out the web page, giving students the means to capture information from the Web. This print capability is important in a classroom or media center setting, where there are many students yet fewer computers with Internet connections, because it allows students to progressively get online, download some information, then free up the computer for another student.

An even more efficient feature is the ability of most browsers to copy both text and images to temporary memory and save the pages to disk. This is usually accomplished by highlighting the text desired and then using the Edit . . . Copy command to place the text in temporary (RAM) memory, and then using the Edit . . . Paste command to place the text into, for instance, a word processing document or email message. Images can also be copied into memory or saved to disk by simply pressing down the right mouse button on Windows computers as the pointer rests on the image (pressing the mouse button on the Macintosh will do the same thing). It is also possible to simply drag images off a web page and into an open file such as a Word document or PowerPoint presentation. Items posted on the Web are automatically owned (copyrighted) by the person who posts them, providing they were not taken illegally from somewhere else. Students should always properly cite their Web sources, using the appropriate electronic citation style (see later in the chapter). These styles usually include the name and address of the website, the author(s), the date of posting or revision, and the date the site was accessed by the student. Most web browsers also include a mail and instant messaging function.

Uniform Resource Locator

The World Wide Web is a disjointed array of billions of web pages located on web servers all over the world. Even though these pages are scattered randomly, it is possible to access many of them (except some military, government, and commercial web pages for obvious reasons), because every web page has a unique URL. Typing the web pages' unique URL in the proper location in a browser sends the browser off to that location to retrieve the web page. The browser connects with the web server only long enough to retrieve the web page. It then frees the web server to serve the page to other individuals. Parts of the web page are stored in the browser on the computer in a storage area (file) called the **cache.** This speeds up the next loading of the page by using the information stored in the cache rather than retrieving it from the distant computer again. The parts of a URL are explained in Figure 11–4. It is imperative that the user types in the URL exactly, noting the use of either upper or lowercase letters in the URL to the right of the single slash following the name of the host computer, along with the use and placement of characters such as the colon, slash, period, tilde, and underscore.

Searching the Web

As stated earlier, several billion web pages are scattered on computers all over the world. Think of the volumes of information available with just a few taps on the keyboard. All you need to know is the URL of the page you want.

Unfortunately it is not that easy, because there is no master list to go to just look up the URL. This is why we rely on search engines. In November 2005 alone, 5.1 billion searches were made (Sullivan, 2006). According to data gathered by Notess (2000), Fast™, the largest search engine, had a database of 300 million URLs. Today, the largest is Google™ with well over 3 billion URLs (Notess, 2002). That may sound impressive, but Notess found that over 22 percent of these URLs are dead (no longer accessible) and up to 25 percent are listed in the database but not yet cataloged or described.

So what are we going to do? First, we keep our own record of URLs. Many times a bookmark file in our browser is not enough. It may soon become overcrowded and unmanageable. We can use file cards or lists created with a word processor. Better yet, we can create a computer database file of our favorite URLs identified by type or category. Reading professional magazines, we make note of any useful URLs. We also ask our colleagues for their favorite URLs.

Search tools are various software programs located on the Internet designed to make finding information on the Internet easier. The two basic categories of search tools are search engines and directories. **Search engines** index the contents of websites using words contained on the site and allow the user to search for information based on a set of search criteria, including keywords and logical connectors (e.g., AND, OR, NOT). **Directories,** or catalogs (subject directories, subject guides, and specialized databases), are organized by subject areas. Search tools do not go out and actively search the Web for us each time we type in a key word. This would be time consuming and difficult to do. If this were the case, the search tool would have to search all of the millions of computers on the Web to find accessible web pages and then search all of these pages for the key word(s) as typed.

Figure 11–4 Uniform Resource Locator (URL)

Examine the component parts of a URL

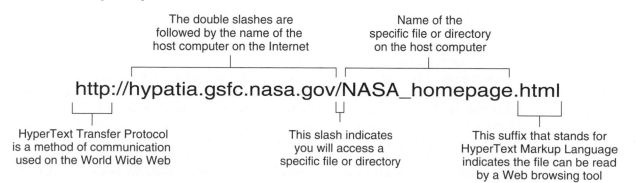

The double slashes are followed by the name of the host computer on the Internet

Name of the specific file or directory on the host computer

http://hypatia.gsfc.nasa.gov/NASA_homepage.html

HyperText Transfer Protocol is a method of communication used on the World Wide Web

This slash indicates you will access a specific file or directory

This suffix that stands for HyperText Markup Language indicates the file can be read by a Web browsing tool

Rather, each search tool relies on a database of websites that they have previously cataloged from the Web. Websites listed in *subject directories* such as Yahoo™ are usually hand selected by reviews and editors and carefully arranged into subject categories. Search engines, on the other hand, utilize software programs, called **spiders** or **robots,** that travel the Web usually by following links on known pages, adding new pages and key words at every step of the way. This finding and cataloging process goes on with little human interaction. Even with all of this, only a total of about 20 percent of the Web is cataloged in all of the search engines and directories around the world combined!

The process of searching is fundamentally similar to that used to search through databases or in online library catalogs. That is, the user enters a search term, and then the directory or search engine looks through its database of Internet sites for the best matches. We should caution you not to just look at the first matches, or hits, because some search engines and directories may list paid sites first.

Directories such as Yahoo™ (*http://www.yahoo.com*) provide additional categories and subcategories of information to assist in narrowing the search. Search engines such as Google™ (*http://www.google.com*) search web pages in their database for a match with any of the words posted on these pages and rely on logical connectors, as well as other qualifiers, to narrow the search. Meta search engines, such as MetaCrawler and DogPile, search other search engines. For example, MetaCrawler (*http://www.metacrawler.com*) searches About.com, Jeeves, Yahoo! Search, Fast, MSN, Google, MIVA, Looksmart, Open-Directory, Overture, and Sprinks simultaneously. There are even specialized meta search engines such as Family Friendly Search (*http://familyfriendlysearch.com*) and GoFish (*http://gofish.com*). Family Friendly Search searches only safe sites for kids such as Yahooligans, AOL Kids, Kids Click, and Saluki Search. GoFish specializes in searching for media, especially videos.

At first glance, it would seem that meta search engines are the ones to use. Unfortunately, they are superficial (see Figure 11–5), barely finding 10 percent of key word citations from each search engine visited (UC Berkeley Library, 2006). Only about 40 percent of the results found in one search engine may be unique to that search engine. About 60 percent will overlap with results of other searches.

When searching, keep in mind two basic rules: (1) *Don't limit* your search to a favorite search engine or directory. Always use several engines and directories for each of your searches. (2) Read the information on how to use that particular search engine or directory. Each search tool uses a slightly different method to search its database.

With so many web pages in the world, it can be difficult to find the right one. Note in Figure 11–5 the number of hits that a simple search using the key word phrase *lesson plans* found.

Interestingly, MetaCrawler™ was searched five times in rapid succession and produced 77, 69, 89, 85, and 66 hits! Adding the search terms *elementary* and *civil war* reduced the number of hits. Unfortunately, the number of hits was still staggering for the most part. Each of these particular search tools are programmed to list their results by relevance, though some had business sites listed near the top. The terms *lesson plans* and *civil war* were grouped by quotation marks so they would be interpreted by the search tool as one term. We entered "*lesson plans*" *elementary* "*civil war*" in the search box in each tool. The order of our three terms did not matter.

It is important to look at sites deeper into the list and not just on the first page. It is also important to use several search tools. It is interesting to note that the four meta search tools had the fewest hits even though they advertise that they use several search tools in each search. The meta search tool Mamma™ found only 32 sites through Google™. Using the same terms, Google™ by itself found 996,000!

Teaching search strategies to students will pay off in a more efficient use of their time while online and will give them experience in the logical cognitive process of defining

Figure 11–5 Search results

Examine the wide variation of results among popular search tools

Search Tool	"lesson plans"	"lesson plans" elementary "civil war"
AllTheWeb	11,200,000	88,200
AltaVista	11,700,000	108,000
Ask	5,932,000	24,100
Earthlink	3,330,000	63,000
Google	56,700,000	996,000
Lycos	5,932,000	24,100
MSN	2,952,653	39,630
My Way	5,932,000	24,100
Meta search tool		
DogPile	89	73
Mamma	72	32
MetaCrawler	89	81
Vivisimo	10,054,446	517,787

and narrowing a search for information. Never do a search for the first time in class or hand out a search assignment that you have not rechecked within the past 24 hours. There are many sites on the Web that you would not want your students to stumble into or have them tell their parents that you stumbled into. It is not uncommon for you to do a search on a term one day and find good sites and a few days later do the same search and find inappropriate sites.

The Invisible Web

The *visible web* is that part of the Web that is searchable by regular search engines. The **invisible web,** in contrast, is unable to be searched by regular search engines.

Most of the invisible web consists of thousands of specialized *searchable databases* that can be searched via the Web. BrightPlanet™, a research company specializing in searching the invisible web, estimates that the invisible web with its over 350,000 specialized databases is 500 times larger than the visible web (Bergman, 2003). Since the largest search engines such as Google™ or NorthernLight™ index no more than 16 percent of the visible web, we are only searching 0.03 percent of the Web or one in 3,000 pages that are really there (BrightPlanet, 2001). If you can search for books in a college library, you are searching one of these databases. Along with library holdings, other databases include newspapers and other publications, museums, medical information, yellow pages, classified listings, job databases, travel schedules, shopping, auctions, and many other specialized listings.

These databases construct the web page with your results on the fly after you type in the search terms. The page you will see does not exist until after you press Enter. At that time, the computer searches for what you are looking for and constructs a web page with the results. This page is called a *dynamic web page,* as opposed to a *static web page* that already exists.

The second group of web pages that comprise the invisible web are *excluded pages.* These are pages that web search engines are not programmed to search or the search engine owner does not want it to search for some reason. Pages are usually excluded because of format. Examples of excluded formats include PDF, Flash, Shockwave, Word,

WordPerfect, and PowerPoint. Google and a few other search engines have reprogrammed their spiders over the last few years to capture and catalog several of these formats including PDF and Word documents. Pages may also be excluded if the page contains script-based commands. Script is a programming language. You can tell a script-based page if the URL contains a question mark.

How do we find information that is held in the invisible Web? As you may have noticed as you read descriptions of the previous database, Web pages like yahoo.com have links to some of these at the bottom of the pages. Jobs, airline schedules, auctions, and people are just a few that they list. You can also enter the search term *invisible web* into a search engine. Many of the hits will contain lists of invisible but searchable databases.

Due to the character of the Internet, we should have definite rules in place to follow when students are searching online. Consider the following.

Online Search Rules

1. Require students to have specific search objectives in mind. Never give students free time to just "surf the Web."
2. Always presearch the Web using keywords and phrases that the students may use.
3. Require students to write full citations of any sites that they use in reports or presentations.
4. Require a bibliography including citations for all pictures, diagrams, sounds, and movies.
5. Do not send all of your students to view the same site at the same time.
6. Always reexamine sites you will show in class beforehand as close to class time as possible. Have a list of alternate sites on hand.
7. Require students to cross-reference information using another medium (e.g., print) when possible to help ensure accuracy.

Filtered Search Engines

Several search engines offer filtered search modes, but each one is a little different. Some allow users to set and password protect the filtering parameters. To invoke the filter option on the Google search engine, click on "Preferences" to the right of the box where you input the search term. The Google Preferences page will appear. Scroll down to "Safesearch Filtering" and choose the mode you would like. It is a good idea to set all of the computers in the classroom to this option. REMEMBER: No Internet filtering device is perfect. Some good sites may be filtered out and some inappropriate sites may not be filtered. Yahooligans! (Figure 11–6) is a student-friendly website for kids to use for searching. Other safe search sites include *Onekey the Kid Safe Search Engine*® (*http://onekey.com*) and *Ask for Kids*® (*http://www.askforkids.com*).

Citations

Once information is found on the Internet, it should be cited appropriately. Users of the American Psychological Association (APA) style can find current, general information in *Electronic References* Formats Recommended by the *American Psychological Association* at *http://www.apastyle.org/elecref.html.* The citation form varies for information retrieved from the Web, online chats, email discussion groups, email, online databases, and online encyclopedias. The basic form of APA citations for the Web contains the same format used for a print source with the Web information placed in a statement at the end of the reference.

Figure 11–6 Yahooligans!
This is a great place for young students to start their search (*http://www.kids.yahoo.com/reference*)

Author, A. A. (2006). *Title of work.* Retrieved month day, year, from source.

Using the above as an example:

American Psychological Association. (2001). *General form for electronic references.* Retrieved June 19, 2006, from *http://www.apastyle.org/elecgeneral.html.*

Users of the Modern Language Association (MLA) style can find current, general information on the MLA website in the frequently asked questions section. The basic form of MLA citation for the Web is as follows:

Author's last name, Full first name. "Document title." *Title of complete work* Date of publication/last revision/site update. Organization or publisher. Date visited.

Using the above as an example:

Johnson, William T. "How shall we know what is Correct?" *Let's Think about Nature May* 17, 2005. June 27, 2006 <*http://sunrise.com/ethics/98767*>.

Figure 11–7 illustrates both APA and MLA citation styles for information found on Kathy Schrock's Guide for Educators website.

349

Figure 11–7 APA and MLA
Compare the two citation styles

APA Style:
> Schrock, K. (1995, June 1). *Kathy Schrock's guide for educators.*
> Retrieved Month Day, Year from
> http://www.school.discovery.com/schrockguide/

MLA Style:
> Schrock, Kathleen. <u>Kathy Schrock's Guide for Educators.</u> 1
> June 1995. Day Month Year Accessed
> <http://www.school.discovery.com/schrockguide/>.

Because the Internet is relatively new, citations are in a state of flux. You may want to check the previous sites or the University of Iowa Guide to Citation Guides site edited by Karla Tonella (*http://bailiwick.lib.uiowa.edu/journalism/cite.html*) for any changes in APA or MLA style.

Evaluating Web Information

Media literacy applies as much to the Internet as to any other medium, such as television or print. Once information has been located, students should have the opportunity to develop skills in evaluating the accuracy of the information, as well as the way it is displayed on the Internet site in order to become critical readers of web pages. A teacher-generated checklist, similar to that suggested in Figure 11–8, containing a few simple criteria can assist the students in evaluating a website.

Figure 11–9 contains a rather sophisticated set of guidelines to evaluate online resources. No list of evaluation guidelines is ever complete and no list contains the one thing to look out for. It is possible for the average website developer to develop a site that passes all of the evaluation guidelines. It is imperative that we teach students to check several sources both on the Web and in print from the library when collecting information for a class or for personal use.

Several excellent sites on the Internet provide examples of evaluation devices and strategies. Figure 11–10 lists site links generated by the Washington (State) Library Media Association, and all sites can be accessed through here. Web page locations sometimes change over time. See if you can search the Web to find the correct URL for each site listed!

Students might also wish to download and save text or graphics and then integrate that information into a report or web page. This raises the issue of copyright of electronic information. Students should realize that information, graphics, sounds, and videos posted on the Web are copyrighted just by the act of putting it there. They should always act under the premise that this information is owned by someone else. This may even be the case at some sites that archive graphics, clip art, sounds, and video. It is not unusual to find such things as the Nike™ swish or the Coca Cola™ logo posted at these sites. Usually, properly cited text or graphics, which are utilized for educational purposes and not redistributed for profit, fall within the "fair use" guidelines of copyright law. Students need to understand that information carries the ownership of the individual or group of persons that originated it, even when it is posted on the Internet. Citation styles have been previously discussed, but it is especially important to note the URL where the information was obtained, along with the author's name if available.

More information on evaluating websites can be found at the Companion Website *http://www.prenhall.com/forcier-descy*

Figure 11–8 **Evaluation checklist**

Evaluating Websites		
URL of the web page: http://		
Does the page load quickly into your computer?	YES	NO
Do the pictures contribute useful information?	YES	NO
Do headings divide the page?	YES	NO
If so, are the headings helpful?	YES	NO
Does the page contain the author's name?	YES	NO
Does it have the author's email address?	YES	NO
Is the information current?	YES	NO
Do you detect a particular bias in the information?	YES	NO
Was the information useful to you?	YES	NO
When was the page created?		
When was it last updated?		

Comments: Describe how you feel about this site. Was it valuable to you? Discuss its appearance and the quality of the information.

_____
_____
_____
_____
_____
_____
_____

WEB PAGE CONSTRUCTION

A favorite activity of students in many schools around the country is the design and construction of one or a series of web pages. At first, the predominant student page was one devoted to the students. Teachers seem to be moving away from that activity and using their students' time more productively. They are using web design and construction as a means of knowledge transfer from their class and students to the world (see WebQuests in this section). Rather than posting personal pages, students and groups of students are posting projects, term papers, and their own research on the Web. Making a WebQuest is a wonderful way to start your students.

Figure 11–9 Evaluation guidelines
Guidelines for evaluating Internet resources
(Adapted from Descy. [1996, February]. Tech Trends. Copyright 1996 by the Association for
Educational Communications and Technology. *(Reprinted with permission.)*

Guidelines for Evaluating Internet-based Resources

Author: Who are the authors in the field? Does this author list any affiliations? Is there a "mail-to" or an e-mail address included? Have you tried to find other information about this author by searching *Who's Who in Education*, Educational Resources Information Center (ERIC), *Journals in Education (JIE)*, or *Current Index to Journals in Education (CIJE)?* Is the author the creator of the information or a compiler of other information resources? Can you find a personal home page or a campus listing for this author?

Producer: Is the producer/affiliation of the page clearly noted? Was it produced by an organization? Is it a well-known professional organization or is it a relative unknown? Are the members professionals, advocates, or consumers? Does this organization have an inherent bias? Is there a way to contact the producer?

Site: Is the URL clearly noted? What is the ending suffix (.edu, .com, .org, .net, and so forth)? Can you find out where it is located? Does it seem to make sense that a producer such as this one would reside on a site such as this?

Publication: Is it a single page or part of a series? Is the remainder of the series by the same author, a collection of authors, or an organization? Is it an abstract or the full text of an article or presentation? Where was the article published or the presentation given? Was is published by or presented at a nationally known organization or conference?

Purpose: What was the purpose of the document? Was it designed to inform others of new research, summarize existing research, advocate a position, or stimulate discussion?

Date of publication: When was the page placed on the Internet? When was it updated?

Arrangement: How difficult was it to find information related to the six guidelines presented earlier in the chapter? Was the information clearly presented in a conspicuous place or was it missing altogether?

Intended audience: Who is the intended audience of this page (professionals, advocates, consumers, and so on)? Would the intended audience change the scope or slant of the information?

Coverage: Does the page cover the information that you need? Does the page include links to other references or backup information? Does the page itself contain substantive information or is it simply a collection of links to other sources?

Writing style/reasoning: Is the information presented in a thoughtful, orderly, well-reasoned manner? Does the information appear to be well researched? Are assumptions and conclusions well documented? Is the information presented as fact or opinion? Can you detect any bias? Do the words used tend to evoke strong emotions?

References: Is the page well documented? Are there links to any primary sources? Is the page referenced to information on the same server or to servers at different sites? How current or relevant are the references?

Hypertext Markup Language

Until just a few years ago, Web construction was done by hand using the markup language HTML. As discussed earlier in the chapter, HTML is a series of tags (enclosed in brackets < >) that tells the browser (Internet Explorer™, Netscape™, etc.) how to display the page on the computer screen. Second or third grade students can produce a web page using HTML code in under an hour. Just as an English teacher might place a ¶ "tag" in your paper to tell you to start a new paragraph, the <br> tag tells the browser to stop displaying the text on a particular line and start displaying the text again on the following line. When you redo your paper you will start a new paragraph where the teacher wants, and not write

Figure 11–10 A reference to evaluation guides

Adapted from Evaluating Websites on the Washington Library Media Association website
www.wlma.org/instruction/evalweb.htm

Evaluating Websites

Evaluation Guides

Evaluation of Information Sources -This page by Alistair Smith contains pointers to criteria for evaluating information resources, particularly those on the Internet. It is intended to be particularly useful to librarians and others who are selecting sites to include in an information resource guide, or informing users as to the qualities they should use in evaluating Internet information.

Evaluating Information Resources, Marquette University - Here are points to consider when evaluating the appropriateness, value and reliability of information sources.

Criteria for Evaluating Information Resources, USC University Libraries - Before beginning to use any new information resource, whether print, online, or Web-based, take a few moments to examine it and ask yourself the following questions. You will make better use of information resources if you do so.

Kathy Schrock's Web Evaluation Surveys -This excellent site gives some survey information to help you evaluate Web sites and think critically about them.

Web Evaluation Form, by Dr. Nancy Everhart - This form provides evaluation activities for looking at web sites. There is a rating scale for currency, content, authority, ease of navigation, experience, graphics, sound & video, treatment, and access.

Teaching Critical Evaluation Skills for World Wide Web Resources - This set of Web pages provides materials to assist in teaching how to evaluate the informational content of Web resources. It focuses on teaching how to develop critical thinking skills which can be applied to evaluating information found on Web pages. Includes a great Powerpoint Presentation. The useful examples page is located at http://www2.widener.edu/Wolfgram-Memorial-Library/webevaluation/examples.htm

Thinking Critically about World Wide Web Resources - The World Wide Web has a lot to offer, but not all sources are equally valuable or reliable. Here are some points to consider, written by Esther Grassian, UCLA College Library.

UCLA College Library Instruction: Hoax? Scholarly Research? Personal Opinion? You Decide! - How critical an observer are you? Learn how to evaluate information sources by doing the following exercise.

---

in the ¶ tag on the paper. In the same way, the browser will break the text at the tag, but not display the <br> tag on the screen.

The following are commonly used tags:

 	tells the browser to stop displaying the text, go to the next line, and start displaying the text again
<p>	tells the browser to insert a blank line
<center>	forces the browser to center all text and graphics entered after the tag
</center>	stops the browser from centering text, graphics, etc; in this case <center> and </center> are paired tags; one tag <center> starts the display (centered text) and the second </center> stops it
<I> and </I>	(also paired tags) instruct the browser to start printing in italics (<I>) and stop printing in italics.</I>
<B> and </B>	turn on and off bold type
<U> and </U>	turn on and off underlining

HTML editors now do all of the tagging. Web pages can vary greatly in layout and content, but they all include some standard HTML tags, regardless if they are written by hand

Figure 11–11 A quick web page
A web page generated by the preceding text and HTML tags

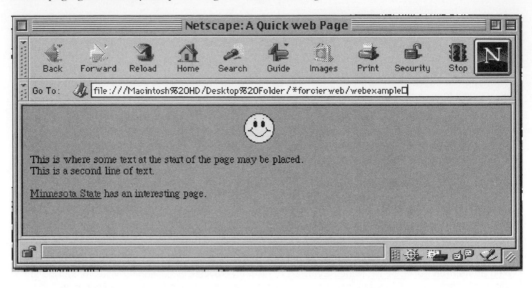

```
<html>
<head>
<title> A Quick web Page</title>
</head>
<body>
<center><img src="smileface.gif"></center>
<p>
This is where some text at the start of the page may be placed.
<br>
This is a second line of text.
<p>
<a href="http://www.mankato.msus.edu">Minnesota State</a> has an interesting
page.
</body>
</html>
```

or by an HTML editor. Read the following text and tags, then look at the rather simple web page they generate in Figure 11–11.

Now let us examine what each of the HTML tags does. (Words in parentheses are comments to help you understand the page and should not be included unless you want them displayed on the page.)

<html>	This tag tells the browser that this page is written in HTML.
<head>	This tag tells the browser that the following information is not to be displayed on the web page itself.
<title>	A Quick web Page</title> This set of tags places the page name at the top of the browser in the title bar.
</head>	This tag tells the browser that we don't want to add anything more to this section.

`<body>`	Everything that follows will be displayed on the web page itself.
`<center>`	Center everything that follows.
`<img src="smileface.gif">`	Find the image called smileface.gif and display it here.
`</center>`	Stop centering.
`<p>`	Insert a blank line.
	"This is where some text at the start of the page may be placed." (this is our text)
` `	Stop displaying the text and move down one line before it displays anything again.
	"This is a second line of text." (more text)
`<p>`	Insert a blank line.
`<a href="`*http://www.mankato.msus.edu*`">`	(This tag tells the browser that a link follows this tag and when it is clicked, to find and display the page listed in this tag.) "Minnesota State" (This text will be our link.)
`</a>`	This tag tells the browser that we are at the end of the link and will resume regular text.
	"has an interesting page." (text)
`</body>`	End of the web page display.
`</html>`	This tag tells the browser that we are finished displaying our HTML document.

Many of the tags are paired. `<a href= . . . .>` starts a link to another web page using its URL (*http://www.mankato.msus.edu*) and the `</a>` tag ends the link. `<center>` starts centering what follows, `</center>` stops the centering, and so forth. Single tags include `<br>` to break a line of text and `<img src="smileface.gif">` referring to a graphic image source (named "smileface.gif") to be placed in that location.

One approach to teaching web page design is to send students, via either email or a text editing document, this set of commands as a boilerplate upon which to build their own page. Of course, there are many other refinements that may be added, and there are some excellent online HTML tutorials on the Web.

"I don't have to know anything about tags," you may say. "HTML editors do all of this for me!" We showed you this example because it is important to have an idea of the underlying structure of HTML. It may be helpful to review a book or online site on the subject before you teach website construction to your students, though you will undoubtedly use an HTML editor and not handwritten HTML tags. By understanding the basic HTML tags, it will help you troubleshoot student web pages and alleviate your fear of the unknown.

HTML Editors

There are three general categories of HTML editors. Some of them are designed specifically for that purpose, such as *Microsoft FrontPage*™. Others are included in regular word processing programs, such as *Microsoft Word*™, and still others are free software that can be downloaded from the Web as part of a browser package, such as *Netscape Composer*™. HTML editors all work about the same and if you have ever made a word processing document into which you have added graphics, you really know all of the basics. Developing a word processing document and making a web page are similar processes. You simply type on the page using the menu found at the top (similar to a word processing menu) to change the font, font size, font color, and other attributes (bold, underline, italics, etc.). Graphics are added in the same way as you add graphics to any word processing document. Figure 11–12 shows the top and bottom menus for the free HTML editor Netscape Composer™. We have pancaked the figure so only these menus are visible.

Figure 11–12 Netscape composer menus

Top and bottom menus on Netscape composer

Figure 11–13 FrontPage® top menus

Notice the similarity to Microsoft Word's menu

Look at the top menu line in Figure 11–12. Starting from the left, we can see the following buttons: new page, open file, save file, publish (sends the page to a predetermined website), browse (light gray) (opens up Navigator™ and shows web page), print page, spell check, insert image, insert table, make link (from highlighted text or image). The second menu from the top has the following buttons: body text (puts in preformatted styles such as paragraph, headings, address, etc.), black box (click to choose text color) and white box (click to choose background color), light gray slash (click to choose text highlight color), −a (decreases text size), +a (increases text size), B (bold text), *I* (italic text), U (underline text), bulleted list, numbered list, move text to left, move text to right, align left, align center, align right, justify.

The second menu from the bottom from left to right: display as working page (this is where you construct the page), show working page with tag icons, show HTML tags and show page as it would look in a Web browser. The very bottom menu is used to navigate around Netscape and is not needed to compose a web page. The icons are from left to right: display Netscape, display mail and newsgroups, display instant messaging, display composer, and display address book. Figure 11–13 shows the top menus for Microsoft FrontPage. If you have used Microsoft Word™, notice how similar it is to FrontPage™ menus and Netscape Communicator™ menus (Figure 11–12).

Before starting the web page construction tutorial, we searched Google.com for clip art and backgrounds. One site had both (*http://www.hellasmultimedia.com/webimages*). Here we found the images, clip art, backgrounds, and lines that we wanted to use in our example. We placed the mouse cursor over the image we wanted to download, held down the right mouse button, and a menu appeared. (On some Macs you only press on the mouse button; on other Macs you have to press the Control key and the mouse button at the same time.) We chose "Download Image to Disk" (some browsers may say something like "Download Image" or "Save Image As") and downloaded the images to a folder on the hard drive. The images we used are shown in Figure 11–14.

Now we want to use the one on the upper right in Figure 11–14, but before we do, let's talk about background images. Unless we have an image that will completely fill

Figure 11–14 Backgrounds, lines, and clip art used in our example

Images downloaded from *http://bellasmultimedia.com/webimages*

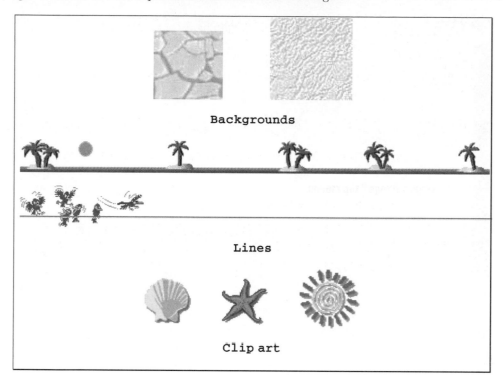

the background of the page, like an image of your school seal, we place a small image in the background and the browser automatically tiles it across and down the page. If we place the left background image (the one that looks like a dozen or so flat stones) on a web page, it will be tiled across and down the page to look like the background in Figure 11–15. In this example, you can see that it is the same little background image pattern used over and over again. Be careful, you may find this background too busy to use.

 **WORKING WITH MICROSOFT WORD®
TO CREATE A WEB PAGE**

As a classroom teacher, you may want to work with your students and create a web page for your class. If you have had no experience with HTML editors, *Microsoft Word®* is a good place to start since you probably already have access to the software. Understand that we are not advocating, by any means, Word as a preferred editor. Once you are comfortable with the concepts, you will want to use more sophisticated programs such as *Netscape Composer®* or *Microsoft FrontPage®*. We will now lead you through the process of creating a web page. To follow this tutorial, you must have access to Word®, part of the *Microsoft Office®* suite. You can download a trial copy from the *http://www.microsoft.com* website. Before beginning this tutorial, copy to your computer the folder *MS Word tutorial files* from the *Tutorials* folder on the *Take-Along CD*.

Figure 11–15 Background image

Small background images are tiled across and down the page

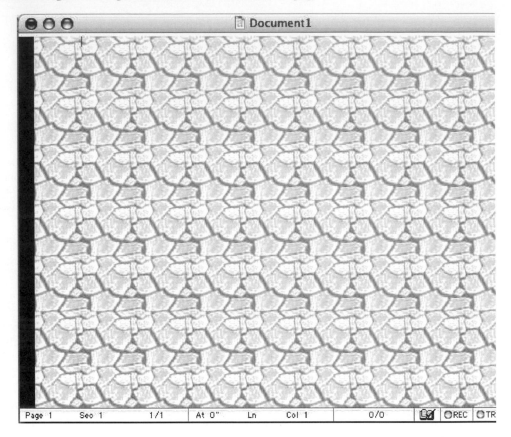

LET'S TRY IT!

A copy of this tutorial may be found in the Tutorials folder in the Take-Along CD

In working through this brief tutorial on creating a web page in *Microsoft Word*®, you will learn the following:

- How to make a web page using Microsoft Word.
- How to add text, backgrounds, hyperlinks, lines, and clip art to a Microsoft Word web page.
- How to save a Microsoft Word document as a web page.

NOTE: Once you have accessed Microsoft Word® and you copy the *MS Word Tutorial Files* folder from the *Tutorials >> MS Word Tutorial* folder on the *Take-Along CD* and save it to your computer, open Microsoft Word® and save the blank document as *mywebpage.doc*. As you progress, you should periodically save this document.

1. CREATE THE BACKGROUND

1.1 Select Format > Background

(From this box you could choose a color or fill effects.)

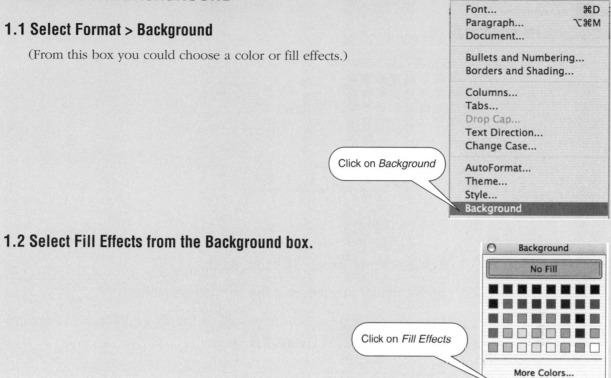

Click on *Background*

1.2 Select Fill Effects from the Background box.

Click on *Fill Effects*

1.3 Select Picture from the Fill Effects box.

(Notice the tabs allowing you to choose a gradient, texture, pattern or a picture.)

Select the background picture that you will be using for your web page called *Sand Background.gif* from the *MS Word Tutorial* folder.

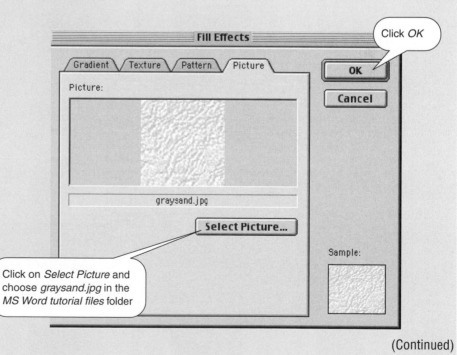

Click OK

Click on *Select Picture* and choose *graysand.jpg* in the *MS Word tutorial files* folder

(Continued)

1.4 Close the Background box.

Click on the *Close button*

Background

No Fill

More Colors...

Fill Effects...

2. TYPE THE TITLE

2.1 Choose the font Times, 36 point, Bold.

2.2 Choose Center aligned from the Formatting toolbar.

2.3 At the top of the page, where you see a blinking cursor, type Forcier and Descy and press the Return key twice.

3. INSERT A PICTURE

(Do not change Center align.)

3.1 Select Insert >> Picture >> From File.

(Choose the *birdsline.gif* file from the *MS Word Tutorial files* folder.)

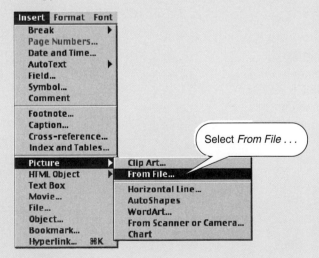

Select *From File . . .*

3.2 Click on the Insert button.

The *birdsline.gif* image will now appear on your Word document.

4. ADDING TEXT

4.1 Press the Return key twice.

4.2 Choose the font Times, 14 point, Bold.

4.3 Choose Left aligned from the Formatting toolbar.

In order to make your page to look like ours, type in the following text:

*Richard Forcier and Don Descy are co-authors of **The Computer as an Educational Tool: Productivity and Problem Solving.** This text is used by over 90 colleges and universities in the USA, Canada, Australia, Europe and the Middle East, making it one of the most popular computer utilization texts in the world.*

Select *birdsline.gif . . .*

FileMaker Tutorial	birdsline.gif
Microsoft Excel Tutorial	Sand Background.gif
MS Word tutorial files	seaisland.gif
Photoshop Elements Tutorial	seashell.gif
	starfish.gif
	sun.gif

. . . then click the *Insert* button

Cancel   Insert

5. ADDING A HYPERLINK

5.1 Highlight the title of the textbook in the paragraph you just typed.

5.2 From the Insert menu, select Hyperlink.

5.3 Type *http://www.prenhall.com/forcier* in the Link to: box at the top of the window and then click OK.

Insert Hyperlink

Link to: http://www.prenhall.com/forcier

Display: The Computer as an Educational Tool: Productivity and Problem Solving.

ScreenTip...

Web Page   Document   E-mail Address

Favorites   History   Launch Web Browser

Enter the Internet address (URL) of the Web page you want to link to. Click Favorites or History to link to a Web page you've visited before or visit frequently.

Anchor:

Locate...

If you want to link to a specific location (anchor) within the Web page, enter the name of the anchor above or click Locate to find it.

Cancel   OK

(Continued)

6. ADDING A SECOND LINE IMAGE

6.1 Place the cursor at the end of the text you wrote on your document and press Return twice.

6.2 Click the Center Align icon on the Formatting toolbar.

6.3 Follow the procedure previously described in step 3. This time choose the image titled seaisland.gif.

6.4 Press the Return key twice.

7. ADDING A TABLE

It is difficult to space images on a web page. Many times we can do this by creating a table and adding either pictures and/or text in the table boxes.

In this case, we want to space four images equally across the page. We also do not want the table to show, so we will make the table borderless. It is much easier than it seems. First, make sure your cursor is Center Aligned.

7.1 Select Table >> Insert >> Table.

The Insert Table window will then appear.

7.2 Change the Number of columns: to 4 and the Number of rows: to 1.

7.3 Now place the cursor in the first cell (make sure it is center aligned!) and insert the image seashell.gif as you previously did in step 3.

Repeat this procedure (remembering to always center align your cursor), inserting *starfish.gif* in the second cell, *sun.gif* in the third cell, and *seashell.gif* again in the last cell.

The table will appear as you see it here.

7.4 Once you have placed all of the images in the cells, click to the left of the table to highlight the entire table.

7.5 Press the small downward-facing triangle to the right of the Border icon. Click on the light gray box to make the table borderless.

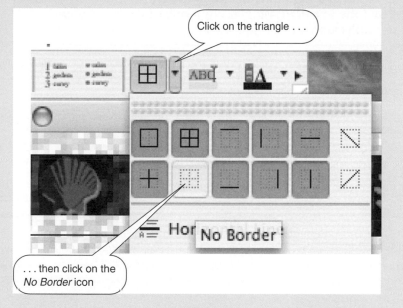

Click on the triangle . . .

. . . then click on the *No Border* icon

No Border

Notice that you can still see the faint gray outline of the table you inserted at the bottom of the page.

7.6 Save this document file one last time.

8. FINALLY, SAVE YOUR DOCUMENT AS A WEB PAGE

8.1 Select File >> Save as Web Page . . . Name this MyWebPage.htm

(The .htm extension lets your browser know that it is a web page.)
Notice that the table borders do not show in the Web page format.

(Continued)

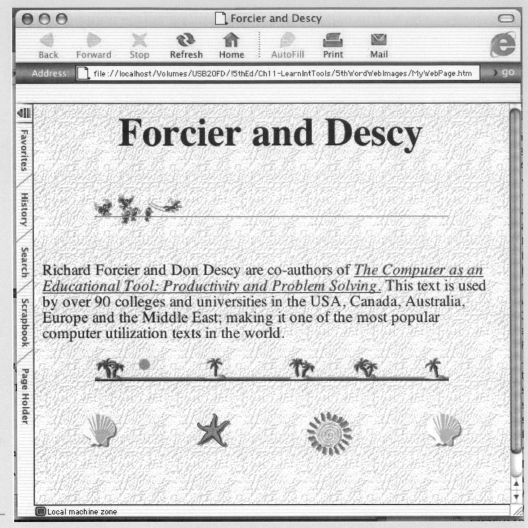

When you close the web page you have just built, notice that the computer has created a folder containing the images you have used along with the file of your web page.

Now that you have completed a web page with *Microsoft Word*®, we encourage you to follow the tutorial on using *Netscape Composer*®found on the *Take-Along* CD.

The major difference between a web page made with an HTML editor and a regular word processing document is something that goes on in the background. As we construct our web page using the HTML editor, the editor is also generating a whole other page containing all of the HTML tags needed to display the page on a browser the way we are constructing it. The HTML tags are also generated when we save our Word® document as a web page. Figure 11–16 shows the tags Netscape Composer® generated in the background as we developed a page for an earlier edition of the text. We are not showing the tags made when we saved our Word document as a web page, because many extra tags were generated that would have been distracting and difficult to understand.

You will also notice that tags written by the HTML editor, though similar, seem to be more confusing than in our handwritten example, because HTML editors add other tags that are not necessary to display the page on a browser. Pages made with HTML editors

Figure 11–16 HTML tags

Tags generated by a web page editor

```
Web page [file:/.../Web_page.html] - Composer

New      Open      Save   Publish   Browse   Print   Spell   Image   Table   Link

<!DOCTYPE html PUBLIC "-//W3C//DTD HTML 4.01 Transitional//EN">
<html>
<head>
  <title>Web page</title>

  <meta http-equiv="content-type"
 content="text/html; charset=ISO-8859-1">
</head>
  <body
 background="file:///Book%204/DED4th/Ch11Internet/4thimages/graysand.jpg">

<div align="center">
<h1>Forcier and Descy</h1>
 <img src="file:///Book%204/DED4th/Ch11Internet/4thimages/birdsline.gif"
 alt="birds on wire" width="582" height="47">
 <br>
 <br>

<div align="left">Richard Forcier and Don Descy are the co-authors of <i><a
 href="http://www.prenhall.com/forcier">The Computer as an Educational Tool:
Productivity and Problem Solving</a>.</i> It is currently in its 4th edition.
The third edition was used in over 60 colleges and universities in the USA,
Canada, Australia and Europe.<br>
 <br>

<div align="center"><img
 src="file:///Book%204/DED4th/Ch11Internet/4thimages/seaislandline.gif"
 alt="chain of Islands in the ocean" width="560" height="36">
 <br>

 Normal   TO Show All Tags   <HTML> Source   XX Preview

Done loading page
```

are said to be "dirty," because they contain these extra tags. We did not show tags produced by Microsoft Word as we saved our document as a Web page, because the tags generated are so dirty and confusing. Microsoft FrontPage™ adds so many of these extra tags that some web masters will not allow pages generated with this editor to be placed on their sites.

The fundamental approach is to begin publishing for the Web using a simple page and then to elaborate as your skills or content needs develop. Publishing on the Web is far more than just another mode of expression; it provides opportunities for interaction among individuals. A few words of caution: Because publishing on the Web is much like publishing in any other medium, the person or student group posting a web page is responsible for the accuracy of the content, which should be free of bias or at least with any biases clearly stated, and should have sources of information such as text and graphics accurately cited. It is also helpful to the viewer of the page to be able to see the name of the person who developed the page, the date on which the page was posted or last revised, and an email address so that the viewer could contact the developer directly. Unless there is good reason, students should not post their photographs and personal information such as complete names and addresses.

LET'S REVIEW

The Internet is a network of networks that spans the globe, serving hundreds of millions of users. The primary resources available are email, email discussion groups, IRC, blogs, and information posted on web pages. The World Wide Web is a global hypertext system that uses the Internet as its transport mechanism. HyperText Markup Language (HTML) provides the coding to display both text and graphics, along with dynamic links both within the document and to other external Internet sites. Each site also has its own Uniform Resource Locator (URL), or address.

Web browser software on the user's machine communicates with web server software at a remote site and receives images and HTML which it puts together to display the web page. Each web server has at least one HTML document, referred to as a web page. The main page of a website is the one usually accessed first and is called its home page.

Search engines are commonly employed to assist the user with the task of finding specific information on the Internet. The user enters a search term or terms, and then the search engine looks through its database of Internet sites for the best matches.

Publishing on the Web begins with a simple page and then elaborates as the user's skills or content needs develop. HTML editors and many word processing applications make it easy for anyone who can use a word processor to also construct a web page. The person or group posting a web page is responsible for using accurate content, free of bias, or at least with any biases clearly stated, and with sources of information such as text or graphics accurately cited.

LET'S PRACTICE

To complete the specified exercises online, go to the Chapter Exercises Module in Chapter 11 of the Companion Website.

1. Research the early history of the Internet. What was the original purpose? How has that changed?

2. Pick out a topic or theme that you wish to explore, and then compare several Internet search engines for their ease of use, cataloging of sites, speed of finding information, and use of logical terms to help narrow the search.

3. Design a form for students to use in evaluating Internet sites for content accuracy or completeness, currency of information, purpose of the site, authorship, date of posting or most recent revision, degree of interactivity, appropriate use of graphics, and useful links to related sites.

4. Using an HTML editor or word processing application, design your own class web page that includes a title, some text, two images, and a hyperlink to another web page.

5. Download demonstration copies of an Internet filtering software package such as CyberPatrol, NetNanny, or Surf Watcher. Compare claims about ease of operation, methods of filtering (e.g., key word), appropriate settings for use, and the relative completeness of filtering inappropriate sites. Would you recommend using one of these packages at your school? Defend your answer.

6. Some people are for and some are against Internet filter applications. Explore the issue, decide which point you seem to favor, and write a short paper defending the opposite view.

7. Team up with a group of students in your class. Have an equal number of groups design a lesson involving the Internet. Share these lessons with the class. Which approach do you prefer? Defend your position to the class.

8. List and discuss four or five ways you could involve your class in web design activities when you are a classroom teacher. What do you feel will be the barriers that might develop to hinder your plans?

9. In Chapter 4 we discussed equitable Internet access. List several ways that lack of Internet access might affect the quality of education in a school or district. Can you think of any ways to work around these problems? Discuss your thoughts with the class.

10. Review a site such as *http://city-mankato.us* or *http://centralpark-ny.us*. How can a ficticious site use this URL? Click on the advertisements. Are they real? How do you know? Is there any way a student would be able to tell that this is a ficticious site? What would students think if this town was located in a southern state?

PORTFOLIO DEVELOPMENT EXERCISES

To complete this exercise online, go to the Digital Portfolio Module in Chapter 11 of the Companion Website.

One of the NETS•S standards covered in this chapter was "Students use telecommunications to collaborate, publish, and interact with peers, experts, and other audiences" under *Category 4: Technology communications tools.* Begin to develop your own portfolio of lesson plans that demonstrates your ability to have your students reach the NETS•S standards.

1. Design a lesson plan activity for elementary, middle school, or high school students in which they interact with peers, experts, and other audiences. This should be a project that could involve individuals in other schools in this country and abroad. How would you go about facilitating this project? How would you go about finding other groups to participate in this project? This lesson should demonstrate that your students have achieved the standard. Be sure to include a system of evaluation for your students' understanding and competence to ensure that they have met this standard.

2. Adapt the lesson plan activity you developed in exercise 1 for students to evaluate each others' work.

GLOSSARY

bookmarks	A feature of web browser programs that allows the user to save and organize the URLs of desired Internet sites
cache	A web file storage area on the computer's hard disk
directories	Catalogs of Internet sites organized by subject areas
email	The electronic transfer of messages and files from one person's computer to another
email discussion group	A group of email addresses given a single name on a computer, sometimes called a *mailing list*
favorites	See *bookmarks*
home page	Usually the first web page accessed at a website, it often includes links to other web pages within that site or at other websites
HyperText Markup Language (HTML)	A programming language that allows the user to post a web document with text, graphics, and dynamic links to other websites
HTML editor	A program designed to streamline the process of building a web page through the automation of adding certain HTML code
HyperText Transfer Protocol (HTTP)	The format by which web documents are transferred over the Internet
Internet	A worldwide network of networks based on the TCP/IP
Internet Service Provider (ISP)	The organization or business that connects individually or group-owned computers to the Internet backbone
invisible Web	That part of the Web that is unable to be searched by regular search engines
LISTSERV™	A registered trademark for a particular brand of software used to create and run email discussion groups
robots	See *spiders*
search engines	Computer applications that automatically search web pages and store key words and text from each page
spiders	Programs used by search engines to travel the Web, usually by following links on known pages, to add new pages and key words at every step of the way
Transmission Control Protocol/ Internet Protocol (TCP/IP)	A set of standards developed to allow different networks to interconnect electronically
Uniform Resource Locator (URL)	The address of any site on the Internet, including gopher and the websites

web browser	Software that finds and displays web pages
web server	Software that allows web pages to be broadcast to the Web
World Wide Web	An Internet navigation system that allows users, through a graphic browser interface, to access information organized on hypertext-linked screens called pages

REFERENCES AND SUGGESTED READINGS

Anthony, T. (2002, December 24). 'IM here'—keeping in touch online. *The FreePress, 119*(222), 8C.

Bergman, M. K. (2003). *The deep web: Surfacing hidden value*. Retrieved online February 17, 2003, from *http://brightplanet.com/deepcontent/tutorials/DeepWeb/index.asp*.

BrightPlanet. (2001, February 22). *The deep web*. Retrieved online February 17, 2003, from *http://brightplanet.com/deepcontent/tutorials/DeepWeb/index.asp*.

Deal, N. (1995). Is the medium the message? Comparing student preconditions of teacher research via written on e-mail forms. Research report by EMERGING TECHNOLOGISTS, Lifelong learning, NECC'95

Descy, D. E. (1999, September). HTML editors: Web pages in minutes. *Tech Trends, 43*(4), 5–7.

Notess, G. R. (2002). *Search engine statistics: Database relative size*. Retrieved online January 19, 2000, from *http://www.notess.com/search/stats/size.html*.

Notess, G. R. (2000). *Search engine statistics: Database relative size*. Retrieved on line February, 21, 2003 from *http://www. searchengineshowdown.com/stats/ size.html*.

Pfaffenberger, B. (2000). *Webster's new world computer user's dictionary* 8th ed. New York: Macmillan.

Poftak, A. (2002, August). Net-wise teens: Safety, ethics, and innovation. *Technology & Learning, 25*(1), 36–49.

Reuters, (2006, April 25). *E-mail and spam clog computers*. Retrieved online May 16, 2006, from *http://www.msnbc.msn.com/id/12480457/*.

Sherman, C. (2005, March 23). *Metacrawlers and metasearch engines*. Retrieved online May 29, 2006, *from http://searchenginewatch.com/links/article. php/2156241*.

Sullivan, D. (2006, January 24). *Nielsen net ratings search engine ratings*. Retrieved online May 29, 2006, from *http://searchenginewatch.com/reports/article.php/2156451*.

Sullivan, D. (2005, January 28). *search engine sizes*. Retrieved online May 29, 2006, from *http://searchenginewatch.com/reports/article.php/2156481*.

UC Berkeley Library (2006). Meta-search engines. Retrieved online December 10, 2006 from *http://www.lib.Berkeley. edu/TeachingLib/Guides/EnteringMetaSearch.html*.

Internet Applications in Education

ADVANCE ORGANIZER

1. What kinds of resources are available on the Internet?

2. What is an acceptable use policy and why is it important for a school to have one?

3. How will filtering software affect many schools?

4. How can students evaluate materials found on the World Wide Web?

5. How can teachers incorporate both directed and exploratory learning styles using the Web?

6. What are examples of good Web-based learning activities?

7. How can instruction be delivered over the Internet?

I. Technology Operations and Concepts
   A. demonstrate introductory knowledge, skills, and understanding of concepts related to technology (as described in the ISTE National Education Technology Standards for Students)
   B. demonstrate continual growth in technology knowledge and skills to stay abreast of current and emerging technologies

II. Planning and designing learning environments and experiences
   A. design developmentally appropriate learning opportunities that apply technology-enhanced instructional strategies to support the diverse needs of learners
   C. identify and locate technology resources and evaluate them for accuracy and suitability

III. Teaching, learning, and the curriculum
   A. facilitate technology-enhanced experiences that address content standards and student technology standards
   B. use technology to support learner-centered strategies that address the diverse needs of students
   C. apply technology to develop students' higher order skills and creativity
   D. manage student learning activities in a technology-enhanced environment

IV. Assessment and evaluation
   B. use technology resources to collect and analyze data, interpret results, and communicate findings to improve instructional practice and maximize student learning

V. Productivity and professional practice
   C. apply technology to increase productivity
   D. use technology to communicate and collaborate with peers, parents, and the larger community in order to nurture student learning

VI. Social, ethical, legal, and human issues
   A. model and teach legal and ethical practice related to technology use
   B. apply technology resources to enable and empower learners with diverse backgrounds, characteristics, and abilities
   C. identify and use technology resources that affirm diversity
   D. promote safe and healthy use of technology resources

LET'S LOOK AT THIS CHAPTER

This chapter discusses the various tools available for use on the Internet and students use of those tools to enhance learning, increase productivity, and prepare and produce creative projects. We discuss some of the ways that students and teachers can use the Internet to research information and collaborate, publish, and interact with individuals from around the world. The Internet is one of a variety of media formats that is used to communicate information and ideas to others around the corner and in distant lands. We also examine acceptable use policies, and the credibility of Web resources encouraging students to evaluate Internet information.

EDUCATION AND THE INTERNET

Telecommunications offers significant advantages to classroom teachers and other educators because it allows them to transcend the isolation that typifies their profession. Teachers of art and music, library media specialists, and other faculty and special subject teachers, who are frequently one of a kind in their buildings, may feel less isolated by sharing teaching strategies and curriculum ideas with distant peers in a daily electronic "convention."

Information is broadcast across electronic networks sooner and in greater quantity than in any other publication medium. Social studies and foreign language teachers are enthusiastic about wide-area computer networking, because it facilitates significant cultural exchanges. Science teachers can expand the scope of their data collection far beyond their local environment by collaborating with classrooms across the country or, indeed, the world.

Telecommunications supports the reform movement in education by facilitating cooperative and interactive learning. Since distance, personal appearance, physical disabilities, and special needs are invisible on the network, students who are set apart from their classmates can participate as equals. Many who are reluctant participants in the classroom become eager contributors when they can compose their inquiries and responses on their own time.

Keep in mind the paradigm shifts explored in Chapter 3 and the dramatic changes in schooling. Telecommunications allows educators to create a virtual classroom without walls, bringing global resources and experiences to their students. Students have access to information resources as never before, as they develop their problem-solving skills and construct their own knowledge.

EVALUATING INTERNET INFORMATION

Media literacy applies as much to the Internet as to any other medium such as television or print. Once information has been located, students should have the opportunity to develop skills in evaluating the accuracy of the information, as well as the way it is displayed on the Internet site, to become critical readers of web pages. A teacher-generated checklist or survey document can assist students in making their evaluation. Figure 11–9 contains a rather thorough and sophisticated set of guidelines to evaluate online resources.

Unfortunately, using a checklist is a good start but still not enough. It is possible to fake just about everything on any of these lists. Did the listed author and/or organization actually contribute any of the information? Is the URL meaningful? One of the authors has a web server on a computer that has seven different URLs associated with it. Two of these URLs even ended with .edu. Is the information accurate? Students have to learn how to discern true from false information. One way to do this is to have them use multiple web and/or print resources to double or triple cross-check the information.

Several excellent sites on the Internet provide examples of evaluation devices and strategies. A Web search will find many articles and discussions about Web credibility. Many great resources can be found under the "Web Credibility" heading at *descy.net*. Four sites listed at that location of particular interest are the Mankato page (blatantly false but still gets a great deal of questions from students), the New Hartford page (false but fools most visitors), the DHMO page (all true . . . but why?), and The End of the Internet (you decide . . . it has to end somewhere).

The Internet is a great source for a wide range of school projects. Students love to use it, but the problem is that there are no editors or librarians to check the quality of information that is found. Anyone can put anything they like on the Internet. As a result, students sometimes inadvertently use biased or inaccurate sources in their research.

Teachers and library media specialists must help students understand that information on the Internet may not be what it seems. It is essential for students to realize that being on the Internet does not make a Website true or useful. To help students choose the best sources for their projects, it is necessary to assist students in learning to evaluate Websites before they use the information that they contain for their papers and projects.

I use both formal and informal methods to help students evaluate Internet sources. I created a Website discussing evaluation techniques at <http://www.crcs.k12.ny.us/lib/hs/evaluating_internet_%20site.htm> to aid in this evaluation. Teachers and media specialists can use this for whole-class lessons, as well as for independent work by students (and other faculty). Besides deciding whether a page appears to be accurate and makes sense, there are several other important questions to ask about a Website:

- What is the purpose of the page? Is it to inform, persuade, sell, or explain?
- Does the information on the site agree with other information I have found?
- Does the information appear to be fact or opinion?
- Does the content of the page seem to be biased or stereotyped?

Asking these and similar questions should help students avoid the accidental use of biased, incorrect, or fake information.

To answer these questions, students should look at the address (URL) to try to learn about the sponsor and location (is it at a .com, .edu, .gov, etc. site) of the page, check the background and credentials of the author, and find out if a site is current and up-to-date. The address (URL) gives important information about the sponsoring organization of a site. Information about the background of the author of a page is usually found on the bottom of a page. The date the page was created or last updated should also usually be found on the bottom of a page. This is a great opportunity to have the students cross-check what they found on the Web using other print and nonprint sources. After evaluating the quality of a Website, the most important question a student should ask themselves is whether a site is useful for his or her project. Students should never forget that they are trying to find the BEST material for their projects.

Joanne Parnes Shawhan, Ph.D.
Media Specialist
Cobleskill-Richmondville High School
Cobleskill, New York

INTEGRATING INTERNET-BASED TOOLS INTO THE CURRICULUM

The Internet is opening up whole new worlds and information resources for both classroom teachers and their students. Teachers have used the power of its many tools to supplement classroom goals and objectives in different ways. We will discuss some of the ideas in this chapter. How we use the Internet in our classrooms is only limited by our imagination. Please remember, though, that there are plenty of places on the Internet that are inappropriate for students. Take precautions also to limit personal information that students may want to send to others.

Frank LaBua/PH College

Email

Email can be used as a means of connecting teacher to teacher, class to class, and student to student. Don't feel that email cannot find a place in your curriculum if you only have one computer and one email account. Proper sharing of this account can make it very useful. Many sites such as *Yahoo.com, hotmail.com,* and *I-Love-Dogs.com* offer free email accounts to anyone who can access them with a web browser.

Email is a wonderful collaborative tool. Students can meet other students, learn about different lands, and share customs and ideas online. Many students have written autobiographies and descriptions of their towns, and even exchanged prices on a shared grocery list with other students and classes around the globe. It is a wonderful way for students to practice writing and collaboration skills. Students have also shared the adventures and communicated with explorers in Africa and the Arctic using email.

Internet Pen Pals (Keypals)

Students can learn about other people and cultures by writing letters and exchanging journal entries and school and local news. Across the nation, continent, and world, students can carry out projects using email and keypals. History, geography, science, and writing skills are but a few of the areas where keypal correspondence can be utilized. The ePALS site illustrated in Figure 12–1 is a good place to start.

Mentor Projects

You may want to start closer to home by linking up students to students or students to adults as mentors and helpers. Do this by establishing an online mentorship program. Pair up high school students to help younger students with their homework or adults to help middle school students for guidance and help. Establish a mentorship program with a college or university class to aid and guide your K–12 students.

Blogs

The word **blog** is really a combination of two words (called a postmanteau!): *web* and *log*. It is an online journaling tool where anyone can place whatever they want. It may be

373

Figure 12-1 ePALS classroom exchange

The ePALS Classroom Exchange site helps find friends all over the world (*http://www.epals.com*)

private, open to select persons, or open to the world. Many blog sites also allow the reader to post comments about the contents right in the blog itself.

Many websites allow users to set up a free blog of their own. It is easy and takes only a few minutes. Blogs are increasingly being used in education by students and teachers alike. In a study on teen use of the Internet, Pew researchers found that 19 percent of online teens keep a blog and 38 percent read them. This compares with 7 percent of adult Internet users having their own blog and 27 percent of online adults reading them (Lenhart & Madden, 2005). Blogging allows students and teachers to carry on group dialogues, reflect and comment on class assignments and happenings, answer questions, and hold group discussions. A fast Web search will yield many sites that discuss setting up a blog and educational uses for both teachers and students. Go to *http://www.ibritt.com/resources/wp_blogs.htm* for a good place to begin.

Podcasting

Podcasting is also a postmanteau. In this case, it is i*Pod* and broad*cast*. Podcasts are recorded audio and/or video files usually in MP3 format that are distributed via Internet download. They can be stored on a computer or a portable music player (hence the reference to the iPod) and replayed when the listener chooses. As with blogs, sites are available for setting up a personal podcasting site. Podcasts are unique in that the receiver can actually subscribe to your (or other) podcast sites and, by doing so, new podcasts will automatically be downloaded to the receiver's computer as they become available. Common podcasts include news and talk shows. Teachers are using podcast to send out lectures and class notes to students. Students are podcasting school work, poetry, and prose.

THE WORLD WIDE WEB

The World Wide Web is probably one of the easiest tools to integrate into your curriculum. There are numerous opportunities to search the Web for information needed for reports or for students' own personal use. Web searching presents us with a wonderful opportunity to integrate a whole series of important lifelong learning activities into classes, including searching techniques (accessing information, limiting searches, reasons for multiple searches, search tool capabilities) and critical evaluation (site and source credibility, author searches, critical reading skills, using non-Internet sources to back up findings). We are able to tap all of our students' higher order thinking skills as described in Bloom's taxonomy (see Chapter 1).

Multicultural Understanding

Students are able to achieve a better understanding and appreciation of other people's cultures using the vast array of information available online. Students from a small town in New York State have found they have much in common with students of American Indian descent living in South Dakota, after examining their website. Email correspondence followed. Other classes have celebrated country-specific holidays found through the Internet as they study worldwide cultures. The Earth Calendar site (Figure 12–2), the Today's Calendar and Clock page (*http://www.ecben.net/calendar.shtml*), and the Kidlink multicultural calendar (*http://www.kidlink.org/KIDPROJ/MCC/*) are good places to look for information.

Group Projects

Schools in many parts of the country and the world have worked together gathering information on weather patterns, insect migration, costs of a set of products in a supermarket, and Civil War history. Each school researches the part of the topic germane to its particular region. The combined data has helped the students understand a product, event, or process from a global perspective. The CIESE Collaborative Classroom Projects site (Figure 12–3) is worth a look. Global Classroom (*www.globalclassroom.org/projects.html*), Global SchoolNet Internet Projects Registry (*www.gsn.org/pr/index.html*), and Global Classroom—Projects and Partners (*www.www.sofweb.vic.edu.au/gc/projects.htm*) may also give you ideas and contacts for group Internet projects.

Figure 12–2 **Earth calendar**

The Earth Calendar helps bring other cultures into the classroom (*http://www.earthcalendar.net*)

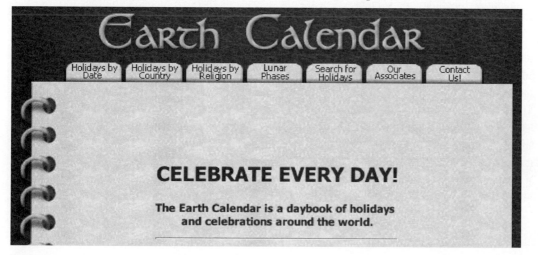

Figure 12–3 CIESE project: down the drain

An Internet project from Stevens Institute of Technology in Hoboken, New Jersey (*http://www. k12science.org/curriculum/drainproj/*)

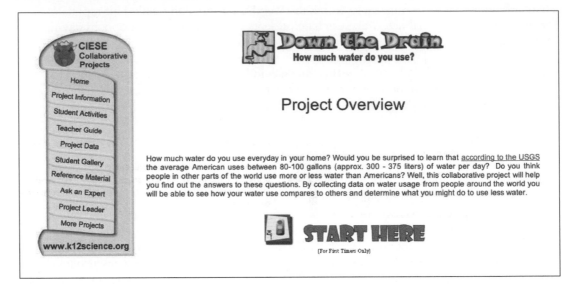

LET'S GO INTO THE CLASSROOM
Mrs. McGowan's First Grade Website

The main purpose of our classroom Website (Figure 12–4) is to provide authentic communication opportunities for my students. It's the "home base" for all our daily Internet activity. Students turn the computers on when they arrive and navigate to our Website. The children access information from various other Websites that I have previewed, and saved links to, on our site. A morning weather report, reached from an image link on the homepage, is a good example. Numerous seasonal, thematic, and subject pages are made available through this linking procedure.

We also get on-line information about other places in the world through class e-mail, our Website guest book, and participation in collaborative on-line projects. One year our class had e-mail pals with a school in Western Australia. My students learned what it's like to have your school built on stilts in case of flooding and what it's like to ride your horse to school instead of taking a car ride or school bus!

However, the main way we communicate with other classes and the general public is by publishing student work on our Web page. The children love seeing their writing and drawings on the screen. So do their families! Some of the most appreciative responses to our Website have come from grandparents living far away. Knowing that so many people will be seeing their work helps motivate the children to do their best.

Our Website also has been hosting collaborative literacy projects. These projects primarily are designed to provide a rich source of on-line reading material for young students. The project resource pages stay on-line as well and can be utilized by other teachers.

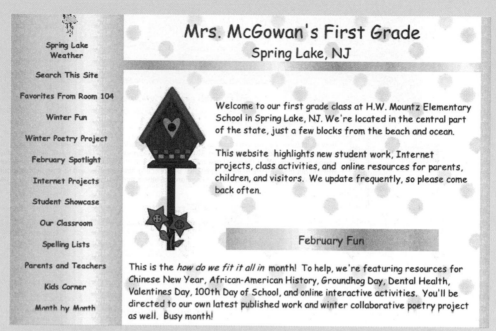

Figure 12–4 Mrs. McGowan's Class

Examine the topics listed on Mrs. McGowan's first grade class web page (*http://www.mrsmcgowan.com/index.html*)

I also use the Website for pages to extend specific classroom lessons. There are on-line quizzes for compound words or math riddles and lists of spelling words to drag and drop into ABC order. Some activities I create and others are shared by teachers from all over the country.

Finally, the Website has become a "supermarket" of resources for students, parents, and other teachers. Our spelling lists, word wall words, schedules, and flashcards are all there for home use. It's a convenient place to find tips on reading with children, critical thinking questions using Bloom's Taxonomy, our state standards, Website building information, holiday puzzles, math projects, rubrics, book lists, and links to other teacher Websites—just to name a few!

Marci McGowan
First Grade Teacher
H. W. Montz Elementary School
Spring Lake, New Jersey

Electronic Field Trips

It is possible for students to tour distant places through many sites on the Web. Distant countries, cities, museums, monuments, zoos, underground New York, and even the sewers of Paris can be toured online. Maps and weather sites can also be used online. Other technology, including video and computer programs such as *Where in the World Is Carmen Sandiego?*, can also be interwoven into these activities. Virtual Tours (*http://www.virtualfreesites.com/tours.html*) contains links to over 300 virtual tours of museums and exhibits around the world, 100 cities, and many U.S. government buildings. The Weather Channel (*http://www.weather.com*) and Mapquest (*http://www.mapquest.com*) both contain useful information to utilize in creating virtual field trips for students. With just

Figure 12–5 **Museum of the history of science**

Students can take a virtual tour of the Institute and Museum of the History of Science in Florence, Italy (*http://www.imss.fi.it/*)

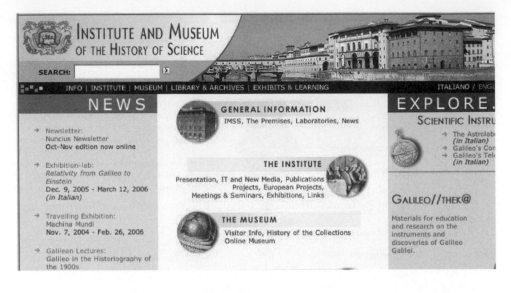

a little typing and a few clicks of the mouse, students can visit their nation's capital and take a virtual tour of the Institute and Museum of the History of Science in Florence, Italy (Figure 12–5).

Research Projects

The Internet allows for up-to-the-minute research on many topics. Newspaper and television websites offer current news and information. Museums and archeological sites offer glimpses into the past. Libraries and historical sites, and universities and government archives, contain records and information needed for research reports.

Parallel Problem Solving

Students in several parts of the country can independently work on the same or similar projects assigned through email, email discussion groups, or the Web. Upon completion, they can exchange methods and results with the other groups.

WebQuests

Bernie Dodge developed the **WebQuest** concept in 1995. A short time later, Tom March developed the first WebQuest. WebQuests are defined as "inquiry-oriented activities in which most or all of the information used by the learner is drawn from the Web" (Dodge & March, 2005). WebQuests may be teacher- or student-designed activities and can last from a few hours to several weeks. WebQuests are great for cooperative learning and learning communities. They may be worked on individually or by a group of students. The group approach will also foster teamwork, sharing, and individual responsibility as well as responsibility to the group as a whole. The majority of information and sites in a WebQuest has been selected and gathered by the WebQuest developer. This directed learning approach guides students through prelinked web pages as they try to find answers and draw conclusions while helping them avoid many of the pitfalls found in general Web surfing. It is an ideal way for students to find and use Web-based information in a safe environment. WebQuests fit nicely into a constructivist classroom atmosphere as students synthesize their own knowledge using a teacher-guided set of activities. "There are wonderful, award-winning WebQuests for every grade level (even PreK)" (Summerville, 2000). WebQuest loosely follows a specific format (see below) and therefore requires preplanning as all media projects do. Many WebQuests have been made by elementary and secondary students to give them practice in data gathering, synthesis of information, problem solving, and web page construction. Chapter 11 explained how to make web pages and link them to other pages and outside sites. This is the only technical expertise you or your students will need. The WebQuest site shown in Figure 12–6 is a great starting point.

WebQuests usually contain the following parts.

1. **Introduction.** This important part of the project is meant to prepare the student for the WebQuest. It should be interesting and make the student want to continue. WebQuest should be fun to do and motivate students to learn and complete the activities.
2. **Task.** This section must focus the students on what they are going to do as the culminating product or performance. This should be an interesting and different assignment, not just write a report or give an oral report. Many developers find this a difficult section to complete. WebQuests do not rely on tests or written reports, but have students show their knowledge in a variety of ways including storytelling, persuasionary presentations, dramatizations, news articles, forming judgments, consensus building, and analytical tasks, to name a few. Students

Figure 12–6 WebQuest page

The WebQuest page at San Diego State University is a great starting point (*http://webquest. sdsu.edu/*)

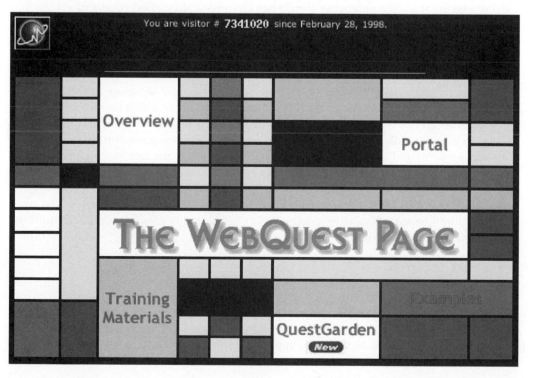

reading *The Ugly Duckling,* for example, might have to write a letter to the duckling explaining how swans are special birds. Students studying states may have to give a talk designed to persuade other students in the class to travel to that state.

3. **Process.** This section outlines how the student will accomplish the task in a step-by-step fashion. Links to reviewed online resources will be given, along with links to web pages that the teacher/students may have developed. Other forms of print and nonprint resources may also be included such as books, videotapes, and filmstrips.

4. **Evaluation.** Evaluation criteria used to grade the student are listed here. Rubrics are often used to help the student meet content and performance standards. A good set of rubrics helps the student by establishing clear goals and matching the assessment to specific tasks. It involves the student in the evaluation process from the beginning. We discussed rubrics earlier in the text.

5. **Conclusion.** This section encourages reflection and brings closure to the WebQuest. Additional links and rhetorical questions encourage students to extend their thinking and encourage further study. You may link it to future work and topics.

6. **Resources.** This section usually consists of a list of resources such as print or other resourses, linked websites, and author-made supplemental web pages that the student will need to complete the task or tasks. It is mostly found in older WebQuests. More often now, this is not a separate section, rather the resources are embedded in the area of immediate need in the prior *Process* section. Many people think that WebQuests should only use Web and Internet resources. This is not true. Many great WebQuests have the student read books; view videos, posters, or maps; manipulate models or sculptures; or even use data gathered on field trips.

7. **Teacher Page.** This section includes much of the systematic design work including standards, target audience, notes on teaching the unit, problems, questions that may arise, and sometimes examples of finished products.

More information on WebQuests, on evaluating websites, a list of educational networks, and various curriculum-related sites can be found on the Companion Website *(http://www.prenhall. com/forcier)*

The first five (or six if you include *Resources*) are usually placed on one web page with links to other outside websites and web pages that the developer has constructed. The *Teacher Page* is usually a separate web page.

Don't be afraid to use WebQuests in your classroom even if developing them yourself seems a big project. There are three accepted ways to go about using them. First, it is perfectly okay to go out on the Web and use a WebQuest that someone else has made—just be sure to give the author full credit. It is also permissible to use someone else's WebQuest as a starting point and modify it to meet the needs of your class, curriculum, and/or location. If you do this, you should email the developer, thank him or her for the ideas, and share your WebQuest. Lastly, you can make your own WebQuest. These are also good projects for one student or a group to develop for a final unit project. Aside from the website shown in Figure 12–7, another great place to get started is *www.thirteen.org/edonline/ concept2class/webquests/index.html.*

Scavenger Hunts

More specific searches can be accomplished by several strategies. One such strategy is the *scavenger hunt.* In this strategy, the students are given a list of terms or concepts to search for that perhaps all relate to the same topic or theme. The students are asked to report back on specific information, along with the URL where they located it. For example,

Students can post research projects such as this one on the Web (*http://isd77.k12.mn.us/ schools/ dakota/conflict/history.htm*) *(Reprinted with permission)*

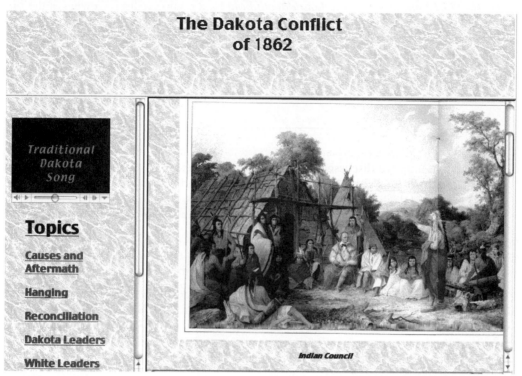

when asked to find the number of airports in Burkina Faso, students must determine what Burkina Faso is, where it is, and the search tool that would most likely yield the answer. Though such a question might relate to a geography lesson, its primary purpose may be to refine search skills and acquaint the students with new information resources.

A second strategy is to give students a specific set of bookmarks that they are to locate and then to provide specific questions or responses to which the students need to respond. Many Internet sites are particularly targeted to students and can provide interactive lessons of their own. Bookmarks can be distributed as simply as having the URLs typed on a handout, or more efficiently in an HTML document that could provide a given order for access along with some teacher annotations.

Web pages can even be *whacked*—that is, copied while online to have their images stored in a data storage device (e.g., a hard drive) for later instructional use by students viewing specifically saved sites. An interesting collaborative strategy is to give individual students, or teams of students, specific portions of an overall task and then to have them email each other to share and combine what they have found. This furthers the concept of knowledge as a shared process of interaction that combines multiple sources and interpretations of information.

Website Displays

Students can research areas of local, national, and international interest and post their research and findings on the Web. Students at Dakota Meadows Middle School in Mankato, Minnesota, did just that. So far they have developed and posted sites on the Holocaust, journals consisting of firsthand accounts and stories from people who lived through World War II (either at home or in the armed services), Vietnam oral histories, and the Dakota Indian uprising (Figure 12–7) around the Mankato area during the middle 1860s (see *www.isd77.k12.mn.us/schools/dakota/dakota.html* for a complete list). Viewers of the uprising site will hear students read the narrative and view colorful images and can listen to a traditional Dakota song.

If you are still wondering how to get started or how to design customized Internet lessons for your particular curriculum, Pacific Bell's Knowledge Network Explorer contains a tool called Filamentality (*http://www.kn.pacbell.com/wired/fil/#intro*). Filamentality is a

LET'S GO INTO THE CLASSROOM
Meaningful Student Web Projects

Today's students are not intimidated by technology; rather they expect to have access to it and use it. Dakota Meadows Middle School opened in 1993 with the goal of integrating computer and other emerging technologies into the student learning experience. Internet technologies help students gain access to information and provide students an opportunity to share their work with others in the school, community, and around the world. Our students use computers, digital video and still cameras, digitizers and scanners, and a wide variety of computer software and programs for producing educational Websites.

Students are more motivated and learning is more effective when they know that their product will be viewed by someone other than the teacher. Students know they must stand behind their work before the world when it is produced for distribution on the Internet. Our grade 8 English students are required to write for an audience other than their teacher. One way to do this is through a student-constructed Web. This project motivates students to write clearly, without error, and to use a vocabulary that can be understood by a worldwide audience. Students have constructed Websites on mini-mysteries (*http://www.isd77.k12.mn.us/schools/dakota/mystery/contents.html*) and community memories of World War II (*http://www.isd77.k12.mn.us/schools/dakota/war/worldwar.html*). In the latter, they interviewed local veterans and individuals living during the 1930s and 40s.

Students further improved their research and writing skills when building *The Dakota Conflict 1862* Website. This Website documents a major local Native American uprising. I had students work in teams against a deadline to produce their piece of the project. Students had to resolve time, as well as content issues within their individual teams. For a number of students, *The Dakota Conflict 1862* project was their first experience with fieldwork and interviewing as information gathering tools. Students learned the history of the *Conflict* and subsequent efforts at native and immigrant reconciliation. This engaged them in an examination of their ideas and attitudes about other times and other peoples. Students also learned to use Website building technologies in order to tell their story. *The Dakota Conflict 1862* Website has been featured in local television and print media and was entered in the *International Schools CyberFair*. Here it won first place in the History category among competing entries from schools from around the globe. Positive community, national, and international feedback has provided students with an incentive to continue designing and producing projects in order to share their work with others beyond the school's walls.

Beth Christensen
Eighth Grade English Teacher
Dakota Meadows Middle School
North Mankato, Minnesota
Minnesota Teacher of the Year, 1996–1997

fill-in-the-blank interactive Web tool that will guide you as you pick a topic, search the Web for suitable sites, and build Web-based activities appropriate for your class.

Prescreened Collections of Websites

One of the first places to look when you are preparing a lesson is websites that contain lists of prescreened sites. These sites usually list the sites by subject and topic. They are a good place for you to find information and also a wonderful place to find websites for students to search. Many times outright web searching is not carried on in the lower grades; instead, teachers send students to particular sites to find information. Many teachers also develop their own web pages containing lists of prescreened sites for students to use in their search for knowledge. *EduHound* is a huge site containing "Everything for Education K12". Clip art, schools and classrooms on the Web, a Spanish section, and a list of prescreened sites can be found here (*www.eduhound.com*).

Kathy Schrock is the technology coordinator at Dennis-Yarmouth Regional School District on Cape Cod, Massachusetts. She has put together a huge site (now sponsored by Discovery Channel School), appropriately called *Kathy Schrock's Guide for Educators* (Figure 12–8). This site should be a required stop for all pre- and inservice teachers. Not only are there thousands of prescreened sites here but also search tools and information, slide shows for training, bulletin board ideas, assessment rubrics, readability graphs, and much more.

Yahooligans!™ (*http://www.yahooligans.yahoo.com*) is a site for students, parents, and teachers. Not only can you find a vast number of prescreened sites for students but also many student activities. The Yahooligans Teachers' Guide contains information on teaching Internet literacy, acceptable use policies, citing Internet sources, and evaluating websites.

Educational and Learning Networks

A number of networks aimed primarily at K–12 education have developed during the past few years.

Classroom Connect. A free site, although you have to register, Classroom Connect (*http://www.classroom.com*) contains a wealth of information on teaching and learning. *Connected University,* an online professional development area, and other areas containing online resources for K–12 teachers are found here.

DiscoverySchool.com. This service of the Discovery networks (Animal Planet, Discovery Channel, Discovery Health, TLC: The Learning Channel, Travel Channel) is dedicated to making teaching and learning a rewarding and exciting adventure for teachers, students, and parents. The site (*http://school.discovery.com*) contains resources for students, teaching materials for teachers, and information for parents about helping their children enjoy learning and excelling in school. Kathy Schrock's guide is located here.

Scholastic Network. This free registration site (*http://teacher.scholastic.com*) was created by the commercial software company of the same name. Certain sections are specifically designed for teachers, students, and parents. You will find wonderful lists of teacher resources, student activities, lesson plans, a *Web Guide* containing thousands of reviewed websites, curriculum integration ideas, and more. Live interviews with such notables as J. K. Rowling (author of the *Harry Potter* series) and General Colin Powell (for a Black History Month special) were presented as well as live practice interviews for prospective teachers.

Figure 12-8 Kathy schrock's guide for educators

This is a must-see website for every teacher and preservice teacher (*http://school.discovery. com/schrockguide/*) (*Reprinted with permission*)

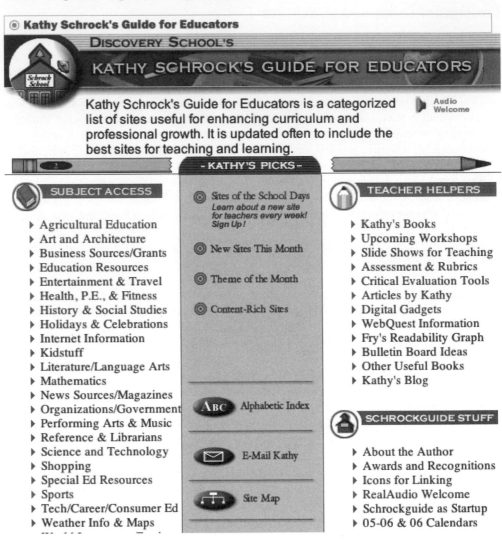

Internet Archives (Databases)

The Educator's Reference Desk. With the reorganization of the U.S. Department of Education, the ERIC Clearinghouse for Information and Technology and the AskERIC Service have been discontinued. Most of the resources previously found there are available at the Educator's Reference Desk (Figure 12–9). This site contains over 2,000 lesson plans and more than 3,000 links for online educational information including discussion groups, online information, and educational organizations. The U.S. Department of Education still keeps the website for searching the ERIC Database at *www.eric.ed.gov*. Many of you have probably used articles and reports in the ERIC database in a library as a basis for reports and presentations in your college courses.

This site contains a wealth of information for teachers (*http://www.eduref.org*)

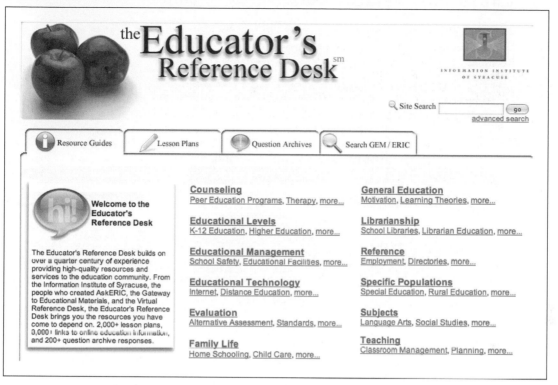

The Library of Congress. The website of the Library of Congress (LOC)(*http://www.loc.gov*) is a wonderful site to visit. Even though only a portion of its 95 million maps, images, audio recordings, and 17 million books are accessible online at this time, the array of information is both interesting and mind-boggling. American Memory, an ongoing project to digitize the LOC's American historical holdings, and THOMAS, a congressional database, are easily accessed here. Another interesting literature site to view is the University of Virginia Library's Electronic Text Center (*http://etext.lib.virginia.edu*). This site contains one of the largest collections of electronic texts in over 13 languages!

One Internet database useful to math and science educators is *The Eisenhower National Clearinghouse (ENC) (goENC.com)*. It proports to be "the largest, most comprehensive resource for K–12 math and science educators." Its purpose is to improve access to the most current materials in math and science resources in the nation. Descriptions and evaluations are available.

WEB PORTALS

A **Web portal,** sometimes just called a *portal,* is a service or website that offers a broad range of services and resources such as email, email discussion group development, forums and chat, search engines, travel information, yellow and white pages, and online shopping malls. Portals can be paid services, free services, and even special pages set up by schools and businesses. They usually act as the first or home page for the particular user's computer. The first portals were paid services such as America Online™, CompuServe™, EarthLink™, and Prodigy™.

Figure 12–10 My yahoo page

Just under 100 categories may be added including such items as lottery results, market performance, and package tracking.

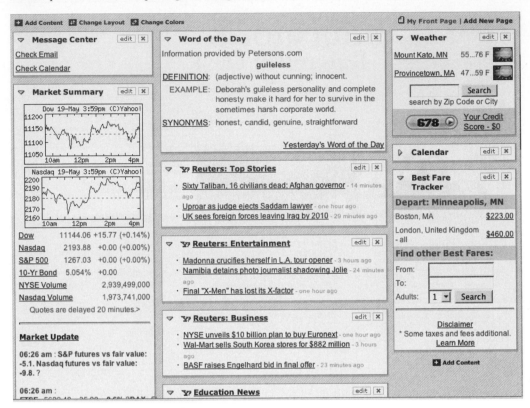

Though most of these commercial companies offer a wide variety of services, their biggest draw is the ability to access the Internet through the service. This industry has been in a state of flux. Increasingly more people are becoming comfortable with telecommunications and are demanding more and faster services. Established companies have gone bankrupt or have merged or been bought out by others. Now many people buy their Internet service from telephone companies or their local cable television system; and because of this, free portals such as Netscape, MSN (also has a paid service), and Yahoo (Figure 12–10) offer many of the same services as the paid portals. Most services also allow the user to customize the main page with weather, news, and other information of interest to the user. Note the wide variety of information available for you to customize your portal home page.

THE INTERNET AS A DISTANCE LEARNING TOOL

One of the newer uses of the Internet is as a medium for the delivery of instruction. A growing trend in electronic distance education (sometimes called *e-learning*) is to encourage instructors to present either their entire course, or its supporting materials, by means of a web page. Students access these pages to read instructional materials, download or submit

Figure 12–11 WebCT

The opening screen of a sample WebCT® course (*http://webct.com*)

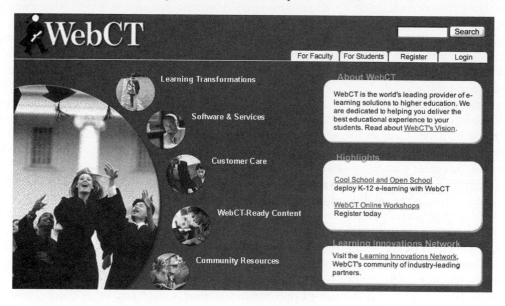

assignments, communicate with both the instructor and other students via email, take tests and quizzes, see how they are doing in class, and just about anything they would be able to do if they were in a real classroom. E-learning software is so inclusive that it is grouped under the title, Course Management System (CMS).

This method of delivery opens many opportunities for instruction of students whose access to education is limited by either distance or physical impairment. Perhaps you have been in a course in which some, if not all, of the course material was presented to you online. All of the Internet tools we described may be utilized in these courses.

Internet distance education communications tools are usually divided into two categories according to the mode. Asynchronous modes of communications do not take place between parties simultaneously. Examples include email, email discussion groups, web pages, and discussion boards that enable students to access them at different times throughout the day and night. Synchronous modes are real-time communications in which the interaction between participants takes place simultaneously, perhaps during a set class time. Synchronous tools would include chat rooms, white boards, live Web cams, and others. Students are online in this mode and participate in learning and discussions together as a group. Email is used to keep students and teachers in touch with each other. Bulletin boards are used to post information. Chat rooms and forums may be used to exchange questions and comments. Complete Web-based software packages can seamlessly integrate all of the above Internet tools to produce a comprehensive course. Figure 12–11 shows an introductory screen for WebCT™, one of these course management programs.

OTHER WEBSITES AND CURRICULUM INFUSION IDEAS

A number of Internet activities have already been mentioned. Student and teacher use of email to communicate with peers or with experts in a given field extends the classroom experience to begin the realization of what is rapidly becoming a "global schoolhouse."

Databases or archives and search engines assist both students and teachers in utilizing the encyclopedic quality of the vast array of content available on the Internet. WebQuests enable students to learn in a safe environment. However, just as it is a myth that merely placing a student in front of a computer will result in substantive learning, it is equally a myth that merely having access to the Internet will result in productive student acquisition and use of information. The immediacy of access, the sheer volume, and the dynamic quality of the information available is very different from that of previous media for storing and displaying knowledge.

Classroom or media center access is usually through the channel of modem-based communications or via a "hard-wired" cable in a local area network. The main differences are the provider costs to the school district, long-distance fees if by modem connection, the speed of information transfer, and the number of connected computers in any given setting. Speed of transfer is often crucial (this is where networked cable communications have the advantage), especially where the number of computers or the time available for student online access is limited. Teachers need to plan the time allotted to Internet access, as well as the placement of connected computers within a classroom. If there is a single computer, then the logistics of providing equity of access to all students or a display that can be viewed by the entire class become very important. Equality of access means that students are not limited by such features as age, gender, socioeconomic background, and experience in working with computers.

Teachers should plan the use of the Internet as they would any other media, with a clear set of objectives, appropriate preparation and integration into the unit of study, and methods of assessing and reporting student performance.

Generalized searches of the Internet are often useful for determining just what is available. Teachers should assist the students beforehand in the ways of stating terms that narrow and define their search if they are to avoid "information overload." Additionally, students need to understand the appropriate methods of citing electronic information, paying special attention to the person or organization posting that information, and when that information was posted or last revised.

The Internet not only allows for student retrieval of information, but also presents many opportunities for educators to grow as professionals. Email communication with other teachers provides for sharing of lesson plans or the solutions to specific classroom problems and issues. Teachers in many different parts of the world can have their classes collaborate and share such things as environmental data, poetry and artwork, and discussions of various cultural points of view. Many professional organizations for educators have web pages posted, and many educational journals and sources of research information can be obtained online. Specialized sources of data provide the raw material for building curriculum and assessment and keep the educator current with local, state, and national standards in their particular content area.

Figures 12–12 through 12–14 illustrate a few of the many websites that are of particular interest to educators. The danger in identifying specific references on the Internet is that this dynamic structure is in a constant state of flux. New sites are added and existing sites are withdrawn. Hopefully, the sites represented in these illustrations possess a fair degree of longevity. Visit the textbook's Companion Website at *http://www.prenhall.com/forcier* to examine a host of curriculum-related sites.

The Children's Literature Web Guide (Figure 12–12) is a valuable resource of children's stories, authors, and book reviews. It contains links to children's authors, stories, awards, movies, and television, as well as organizations.

CIA Publications (Figure 12–13), maintained by the Central Intelligence Agency, is an excellent resource for any geography or current events class. The high-quality

Figure 12–12 Children's literature web guide

This is an extremely useful resource housed at the University of Calgary (*http://www.ucalgary.ca/~dkbrown*)

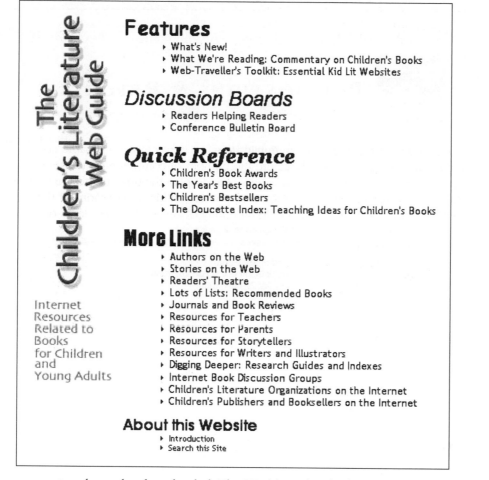

maps are current and may be downloaded. The World Factbook alone is worth a visit to this site.

edHelper.com (Figure 12–14) is just one of the many sites for teachers. Here you can find lesson plans, worksheets and worksheet generators, WebQuest puzzles and exams, and puzzle and exam generators, and a host of other teacher helpers divided into preK through twelfth grade areas. SAT and test prep worksheets are included along with links to the latest education news for teachers.

Perhaps most important, the Internet offers the means for a teacher to connect to a global educational system and to transition from being the source of any and all information in the classroom to being a facilitator of student skills in locating, retrieving, evaluating, assimilating, repurposing, and displaying the ever-increasing amount of information available on the Internet.

In closing, we would refer you to a wealth of additional information found in 14 All Aboard the Internet columns written by Don Descy and published in *Tech Trends* magazine, a publication of the Association for Educational Communications and Technology (AECT). Each column, included on *the Take-Along CD*, was specifically chosen to increase your knowledge of topics covered in the text.

Figure 12–13 CIA

CIA documents provide an excellent source of information on world geography (*http://www.cia.gov/cia/publications/*)

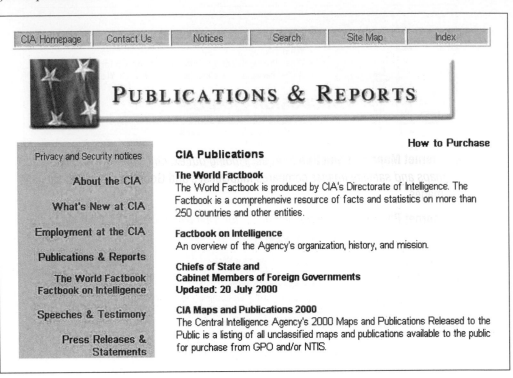

Figure 12–14 edHelper.com

This site has thousands of lesson plans and teacher helpers (*http://www.edhelper.com/*)

Lesson Plans - Worksheets - Teacher's Lesson Plans - WebQuests - Primary Teacher Resources - Math Lesson Plans - Writing Lesson Plans - Reading Lesson Plans - Science Lesson Plans - Technology Lesson Plans - Social Studies Lesson Plans - ...

11443 Lesson Plans, **1296** WebQuests, **5000**
Free Worksheet Generators, 1600 Word and Critical Thinking Problems, Exams and Puzzles for Standardized Tests.

The spelling and vocabulary sections now include new worksheets and tools!
New Word Stories Math Problems Section!
Addition, Subtraction, Multiplication, and Division worksheets now use bigger fonts!
Language Arts Worksheets   Contractions
New **Animal Worksheets**   Solar System Worksheets   Weather Worksheets   Plants
New Biomes: Rainforests, Deserts, Polar Regions.
Reading + Math + Vocabulary + Spelling + Writing = **edHelper's New Reading Comprehension Section**
New Phonics Section with Printables and Worksheets

The Valentine
Scavenger Hunt
Now Playing!

January Theme Units   Winter Theme Unit   Penguins Theme Unit
February Theme Units   Groundhog Day   Valentine's Day   Black History

 Chinese New Year Theme Unit
Using Chinese characters to learn about place value and more!

Build a puzzle: **Use Your Own Words** (Build Spelling and Vocabulary Worksheets) | Word Find | Crossword | Spelling | Math Crossnumber | Math Box | Math Sequences | Bingo | Number Word Searches | Missing Digits | Math Words | Word Stories | **Critical Thinking Puzzles**

All Aboard the Internet Columns as an Additional Resource

1. **Alternate Web Browsers.** *X marks the spot for an opera and for lighting a fire with the fox!* is a discussion of alternate web browsers such as Opera and Firefox.

2. **Blogs and Blogging.** *Let's Put It In Writing for Everyone to See: The Blog* presents a coverage of what they are, how they are used, and how to start a blog.

3. **Google Can Do That?** *Google-eyed over Google!* is a discussion of many of Google's little tricks. Most people just think that Google is just a search engine. It is really much more.

4. **Internet Maps and Satellite Images.** *Finding out exactly where we are: Internet maps and satellite images* compares MapQuest's and Google's maps and satellite images.

5. **Internet Phones.** *Calling the world . . . .for free!* discusses Internet phone programs and how to get started using them for free.

6. **Internet Uses for Everyone.** *Becoming a Digital Being* reviews many uses of the Internet in everyday life.

7. **Introduction to RSS.** *Introducing RSS: Your one stop for news and information* explains the technology that allows you to "subscribe" to a text or video document. When it is updated or when something new is added, it downloads the information to your computer automatically allowing you to keep up-to-date with news and information.

8. **Mobile Internet.** *E to go: The Internet in your pocket* covers Internet feeds to mobile phones and handheld computers.

9. **Podcasting.** *Podcasting: Online Media Delivery . . . with a Twist* presents a complete discussion of Podcasting. What is it? What is available? and How can you get started? are all covered.

10. **Spyware, Malware, Adware.** *Peek a boo . . . I'm watching you: Spyware* may save you time, money, and headaches. If you have a computer and it is attached to the Internet . . . even for a few short minutes . . . it has probably become infected with Spyware, Malware, and Adware.

11. **The Wiki: True Democracy on the Net.** *The Wiki: True Web Democracy* explains how Wiki's allow users to change or modify information people put on the Web. The Wiktionary and Wikopedia are popular, informative and easily modified by everyone.

12. **Video Over the Net.** *Video: From the Big Screen to the Small Screen, to the Smaller Screen* discusses video available on the Internet ranging from sports to education, commercial and homemade.

13. **Web Page Add-ons.** *Neat Little Web Page Add-ons* suggests little add-ons to make your web page fun and friendly.

14. **Web Searching.** *Searching the Web: From the visible to the invisible* reviews web directories and search engines along with finding hidden information on the invisible web.

A copy of the following *All Aboard the Internet* columns may be found in the Tech Trends folder in the Take-Along CD

LET'S REVIEW

Telecommunications offers significant advantages to the educator who wishes to collaborate with colleagues, access current information, and expose students to a broad range of cultures and curricular resources. Electronic networks overcome traditional barriers of social and geographic isolation, facilitate interactive and cooperative learning, and serve as highly effective motivators to reluctant writers. In particular, the Internet allows students to construct their own knowledge, promotes the use of technology as a powerful resource tool, enables collaboration between and among students through various projects and thematic units, provides a global perspective and interchange of ideas, allows teachers to individualize student instruction, and encourages the use of technology as a tool and enabler.

To take advantage of telecommunications, teachers must move from seeing the computer as a static piece of equipment they use to process data to seeing the computer as a vehicle capable of gathering information and transporting them and their students to distant places around the globe.

LET'S PRACTICE

To complete the specified exercises online, go to the Chapter Exercises Module in Chapter 12 of the Companion Website.

1. Put together an Internet scavenger hunt for a particular theme or content area. This should include descriptions of the relevant information to be found, a space for the answer, and another space for the recording of the URL. This activity may need to include instructions on appropriate search strategies.

2. Pick out a topic or theme that you wish to explore, find five appropriate sites, and discuss how you know that the information you found was credible.

3. Design a form for students to use in evaluating Internet sites for content accuracy or completeness, currency of information, purpose of the site, authorship, date of posting or most recent revision, degree of interactivity, appropriate use of graphics, and useful links to related sites.

4. Go to *descy.net* and click on and review the Mankato home page and the New Hartford home page, the Bermese Mountain Dog home page and the central park home page. Which of these sites is true and which is false? What techniques did the website author use to try to fool you into believing

the information is credible on the site(s) you thought were false?

5. Write a short paper discussing the pros and cons concerning government-mandated filtering of websites. Be prepared to defend yourself in class.

6. Write a list of 10 statements that you could post in your classroom regarding proper student use of the Internet.

7. Search the Internet for information about WebQuests. Using the grade level that you plan to teach, develop a short WebQuest that you might be able to use. Using what you learned in Chapter 11, could you make this WebQuest?

8. How will the Internet and/or the Web help your students understand cultural diversity in this country and around the world? Find and list several sites that might be helpful to you. Be prepared to share your comments and sites in class.

9. Explore Kathy Schrock's Guide for Educators. What feature of the site did you find most useful?

10. Search for a site that lists information that you can use in the grade level or subject you would like to teach after you graduate. Discuss this site with others in the class.

PORTFOLIO DEVELOPMENT EXERCISES

To complete this exercise online, go to the Digital Portfolio Module in Chapter 12 of the Companion Website.

One of the NETS•S standards covered in this chapter was "Students use technology to locate, evaluate, and collect information from a variety of sources" under *Category 5: Technology research tools*. Begin to develop your own portfolio of lesson plans that demonstrates your ability to have your students reach the NETS•S standards.

1. Design a lesson plan activity for elementary, middle school, or high school students in which they interact with peers, experts, and other audiences. This should be a project that could involve individuals in other schools in this country and abroad. How would you go about facilitating this project? How would you go about finding other groups to participate in this project? This lesson should demonstrate that your students have achieved the standard. Be sure to include a system of evaluation for your students' understanding and competence to ensure that they have met this standard.

2. Adapt the lesson plan activity you developed in exercise 1 for students to evaluate each others' work.

GLOSSARY

blog	We*b* and *log* is an online journaling tool where anyone can place whatever they want
podcasting	i*Pod* and broad*cast* are recorded audio and/or video files that are distributed via Internet download
Web portal	A website that offers a broad range of services and resources
WebQuest	Defined as "inquiry-oriented activities in which most or all of the information used by the learner is drawn from the Web"

REFERENCES AND SUGGESTED READINGS

Brandt, D. S. (1996). Evaluating information on the Internet. *Computers in Libraries, 16*(5), 44–46.

Descy, D. E. (1996, September). Evaluating Internet resources. *Tech Trends, 41*(4), 3–5.

Descy, D. E. (2004, May/June). Let's put it in writing for everyone to see: The blog. *Tech Trends, 48*(3), 4–5.

Descy, D. E. (2004, January). Organizing the Internet: Safe passage through a minefield of information. *Library Trends, 51*(4), 46–48.

Descy, D. E. (2005, September/October). Podcasting: Online media delivery . . . with a twist. *Tech Trends, 49*(5), 4–6.

Dodge, B., & March, T. (2005). *The WebQuest page.* Retrieved online July 15, 2006, from *http://webquest.sdsu.edu.*

Eastman, J. N., Nickel, T., Du Plessis, J., & Smith, L. D. (2000, April). An incremental approach to implementing a Web course. *TechTrends, 44*(3), 40–45.

Kennedy, K. (2003). *Writing with web logs.* Retrieved online January 16, 2006, from the *http://www.techlearning.com/db_area/archives/TL/2003/02/blogs.html.*

Lamb, A. (1999). *Building treehouses for learning* (2nd). Emporia, KS: Vision to Action.

Lenhart, A., & Madden, M. (December, 2005). Teen content creators and consumers. *Pew/Internet & American life project.* Retrieved online February 2006, from *http://www.perinternet.org/pdfs/PIP_Teens_Content_Creation.pdf.*

Poftak, A. (2002, August). Net-wise teens: Safety, ethics, and innovation. *Technology & Learning, 25*(1), 36–49.

Summerville, J. (2000, March). WebQuests: An aspect of technology integration for training preservice teachers. *TechTrends, 44*(2), 31–35.

Epilogue

A Peek at the Classroom of 2015

by David Warlick

Kathy Schrock opened this book with a review of our evolving educational technologies. It is an important topic, because there is much in how technology is used to promote learning that does not change. The tools change. Taking what has happened in the past, some of the innovative techniques of today, and factoring in some of the emerging technologies, I am going to suggest an image of the classroom of 2015, and take you on a tour. There are several points we need to agree on first.

1. No prediction of the future can possibly be accurate, and this has never been more true. If someone had suggested to a classroom teacher in 1995, that by 2005 students would be entering their classrooms with multimedia laptop computers equipped with image, audio, and video editing software, and capable of accessing billions of pages of content through the air of the classroom, that person would not have been believed. In 1995, many teachers had not even heard of the Internet.

2. The classroom that I am suggesting will not depend on advances in technology or even expense, as much as it depends on the vision and courage of education and political leaders. Much of what I suggest is already happening to some degree in some places, because of visionary leadership.

3. I am assuming that philosophies of teaching and learning have changed dramatically. Perhaps it happened as a result of our decoding the video game experience, discovering the precise elements of gaming that so engages our students and through which they accomplish deep learning. It may come from other research. But our definitions of teaching, learning, the classroom, the textbook, etc., have all changed.

A TOUR OF THE CLASSROOM

It's early and the morning sun lights up the room, revealing a middle school classroom that, at this hour, is empty of students. Our first impression, upon gazing around the room, is that it seems to display less technology than its counterpart of 10 years ago. There are no computers, printers, scanners, or displays. Just desks and tables.

The furniture appears to be designed primarily for comfort. As I sit in a chair, I find that the seat conforms to my seated shape and supports my back. Much of the furniture's materials are nano-engineered producing surfaces that can be stiff or pliable, hard, or soft. The walls are also covered with nano-materials that repel dirt and smudges.

Along the edges of the ceiling are devices that appear to be track lighting. Instead, they are small LCD projectors that are connected to the school network, enabling the display of computer generated content on any wall of the room. Some schools are already experimenting with walls covered with e-/paper, but that is still a bit expensive and the resolution has not yet reached that of LCD projectors.

All of the furniture can be easily moved around. There are no wheels, but the bottoms of the chair and table legs are made of a nano-material that makes them easy to slide along the floor unless the weight of a person is resting on them.

Suddenly, several of the LCD projectors click into action and information starts to appear on one of the walls. A news program appears, the anchor person delivering the news in Spanish. To the right of the newscast appears a map of the United States, with animated weather symbols, illustrating rain in the Northwest and Southeast, but clear skies across most of the rest of the country. Temperatures are dipping down in the Midwest in reaction to a corresponding dip in the jet stream.

On another wall, a grid-style rubric appears, describing how the students' current assignment will be evaluated. The class contributed to the design of the rubric, and their projects will be judged by students in five other classrooms in three countries.

To the left of the newscast, a list appears of topics that are of current interest to the classroom. After a couple of seconds, each topic unfolds into a list of news items that have recently been reported—some only minutes old—that are related in some way to the topics. This news listing continues to update through the day.

The content that is appearing, seemingly by magic, is actually being selected and laid out on the wall by the classroom teacher, who is still sitting at her breakfast table, three miles away, with her tablet. The display is also syndicated so that the students in her classroom can receive the display on their tablets, though very few of them do, mostly opting for their own personal displays of information.

As the audio of the newscaster dies down, and is replaced by Scottish music, being narrowcasted by a podcast station run by a classroom in Northern Scotland, the teacher's schedule appears on a third wall. The schedule indicates four hours of instructional supervision in the morning, and appointments and professional activities in the afternoon, consisting of research, instructional media development, catching up on correspondence, and doing any professional writing that she may be involved in.

Forty-five minutes later, students begin to arrive in the classroom, sliding their chairs and desks around into small groups, chatting, and working their tablets. A larger number of students have gathered in the school media center, where there is much more technology visible. Each table holds a larger LCD panel. There is also a small stage in one corner and one wall is occupied by wooden (simulated) book shelves, covered mostly with books of fiction, many of them donated by local residents. The ceiling here is also lined with LCD projectors.

Students are gathered at the tables, focused on something happening on their table's large display, pointing, and discussing what they are seeing. Many of the students are watching media that they have captured or produced for personal reasons, but a significant number are discussing current projects that have been assigned by their teachers. Two professional media center staff members are wandering around the large room, greeting the groups of students and asking if their assistance is needed. A couple ask questions, mostly seeking sources of information that they need for their work, both personal and instructional.

Back in the classroom, the teacher has arrived and she has claimed one of the desks and chairs for her work, pulling her tablet out of her tote bag and bringing up the presentation media that she will be using. She then replaces the current arrangement of content on the walls, except for the evaluation rubric, and with a real-time video display of their class. Small video cameras are conspicuously mounted in various locations and are used to facilitate teleconferences with other classes and virtually any other location appropriate to the learning at hand. Displaying the classroom image on the current front wall is the signal to the class that it is time to begin the morning's first session.

Students began to seat themselves, moving chairs and desks into position to face the teacher. Their presence has been registered as they entered the classroom, a sensor detecting their presences from personal RFID chips installed with their tablets. As they click on their tablets, they automatically flash to a display that has been directed to them by the teacher. She immediately begins the discussion, an exploration of the conditions that sparked the American Declaration of Independence and the Revolutionary War.

The tablets used by the teacher and students are computers, capable of a wide range of processes designed to access, manage, process, and display information, mostly coming from the global Internet. Most of the content that the students use in their classes, though technically stored on the Internet, has been selected and organized by the teacher. Some of the information is a result of ongoing research on the Internet, but much of it comes from content companies who rent access to the information—and many of these companies used to be textbook publishers.

Although the teacher drives much of the content of the class, an explicit part of being a student is to enhance and remix the content with information that they have selected or produced. Each student is constructing a personal digital textbook, so to speak, and each student has access to each others digital textbook and can annotate the information.

The tablets are equipped with a microphone that can record audio, pick out and distinguish the voices of those speaking, and transcribe the speech into searchable text, attributing the text to the speaker. This feature is not often used in the classroom, since the room itself records and transcribes all presentations and discussions. The tablets are also equipped with video cameras and 3D VR accessories, so that learners can enjoy rich media, fully immersive, real-time communication and simulations.

After an introduction, the wall next to the teacher's position lights up with a real-time video display, a scene, seemingly out of the past. The classroom has connected to a room at Colonial Williamsburg, where several of the re-enactors who work at the living museum in the restored Virginia town sit ready to interact with students. The Colonial Williamsburg Foundation is hosting occasional video conferences with classrooms around the world, talking about life in America hundreds of years ago, and answering questions posed by students.

Each session like this involves hundreds of classes, but since it is impractical to answer questions from every class, only three have been selected to interact directly with the historians. Over the past weeks, a team of students in each of the participating classes have collaborated with a wiki to compile a list of questions for the designated classes to pose to the historians.

Formal education has changed in some significant, powerful, and fundamental ways. Educators and the communities that they live in have come to consensus that the purpose of education is to:

1. Establish a context for their experience as children and adults based on where and when they live; the cultural, social, and physical characteristics of their environment; the ways that their environment affects them and the affects that they have on their environment.
2. Help students to become proficient in the information skills required to be effective and responsible citizens of their communities (local and global), and to continue to adapt and prosper in a rapidly changing world.

Educators have agreed that students learn best:

1. When information is seen less as a product to be consumed and memorized, and more as a raw material to be worked and even played.
2. When they have input in how and what they are taught, and complete control over other aspects of their learning.
3. When they work in classrooms that are richly connected to the world they are learning about, where their classroom walls are virtually invisible.
4. When taught by teachers who are confident instructional leaders with the resources and professional time to continue to adapt their classrooms to a rapidly changing world, and teachers who are respected by their communities for the importance of their work.

David Warlick Technology Consultant & Author Raleigh, North Carolina davidwarlick.com Landmarks for Schools http://landmark-project.com

Glossary

The page location for these term can be found in the index.

A

absolute reference A formula is meant to always refer to an exact cell regardless of the placement of the formula cell within the spreadsheet

abstract Symbolizing an object, event, or occurrence that can be observed by the learner

acceptable use policies (AUPs) Outline proper Internet use and student responsibilities and require permission forms signed by both parent and student before allowing student access to the Internet

action The programmed result of clicking on a hypermedia button

arcs model A model designed by Keller to describe the four components of motivation

action research The teacher as researcher investigates a problem, usually arising from some classroom practice. Results are applicable only to the setting in which the research was conducted

active cell The cell that is selected and ready for data entry or editing

ASSURE model A model to aid in the planning and delivery of instruction

authentic assessment Consists of assessment tasks that resemble real-world situations

authority list A list of approved headings, names, terms, and so on, designed to control what is entered into a field

B

bar code reader A device that translates the sequence of spaced thick and thin lines to the computer, enabling it to identify an object

behaviorism A theory of learning that perceives the teacher as the manipulator of an environment that is experienced by the learner

binary Consisting of two parts; limited to two conditions or states of being

bit The single digit of a binary number, either 0 or 1; derived from the words *b*inary dig*it*

bit-mapped graphics Computer-generated images composed of bits, or screen pixels, that are turned on (black or colored) and bits that are turned off (white or clear)

blog We*b* and *log* is an online journaling tool where anyone can place whatever they want

boilerplate Material, such as paragraphs of text, that can be used repeatedly in many documents without modification

bookmarks A feature of web browser programs that allows the user to save and organize the URLs of desired Internet sites

Boolean connectors Words such as AND, OR, and NOT used to connect search terms

bps A measure of data transmission speed between computers in *b*its *p*er *s*econd

branching A design of some programs that uses techniques to provide multiple alternative paths, or branches, for remediation or acceleration

browser A software program used to access and view sites on the Web

burner A term used to describe a drive that records data onto optical discs such as a CD or a DVD

button A visible object or an invisible area of the screen, often covering images or text, that can be programmed using a scripting language to perform certain actions

byte A grouping of bits (in groups of 8, 16, 32, or more); the code represents one alpha or a numeric character of data

C

cable modem A peripheral device that connects a computer to a television cable system

cache A web file storage area on the computer's hard disk

card One screen or frame of a hypermedia presentation

cell The intersection of a row and a column in a spreadsheet

central processing unit (CPU) A chip in the computer where all parts of the system are linked together and where the calculations and manipulation of data take place

checklists Simple ways of observing and categorizing behaviors in a bimodal (observed/not observed) manner

chip A small piece of silicon housing an integrated circuit that may contain tens of thousands of miniaturized transistors and other electronic components

clip art Prepared files of line drawings and images available on disk that are intended to be incorporated into the user's own work

clock speed The number of electronic pulses per second that a CPU will process

computer-assisted instruction (CAI) The direct instructional interaction between computer and student designed to produce the transmission of information

computer literacy The study of the development and functional use of the computer, as well as related societal issues

computer-managed instruction (CMI) Use of the computer as a diagnostic, prescriptive, and organizational tool to gather, store, manipulate, analyze, and report information relative to the student and the curriculum

concrete Actual, direct, purposeful happenings involving the learner as a participant

constructivism A theory of learning that holds that students interact with the real-life experiences and construct mental structures that provide an understanding of their environment

copyright Laws designed to protect the financial interests of the creators, producers, and distributors of original works of art and information

cropping Controlling the size of an image without affecting the size of any of its components

D

database The collection of related data records stored and accessed electronically by computer

database manager Software that is designed to manage electronic data files

data entry bar See *formula bar*

debugging The process of removing all logic and construction errors

desktop presentation The design, creation, and display of textual and graphic information under the control of a personal computer often with the use of a video projector

desktop publishing Usually refers to the use of software that contains an extensive set of text and graphics manipulation commands and includes advanced page layout capabilities

digital Electrical current flowing in very discrete units usually depicted as individual packets, 0s and 1s or on/off units

digital camera A device that captures and stores still images in a digital format

digital multimedia A multimedia design that allows a computer user to combine and control a number of instructional resources in order to present information

digital portfolio A portfolio in which all of the components are in a digital format enabling them to be accessed by a computer. Often stored on CD-ROMs

digital subscriber line (DSL) A service available from some phone companies for fast Internet access

digital video camera A device that captures and stores moving images in a digital format

directories Catalogs of Internet sites organized by subject areas

dissolve Moving from one screen to the next by having one visual fade out as the second fades in

documentation Written explanations supporting program maintenance and use

drill and practice A category of computer software that uses the teaching strategy to reinforce instruction by providing repetition necessary to move acquired skills and concepts into long-term memory

driver A small program added to the operating system that allows it to control certain hardware peripherals (e.g., a printer)

dot matrix printer An impact printer that uses a series of electrically hammered pins to create characters composed of a pattern of dots

dots per inch (dpi) The number of discrete elements produced by a printer

E

electronic conferences Electronic forums usually organized around specific topics designed to allow the exchange of information by a number of simultaneous users

electronic portfolio A portfolio in which all of the components are in an electronic format. Items may be in a digital (scanned images, word-processed documents, etc.) and/or analog (videotape, audiotape) format

email The electronic transfer of messages and files from one person's computer to another

email discussion group A group of email addresses given a single name on a computer, sometimes called a *mailing list*

extension A small program added to the operating system that allows the application software to interact with the operating system

external memory The auxiliary storage of programs and data, often on a removable medium

F

favorites See *bookmarks*

field The group of related characters treated as a unit within a record—for example, the last name of a student; the smallest, most discrete element of a file

file A collection of related records treated as a unit

file management A systematic approach to the storage, manipulation, and retrieval of information stored as data items in the form of records in a file

file manager Software that is designed to create and to manage data files, also now called a *database manager*

FireWire A very-high-speed connection between peripherals and the computer that allows for the transfer of large amounts of data

firmware Software that is permanently stored on a computer chip

flash drive An ultra-small, pocket-sized removable memory device

floppy disk An external storage medium made of flexible polyester film with magnetic properties

font The collection of characteristics applied to a typeface in a particular size and style

form See *layout*

formula bar The area at the top of the screen that displays the content of the active cell and that can be edited

fragmented The dispersal of files stored on disk into segments scattered at various points on the disk

freeware Software that may be copied and distributed free of charge

functions Built-in mathematical formulas used to calculate cell values

G

gaming A strategy that includes the elements of a set of rules and competition against others or against a standard

gigabyte (GB) One thousand megabytes, or one billion bytes, used as a reference to memory storage capacity

gradient fill A pattern that begins with a certain opacity or density of pattern at a determined point and gradually fades to one that is less dense or increases to one that is more dense

graphical user interface (GUI) The on-screen use of pictorial representations (icons) of objects

graphics Photographic and nonphotographic representations of an object or event

graphics tablet A flat input device on which the user writes

H

hard disk An external storage medium consisting of a rigid platter coated with a magnetic emulsion and not removable from the disk drive

hardware Tangible computer parts such as a keyboard, mouse, disk drive, and printer

home page Usually the first web page accessed at a website, it often includes links to other web pages within that site or at other websites

hot-swappable The ability to plug or unplug peripherals from the computer system without having to shut down and restart the computer

hypermedia A multimedia presentation that contains links or buttons that will allow the product to be presented in a nonlinear fashion

hypertext A term synonymous with hypermedia but emphasizes textual links instead of buttons

HyperText Markup Language (HTML) A programming language that allows the user to post a World Wide Web document with text, graphics, and dynamic links to other websites

HTML editor A program designed to streamline the process of building a web page through the automation of adding certain HTML language code

HyperText Transfer Protocol (HTTP) The format by which World Wide Web documents are transferred over the Internet

I

icon A pictorial representation of an object

information literacy The study of how we find, analyze, understand, and use information

ink-jet printer A printer that uses a series of electronically controlled nozzles to create characters composed of a pattern of dots squirted onto the paper

input peripherals Equipment whose function is to enter data into the computer

instructional games A category of software that is highly competitive, is intriguing, may include elements of speed or time, and often involves some type of fantasy atmosphere

integrated circuit An electronic component made up of circuit elements constructed on a single piece of silicon

integrated learning system (ILS) A hardware and software package designed to present and manage the scope and sequence of one or several content areas. These content areas may encompass several years of instruction

integration literacy The study of how we use a variety of technologies and methods to enhance teaching and learning

intellectual property Something conceived in the mind of an individual and made available to others

Internet A worldwide network of interconnected networks all based on TCP/IP

Internet Service Provider (ISP) The organization or business that connects individually or group-owned computers to the Internet backbone

interpolation A process in which the scanner software makes up pixels without actually capturing greater detail from the scanned image

invisible Web That part of the Web that is unable to be searched by regular search engines

K

Kbps A measure of a modem's data transmission speed between computers in thousands of bits per second

keyboard The primary input device for the computer; it generates a digital code that can be understood by the microprocessor

kilobyte (K) One thousand bytes (actually 1,024 in computer terms); used as a reference to memory capacity

L

labels The text descriptors related to adjacent data

laser printer A printer that uses a laser beam to create an image on a photosensitive drum and transfers this by means of carbon toner to paper

layout The selection and positioning of fields and their labels for screen or printed use

linear Proceeding in a step-by-step, sequential manner

LISTSERV™ A registered trademark for a particular brand of software used to create and run email discussion groups

local area network (LAN) A network composed of devices located in close proximity to one another

logical search The ability to apply logical operators to a search—for example, "Find all words that contain 'th'" or "Find all values greater than 100."

lossless compression A file compression technique through which no information is lost though the file is smaller

lossy compression A file compression technique that discards information it judges unnecessary

lumens A measure of a video projector's output affecting the brightness of the screen image

M

Mbps A measure of a modem's data transmission speed between computers in millions of bits per second

mechanical spacing Letter spacing that requires letters within a word to be equally distant from each other regardless of the letter shape

media literacy The study of how we find, analyze, understand, and use information and how we can communicate this information in a variety of forms

Megabyte (MB) One thousand kilobytes or one million bytes, used as a reference to memory capacity

Megapixel One million pixels

microdiskette A 3 1/2-inch format that houses a magnetic disk in a rigid plastic protective case

modem A device that translates digital computer information into analog signals that can be transmitted over telephone or cable lines and translates analog signals into a digital form that can be processed by a computer

monospaced See *mechanical spacing*

mouse A handheld device connected to the input port of a computer, which moves a pointer on the screen

multilevel sort A series of second, third, and so on levels of sorts performed after a primary one has been performed—for example, sorting a group of students by first name after they were first sorted by last name

multimedia A technique that conveys information in a multisensory manner

multimedia instruction The technique of accessing, organizing, and displaying textual, graphic, audio, and video information under the control of a computer allowing a teacher to convey information in a multisensory manner

multimedia learning The technique of accessing, organizing, and displaying textual, graphic, audio, and video information under the control of a computer to meet student needs in conveying information in a multisensory manner

N

nested sort See *multilevel sort*

network The interconnection of computers to allow multiple users to access software and to exchange information

noise Anything that deteriorates the quality of the signal or message

O

operating system An operating system enables the central processing unit (CPU) to control and communicate with internal and external devices

optical character recognition (OCR) Software that allows scanners to digitize text so that it can be used and manipulated as regular text in a word processor

optical spacing Letter spacing that requires letters within a word to have equal surface areas in the spaces between each other, thereby taking letter shapes into account

optical storage device Storage peripherals that are written to and accessed by laser light beams such as CD-ROMs and DVDs

orphans Single lines of text that occur at the bottoms of pages

output peripherals Equipment that displays information from the computer

P

pen drive See *flash drive*

performance-based assessment See *authentic assessment*

pixel Abbreviation for *picture element*. One pixel is a single point in a graphic image

podcasting *iPod* and broad*cast* are recorded audio and/or video files that are distributed via Internet download

ppi The number of **p**ixels **p**er **i**nch affects the resolution or sharpness of an image

print formatter The part of a word processing program that delivers the text file to the printer and ensures that it is printed correctly on paper

problem-solving software A category of software that presents students with a problem for which they must state the hypothesis, plan strategies, and follow some set of procedures to achieve a final goal or outcome

project-based learning An authentic assessment model for teaching in which projects are used to assess student learning

proportional-spaced See *optical spacing*

public access catalog (PAC) A computer-based system that provides users access to a library's holdings

Q

quartile analysis The ranking of performance measures from high to low and the separation of the measures into four groups to study performance by high, medium, and low achievers

query See *logical search*

R

RAM Random-access memory; volatile internal memory that is erased if power to the computer system is interrupted

rating scales Complex measures where each observation is placed on a scale, usually of numerical values, that measures the degree to which a student completes a task

record A group of related fields treated as a unit. For example, in a student file, a record might be all the information stored relating to a given student

relational database manager Software designed to manage a collection of related electronic data files

resolution The sharpness of an image. Used to describe output from graphic images, monitors, and printers

robots See *spiders*

ROM Read-only memory; constant memory contained in an integrated circuit or chip that cannot be modified by the user

rubric A scoring matrix that differentiates the quality of learning using a graduated scale of exemplar behaviors

S

scaling Controlling the size of an image and, in direct proportion, all of its components

scanner An input peripheral that digitizes photos, line drawings, and text by reflecting light off their surface

search engines Computer applications that automatically search web pages and store keywords and text from each page

shareware Software distributed free of charge with conditions that usually include a payment made to the authors if software continues to be used after a trial period

simulation A category of computer software that uses a teaching strategy based on role-playing within structured environments providing an environment for discovery learning

size The height of a letter expressed in points

software Information and directions to control the computer; a computer program preserved on a recording medium

speech recognition device A software program with accompanying microphone that changes the spoken word into text and can be used in a word processing program

spiders Programs used by search engines to travel the Web, usually by following links on known pages, to add new pages and keywords at every step of the way

spreadsheet Software that accepts data in a matrix of columns and rows, with their intersections called cells. Often used with numeric data to forecast results of decisions

stack A group of cards linked together to form a complete hypermedia presentation

stationery Sometimes used as a replacement for template

style (1) A set of characteristics that can be applied to text in a word processor. (2) When dealing strictly with the appearance of text, style pertains more narrowly to the appearance of a particular typeface

T

template A blank preformatted file design; see also *boilerplate*

text editor The part of a word processing program that allows the user to manipulate text on a screen display

text-wrapped graphics The format feature that allows the program to wrap lines of text around the edges of graphics

thumb drive See *flash drive*

trackpad A pressure-sensitive pad, often found on laptop computers, on which the user presses a finger in order to move a pointer on the screen

transistor A small electronic device that controls current flow and does not require a vacuum to operate

Transmission Control Protocol/Internet Protocol (TCP/IP) A set of standards developed to allow different networks to interconnect electronically

tutorial A category of computer software that uses the teaching strategy in which the student's level of knowledge is first determined before new information is introduced along with learning guidance

typeface The design or appearance of a particular letter type and the name given to that design

U

Uniform Resource Locator (URL) The address of any site on the Internet, including gopher and the websites

uninterruptible power supply (UPS) A device that provides emergency power from batteries in the event of an AC power failure

Universal Product Code (UPC) A sequence of thick and thin lines on consumer products spaced to identify a specific item, read by an optical bar code reader

Universal Serial Bus (USB) A powerful, cross-platform communication standard developed to link the computer to external devices

user interface The interaction between human and machine

V

vacuum tube A sealed electronic device designed to regulate current flow

vector graphics Computer-generated images determined by formulas that create discrete objects of a certain size and position

video monitor A television set that has been manufactured to accept a video signal

video projector A device that accepts a video signal and projects an image onto a screen

virtual reality (VR) A computer-generated simulated environment with which a user can interact

visual literacy The study of how we interpret, understand, and create visual messages and information

volatile memory Internal memory that is available and accessible to the user and requires a constant source of power to maintain itself

W

web browser Software that finds and displays web pages

web-enhanced cell phones A cellular telephone able to send and receive data to and from the web

web filter Blocking program that screens out undesirable content but may also block an educationally valid search term that possesses meanings other than those appropriate for students of a specific age or ability

web portal A website that offers a broad range of services and resources

WebQuest Defined as "inquiry-oriented activities in which most or all of the information used by the learner is drawn from the Web"

web server Software that allows web pages to be broadcast to the Web

wide area network (WAN) A network that spans great distances or covers a wide geographic area

widows Single lines of text that occur at the tops of pages

Wi-Fi (Wireless Fidelity) A generic term for any device that uses one of the IEEE 802.11 wireless transmission standards

wipe Moving from one slide to the next by having one slide replace the next by covering it and pushing it off the screen as from left to right or top to bottom

word processor Software, with accompanying hardware, used primarily to facilitate the creation, editing, formatting, saving, and printing of information in electronic and hard copy form

word wrap A process of monitoring the entry of words so that words are not split on the right side of the screen

World Wide Web (WWW) An Internet navigation system that allows users, through a graphic browser interface, to access information organized on hypertext-linked screens called pages

WYSIWYG (**W**hat **Y**ou **S**ee **I**s **W**hat **Y**ou **G**et) Pronounced "wizzy wig," the exact screen replication of what will be printed on paper

Name Index

Subject Index

A

AASL (American Association of School Librarians), 109

AAUP (American Association of University Women), 136

abstract thought, 11

acceptable use policies (AUPs), 139–140
  classroom case, 140

accommodation, 11

action research, 91–93

actions, multimedia, 307

active cells, spreadsheet, 243

ADA (Americans with Disabilities Act), 128

adaptive technology, 127

Adobe Illustrator, 85, 173, 183

advertisements, creating, classroom case, 235–236

AECT (Association for Educational Communications and Technology), 109, 177, 389

affluence, and equity, 131, 133–134

AirPort, 162

"All Aboard the Internet" columns, 389, 391

American Association of School Librarians (AASL), 109

American Association of University Women (AAUP), 136

American Memory database, 385

American Psychological Association (APA), 348, 349

American Sign Language (ASL), 128

Americans with Disabilities Act (ADA), 128

America Online, 385

AOL/Netscape, 342

APA (American Psychological Association), 348–349

Apache, 343

Apple Computer, 100, 105, 106, 157, 162, 327

Apple Safari, 343, 344

AppleWorks, 37, 85, 183, 262

ARCS model, 27

area graphs, 257

ARPAnet, 105, 337

art, multimedia software for, 309

Arthur's Kindergarten, 58

Arthur's 1st Grade, 58

Arthur's 2nd Grade, 58

artifacts, portfolio, 21–22

Ask for Kids, 348

ASL (American Sign Language), 128

assessment, 17–23
  authentic, 17
  digital portfolios, 17–18, 21–22
  portfolio programs, 22–23

assimilation, 11

assistive technology, 127

Association for Educational Communications and Technology (AECT), 109, 177, 389

ASSURE model, 30

Atkinson, Richard, 6

at-risk students. *See* special needs students

audio processing, tools for, 115

Ausubel, David, 6

authentic assessment, 17

authentic inquiry, 14

authoring, multimedia, 86, 88. *See also* multimedia tools

authority lists, database, 291

Authorware Professional, 328

Avid Express Pro, 176

AVI file format, 190

B

Ballistic, 54–55

bar code readers, 148

bar graphs, 253

behaviorism, 6

behaviorist perspective, 5, 6–11
  and constructivist approach, compared, 12

Bell Telephone Laboratories, 28

bias. *See* equity

Big Books, 232

Big Box of Art, The, 187

binary code, 105

bit-mapped graphics, 181–183

bits, 105

Blackberry, 160

blocking, Internet, 139–140

blogs, 342–343, 373–374

Bloom, Benjamin, 29–30, 395

Bloom's taxonomy, 29–30, 375

Bluetooth wireless device, 163

BMP file format, 189

bodily-kinesthetic intelligence, 24, 25

boilerplates, 228

Bookmarks, *Netscape Navigator,* 344

Boolean connectors, 283–284

branching programs, 50

Briggs, Katherine, 26

Briggs Myers, Isabel, 26

BrightPlanet, 347

Bruner, Jerome, 6

budget, management of, 89

burners, CD, 156

buttons, multimedia, 307

bytes, 105

C

cable modems, 153

cache, 345

CAI (computer-assisted instruction), 7, 45

California State University at Long Beach, 92

cameras
  and literacy, 176–177
  digital, 149, 173–176

Canvas, 173, 183

cards, multimedia, 307

Carmen Sandiego series, 56–57

CD-audio data storage devices, 156

CD-Recordable (CD-R) devices, 156

CD-Rewritable (CD-RW) devices, 156

CD-ROM data storage devices, 21, 22, 156

Cellflix Festival, 160

cell phones, 106, 160

cells, spreadsheet, 242–243

Central Intelligence Agency (CIA), 388, 390

central processing unit (CPU), 146, 153

CERN, European Particle Physics Laboratory, 106

change, institutional, 110

charts and graphs, 252–258

Chase Active Learning Grant, 130

checklists, 17

Children's Internet Protection Act (CIPA), 139

Children's Literature Web Guide, 388, 389

chips, 105

CIA (Central Intelligence Agency), 388, 390
  Publications, 388–389, 390

CIESE Collaborative Classroom Projects site, 375, 376

CIPA (Children's Internet Protection Act), 139

citations, source, 348–350

Classroom Connect network, 383

classroom contexts. *See* social contexts

classroom management. *See* management, classroom and school

classroom newsletters, 230

classrooms, future, 395–398

clip art, 187–189

clock speed, 153

ClueFinders Math Adventures, 58

CMI (computer managed instruction), 45

cognitive styles, 26

Cold War, 105, 337

collaboration, 15–16

collaborative research, 91

column graphs, 253, 255, 257, 258

Commodore computers, 105

"What students should know and be able to do to learn effectively and live productively in an increasingly digital world …"

1. Creativity and Innovation

Students demonstrate creative thinking, construct knowledge, and develop innovative products and processes using technology. Students:

a. apply existing knowledge to generate new ideas, products, or processes.
b. create original works as a means of personal or group expression.
c. use models and simulations to explore complex systems and issues.
d. identify trends and forecast possibilities.

2. Communication and Collaboration

Students use digital media and environments to communicate and work collaboratively, including at a distance, to support individual learning and contribute to the learning of others. Students:

a. interact, collaborate, and publish with peers, experts or others employing a variety of digital environments and media.
b. communicate information and ideas effectively to multiple audiences using a variety of media and formats.
c. develop cultural understanding and global awareness by engaging with learners of other cultures.
d. contribute to project teams to produce original works or solve problems.

3. Research and Information Fluency

Students apply digital tools to gather, evaluate, and use information. Students:

a. plan strategies to guide inquiry.
b. locate, organize, analyze, evaluate, synthesize, and ethically use information from a variety of sources and media.
c. evaluate and select information sources and digital tools based on the appropriateness to specific tasks.
d. process data and report results.

4. Critical Thinking, Problem-Solving & Decision-Making

Students use critical thinking skills to plan and conduct research, manage projects, solve problems and make informed decisions using appropriate digital tools and resources. Students:

a. identify and define authentic problems and significant questions for investigation.
b. plan and manage activities to develop a solution or complete a project.
c. collect and analyze data to identify solutions and/or make informed decisions.
d. use multiple processes and diverse perspectives to explore alternative solutions.

5. Digital Citizenship

Students understand human, cultural, and societal issues related to technology and practice legal and ethical behavior. Students:

a. advocate and practice safe, legal, and responsible use of information and technology.
b. exhibit a positive attitude toward using technology that supports collaboration, learning, and productivity.
c. demonstrate personal responsibility for lifelong learning.
d. exhibit leadership for digital citizenship.

6. Technology Operations and Concepts

Students demonstrate a sound understanding of technology concepts, systems and operations. Students:

a. understand and use technology systems.
b. select and use applications effectively and productively.
c. troubleshoot systems and applications.
d. transfer current knowledge to learning of new technologies.